Buying a Home
in
France
2005

A Survival Handbook

by
David Hampshire

SURVIVAL BOOKS • LONDON • ENGLAND

Hope this helps!
Matt x

KU-175-755

all the best for the future.
Ross x

Here's to good
weather + nice
wine! lots of love
Dosh xx

wow! Congratulation
and how exciting!
Best regards,
Amit ☺

Why not N2?>
Ceu

Have fun
looking!
love sheryl x

Be sure we
your French house-
warming party!!!
Hope you have an
amazing married life!!
Cass
x

lots of love
Naomi
xx

Happy Hunting
Mike .

good luck hunting!
Shelly xx

Lots of love
Vicki xx

Happy hunting
All good wishes
Regina .

First published 1996
Second Edition 1999
Third Edition 2002
Fourth Edition 2003
Fifth Edition 2004

Survival Books Limited, 1st Floor,
60 St James's Street, London SW1A 1ZN, United Kingdom
☎ +44 (0)20-7493 4244, ▤ +44 (0)20-7491 0605
✉ info@survivalbooks.net
🖥 www.survivalbooks.net
To order books, please refer to page 389.

British Library Cataloguing in Publication Data.
A CIP record for this book is available
from the British Library.
ISBN 1 901130 48 7

Printed and bound in Finland by WS Bookwell Ltd

ACKNOWLEDGEMENTS

My sincere thanks to all who contributed to the successful publication of the fifth edition of this book: in particular, Joe Laredo (research for this edition), Grania Rogers (proofreading this edition), Kerry Laredo (desktop publishing), Graham Platt of Fox Hayes solicitors for information about house buying fees, Howard Farmer of 1st for French Property, Ingram Monk of Internet French Property and Bob Mulcahy of the KBM Consultancy for information about the current state of the French property market, and everyone else who provided information or contributed in any way. I would also like to thank Roger Moss of *Everything France* magazine and Carolyn Cohen and Penny Zoldan of Latitudes for providing photographs. Finally, a special thank-you to Jim Watson for the superb illustrations, cartoons, maps and cover design.

TITLES BY SURVIVAL BOOKS

Alien's Guides
Britain; France

The Best Places To Buy A Home
France; Spain

Buying A Home
Abroad; Florida;
France; Greece & Cyprus;
Ireland; Italy; Portugal;
South Africa;
Spain

Foreigners Abroad: Triumphs & Disasters
France; Spain

Lifeline Regional Guides
Costa del Sol; Dordogne/Lot;
Poitou-Charentes

Living And Working
Abroad; America; Australia;
Britain; Canada; The European
Union; The Far East; France;
Germany; The Gulf States & Saudi
Arabia; Holland, Belgium &
Luxembourg; Ireland; Italy; London;
New Zealand; Spain; Switzerland

Other Titles
Buying, Selling & Letting
Property; How To Avoid Holiday
& Travel Disasters; Renovating &
Maintaining Your French Home;
Retiring Abroad; Rioja And Its
Wines; The Wines Of Spain

Order forms are on page 389.

WHAT READERS & REVIEWERS

When you buy a model plane for your child, a video recorder, or some new computer gizmo, you get with it a leaflet or booklet pleading 'Read Me First', or bearing large friendly letters or bold type saying 'IMPORTANT – follow the instructions carefully'. This book should be similarly supplied to all those entering France with anything more durable than a 5-day return ticket. It is worth reading even if you are just visiting briefly, or if you have lived here for years and feel totally knowledgeable and secure. But if you need to find out how France works then it is indispensable. Native French people probably have a less thorough understanding of how their country functions. – Where it is most essential, the book is most up to the minute.

LIVING FRANCE

Rarely has a 'survival guide' contained such useful advice. This book dispels doubts for first-time travellers, yet is also useful for seasoned globetrotters – In a word, if you're planning to move to the USA or go there for a long-term stay, then buy this book both for general reading and as a ready-reference.

AMERICAN CITIZENS ABROAD

It is everything you always wanted to ask but didn't for fear of the contemptuous put down – The best English-language guide – Its pages are stuffed with practical information on everyday subjects and are designed to complement the traditional guidebook.

SWISS NEWS

A complete revelation to me – I found it both enlightening and interesting, not to mention amusing.

CAROLE CLARK

Let's say it at once. David Hampshire's *Living and Working in France* is the best handbook ever produced for visitors and foreign residents in this country; indeed, my discussion with locals showed that it has much to teach even those born and bred in l'Hexagone. – It is Hampshire's meticulous detail which lifts his work way beyond the range of other books with similar titles. Often you think of a supplementary question and search for the answer in vain. With Hampshire this is rarely the case. – He writes with great clarity (and gives French equivalents of all key terms), a touch of humour and a ready eye for the odd (and often illuminating) fact. – This book is absolutely indispensable.

THE RIVIERA REPORTER

A mine of information – I may have avoided some embarrassments and frights if I had read it prior to my first Swiss encounters – Deserves an honoured place on any newcomer's bookshelf.

ENGLISH TEACHERS ASSOCIATION, SWITZERLAND

Have Said About Survival Books

What a great work, wealth of useful information, well-balanced wording and accuracy in details. My compliments!

THOMAS MÜLLER

This handbook has all the practical information one needs to set up home in the UK – The sheer volume of information is almost daunting – Highly recommended for anyone moving to the UK.

AMERICAN CITIZENS ABROAD

A very good book which has answered so many questions and even some I hadn't thought of – I would certainly recommend it.

BRIAN FAIRMAN

We would like to congratulate you on this work: it is really super! We hand it out to our expatriates and they read it with great interest and pleasure.

ICI (SWITZERLAND) AG

Covers just about all the things you want to know on the subject – In answer to the desert island question about the one how-to book on France, this book would be it – Almost 500 pages of solid accurate reading – This book is about enjoyment as much as survival.

THE RECORDER

It's so funny – I love it and definitely need a copy of my own – Thanks very much for having written such a humorous and helpful book.

HEIDI GUILIANI

A must for all foreigners coming to Switzerland.

ANTOINETTE O'DONOGHUE

A comprehensive guide to all things French, written in a highly readable and amusing style, for anyone planning to live, work or retire in France.

THE TIMES

A concise, thorough account of the DOs and DON'Ts for a foreigner in Switzerland – Crammed with useful information and lightened with humorous quips which make the facts more readable.

AMERICAN CITIZENS ABROAD

Covers every conceivable question that may be asked concerning everyday life – I know of no other book that could take the place of this one.

FRANCE IN PRINT

Hats off to *Living and Working in Switzerland*!

RONNIE ALMEIDA

CONTENTS

IMPORTANT NOTE

France is a large country with myriad faces and many ethnic groups, religions and customs. Although ostensibly the same throughout the country, rules and regulations tend to be open to local interpretation (Paris is a law unto itself!), and are sometimes even formulated on the spot. **I cannot recommend too strongly that you check with an official and reliable source (not always the same) before making major decisions or undertaking an irreversible course of action. Don't believe everything you're told or read, even, dare I say it, herein!** To help you obtain further information and verify data with official sources, useful addresses, references and websites have been included in most chapters and **Appendices A, B** and **C**. Important points have been emphasised throughout the book **in bold print**, some of which it would be expensive or even dangerous to disregard. **Ignore them at your cost or peril.** Unless specifically stated, the reference to any company, organisation, product or publication in this book doesn't constitute an endorsement or recommendation. Any reference to any place or person (living or dead) is purely coincidental.

THE AUTHOR

David Hampshire was born in the United Kingdom, where after serving in the Royal Air Force he was employed for many years in the computer industry. He has lived and worked in many countries, including Australia, France, Germany, Malaysia, the Netherlands, Singapore, Switzerland and Spain, where he now resides most of the year. It was while working in Switzerland that he wrote his first book, *Living and Working in Switzerland*, in 1987. David is the author of around 15 books, including *Buying a Home in France*, *Buying a Home in Italy*, *Buying a Home in Spain*, *Buying, Selling & Letting Property*, *Living and Working in France*, *Living and Working in Spain* and *Retiring Abroad*.

AUTHOR'S NOTES

- Frequent references are made in this book to the European Union (EU), which comprises Austria, Belgium, Cyprus, the Czech Republic, Denmark, Estonia, Finland, France, Germany, Greece, Hungary, Ireland, Italy, Latvia, Lithuania, Luxembourg, Malta, the Netherlands, Poland, Portugal, Slovakia, Slovenia, Spain, Sweden and the United Kingdom, and the European Economic Area (EEA), which includes the EU countries plus Iceland, Liechtenstein and Norway.

- Times are shown using the 24-hour clock, which is the usual way of expressing the time in France.

- Prices quoted should be taken only as estimates, although they were correct when going to print and usually don't change greatly. Prices are quoted inclusive of tax (which is the method generally used in France) unless otherwise stated.

- His/he/him/man/men (etc.) also mean her/she/her/woman/women. This is done simply to make life easier for the reader and, in particular, the author, and **isn't** intended to be sexist.

- British English is used throughout, but American English equivalents are given where appropriate.

- The French translation of key words and phrases is shown in brackets in *italics*. Note that the French is given in the singular, except when the plural is the standard word or phrase.

- Warnings and important points are shown in **bold** type.

- The following symbols are used in this book: ☎ (telephone), 🖷 (fax), 🖳 (internet) and ✉ (email).

- Lists of **Useful Addresses**, **Further Reading** and **Useful Websites** are contained in **Appendices A, B** and **C** respectively.

- Imperial/metric conversion tables are included in **Appendix D**.

- Maps of France showing the regions and departments, airports and ports, the high-speed train (*TGV*) network, and motorways and other major roads are included in **Appendix E**. A geographical map of France is shown on page 6.

- A table showing the scheduled airline services between France and the UK/Ireland can be found in **Appendix F**.

- A glossary of property, mortgage and other terms used in this book is included in **Appendix G**.

INTRODUCTION

Since it was first published in 1996, *Buying a Home in France* has been the most comprehensive and up-to-date book for homebuyers in France. To make the information more accessible and helpful, we totally re-designed and enlarged the fourth edition and since 2003 have published a new edition annually, thus ensuring that you always have the most up-to-date information at your fingertips.

Whether you want a villa, farmhouse, townhouse or an apartment, a holiday or permanent home, this book will help make your dreams come true. The purpose of *Buying a Home in France* is to provide you with the information necessary to help you choose the most favourable location and the most appropriate home **to satisfy your individual requirements**. Most importantly, it will help you avoid the pitfalls and risks associated with buying a home in France, which for most people is one of the largest financial transactions they will undertake during their lifetimes.

You may already own a property in your home country; however, buying a home in France (or in any foreign country) is a different matter altogether. One of the most common mistakes many people make when buying a home in France is to assume that the laws and purchase procedures are the same as in their home country. **This is almost certainly not the case!** Despite some reports to the contrary, buying property in France is generally safe and needn't be a lottery. However, if you don't obtain legal advice and follow the rules provided for your protection, a purchase can result in a serious financial loss, as many people have discovered to their cost.

Before buying a home in France you need to ask yourself exactly why you want to buy there? Is your primary concern a long-term investment or do you wish to work or retire there? Where and what can you afford to buy? Do you plan to let your home to offset the running costs? How will French taxes affect your investment? *Buying a Home in France* will help you answer these and many other questions. It won't, however, tell you where to live, what to buy, or, having made your decision, whether you will be happy – that part is up to you!

For many people, buying a home in France has previously been a case of pot luck. However, with a copy of *Buying a Home in France* to hand you'll have a wealth of priceless information at your fingertips – information derived from a variety of sources, both official and unofficial, not least the hard won personal experiences of the author, his friends, colleagues and acquaintances. Furthermore, this book will reduce the risk of making an expensive mistake that you may bitterly regret later, and help you make informed decisions and calculated judgements, instead of costly mistakes and uneducated guesses (forewarned is forearmed!). **Most importantly, it will help you save money and repay your investment many times over.**

Buying a property in France is a wonderful way to make new friends, broaden your horizons and revitalise your life – and it provides a welcome bolt-hole to recuperate from the stresses and strains of modern life. I trust this book will help you avoid the pitfalls and smooth your way to many happy years in your new French home, secure in the knowledge that you've made the right decision.

Bon courage!

David Hampshire
November 2004

1.

MAJOR CONSIDERATIONS

Buying a home abroad is not only a major financial commitment, but also a decision that can have a huge influence on other aspects of your life, including your health, security and safety, your family relationships and friendships, your lifestyle, your opinions and your outlook. You also need to take into consideration any restrictions that might affect your choice of location and type of property, such as whether you will need (or be able) to learn another language, whether you will be able (or permitted) to find work, whether you can adapt to and enjoy the climate, whether you will be able to take your pets with you, and not least, whether you will be able to afford the kind of home (and lifestyle) that you want. In order to ensure that you're making the right move, it's as well to face these and other major considerations before making any irrevocable decisions.

WHY FRANCE?

There are many excellent reasons for buying a home in France. It's one of the most beautiful countries in Europe, if not **the** most beautiful, and has the most varied landscape, offering something for everyone: magnificent beaches for sun-worshippers; spectacular countryside for nature lovers; mountains and seas for sports fans. It also offers vibrant Parisian night-life for the jet set, some of the world's greatest wines for connoisseurs, *haute cuisine* for gourmets, an abundance of culture for art lovers, and tranquillity for the stressed.

In France, the pursuit of *la bonne vie* is a serious business and even *bons viveurs* (*bons vivants* in French) are spoilt for choice (most French people rate the pursuit of pleasure and style way ahead of success and wealth). Nowhere else in the world is there such an exhilarating mixture of natural beauty, culture, tradition, sophistication and style. It's often said that when buying property in France you aren't buying a home but a lifestyle! As a location for a holiday, retirement or permanent home, France has few rivals and in addition to the incomparable choice of properties and excellent value for money, it offers a generally fine climate for most of the year, particularly in the south.

Nevertheless, it's important to ask yourself **exactly** why you want to buy a home there. For example, are you primarily looking for a sound investment or do you plan to work or start a business in France? Are you seeking a holiday or retirement home? If you're seeking a second home, will it be mainly used for long weekends or for lengthier stays? Do you plan to let it to offset the mortgage and running costs? If so, how important is the property income? You need to answer these and many other questions before deciding on the best (and most appropriate) place to buy a home in France.

Often buyers have a variety of reasons for buying a home in France; for example, many people buy a holiday home with a view to living there permanently or semi-permanently when they retire. If this is the case, there are many more factors to take into account than if you're 'simply' buying a holiday home that you will occupy for just a few weeks a year (when it's usually wiser not to buy at all!). If, on the other hand, you plan to work or start a business in France, you will be faced with a completely different set of criteria. An increasing number of people live in France and work in another European country (e.g. neighbouring England, Belgium, Luxembourg, Germany, Switzerland and Italy), commuting back and forth by road, rail or air.

Can you really afford to buy a home in France? What about the future? Is your income secure and protected against inflation and currency fluctuations? In the '80s, many foreigners purchased holiday homes in France by taking out second mortgages on their family homes and stretching their financial resources to the limits. Not surprisingly, when the recession struck in the early '90s many people had their homes repossessed or were forced to sell at a huge loss when they were no longer able to meet the mortgage payments.

 You shouldn't expect to make a quick profit when buying property in France and should look upon it as an investment in your family's future happiness, rather than merely in financial terms.

Property values in France generally increase at an average of less than 5 per cent a year or in line with inflation (with no increase in real terms). In some fashionable resorts and developments, prices rise faster than average, although this is usually reflected in much higher purchase prices. For example, prices increased by over 20 per cent per annum in some parts of the Côte d'Azur in the late '90s and early 21st century. Generally, however, there's a stable property market in most of France, which acts as a discouragement to speculators wishing to make a 'fast buck', particularly when you consider that capital gains tax can wipe out much of the profit made on the sale of a second home. Bear in mind that you must also recover the costs associated with buying a home when you sell; these are particularly high in France.

SURVIVAL TIP
Before making any irrevocable decisions about buying a home in France, you should do extensive research (see page 19), study the possible pitfalls (see page 20), and be prepared to rent for a period before buying (see page 108).

Advantages & Disadvantages

There are both advantages and disadvantages to buying a home in France, although for most people the benefits far outweigh any drawbacks. France has many attractions: much of the country enjoys a sunny and warm climate all year round, with over 300 days of sunshine annually and high temperatures in southern areas; access to your French home from home has never been easier or cheaper, especially from the UK, thanks mainly to the proliferation of low cost flights offered by airlines such as BMIbaby, Flybe and Ryanair (see page 95), but also to the Eurotunnel, new high-speed cross-Channel operators and the widespread freezing of ferry prices (see page 98); France's motorway network is second to none (although expensive to use) and is constantly being improved, and most regions can now be reached by motorway (see page 103); Europe's fastest trains (*TGV*) not only serve an increasing number of major towns and cities, but also link with a Europe-wide network via the new hub at Lille, and the government has recently 'ordered' the (nationalised) railway operators to compete with the low-cost airlines, so lower train fares can be expected (see page 101).

France is famous for its huge variety of cultural and leisure activities, and the French, although not renowned for their friendliness and hospitality, are generally welcoming to foreigners who make the effort to integrate. The standard of living is generally high and the cost of living reasonable by Western European standards, including very good value homes (in less fashionable areas). Although prices have risen in many popular areas recently, property remains far cheaper than its equivalent in the UK, for example, with the bonus that it's often accompanied by generous amounts of land (see **Cost Of Property** on page 29).

Among the many other advantages of buying a home in France are good rental possibilities, good local tradesmen and services (particularly in resort areas), fine food and wine (some would argue, the best in the world) at reasonable prices, a relaxed pace of life in rural areas, one of the world's best healthcare systems, plenty of open space, and some of the most beautiful scenery in Europe all around you.

Naturally, there are also a few disadvantages, including communication problems if you don't speak French, the high purchase costs associated with buying a home in France, unexpected renovation and restoration costs (if you don't do your homework), a high rate of burglary in some areas, overcrowding in popular tourist areas during the peak summer season, traffic congestion and pollution in many towns and cities, and the expense of getting to and from France if you own a holiday home there and don't live in a nearby country with good air connections.

RESEARCH

A successful purchase is much more likely if you thoroughly investigate the various regions, the types of property available, prices and relative values, and the procedure for buying property in France.

SURVIVAL TIP **The secret of successfully buying a home in France** **is research, research and more research.**

It's all too easy to fall in love with the beauty and ambience of France and to sign a contract without giving it sufficient thought. If you're uncertain, don't allow yourself to be rushed into making a decision, by fears of an imminent price rise or because someone else is supposedly interested in a property. Although many people dream of buying a holiday or retirement home in France, it's vital to do your homework thoroughly and avoid the 'dream sellers' (often fellow countrymen) who will happily prey on your ignorance and tell you anything in order to sell you a property. Many people make expensive (and even catastrophic) mistakes when buying homes in France, usually because they do insufficient research and are in too much of a hurry, often setting themselves ridiculous deadlines such as buying a home during a long weekend or a week's holiday, although they wouldn't dream of acting so rashly when buying a property in their home country!

 It isn't uncommon for buyers to regret their decision after a few months or years and wish they had purchased a different kind of property in a different region (or even in a different country!).

If possible, you should take advice from people who already own a house in France, from whom you can usually obtain invaluable information (often based on their own mistakes). Much of this advice is included in this book (and its companion volume, *Foreigners in France: Triumphs & Disasters*), but you will **really** believe it if you hear it 'from the horse's mouth'! You should also read books especially written for those planning to live or work in France (such as *Living and Working in France*, also by David Hampshire). It helps to study specialist property magazines and newspapers such as *French Property News* and *Focus on France* (see **Appendix B** for a list), and to visit property exhibitions such as those organised by Outbound Publishing and French Property News in the UK (see **Appendix B**). There are also a number of websites where you can obtain information and advice from other expatriates (see **Appendix C**).

> **SURVIVAL TIP**
> Bear in mind that the cost of investing in a few books
> or magazines (and other research) is tiny compared with
> the expense of making a big mistake. Nevertheless,
> don't believe everything you read!

AVOIDING PROBLEMS

The problems associated with buying property abroad have been highlighted in the last decade or so, during which the property market in many countries has gone from boom to bust and back again. From a legal viewpoint, France is one of the safest places in the world in which to buy a home, and buyers have a high degree of protection under French law, irrespective of whether they're French citizens or foreign non-residents. Nevertheless, you should take the usual precautions regarding offers, agreements, contracts, deposits and obtaining proper title to a property.

The most common problems experienced by buyers in France include:

- **Buying in the wrong place:** Do your homework (see **Regions** on page 58, **Location** on page 85 and **Research** above) and rent first (see **Renting Before Buying** on page 108).

 The wrong decision regarding location is one of the main causes of disenchantment among foreigners who have purchased property in France.

- **Buying a home that's difficult or impossible to sell:** If there's a chance that you will need to sell (and recoup your investment) in the short to medium term, it's important to buy a home that will be easy to sell. A property with broad appeal in a popular area (particularly a waterside property) usually fills the bill; it will need to be very special to sell quickly in less popular areas. A modest, reasonably priced property is likely to be much easier to sell than a large, expensive home, particularly one needing restoration or modernisation. In most areas there's a small market for renovated rural property. There are usually many buyers in the €50,000 to €75,000 price range, but they become much scarcer at around €150,000 unless a property is exceptional, i.e. outstandingly attractive, in a popular area and with a superb situation. In some areas, even desirable properties remain on the market for a number of years.

● **Buying a house and garden much larger than you need because it seems to offer such good value:** Although buying a house with umpteen rooms and several acres of land may seem like a good investment, bear in mind that, should you wish to sell, buyers may be thin on the ground (see above), particularly if the price has doubled or trebled after the cost of renovation (see below). You should think carefully about what you're going to do with a large house and garden. Both will require a lot of maintenance, and your heating costs will be high. After you've installed a swimming pool, tennis court and croquet lawn, you still have a lot of change left out of even a couple of acres. Do you like gardening or are you prepared to live in a jungle? Can you afford to pay a gardener? Of course you can always plant an orchard or vineyard, create a lake or take up farming!

Don't, on the other hand, buy a property that's too small; when you have a home in France, you will inevitably discover that you have many more relatives and friends than you realised!

● **Paying too much:** Foreign buyers, particularly the British, are often tempted to pay more than the true market value of a property because it's so cheap compared to a similar property in their home country and they're reluctant to negotiate for fear of losing it. Some French vendors and agents take advantage of this tendency by asking inflated prices.

SURVIVAL TIP
Before buying a property from an agent advertising in the foreign (i.e. non-French) press, check the prices of similar properties offered by French agents and *notaires* to ensure that you're getting good value.

See **Cost Of Property** on page 29, **Property Prices** on page 121 and **Negotiating The Price** on page 123.

● **Grossly underestimating restoration and modernisation costs:** A tumbledown house for €50,000 can seem a steal, but renovation can cost as much as new building, as well as taking time and causing headaches (see **Renovation & Restoration** on page 167).

● **Buying a property for business, e.g. to convert to *gîtes*, and being too optimistic about the income:** The letting season can be as little as 15 weeks in some areas, which means it's difficult or impossible to cover the cost of maintaining a home, let alone make a living (see **Chapter 9**).

● **Not having a survey done on an old property:** As surveys aren't a matter of course in France, many people assume they aren't necessary – often with disastrous consequences (see **Inspections & Surveys** on page 154).

- **Not taking legal advice:** Another common assumption among foreign buyers in France is that the *notaire* handling a sale will look after their interests and ensure that they don't run into problems, which isn't necessarily the case (see **Legal Advice** below).

- **Not including necessary conditional clauses in a contract:** As above, the *notaire* handling the sale won't necessarily safeguard your interests by inserting provisos in the purchase contract (see **Contracts** on page 204).

- **Taking on too large a mortgage:** French lenders are offering larger and longer mortgages, particularly to foreign buyers, which can tempt them into borrowing more than they can afford to repay (see **Chapter 4**).

If you're looking for a holiday home, you may be better off not buying a house or apartment outright but may wish to consider purchasing a mobile home (see page 173) or investing in a scheme that restricts your occupancy of a property to a number of weeks each year, such as part-ownership, leaseback or timesharing (see page 145).

 Don't rush into any of these schemes without fully researching the market, and before you're absolutely clear about what you want and what you can realistically expect to get for your money.

Although it isn't possible to insure against making a poor decision, it is possible to insure against certain unforeseen problems, such as boundary disputes, unknown rights of way over or use of a property and planning restrictions by means of a policy called *Assur-titre*, offered by some French estate agents and French-based UK insurers London & European (☎ 02 32 32 95 60, 🖳 www.europeantitle.com).

Legal Advice

The vast majority of people who buy homes in France don't obtain independent legal advice, and most of those who experience problems have taken no precautions whatsoever. Of those that do take legal advice, many do so only **after** having paid a deposit and signed a contract or, more commonly, after they've run into problems.

> **SURVIVAL TIP**
> The most important thing to do before buying
> property in France (or indeed anywhere) is to obtain
> expert, independent legal advice from someone
> who's familiar with French law.

As when buying property in any country, you should never pay any money or sign anything without first taking legal advice in a language in which you're fluent from an experienced lawyer. You will find that the small cost (in comparison to the price of a home) of obtaining legal advice is excellent value, if only for the peace of mind it affords. Trying to cut corners to save a few euros on legal costs is foolhardy in the extreme when a large sum of money is at stake.

You may be able to obtain a list of lawyers who speak your language and are experienced in handling French property sales, either in France or in your home country, e.g. British buyers can obtain a list from the Law Society in the UK. Specialist lawyers advertise in Francophile newspapers and magazines (see **Appendix B**).

There are professionals speaking English and other languages in all areas of France, and many expatriate professionals (e.g. architects and surveyors) also practise there. However, don't assume that because you're dealing with a fellow countryman he will offer you a better deal or do a better job than a French person (the contrary may be true). It's wise to check the credentials of all professionals you employ, whether French or foreign.

It's **never** wise to rely solely on advice proffered by those with a financial interest in selling you a property, such as a builder or estate agent, although their advice may be excellent and totally unbiased.

Finance

You should have your finance in place before you start looking for a property and, if you need a mortgage, obtain a mortgage guarantee certificate from a lender that guarantees you a mortgage at a certain rate, which is usually subject to a valuation (see **Mortgages** on page 194). There's a mandatory conditional clause in French contracts that allows buyers to withdraw from a contract and have their deposit returned if they're unable to obtain a mortgage, although this applies only in certain circumstances. If you're buying a property for restoration, note that most lenders won't make a loan against a property that they consider uninhabitable (e.g. lacking access or sanitation) and they may require 'proof' that the restoration costs won't exceed 40 per cent of the purchase price (in which case a little inventiveness may be required on your part!); you might also be required to use French-registered builders, which is recommended in any case (see **DIY Or Builders?** on page 168). You will also need a 10 per cent deposit when buying a property more than five years old plus the fees and taxes associated with buying, which can be up to 40 per cent of the purchase price (see **Fees** on page 127).

BUYING FOR INVESTMENT

With prices now rising faster than inflation in most areas and at several times the rate of inflation in many, property is becoming an attractive investment proposition, particularly in popular areas such as the Mediterranean coast and parts of Brittany and the west coast. There are various kinds of property investment. Your family home is an investment, in that it provides you with rent-free accommodation. It may also yield a return in terms of increased value (a capital gain), although that gain may be difficult to realise unless you trade down or move to another region or country where property is cheaper. Of course, if you buy property other than for your own regular use, e.g. a holiday home, you will be in a position to benefit from a more tangible return on your investment. There are four main categories of investment property:

● A holiday home, which can provide your family and friends with rent-free holiday accommodation while (hopefully) maintaining or increasing its value; you may also be able to let it to generate supplementary income.

● A home for your children or relatives, which may increase in value and could also be let when not in use to provide an income.

● A business property, which could be anything from a private home with bed and breakfast or guest accommodation to a shop or office.

● A property purchased purely for investment, which could be a capital investment or provide a regular income, or both. In recent years, many people have invested in property to provide an income on their retirement.

A property investment should be considered over the medium to long term, i.e. a minimum of five and preferably 10 to 15 years, as you need to recoup the high purchase costs – up to 40 per cent of the value of a home (see **Fees** on page 127) – when you sell. You also need to take into account income tax if a property is let (see **Taxation Of Property Income** on page 242) and capital gains tax (see page 251) when you sell a second home. **Bear in mind that property isn't always 'as safe as houses' and property investments can be risky over the short to medium term**.

When buying to let, you must ensure that the rent will cover the mortgage (if applicable), running costs and periods when the property isn't let. Bear in mind that rental rates and 'lettability' vary according to the region and town, and that an area with high rents and occupancy rates one year may not be so fruitful the next. Gross rental yields (the annual rent as a percentage of a property's value) are from around 5 to 10 per cent a year in most areas (although gross yields of 15 per cent or more are possible); net yields (after expenses have been deducted) are 2 to 3 per cent lower.

Before deciding to invest in a property, you should ask yourself the following questions:

- Can I afford to tie up capital for at least five years?
- How likely is it that the value of the property will rise during this period, and will it outstrip inflation?
- Can I rely on a regular income from my investment? If so, how easy will it be to generate that income, e.g. to find tenants? Will I be able to pay the mortgage if the property is empty and, if so, for how long?
- Am I aware of all the risks involved and how comfortable am I with taking those risks?
- Do I have enough information to make an objective decision?

See also **Location** on page 85, **Mortgages** on page 194 and **Chapter 9.**

CLIMATE

France is the only country in Europe that has several distinct climatic zones (three or four according to interpretation): maritime along the west and north-west coast (and making its influence felt as far inland as the departments of Dordogne, Lot, Tarn and Tarn-et-Garonne), continental in central and eastern areas, and Mediterranean in the south-east and in Corsica, with a mountain climate in the Alps, Pyrenees, Massif Central and Vosges and numerous micro-climates making certain areas warmer, drier, wetter or colder than you might expect. The Alps and Pyrenees in particular experience extremes of weather, and there can be violent winds and storms in the south and north-west.

It therefore isn't easy to generalise about weather (*temps*) and, if you're planning to live in France and don't know whether the climate in a particular region will suit you, it's advisable to rent accommodation until you're absolutely sure, as the extremes of hot and cold in some areas are too much for some people. If you're seeking 'guaranteed' sun you need to head south. Generally the Loire river is considered to be the point where the cooler northern European climate gradually begins to change to the warmer southern climate. Spring and autumn are usually fine throughout France, although the length of the seasons vary depending on the region and altitude. In Paris, it's rare for the temperature to fall below minus 5°C (41°F) in winter or to rise above 30°C (86°F) in summer. However, Paris gets its fair share of rain. The expression 'raining cats and dogs' (*pleuvoir des chats et des chiens*) was coined here, when during periods of heavy rainfall dead cats and dogs were flushed out of the sewers into the streets!

The west and north-west (e.g. Brittany and Normandy) have a maritime climate tempered by the Atlantic and the Gulf Stream, with mild winters and warm summers, and most rainfall in spring and autumn. The area around La Rochelle in the west enjoys a pleasant micro-climate and is the second sunniest area of France after the Côte d'Azur. Many people consider the western Atlantic coast to have the best summer climate in France, with the heat tempered by cool sea breezes. The Massif Central (which acts as a weather barrier between north and south) and eastern France have a moderate continental climate with cold winters and hot and stormy summers. However, the centre and eastern upland areas have an extreme continental climate with freezing winters and sweltering summers. The northern Massif is prone to huge variations in temperature and it was here that an amazing 41°C (106°F) minimum/maximum temperature difference was recorded **in one day** (on 10th August 1885).

The Midi, stretching from the Pyreneesto the Alps, is hot and dry except for early spring, when there's usually heavy rainfall; the Cévennes region is the wettest with some 200cm (79in) of rain a year. Languedoc has hot dry summers and much colder winters than the French Riviera, with snow often remaining until May in the mountainous inland areas. The Riviera enjoys a Mediterranean climate of mild winters, daytime temperatures rarely dropping below 10°C (50°F), and humid and very hot summers, with the temperature often rising above 30°C (86°F). The average sunshine on the French Riviera is five hours in January and 12 hours in July. Note, however, that it isn't always warm and sunny on the Riviera and it can get quite cold and wet in some areas in winter.

The higher you go, the colder it gets, so if you don't like cold and snow, don't live up a mountain, e.g. in the Alps, Pyrenees, Vosges, Auvergne or Jura mountains. The mountains of the Alps and Pyrenees experience extremes of weather with heavy snow in winter and hot summers, although the western Pyrenees have surprisingly mild winters. The natural barrier of the Alps disrupts normal weather patterns and there are often significant local climatic variations. Central and eastern France have the coldest winters and consequently the highest heating bills. One of the most unpleasant aspects of very cold winters is motoring. If you need to commute in winter, bear in mind that roads are inevitably treacherous at times and can be frightening if you aren't used to driving on ice and snow (fog is also a particular hazard).

Average annual sunshine hours and days' rainfall in selected towns and cities are shown below:

Town/City	Region	Sunshine Hours	Days' Rainfall
Bordeaux	Aquitaine	2,084	125
Carcassonne	Languedoc-Roussillon	2,506	94
Clermont-Ferrand	Auvergne	1,907	90
Limoges	Limousin	1,974	135
Nantes	Pays-de-la-Loire	1,956	118
Nice	Provence-Alpes-Côte-d'Azur	2,694	64
Paris	Ile-de-France	1,800	112
Poitiers	Poitou-Charentes	1,930	113
Quimper	Brittany	1,749	146
Rouen	Upper Normandy	1,687	131
Toulouse	Midi-Pyrénées	2,047	101
Vannes	Brittany	2,024	131

France occasionally experiences extreme and unpredictable weather, which has become a favourite topic of conversation in some areas. Freak conditions combined to create violent storms in the south of France in recent years, e.g. in 1992 winds of 150km (93mph) an hour and flash floods resulted in over 40 deaths, and 63 communes being declared disaster areas. They were the worst storms in living memory and of a ferocity experienced only once every 50 years. In some areas 30cm (12in) of rain fell in three hours and half the annual rainfall for the region fell in just ten hours. Wherever you live, if you're anywhere near a waterway you should ensure that you have insurance against floods.

France experiences many violent cold and dry winds (*vent violent*) including the *Mistral* and the *Tramontane*. The *Mistral* is a bitterly cold wind that blows down the southern end of the Rhône valley into the Camargue and Marseille. The *Tramontane* affects the coastal region from Perpignan, near the Pyrenees, to Narbonne. Corsica is buffeted by many winds including the two aforementioned, the *Mezzogiorno* and *Scirocco*.

Average daily maximum/minimum temperatures for selected cities in Centigrade and Fahrenheit (in brackets) are:

City	Spring	Summer	Autumn	Winter
Bordeaux	17/6 (63/43)	25/14 (77/57)	18/8 (64/46)	9/2 (48/36)
Boulogne	12/6 (54/43)	20/14 (68/57)	14/10 (57/50)	6/2 (43/36)
Lyon	16/6 (61/43)	27/15 (81/59)	16/7 (61/45)	5/-1 (41/30)
Nantes	15/6 (59/43)	24/14 (75/57)	16/8 (61/45)	8/2 (46/36)

Nice	17/9 (63/48)	27/18 (81/64)	21/12 (70/54)	13/4 (55/39)
Paris	16/6 (61/43)	25/15 (77/59)	16/6 (57/43)	6/1 (43/34)
Strasbourg	16/5 (61/41)	25/13 (77/55)	14/6 (57/43)	1/-2 (34/28)

A quick way to make a **rough** conversion from Centigrade to Fahrenheit is to multiply by two and add 30 (see also **Appendix D**). Weather forecasts (*météo*) are broadcast on TV and radio stations and published in daily newspapers. You can obtain weather forecasts by telephone (e.g. ☎ 3201 – €0.46 per minute – 3250 – €0.34 per minute – or 08 92 68 08 08 (or 08 92 68 02 followed by a two-digit department code for a local forecast), 08 99 70 08 08, 08 99 70 11 00 or 08 99 70 12 34 – all premium rate numbers) or Minitel (3615 METEO) or via the internet (e.g. 🖳 www. meteo.fr or www.meteoconsult.fr). Note that French weather forecasts now include an index for afternoon ultra-violet light levels: 1 is the lowest, 10 the highest.

ECONOMY

When you're contemplating buying a property abroad, the financial implications of the purchase are usually one of your main considerations. These include not only the state of the French and eurozone economies but also that of your home country (or the country where you earn your income). The state of the economy in your home country (and your assets and job security there) may dictate how much you can afford to spend on the purchase, whether you can maintain your mortgage payments and the upkeep of a property, and how often you can afford to visit France.

France is one of the wealthiest countries in the world, with one of the highest per capita Gross Domestic Products per head (currently just under US$26,000 (E20,000) in the European Union. Inflation is running at under 2 per cent (there has been only a 10.5 per cent increase in the retail price index since 1998), and in late 2004 the Eurozone interest rate was 2.5 per cent and the European Central Bank (ECB) base rate stood at 3.25 per cent. France has experienced an economic transformation in the last few decades, during which its traditional industries have been thoroughly modernised and a wealth of new high-tech industries have been created, although increasing competition, particularly from the Far East, has meant that traditional industries such as steel, shipbuilding, textiles and motor vehicles have become less competitive. France's industrial output has been in decline since the mid-'90s. However, manufacturing remains important, particularly that of ships, cars, aeroplanes and defence equipment. The Saint-Nazaire shipyards near Nantes recently completed the largest-ever cruise liner, the Queen Mary 2, and the industrial park at Blagnac near Toulouse, where the new 550-seat Airbus A380 is being built, is expected to employ around 9,000 people.

Less labour and capital intensive industries such as electronics, pharmaceuticals and communications have flourished since the '80s, although the largest growth in recent years has been in service industries, e.g. banking, insurance and advertising, which now account for over 70 per cent of Gross Domestic Product (GDP) compared with industry at around 26 per cent and agriculture at a mere 3 per cent. (France is nevertheless Europe's largest agricultural producer with 23 per cent of total EU production.) France's answer to California's Silicon Valley, Sophia Antipolis on the Côte d'Azur, is the largest technology park in Europe with some 1,200 companies employing 23,000 people; a second park is under construction.

Since the start of the new millennium, France has maintained its large trade surplus, although it's still struggling to reduce the national debt in order to meet an EU ruling that all member states must have 'balanced books' (the national debt is €840 billion or over €2,700 for every man, woman and child). Nevertheless, since the economic difficulties encountered in Germany, France has been regarded by many as Europe's 'benchmark' economy (although the introduction of the 35-hour week, which was predicted to earn the economy over €2 billion, actually cost almost €1 billion!).

COST OF PROPERTY

After a slump in the '90s, property prices in France have begun to rise again, in some cases dramatically: in the first two years of the century, annual increases of 20 per cent weren't unusual in the most popular areas (e.g. the Côte d'Azur, where available property is now in short supply), although since then price rises have generally been less dramatic: a recent survey by the Royal Institution of Chartered Surveyors found that French house prices overall rose by 9 per cent in 2003, with higher increases common in the south. Nevertheless, French property remains excellent value compared with the UK and Spain, particularly rural properties. In general, prices are between 35 and 60 per cent of those in the UK, and there are still bargains to be found in many areas. (The best bargains are often to be had at auction – see page 126 – where properties repossessed by banks are sold.)

As in most countries, property is cheapest in rural areas, where the exodus in the last 30 years has left the countryside with a surfeit of empty properties (and where employment prospects are poor or non-existent). The French tend to live close to their work and the idea of commuting long distances doesn't appeal to them. With the exception of major commuter areas such as the Seine Valley and a few popular holiday areas such as Provence, Dordogne, the Alps and most coastal areas, the price of rural property in France is relatively low.

Prices have been driven up by foreign buyers particularly in border regions such as the Rhine departments, Savoy and the Lyon-Grenoble-Annecy triangle, and some areas in the south-west, e.g. the Dordogne. However, prices are highest in areas where the French demand for holiday homes is strongest, which generally includes anywhere along the Atlantic and Mediterranean coasts. Note that you usually pay a premium for a property with a sea view, although it's also easier to resell. Coastal and city properties can cost up to two or three times the price of similar inland rural properties. Property on the Côte d'Azur is among the most expensive in the world, and Paris isn't far behind.

Properties in traditionally popular places, such as Provence, Dordogne and Brittany, will probably always show a steady increase in value, as it's unlikely that these regions will lose their appeal to foreign (and particularly British) buyers, but there are other parts of France waiting in the wings that could soon (and suddenly) increase in popularity and where prices could therefore jump dramatically. These include the departments of Ariège, Aveyron, Gers and Mayenne, the Auvergne and Limousin regions, Burgundy and the Roussillon coast. Note, however, that in some remote areas (e.g. in the Auvergne) the local people may be hostile to foreign buyers and integration can be difficult. Those looking for a French idyll who cannot afford Provence prices (where villas start at around €300,000) but don't want to buy in the back of beyond should consider the Pays de la Loire and Poitou-Charentes regions, which are increasingly popular but not yet overrun with foreigners.

While it's no longer possible to find a perfectly restored country cottage for next to nothing, there are still properties to be had in Brittany, Normandy, Poitou-Charentes and other areas for as little as €25,000 (£18,000/$30,000), although they will need complete renovation, which could cost at least twice as much again. A modest €75,000 (£50,000/$85,000) will buy you a small modern house or quite a large property in need of renovation in Normandy or Brittany, the Auvergne, Limousin, Poitou-Charentes or Rhône-Alpes, a one-bedroom apartment on the Côte d'Azur or even a (tiny) studio flat in Paris, while for €150,000 (£100,000/$170,000) you can purchase a detached, three-bedroom house in Dordogne or Provence or an extensive property with acres of land in many other parts of the country. Those with a few hundred thousand euros to spend can stretch to a *maison de maître*, a *manoir*, a *château* or even an entire hamlet (*hameau*), which in remote areas such as the Cévennes or the departments of Lozère and Ardèche in the south-east, can be picked up for €500,000 or less (you can even find them in Nord-Pas-de-Calais) – ideal if you really want to get away from the neighbours!

For details of property prices in different areas, see **Property Prices** on page 121 and *The Best Places to Buy a Home in France* (Survival Books).

COST OF LIVING

No doubt you'd like to try to estimate how far your euros will stretch and how much money (if any) you will have left after paying your bills. Inflation in France in mid-2004 was around 1.9 per cent and is expected to fall to around 1.5 per cent in 2005. Salaries are generally high and the French enjoy a high standard of living and, although some 1.7 million people live below the official poverty line (i.e. earn less than €600 per month), many of these are part-time workers. On the other hand, social security costs are very high, particularly for the self-employed, and the combined burden of social security, income tax and indirect taxes make French taxes among the highest in the EU.

Anyone planning to live in France, particularly retirees, should take care not to underestimate the cost of living, which has increased considerably in the last decade. France is a relatively expensive country by American standards, particularly if your income is earned in US$, and in recent years many US visitors have found it difficult or impossible to remain within their budgets. (Americans will be particularly shocked by the price of gasoline, electricity, clothing, paper products and English-language books.) With the exception of Paris and other major cities, where the higher cost of living is offset by higher salaries, the cost of living in France is similar to that of Germany, some 25 per cent lower than in the UK and around 25 per cent higher than the USA. You should, however, be wary of published cost of living comparisons with other countries, which are often wildly inaccurate (and often include irrelevant items which distort the results).

It's difficult to calculate an average cost of living in France, as it depends on each individual's circumstances and lifestyle. The difference in your food bill, for example, will depend on what you eat and where you lived before arriving in France. Food costs around 50 per cent more than in the USA but is similar overall to most other western European countries, although you may need to modify your diet. From €300 to €500 should feed two adults for a month, excluding fillet steak, caviar and alcohol (other than a moderate amount of inexpensive beer or wine). Shopping abroad for selected 'luxury' items, such as stereo equipment, household apparatus, electrical and electronic goods, computers and photographic equipment, can result in significant savings (see page 308).

Approximate **minimum** monthly major expenses for an average single person, couple or family with two children are shown in the table below (most people will no doubt agree that the figures are either too high or too low!). When calculating your cost of living, deduct **at least** 15 per cent for social security contributions and the appropriate percentage for income tax (see page 238) from your gross salary. The numbers in brackets refer to the notes following the table.

	Monthly Costs (€)		
	Single	Couple	Couple with 2 Children
Housing (1)	425	575	750
Food (2)	200	375	475
Utilities (3)	50	80	110
Leisure (4)	100	160	200
Transport (5)	100	100	130
Insurance (6)	75	110	135
Clothing	50	100	200
TOTAL	**1,000**	**1,500**	**2,000**

1. Rent or mortgage payments for a modern or modernised apartment or house in an average suburb, excluding Paris and other high-cost areas. The properties envisaged are a studio or one-bedroom apartment for a single person, a two-bedroom property for a couple and a three-bedroom property for a couple with two children.
2. Doesn't include luxuries or expensive alcoholic drinks.
3. Includes electricity, gas, water, telephone, cable TV and heating costs.
4. Includes entertainment, restaurant meals, sports and holiday expenses, newspapers and magazines.
5. Includes running costs for an average family car plus third party insurance, annual taxes, petrol, servicing and repairs, but excludes depreciation and credit purchase costs.
6. Includes 'voluntary' insurance such as supplementary health, home contents, travel, car breakdown and life insurance.

PERMITS & VISAS

Before making any plans to visit France or live or work there, you must ensure that you have the necessary identity card or passport (with a visa if necessary) and, if you're planning to stay long-term, the appropriate documentation to obtain a residence and/or work permit. There are different requirements for different nationalities and circumstances, as detailed below.

French bureaucracy (euphemistically called *administration*) is legendary, and you should be prepared for frustration caused by time-wasting and blatant obstruction on the part of officials. (This isn't necessarily xenophobia – they treat their fellow countrymen in the same way!) Note also that immigration is an inflammatory issue in France, where non-EU citizens are regarded with particular suspicion.

 Permit infringements are taken very seriously by the French authorities, and there are penalties for breaches of regulations, including fines and even deportation for flagrant abuses.

While in France, you should carry your passport or residence permit (if you have one), which serves as an identity card, at all times. You can be asked to produce identifaction papers at any time by the police or other officials and, if you don't have them, you can be taken to a police station and interrogated.

SURVIVAL TIP
Immigration is a complex and ever-changing
subject, and the information in this chapter is intended
only as a general guide. You shouldn't base any
decisions or actions on the information contained herein
without confirming it with an official and reliable
source, such as a French consulate.

Visitors

Citizens of other EU countries can visit France for up to 90 days with a national identity card or passport only. Visitors from EU countries plus Andorra, Canada, Cyprus, the Czech Republic, Hungary, Iceland, Japan, Malta, Monaco, New Zealand, Norway, Singapore, the Slovak Republic, South Korea, Switzerland and the US don't require a visa, although French immigration authorities may require non-EU visitors to show a return ticket and proof of accommodation, health insurance and financial resources. All other nationalities need a visa to visit France (see **Visas** below).

EU nationals who visit France to seek employment or start a business therefore have 90 days in which to find a job and apply for a residence permit (see page 36). If they haven't found employment within this period and don't have sufficient funds to support themselves, the application will be refused.

Retired and non-active EU nationals don't require a visa before moving to France, but they must apply for a residence permit within a week of arriving (see page 36).

If you're a non-EU national, it isn't normally possible to enter France as a tourist and change your status to that of an employee, student or resident. You must return to your country of residence and apply for a long-stay visa (see below).

Note that you must spend at least 90 days outside France before you're eligible for another 90-day period in the country. If you're likely to want to return and require proof that you've spent the required period abroad, you should have your passport stamped at a police station, customs office or an office of the national police (*gendarmerie*) near your point of entry into France. You should ask to make a declaration of your entry (*déclaration d'entrée sur le territoire français*). Note also that you may not remain in France for more than 180 days in a year.

Non-EU citizens (except citizens of Andorra, Monaco and Switzerland and spouses of French citizens) who are staying with friends or family must obtain a 'certificate of accommodation' (*attestation d'accueil* – formerly *certificat d'hébergement* and sometimes referred to as *attestation d'hébergement!*), valid for 90 days, before departure and present it on arrival in France. Your hosts must apply for the *attestation* at their local town hall, police station or gendarmerie up to six months in advance of your arrival and post to you.

Visas

Visitors from EU countries plus Andorra, Canada, Cyprus, the Czech Republic, Hungary, Iceland, Japan, Malta, Monaco, New Zealand, Norway, Singapore, the Slovak Republic, South Korea, Switzerland and the US don't require a visa to enter France. Other nationals need a visa to enter the country, either as visitors or for any other purpose. Note, however, that some countries (e.g. Ireland and Italy) allow foreigners with close ancestors (e.g. a grandfather) who were born there to apply for a passport for that country, which can allow non-EU citizens to become 'members' of the EU. Visas may be valid for a single entry only or for multiple entries within a limited period. A visa is stamped in your passport, which must be valid for at least 90 days **after** the date you intend to leave France.

The following websites provide further details about visas in France: ⌨ www.diplomatie.fr (in English, including a facility for finding out which type of visa you need); ⌨ www.afii.fr (in English), the Invest in

France website, which has general information on settling in France as well as details about visas; 🖳 www.edufrance.fr, which contains general information about studying in France, including visa requirements for students. For details of the application procedure, see *Living and Working in France* (Survival Books – seee page 389).

There are two main types of visa in France, as described below.

Short-Stay Visas

A short-stay visa (*visa de court séjour*, sometimes referred to as a 'Schengen Visa') is valid for 90 days and is usually valid for multiple entries as well as for free circulation within the group of EU nations that are signatories to the Schengen agreement (i.e. Austria, Belgium, Denmark, Finland, France, Germany, Greece, Italy, Luxembourg, the Netherlands, Portugal, Spain and Sweden).

Another type of short-stay visa, often issued to businessmen, is a *visa de circulation*. It allows multiple stays of up to 90 days over a period of three years, with a maximum of 180 days in any calendar year.

Transit visas valid for three days are issued to rail and some airline passengers travelling through France.

A short-stay visa costs from €25 to €50, depending on the type.

Long-Stay Visa

A long-stay visa isn't necessary for EU nationals planning to stay longer than 90 days in France, although they must apply for a residence permit (see page 36). A non-EU national intending to remain in France for more than 90 days, whether to work, study or merely holiday, must obtain a long-stay visa (*visa de long séjour*) **before** arriving in France and must apply for a residence permit within a week of arrival. If you arrive in France without a long-stay visa, it's almost impossible to change your status after arrival and, if you wish to remain for longer than 90 days, you must return to your country of residence and apply for a long-stay visa.

Non-EU parents with children aged under 18 must also obtain long-stay visas for their children. Non-EU retirees should make a visa application to their local French consulate at least four months before their planned departure date.

Retired and non-active EU nationals are issued temporary residence permits, which must be renewed each year; they must provide proof that they have an adequate income or financial resources to live in France without working or becoming a burden on the state. The minimum amount necessary is roughly equivalent to the French minimum wage of €1,011 per month (around €12,000 per year), although it should be less if you aren't paying a mortgage or rent. It's normally necessary for non-EU retirees to show proof of private health insurance.

 If you require a visa to enter France and attempt to enter without one, you will be refused entry. If you're in doubt as to whether you require a visa to enter France, enquire at a French consulate before making travel plans.

Alternatively you can go to the French Ministry of Foreign Affairs website (Ministère des Affaires Etrangères, 💻 www.diplomatie.fr), where you can enter information about your situation to find the visa you require.

RESIDENCE PERMITS

All foreigners remaining in France for longer than 90 days in succession (for any reason) require a residence permit (*titre de séjour*). Where applicable, a residence permit holder's dependants are also granted a permit. Different types of residence permit are issued according to your status, including permits for long-stay visitors (*visiteur*), salaried employees (*salarié*), transferees (*détaché*), family members (*membre de famille*), students (*étudiant*) and traders (*commerçant*). A combined residence and work permit (*carte unique de séjour et de travail* or *carte de séjour salarié*) is issued to non-EU nationals taking up permanent employment in France. For details of the application and renewal procedures, see *Living and Working in France* (Survival Books – see page 389).

  There are two main categories of residence permit in France: a *carte de séjour* and a *carte de résident*. The *carte de séjour* is referred to below as a temporary residence permit and the *carte de résident* as a permanent residence permit.

Temporary Residence Permit

Until November 2003, a temporary residence permit (*carte de séjour*) was required by all foreigners aged 18 and above, both EU and non-EU nationals, who were to remain in France for more than 90 days (around 120,000 are issued each year). A new law (called the *loi Sarkozy*) introduced in November 2003 is generally believed to have waived the requirement for EU citizens to obtain a carte de séjour, although the actual wording of the law is ambiguous. EU citizens are therefore advised to contact their departmental *préfecture* in order to check whether a *carte de séjour* is required – particularly as you can be fined up to €1,500 for failing to apply for one! The information below is provided on the assumption that a *carte de séjour* is required.

 Whether or not you require a *carte de séjour*, you must meet the criteria for residence in France, i.e. adequate financial means of support and, unless you qualify for state health benefits, private health insurance.

The period of validity of a temporary residence permit varies according to your circumstances, e.g. a year (for EU nationals who are unemployed and non-EU employees), five years (for pensioners and 'non-active' EU nationals) to ten years (for EU nationals).

A residence permit automatically becomes invalid if you spend over six months outside France and it can be revoked at any time if you no longer meet the conditions for which it was issued (or if you obtained a permit fraudulently). After three years of continuous residence in France, the holder of a temporary residence permit can obtain a permanent residence permit (see below).

Permanent Residence Permit

A permanent residence permit (*carte de résident*) is usually issued to foreigners who have lived in France for three consecutive years and speak fluent French, (the exception is the foreign spouse of a French resident, who's automatically granted a permanent residence permit after one year of marriage). It's valid for ten years and renewable provided the holder can furnish proof that he's practising a profession in France or has sufficient financial resources to maintain himself and his dependants. A permanent residence permit authorises the holder to undertake any professional activity (subject to qualifications and registration) in any French department, even if employment was previously forbidden.

WORKING

If there's a possibility that you or any family members will wish to work in France, you must ensure that it will be possible before buying a home. If you don't qualify to live and work in France by birthright, family relationship or as a national of an EU or European Economic Area (EEA) country, you must obtain a work permit. Note that obtaining permission can be difficult or impossible. France has had a virtual freeze on the employment of non-EU nationals for many years; their employment must be approved by the French labour authorities (Agence Nationale Pour l'Emploi/ANPE), and there are restrictions as to the type of work they can do and the department(s) where they can work. Exceptions are foreigners with a permanent residence permit (issued after three years' residence), spouses of French citizens, and students who've studied in France for the preceding two years and have a parent who has lived in France for at least four years.

If you're a national of an EU country, you don't require official approval to live or work in France, although you may still require a residence permit (see page 36). If you visit France to look for a job, you have three months to find employment or set up in business. Once employment has been found, you must apply for a residence permit within a week.

Before moving to France to work, you should dispassionately examine your motives and credentials, and ask yourself the following questions:

- What kind of work can I realistically expect to do?
- Are my qualifications and experience recognised in France?
- How old am I? (Although discrimination on the basis of your age, physical appearance, name and sexual preference is illegal, age discrimination is rife in France, where only 38 per cent of men aged 55 to 64 work – the lowest percentage in Europe.)
- How good is my French? Unless your French is fluent, you won't be competing on equal terms with the French (you won't anyway, but that's a different matter!). Most French employers aren't interested in employing anyone without, at the very least, an adequate working knowledge of French.
- Are there any jobs in my profession or trade in the area where I wish to live? (Employment prospects in different regions of France are outlined in *The Best Places to Buy a Home in France*, published by Survival Books – see page 389).
- Could I be self-employed or start my own business?

The answers to these questions can be disheartening, but it's better to ask them before moving to France than afterwards.

Many people turn to self-employment or start a business to make a living, although this path is strewn with pitfalls for the newcomer.

 It's difficult for non-EU nationals to obtain a residence permit to work on a self-employed basis or start a business in France.

While hoping for the best, you should plan for the worst and have a contingency plan and sufficient funds to last until you're established (this also applies to employees). If you're planning to start a business you must also do battle with the notoriously obstructive French bureaucracy. For further details of working in France, see *Living and Working in France* (Survival Books – see page 389).

RETIREMENT

After Spain, France is the most popular destination for Britons looking to retire abroad. If you're planning to retire to France or move to France with a view to retiring there, you need to take certain special considerations into account, including those listed below. You should also think carefully whether you want to be living in a 'foreign' country in your final years and what would happen if your spouse or partner died before you .

 Many people who retire to France return home after deciding that they would rather spend their last years in more familiar surroundings.

Visas & Permits

Although retired and non-active EU nationals don't require a long-stay visa in order to move to France, a residence permit may be necessary and an application should be made within a week of your arrival (see page 36). Non-EU retirees intending to remain in France for more than 90 days must obtain a long-stay visa (*visa de long séjour*) **before** arriving in France and must also apply for a residence permit within a week of arrival. Non-EU retirees are issued temporary residence permits, which must be renewed each year.

Financial Resources

All non-employed residents, whether EU or non-EU citizens, must provide proof that they have an adequate income or financial resources to live in France without working or becoming a burden on the state. The minimum amount necessary is roughly equivalent to the French minimum wage of €1,091 per month (around €13,000 per year), although it should be less if you aren't paying a mortgage or rent. It's normally necessary for non-EU retirees to show proof of private health insurance.

If you plan to retire to France, you should ensure that your income is (and will remain) sufficient to live on, bearing in mind devaluations if your pension or income isn't paid in euros, rises in the cost of living (see page 31), and unforeseen expenses such as medical bills or anything else that may reduce your income, e.g. stock market crashes.

 Note that retirees often under-estimate the cost of living (see page 31) in France and many are forced to return to their home countries after a year or two.

Pensions & Social Security Benefits

Retirees receiving a state pension from another EU country can continue to receive it while in France and are entitled to the same health benefits as French retirees. Americans who retire in France can receive their pensions (and other benefits) via the Social Security department of the French Embassy in Paris (see **Appendix A** for address). Note, however, that tax-free lump sums from a foreign (e.g. UK) pension fund are regarded as taxable income in France. The rules regarding the the commutation of occupational pension scheme funds are complicated and you should seek expert legal advice.

EU retirees over 65 (over 60 in the case of women) going to live permanently in France can receive French social security benefits and aren't required to make contributions in France, although they must still register (and present forms E106 and E121). Note that since 1st January 2002 you're required to have a form E121 for **each** member of your household.

EU citizens who retire before qualifying for a state pension can receive French social security health cover for two years by obtaining a form E106 from their country's social security department (see page 40 for further details).

British pensioners who were receiving a winter fuel allowance in the UK can continue to receive it from the Winter Fuel Payments Centre, Southgate House, Cardiff CF91 1ZH (☎ 029-2042 8635).

If you're receiving a state pension in another EU country, you may be subject to an annual check that you're still receiving a pension. If you're of retirement age but are still working, you may qualify for an E106 and obtain health benefits for up to 30 months. If you don't qualify for either an E106 or an E121, you're still eligible for *CMU* (see **Health Insurance** below).

If you intend to retire while in France, you should check regularly that your pension contributions are up to date, either in France or in your previous country of residence. If you won't be entitled to a full French state pension (e.g. you won't have worked there for sufficient years), you may be able to continue to make contributions to your pension in your previous country of residence. Britons should contact the International Services department of the Inland Revenue NI Contributions Office, Benton Park View, Longbenton, Newcastle-upon-Tyne NE98 1ZZ (☎ 0845-915 4811). A French state pension is paid only when you cease full-time employment. It isn't paid automatically and you must make an application to your regional sickness insurance fund office (Caisse Régionale d'Assurance Maladie/CRAM).

Health Insurance

If you require just health insurance, it's **much** cheaper to take out private health insurance than to pay high French social security payments. Private health policies also offer a greater choice of health facilities and may provide a wider range of benefits than social security. On the other hand, as soon as you take up residence in France, you're obliged to 'join' (i.e. contribute to) the French social security system (*sécurité sociale*, commonly known as *la sécu*), which normally covers you for only a proportion of your medical expenses, so that you may wish to take out a complementary health insurance or 'top-up' policy (*assurance complémentaire maladie*, commonly known as *une mutuelle*); this normally (but not always) covers the balance of costs.

If you're living legally in France but aren't covered by French social security (directly or through a reciprocal health agreement) or a private health insurance policy, you may be entitled to free universal medical cover (*couverture maladie universelle/CMU*), a programme introduced in January 2000 and intended to ensure medical cover for all French residents. Information is available from your local CPAM office and on a dedicated government website (⌨ www.cmu.fr).

Taxes

If you spend more than 183 days in France, you become liable for French tax on your worldwide income (see **Liability** on page 239) but may still be liable for inheritance tax in your home country. French residential tax (see page 249) isn't paid by certain retirees whose income in the preceding year was below around €7,000 (plus around €1,800 for each dependant).

Mobility

If you're contemplating buying a rural property, consider how you will get to the nearest amenities and services, e.g. shops, doctor and dentist (see **Location** on page 85).

There's little point in choosing an isolated spot or somewhere with a limited public transport system, when in a few years' time you may have to rely on local bus, taxi or train services to get about.

You should also consider the terrain of your chosen home, as a location with lots of hills or steps could become an insurmountable problem if you have mobility problems or become disabled. A home in a town is usually a much better proposition for retirees than a country home. It's particularly important for retirees to thoroughly research an area and rent for a period before buying (see **Research** on page 19 and **Renting Before Buying** on page 108). See also **Retirement Homes** on page 144.

LANGUAGE

If you want to make the most of the French way of life and your time in France, it's essential to learn French as soon as possible. For people living in France permanently, learning French isn't an option, but a necessity and you should take evening classes or a language course **before you leave home**, as you will probably be too busy for the first few months after your move, when you most need the language.

SURVIVAL TIP
Your business and social enjoyment and
success in France will be directly related to the degree
to which you master French.

If you come to France without being able to speak French, you will be excluded from everyday life and will feel uncomfortable until you can understand what's going on around you.

 The most common reason for negative experiences among foreigners in France, both visitors and residents alike, is that they cannot (or won't) speak French.

However bad your grammar, however poor your vocabulary and however terrible your accent, an attempt to speak French will be much better appreciated than your fluent English. Don't, however, be surprised when the French wince at your torture of their beloved tongue or correct you in public for minor grammatical or pronunciation errors! (The French honestly believe they're doing you a favour by pointing out your mistakes to you while they're fresh in your mind! This also explains much of their hesitance to use English in public, for fear of being corrected themselves.) You **must** learn French if you wish to have French friends.

Note that France has a number of regional languages, including Alsatian (spoken in Alsace), Basque (south-west), Breton (Brittany), Catalan and Occitan (Languedoc-Roussillon) and Corsican (Corsica), although you won't need to learn anything other than French in any part of France. On the other hand, however fluent your French, you may still have problems understanding some accents – particularly those of the south of France – and local dialects (*patois*).

Learning French

Although it isn't easy, even the most non-linguistic person can acquire a working knowledge of French. All that's required is a little hard work, perseverance and some help, particularly if you have only English-speaking colleagues and friends. If you don't already speak good French, don't expect to learn it quickly, even if you already have a basic knowledge and take intensive lessons. It's common for foreigners not to be fluent even after a year or more of intensive lessons in France. If your expectations are unrealistic, you will become frustrated, which can affect your confidence. **It takes a long time to reach the level of fluency needed to be able to work in French.**

If you don't speak French fluently, you should begin French lessons **before** your arrival in France and continue them once you're there.

Language Schools & Courses

Most people can teach themselves a great deal through the use of books, tapes, videos and even computer-based courses. However, even the best students require some help. Teaching French is big business in France, with classes offered by language schools, French and foreign colleges and universities, private and international schools, foreign and international organisations (such as the British Institute in Paris), local associations and clubs, and private teachers.

There are many language schools (*école de langues*) in French cities and large towns, most French universities provide language courses, and many organisations offer holiday courses year-round, particularly for children and young adults (it's best to stay with a local French family). Tuition ranges from courses for complete beginners, through specialised business or cultural courses to university-level courses leading to recognised diplomas. If you already speak French but need conversational practice, you may prefer to enrol in an art or craft course at a local institute or club. You can also learn French via a telephone language course, which is particularly practical for busy executives and those who don't live near a language school.

One of the most famous French language teaching organisations is the Alliance Française (AF), 101 boulevard Raspail, 75270 Paris Cedex 06 (☎ 01 42 84 90 00, 🖥 www.alliancefr.org), a state-approved, non-profit organisation with over 1,000 centres in 138 countries, including 32 in France, mainly in large towns and cities. The AF runs general, special and intensive courses, and can also arrange homestays in France with a family.

Another non-profit organisation is Centre d'Échanges Internationaux, 1 rue Gozlin, 75006 Paris (☎ 01 43 29 60 20, 🖥 www.cei4vents.org for junior courses; 🖥 www.cei-frenchcentre.com for adult courses), offering intensive French language courses for juniors (13 to 18 years) and adults throughout France. Courses include accommodation in the organisation's own centres, with a French family, or in a hotel, bed and breakfast, or self-catering studio. Junior courses can be combined with tuition in a variety of sports and other activities, including horse riding, tennis, windsurfing, canoeing, diving and dancing.

Another well-known school is Berlitz (☎ 01 40 74 00 17, 🖥 www.berlitz.com), which has around 16 schools in France, including five in the Paris area. The British organisation CESA Languages Abroad (UK ☎ 01872-225300, 🖥 www.cesalanguages.com) offers advice and arranges language courses. In some areas, the *centre culturel* provides free French lessons to foreigners.

Most language schools run various classes depending on your language ability, how many hours you wish to study a week, how much money you want to spend and how quickly you wish to learn. Language classes generally fall into the following categories: Extensive (4 to 10 hours per week); Intensive (15 to 20 hours); Total Immersion (20 to 40 or more).

Unless you desperately need to learn French quickly, it's better to arrange your lessons over a long period. Don't commit yourself to a long course of study, particularly an expensive one, before ensuring that it's the right course. The cost for a one-week total immersion course is usually between €2,500 and €3,000! Most schools offer free tests to help you find your appropriate level and a free introductory lesson.

Private Lessons

You may prefer to have private lessons, a quicker, although more expensive way of learning a language. The main advantage of private lessons is that you learn at your own speed and aren't held back by slow learners or left floundering in the wake of the class genius. You can advertise for a teacher in your local newspapers, on shopping centre/supermarket bulletin boards and university notice boards, and through your or your spouse's employer. Otherwise, look for advertisements in the English-language press (see **Appendix B**). Don't forget to ask your friends, neighbours and colleagues if they can recommend a private teacher.

Private lessons by the hour cost from around €50 at a school or €15 to €35 with a private tutor, although you may find someone willing to 'trade' French lessons for English lessons. In some areas (particularly in Paris), there are discussion groups which meet regularly to talk in French and other languages; these are usually also advertised in the English-language press.

Self-Help

There are numerous self-study French courses available, including those offered by the BBC (🖳 www.bbc.co.uk/education/languages/french), Eurotalk (🖳 www.eurotalk.co.uk) and Linguaphone (🖳 www.lingua phone.co.uk). A quarterly publication, *Bien-dire*, is aimed at adult learners (🖳 www.learning french.com).

There are several things you can do to speed up your language learning, including watching television (particularly quiz shows where the words appear on the screen as they're spoken) and DVDs (where you can programme French or English subtitles), reading (especially children's books and product catalogues, where the words are accompanied by pictures), joining a club or association, and (most enjoyable) making French friends!

Information

Our sister-publication, *The Best Places to Buy a Home in France* (Survival Books), includes lists of language schools in the most popular regions of France. A comprehensive list of schools, institutions and organisations providing French language courses throughout France is contained in a booklet, *Cours de Français Langue étrangère et Stages pédagogie de Français Langue étrangère en France*. It includes information about the type of course, organisation, dates, costs and other practical information, and is available from French consulates or from the Association pour la Diffusion de la Pensée Française (ADPF), 6 rue Ferrus, 75683 Paris Cedex 14 (☎ 01 43 13 11 00, 🖳 www.adpf.asso.fr).

HEALTH

One of the most important aspects of living in France (or anywhere else for that matter) is maintaining good health, and France is among the world's 'healthiest' countries. Despite the common stereotype of the

French as wine-swilling gourmets stuffing themselves with rich foods, many have become health freaks in recent years. Fitness and health centres flourish in most towns, and even jogging (*footing*) has become fashionable in recent years. Smoking has declined considerably and is now a minority habit, although still more prevalent than in many other European countries.

On the other hand, air pollution (caused by vehicles, not smokers!) is an increasing problem in Paris and other French cities – particularly Grenoble, Lyon and Strasbourg – where it's blamed for a sharp rise in asthma cases. It's estimated that around 16,000 French people die prematurely each year as a result of air pollution. There's also a high and increasing rate of stress in French cities.

The incidence of heart disease in France is among the lowest in the world, a fact that has recently been officially contributed in part to the largely Mediterranean diet and high consumption of red wine. However, the French have a high incidence of cirrhosis of the liver and other problems associated with excessive alcohol consumption, and there has recently been an increase in the number of sufferers from Alzheimer's disease to over half a million (it affects around 10 per cent of those over 65 and 50 per cent of those over 85).

Overall, average life expectancy at birth in France has risen almost five years in the last two decades and is now the highest in the world after Japan: around 83 years for women, compared with the EU average of 81.4, and 75.3 for men, which is the EU average (almost half of male deaths between 15 and 45 are due to road accidents and suicide, and France has Europe's highest suicide rate by over 65s – over 3,000 per year). Amazingly, a child born in France in 2004 has an even chance of living to be 100. In fact people are now living so long that a new 'category' of person has been created, *le quatrième âge*, which refers to those over 75. At the other end of the scale, the infant mortality rate in France has been halved since 1990 to around 4.4 deaths before the age of one year per 1,000 live births (around the European average).

Among expatriates, sunstroke, change of diet, too much rich food and (surprise, surprise) too much alcohol are the most common causes of health problems. Nevertheless, when you've had too much of *la bonne vie*, you can take yourself off to a French spa for a few weeks to rejuvenate your system (in preparation for another bout of over-indulgence). Among the most popular treatments offered is thalassotherapy (*thalassothérapie*), a sea water 'cure' recommended for arthritis, circulation problems, depression and fatigue. You can safely drink the water in France unless it's labelled as non-drinking (*eau non-potable*), although the wine (especially the 1973 Château Mouton Rothschild) is more enjoyable.

The quality of healthcare and healthcare facilities in France is among the best in the world. The standard of hospital treatment is second to none, and there are virtually no waiting lists for operations or hospital beds. Public and private medicine operate alongside one another and there's no difference in the quality of treatment provided by public hospitals and private establishments, although the former may have more medical equipment. Local hospital services, particularly hospitals with casualty departments, can be limited in rural areas. Nevertheless, private treatment costs around half or even a third as much as similar treatment in the UK (e.g. around £900 for a cataract operation, compared with £3,000 in the UK).

France devotes a greater proportion of its GDP to health than to defence or education, the lion's share being spent on medicines rather than hospitals. They spend around 10 per cent of their national income on healthcare and are the world's second-largest spenders after the US. As a result, the cost of the public health service has spiralled out of control and the government has recently introduced measures designed to save money, including 'black listing' dozens of medicines (i.e. no longer reimbursing their cost) and 'encouraging' doctors to prescribe generic medicines rather than branded products. Though most French people recognise the need for reform, they're reluctant to lose hospitals, unlimited second opinions and an endless supply of free pills. (The French are famous for their hypochondria – famously satirised by Molière in *Le Malade Imaginaire*).

In general, French healthcare places the emphasis on preventive medicine rather than treating sickness, as in many other countries. Alternative medicine (*médecine douce*) is popular, particularly acupuncture and homeopathy. These treatments are recognised by France's medical council (Ordre des Médecins) and reimbursed by the national health service when prescribed by a doctor. France is the world leader in homeopathy, and some 15 per cent of the population regularly consult homeopathic doctors. Other types of treatment such as osteopathy and chiropractic are available but may not be reimbursed. (The practice of osteopathy and chiropractic by anyone other than a registered doctor was until recently illegal.)

If you're planning to take up residence, even if for part of the year only, it's wise to have a health check before your arrival (see page 222), particularly if you have a record of poor health or are elderly.

Most foreign medicines have an equivalent in France, although particular brands may be difficult or impossible to obtain. Note that the brand names for medicines often vary from country to country, so if you regularly take a particular medicine you should ask your doctor for the generic name. If you wish to match a medicine prescribed abroad, you need a current prescription with the medicine's trade name, the manufacturer's name, the chemical name and the dosage. A chemist may propose a generic product which is cheaper than the brand on your prescription (as part of the government's scheme to reduce health spending) but you aren't obliged to accept the alternative product. Generic products are up to a third cheaper than branded products and are usually identified by the prefix 'Gé'. Note, however, that social security reimbursement will be based on the generic equivalent of branded medicines (if one exists).

It's possible to have medicines sent from abroad, and no import duty or value added tax (*TVA*) is payable. If you're visiting France for a short period, you should take sufficient medicines to cover the length of your stay. In an emergency a local doctor will write a prescription (*ordonnance*) that can be filled by a local chemist, or a hospital may refill a prescription from its own pharmacy.

For further information about health services in France, see *Living and Working in France* (Survival Books); for details of services in particular regions, refer to *The Best Places to Buy a Home in France* (Survival Books). See also **Health Insurance** on page 263.

PETS

If you're exporting a cat, dog, rabbit, guinea pig, mouse, rat or ferret to France from the UK, you should obtain a 'passport' for it confirming that it has been microchipped and that its vaccinations are up to date. You must then continue to have it vaccinated regularly while in France.

 If you fail to do this and want to bring your pets back to the UK at any time, they will need to be quarantined for six months.

The cost of a pet passport (i.e. the tests and vaccinations required to obtain one) is around £150, plus £60 per year for follow-up vaccinations and around £20 for a border check on re-entry to the UK. Details of the scheme, known as PETS, can be obtained from the Department for Environment, Food and Rural Affairs (see **Further Information** below).

You can take up to three animals into France at any one time, one of which may be a puppy (three to six months old), although no dogs or cats under three months of age may be imported. Two parrot-like birds (psittacidaes) can be imported into France and up to ten smaller species; all require health certificates issued within five days of departure. Other animals require special import permits from the French Ministry of Agriculture.

If you're transporting a pet to France by ship or ferry, you should notify the ferry company. Some companies insist that pets are left in vehicles (if applicable), while others allow pets to be kept in cabins. If your pet is of nervous disposition or unused to travelling, it's best to tranquillise it on a long sea crossing. Pets can also be transported by air and certain pets can be carried with you (in an approved container), for which there's a charge (e.g. around €100 one-way from the US).

There are companies that will accommodate your pets while you move, take care of all export requirements and ship them to you when you've settled in, e.g. Pinehawk Kennels & Livestock Shippers (☎ 01223-290249) in the UK.

SURVIVAL TIP

If you plan to take a pet (*animal domestique*) to France, it's important to check the latest regulations. Make sure that you have the correct papers, not only for France but for all the countries you will pass through to reach France. Particular consideration must be given before exporting a pet from a country with strict quarantine regulations in case you wish to re-import it later (see below).

With a pet passport, you can reimport your pets to their country of origin, but you may have to make arrangements well in advance. For example, a pet must be blood tested at least six months before it can be taken to the UK.

Vaccinations

France has almost eradicated rabies in the last 20 years by vaccinating foxes and it could disappear in the next few years, although there have recently been a number of reported cases in dogs (one in 2001, one in 2002 and three in the first half of 2004 – two in the south-west and one in Brittany). Although there's generally no quarantine period for animals imported into France, there are therefore strict vaccination requirements for dogs in certain departments, where they must be vaccinated against rabies and have a *certificat contre la rage* or have a health certificate (*certificat de bonne santé*) signed by an approved veterinary surgeon issued no more than five days before their arrival. Resident dogs need an annual rabies booster and it's recommended that they're also vaccinated against the following diseases:

● *Babesia canis*, also known as *Piroplasma canis* or Canine piroplasmosis (*la piroplasmose*), a parasitic disease carried by ticks (*tiques**) that also affects horses and cattle;

- Distemper or Carré's disease (*la maladie de Carré*, also known as *la maladie des jeunes chiens* and *la maladie du jeune âge*, as it mainly affects young animals), a potentially fatal viral infection;
- *Hepatitis contagiosa canis* or Rubarth's disease (*l'hépatite de Rubarth*), an acute viral disease which attacks the liver;
- Leptosporosis (*la leptospirose*), a bacterial disease which can be transmitted to humans and can be fatal;
- Parvovirus or Parvo (*la parvovirose*), an intestinal virus;
- Tracheobronchitis, known as kennel cough (*la toux de chenil*), which is one of the most common canine diseases and can lead to fatal complications.

* Ticks are a problem in many parts of France and can be lethal. You should invest in a tick-remover (around €3.50 from your vet) and treat your pets regularly with a preventive such as Frontline.

Vaccinations are initially in two stages, a 'booster' being administered three or four weeks after the initial injection; a single annual renewal is required. Each injection costs between around €35 and €60, depending on the vet. Serums must be administered separately.

Cats aren't required to have regular rabies vaccinations, although if you let your cat roam free outside your home it's advisable to have it vaccinated annually. Cats must, however, be vaccinated against feline gastro-enteritis and flu. (A rabies vaccination is compulsory for animals entering Corsica or being taken to campsites or holiday parks.) All vaccinations must be registered with your veterinary surgeon (*vétérinaire*) and be listed on your pet's vaccination card or (preferably) in a *livret international de santé*, which must also certify that the animal has been confined to countries that have been rabies-free for at least three years.

Sterilisation

Sterilisation of pets isn't common practice in France, where stray dogs and cats are a problem in many areas. Nevertheless, vets are familiar with the procedures, which are usually straightforward.

Sterilisation of bitches and female cats not only prevents them from becoming pregnant but can also protect them against the canine equivalent of breast cancer (*le cancer des mamelles*), provided the operation is carried out before the animal's first heat. Sterilisation offers some protection against cancer if carried out between the first and second heats but none after the second.

Sterilising a bitch costs between around €130 and €300 depending on the size of the animal and the vet; sterilisation of female cats costs around €120.

Castration of male dogs and cats costs approximately half as much and can be beneficial in cases where an animal is prone to running away or is aggressive or to reduce the smell of its urine.

Dogs

Dogs and cats don't wear identification discs in France and there's no system of licensing. However, all dogs born after 6th January 1999 must be given an official identifying number, either in the form of a tattoo or contained in a microchip inserted under their skin. This rule is designed to make it easier to find the owners of stray dogs and to reduce the incidence of 'dog trafficking'. Around 100,000 dogs are abandoned by their owners every year, many at the start of the long summer holiday or after the hunting season is over, and stray dogs are regularly rounded up and taken to the local pound to be destroyed. A further 60,000 dogs are stolen each year and certain breeds are highly prized. It's therefore recommended to have your dog tattooed or chipped even if it was born before this date.

Some vets favour tattooing (*tatouage*) because the number is visible, whereas reading a microchip (*puce*) requires a special machine. Others recommend microchipping because a tattoo can be removed or wear off.

The costs of the two procedures are similar, although charges aren't fixed and vary considerably according to the veterinary practice – between around €25 and €75 for tattooing and from €35 to €70 for microchipping.

If you find a dog, look to see whether it's tattooed. If not, you can take it to a vet to have it checked for a microchip. If its owner refuses to take it back, you can prosecute him.

Instead of buying a dog, you can obtain one from a pound (*fourrière*) or an SPA (Société Pour la Protection des Animaux) centre, both of which are listed in the yellow pages under *Animaux (refuges, fourrières)*.

Dogs must be kept on leads in most public parks and gardens in France and there are large fines for dog owners who don't comply. Dogs are forbidden in some parks, even when on leads. On public transport, small pets must usually be carried in a basket or cage if a fare is to be avoided (but the SNCF has a standard charge of €5 and charges half second class fare for uncaged dogs weighing over 6kg). Some 500,000 people are bitten by dogs each year, 60,000 of whom are hospitalised, and certain breeds of dog (e.g. pit-bull terriers) must be muzzled in public places.

French hotels usually quote a rate for pets (e.g. €8 per night), most restaurants allow dogs and many provide food and water (some even allow owners to seat their pets at the table!). There are even exclusive dog restaurants in France. Although food shops make an effort to bar pets, it isn't unusual to see a supermarket trolley containing a dog (the French don't take much notice of 'no dogs' signs). There's usually no discrimination against dogs when renting accommodation, although they may be prohibited in furnished apartments.

Note that allowing your pooch to poop on the pavement is illegal and you can be fined up to €450 if you don't 'scoop' up after it.

Kennels & Catteries

There are many kennels and catteries (*refuge pour animaux* or *pension canine/féline*), where fees are around €6 per day for cats and €9 for dogs. A free list of over 300 kennels and catteries, *Le Guide pratique Royal Canin*, is available from the publisher, a pet food company (☎ 08 00 41 51 61), or you can search for a suitable kennel on the Royal Canin website (🖥 www.royalcanin.fr). If you plan to leave your pet at a kennel or cattery, book well in advance, particularly for school holiday periods.

Vets & Insurance

Veterinary surgeons are well trained in France, where it's a highly popular and well paid profession. Emergency veterinary care is available in major cities, where there are also animal hospitals (*hôpital pour animaux*) and vets on 24-hour call for emergencies. A visit to a vet usually costs €23 to €30. Some vets also make house calls, for which there's a minimum charge of €62 to €78. Taxi and ambulance services are also provided for pets.

Medical treatment for dogs can be just as expensive as human treatment (e.g. €200 for a scan and over €500 for a major operation) – and it isn't reimbursed by social security. Health insurance for pets is available from a number of insurance companies but in most cases provides only partial cover.

There are essentially two types of pet insurance: insurance against accidents and insurance against illness and accidents. The former costs around €70 or €80 per year and covers only medical and surgical costs resulting from accidental injury, e.g. a broken bone, poisoning or a bite by another dog. The latter, which costs at least twice as much, also covers the treatment of certain illnesses and diseases.

As with human health insurance, you should check exactly what is and isn't covered and what conditions apply. Certain treatment may be excluded, e.g. vaccinations, sterilisation or castration, dental treatment and cancer screening, as may certain hereditary diseases. Conditions may include an upper age limit (usually nine or ten years for dogs), a waiting period (of up to four months) before insurance becomes effective, an annual claim limit (generally between €800 and €1,600) and an excess or deductible (*franchise*), which often applies to every claim and can be as much as 30 per cent.

Pet insurance doesn't cover you for third-party liability, e.g. if your pet bites someone or causes an accident, which should be included in your household insurance (see page 273); check with your insurer.

Further Information

For the latest regulations regarding the importation and keeping of pets in France contact the Sous-Direction de la Santé et de la Protection Animales, Ministère de l'Agriculture, de la Pêche et de l'Alimentation, 251 rue de Vaugirard, 75732 Paris Cedex 15 (☎ 01 49 55 40 93).

Details of the British pet passport scheme can be obtained from the Department for Environment, Food and Rural Affairs (DEFRA), Ergon House, 17 Smith Square, London SW1P 3JR (☎ 020-7238 6951 or 0845-933 5577, 🖳 www.defra.gov.uk). General information can be obtained in the UK from Dogs Away (☎ 020-8441 9311, www.dogsaway.co.uk), Pets Will Travel (🖳 www.petswilltravel.co.uk), the Quarantine Abolition Fighting Fund (☎ 01243-264173) and Travelpets (☎ 020-7499 4979, www.travelpets.net). Eurotunnel has details of vets and blood labs in France that are approved by DEFRA (☎ 0870-5353535, 🖳 www. eurotunnel.com).

A useful book is *Travel Tips for Cats and Dogs* by David Prydie (Ringpress Books).

2.

THE BEST PLACE TO LIVE

Once you've decided to buy a home in France, your first task will be to choose the region and what sort of home. France is a world unto itself, and deciding where to live can be difficult and the choice overwhelming.

SURVIVAL TIP
If you're unsure where and what to buy, the best decision is to rent for a period (see page 108).

The secret of successfully buying a home in France (or anywhere else for that matter) is research, research and more research, preferably before you even set foot there (see page 19). You may be fortunate and buy the first property you see without doing any homework and live happily ever after. However, a successful purchase is much more likely if you thoroughly investigate the towns and communities in your chosen area, compare the range and prices of properties and their relative values, and study the procedure for buying property. It's a lucky person who happens upon the ideal home, and you have a much better chance of finding your dream home if you do your homework thoroughly.

France is a huge country (the largest in western Europe) with a vast array of landscapes, including low-lying areas in the north and west, mountains in the centre, east and south-east, forests, farmland and wetlands (see **Geography** below). It's also the only country in Europe that has three (or four) climatic zones as well as numerous micro-climates (see **Climate** on page 25), making your choice of location less than straightforward.

Unlike most Western countries, France is still largely rural. Some 25 per cent of the population lives in rural areas, a percentage which has hardly changed in half a century, and average population density is among the lowest in Europe at around 100 people per km^2 (260 per mi^2). There are over 32,600 French villages with fewer than 1,000 inhabitants, which means that a 'rural idyll' can be a reality in most parts of the country, and complete isolation is a possibility in some areas (e.g. Lozère in the Massif Central). On the other hand, there are bustling cities, although Paris, with a population of almost 11 million, is the only really large city. Only three other cities have populations of over 1 million (Lyon 1.6 million, Marseille 1.4 million and Lille 1.1 million), and only five more (Toulouse, Bordeaux, Nantes, Strasbourg and Nice) have over half a million inhabitants.

GEOGRAPHY

France, often referred to as *l'hexagone* on account of its hexagonal shape (the French are known as *les hexagonaux*), is the largest country in

Western Europe. Mainland France (*la métropole*) covers an area of almost 550,000km^2 (212,300mi^2), stretching 1,050km (650mi) from north to south and almost the same distance from west to east (from the tip of Brittany to Strasbourg). Its land and sea border extends for 4,800km (around 3,000mi) and includes some 3,200km (2,000mi) of sea coast. France is bordered by Andorra, Belgium, Germany, Italy, Luxembourg, Spain and Switzerland, and the opening of the Channel Tunnel in 1994 connected it with the UK (although only by rail). Its borders are largely determined by geographical barriers, including the English Channel (*la Manche*) in the north, the Atlantic Ocean in the west, the Pyrenees and the Mediterranean in the south, and the Alps and the Rhine in the east.

Mainland France is divided into 22 regions and 94 departments, the Mediterranean island of Corsica (*Corse*) comprising a further two departments (see map on page 359). Corsica is situated 160km (99mi) from France and 80km (50mi) from Italy, covering 8,721km^2 (3,367mi^2) and with a coastline of 1,000km (620mi). There are also six overseas departments (*département d'outre-mer/DOM*) – French Guiana (*Guyane*), Guadeloupe, Martinique, Mayotte, Réunion and Saint-Pierre-et-Miquelon – and three overseas territories (*territoires d'outre-mer/TOM*) – French Polynesia (*Polynésie-française*), New Caledonia (*Nouvelle Calédonie*) and the Wallis and Futuna islands. (Although situated within France, Monaco is an independent principality and isn't governed by France.)

The north and west of France is mostly low-lying. The Paris basin in the centre of the country occupies a third of France's land area and is one of Europe's most fertile agricultural regions. The Massif Central in the centre of France is noted for its extinct volcanoes, hot springs and many rivers. In general the south and south-east of France are mountainous, although despite its many mountain ranges (Alps, Auvergne, Jura, Massif Central, Pyrenees and Vosges), France is largely a lowland country with most of its area less than 200m (700ft) above sea level. The Massif Central has many peaks rising above 1,500m (5,000ft) and Mont Blanc (at 4,810m/15,781ft Europe's highest mountain excluding those of the former USSR), is situated in the French Alps. Almost 90 per cent of the land is productive, with around one-third cultivated, one-quarter pasture and one-quarter forest.

France has a comprehensive network of rivers and canals comprising some 40 per cent of European waterways, including the Garonne, Loire, Rhine, Rhône and the Seine. The Loire, 1,020km (634mi) in length, is France's longest river. In recent decades, however, France has lost half its wetlands (*zones humides*), which now account for a mere 2.5 per cent of the country's area.

A geographical map of France is shown on page 6; a map of the regions and departments is included in **Appendix E**.

REGIONS

Alsace

Alsace (population 1.73 million) is one of the smallest regions containing just two departments: Bas-Rhin (67) and Haut-Rhin (68) – Lower and Upper Rhine. It's located in the extreme east bordering Germany, to which it has belonged at various times in its colourful history. Not surprisingly it has a Germanic feel, which is reflected in its architecture, cuisine, dress, dialects (German is still widely spoken), names and people (called Alsatians). Sandwiched  between the Vosges mountains and the Rhine, Alsace is gloriously scenic and largely unspoiled, with delightful hills (cross-country skiing is a popular winter sport), dense forests, rich farmland and pretty vineyards. It's noted for its many picturesque villages, particularly on the Wine Road (*Route du Vin*) stretching from Marlenheim west of Strasbourg down to Thann beyond Mulhouse. Alsace is famous for its beer (such as Kronenbourg) and white wines. Perhaps surprisingly, Alsace has more Michelin restaurant stars than any other region of France!

The regional capital is Strasbourg (67), home of the European Parliament, the European Court and the European Commission on Human Rights. Other notable towns include Colmar and Mulhouse, a prominent industrial city. Property prices are higher than the average for France and there are few bargains to be found. Rundown or derelict rural properties for sale are rare in Alsace, where (unlike many other regions) there hasn't been a mass exodus from the farms and countryside. The region has excellent road connections with Paris, the south of France, Germany and Switzerland.

Aquitaine

Aquitaine (population 2.91 million) is made up of the following departments: Dordogne (24), Gironde (33), Lot-et-Garonne (47), Landes (40) and Pyrénées-Atlantiques (64). Aquitaine owes its name to the Romans, who logically named the area Aquitania, as it had many rivers running through it (to which canals were later added). It has had a somewhat chequered history and, like Normandy, was once ruled by

the kings of England (or vice versa), although it has been under French rule since 1650. The region, which covers an area of 41,310km² (16,135mi²) and has a population of 2.7 million, is largely agricultural, unspoiled and sparsely populated, and it's noted for its temperate climate. Crops include corn and peppers (the hot variety), which are hung from the window ledges and beams of houses to dry. Aquitaine is one of the most varied regions of France; although predominantly flat (the majority of the region lies less than 250m/825ft above sea level), the land rises in the south at the foothills of the Pyrenees. It has over 270km (170mi) of spectacular beaches along the Atlantic coastline, known as the *Côte d'Argent* ('Silver Coast'), 30km (20mi) of which are considered to offer the best surfing in Europe.

Aquitaine is perhaps most famous for its wines, beaches, surfing and of course, Eleanor of Aquitaine, mother of Richard the Lionheart. In the north of the region is the Bassin d'Arcachon, a natural inland sea with the largest beach in Europe (where incidentally 90 per cent of French oysters are grown), while the south of Aquitaine includes the so-called *Landes de Gascogne*. 'The Landes' is a flat, sandy plain (*lande* means 'moor'), roughly triangular, bounded by the sea and dunes to the west and stretching from Bordeaux (33) in the north to Dax (40) and the Golfe de Gascogne in the south and east as far as Nérac (47) and therefore covering roughly the whole of the department of Landes, as well as a good deal of Gironde and parts of Lot-et-Garonne. It was transformed during the 19th century by the planting of pine trees, which now cover virtually the entire area, creating purportedly the largest forest in Europe (the trees are now used for making paper). Part of the forest, corresponding roughly to the basin of the river Eyre, was designated a regional park (the Parc régional des Landes de Gascogne) in 1970. The Landes is known as '*le pays de la bonne bouffe*' ('the land of good grub'), where traditional dishes include *cruchade* (a dessert), *garbure* (soup), *millas* (corn-cake) and *saupiquet* (fried ham). Gironde to the north is also generally flat (its highest point is just 165m/535ft) and much of the land is given over to vineyards.

Pyrénées-Atlantiques is part of the Basque Country (*Pays basque*), which extends from around 160km (100mi) south of Bordeaux, where the Landes give way to the foothills of the Pyrenees, across the mountains into Spain and east along the river Nive as far as Saint-Jean-Pied-de-Port. The Basque Country has its own language, style of architecture, sport (*pelota*) and traditions and is itself divided into ancient 'regions', such as Labourd, Soule and Basse-Navarre. Apart from the conurbation of Bayonne, Anglet and Biarritz (known locally as the 'BAB'), where property is fairly expensive, Pyrénées-Atlantiques is sparsely populated. To the east of the Basque Country is Béarn (famous for its *sauce béarnaise*), another ancient 'region' (its capital is Orthez) surrounding the valleys of the Aspe, Barétous and Ossau in the east of Pyrénées-Atlantiques. The inland department of Lot-et-Garonne is undulating and largely rural and agricultural. It's one of the largest fruit-growing areas in France, producing apples, apricots, melons, nectarines, peaches, plums (including the mouth-watering *prunes d'agenais*) and strawberries, as well as tobacco, among other crops. (There's a famous fruit fair at Prayssas, between Agen and Villeneuve-sur-Lot.) Aquitaine as a whole is 45 per cent woodland (not surprisingly, the highest percentage in France), 30 per cent grassland, 20 per cent arable land and 25 per cent other uses, including urban areas.

With the exception of Dordogne (see below), Aquitaine hasn't been especially popular with foreign property buyers, but with access becoming easier by air, rail and road, coupled with low increases in property prices, a pleasant climate and (of course) wonderful wines and food, the region has seen an increase in the purchase of second and retirement homes – especially by the British and other Europeans.

Dordogne

One of the most popular French departments among foreign homebuyers (particularly the British) is Dordogne. The ancient province of Périgord, Dordogne is France's third-largest department, covering an area of 9,060km^2 (3,533mi^2), and has a population of just under 400,000. Like many French departments, Dordogne is named after the main river flowing through it. It's split into four territories. In the north is 'Green Périgord', so called because of its green valleys irrigated by a multitude of streams. This territory contains the Périgord-Limousin Regional Natural Park and its main towns include Brantôme, Nontron and Riberac. In the centre is 'White Périgord', which takes its name from the limestone plateaux and contains the departmental capital, Périgueux. In the south-west corner of Dordogne is the newly identified territory of 'Purple Périgord', which includes the Bergerac area, famous for its wine grapes (hence 'purple'), and French and English fortified towns, castles and *châteaux* built during the Hundred Years War (Dordogne boasts some 10 per cent of France's 40,000 *châteaux*). In the south-east is 'Black Périgord', so called on account of the ancient oak trees covering large parts of the area and home to the valleys of the rivers Dordogne and Vézère. Perhaps the territory best known to foreigners, Black Périgord has been inhabited since prehistory and contains the famous caves at Lascaux and Les Eyzies (among others) and the picturesque towns of Saint-Cyprien and Sarlat-la-Canéda.

Dordogne has for a long time been a holiday and migration destination for Britons (the French call the area around Ribérac 'little England') and more recently Dutch and Germans. During the late 1980s, the demand was so great for ruined farms and houses that a mini-boom was created. Prices are more reasonable now and bargains can still be found, but it's still the most expensive department in this area for the simple reason that it's one of the most scenic departments in France and contains some of the country's prettiest and most dramatic towns and villages, including Brantôme, Domme, La Roque-Gageac, Sarlat-la-Canéda and Trémolat. Domme and Sarlat are the jewels of Dordogne and are so popular that they're in danger of being ruined by tourism (it's almost impossible to find a grocer amongst the tourist shops and artist's galleries along the main road in Domme).

Most of what makes Dordogne memorable is to be found in a 15km (10mi) stretch of the river between Bergerac and Souillac (in Lot), but every village has historical buildings, whether churches, *châteaux* or ordinary houses inhabited by the same family for generations. Dordogne is also a treasure trove of caves filled with prehistoric paintings up to 30,000 years old. Lascaux and Les Eyzies are the two major sites and perhaps the best known. The river itself provides other distractions for inhabitants and holidaymakers, although the latter can be a nuisance to the former in high season. Local cuisine includes truffles and *pâté de foie gras* (the best French *foie gras* is considered to come from Sarlat) and is noted for its duck and goose dishes.

Auvergne

Situated south of the centre of France, the Auvergne (population 1.31 million) covers an area of 26,000km² (16,250mi²) at the heart of the Massif Central (the volcanic region in the centre of France) and has a population of 1.3 million. The Auvergne includes the departments of Allier (03), Cantal (15), Haute-Loire (43) and Puy-de-Dôme (63). In the area around Clermont-Ferrand (63), the mountains reach a peak of 1,885m (6,180ft). From north to  south, with a small ascent around the Plateau Millevaches (978m/3,200ft) the terrain becomes flatter and rockier. The Auvergne is 25 per cent woodland, 45 per cent grassland, 20 per cent arable land and 10 per cent other uses (including urban areas). Economically, the Auvergne is a relatively poor region, and the department of Haute-

Loire in particular is suffering from the decline of agriculture and an ageing population.

The main towns are Ambert, Aurillac, Clermont-Ferrand, Le Puy-en-Velay, Moulins and Vichy. The region is unique in France, as Europe's largest group of volcanoes (now extinct) have created a landscape of mountains (Mont Dore reaches 1,885m/6,180ft), craters, lakes, rivers (the Dordogne springs from near Mont-Dore), springs (including Arvie, Mont-Dore, Saint-Yorre, Vichy and Volvic), spas and lava flows, all of which combine to create a huge geological park. The region contains two regional parks and two nature parks, and in February 2002 a volcano theme park opened, including volcano-related exhibits and a guided tour around the crater of an extinct volcano.

This natural heritage is complemented by a rich cultural and historical heritage: more than 500 Romanesque churches (some of which are considered France's best), almost 50 *châteaux* and ten spa towns. The Auvergne also contains ten of the 'most beautiful villages of France', four of which are in Haute-Loire. The regional capital, Clermont-Ferrand (headquarters of Michelin, the tyre manufacturer and tourist guide producer), is mainly built from dark basalt, making an impressive and unusual townscape. There are nine ski centres, 200km (125mi) of downhill runs and more than 800km (500mi) of cross-country trails.

Water plays an important part in the economy of the region. Many lakes have formed in valleys blocked by lava streams, e.g. at Aydat and Guéry, or where volcanoes have erupted in valleys, e.g. at Chambon and Montcineyre. Many anglers and watersports enthusiasts use these lakes, along with rivers such as the Allier and the Cher. The many hot springs in the area also owe their existence to volcanic activity. Water temperature ranges from 10°C (50°F) to over 80°C (Chaudes-Aigues is the hottest spring in Europe at 82.3°C/180°F) and the springs are sought after by people who wish to 'take a cure'. Vichy, in Allier, is probably the best known spa town, having waters that are used for drinking and for balneology, and is also famous for its bottled water.

The region is predominantly agricultural with tourism slowly becoming more important. Cows are much in evidence and are used both for meat and for milk, which is made into a number of well known cheeses: Bleu d'Auvergne, Cantal, Forme d'Ambert and Saint-Nectaire. Green lentils have been cultivated in Puy-en-Velay (43) since Gallo-Roman times and are the first vegetable to be given a quality classification as for wine. Excellent wine (both red and white) is also made from the Saint-Pourçain vineyard (one of the oldest in France) stretched along the banks of the Allier.

Burgundy

Burgundy (*Bourgogne*) has a population of 1.61 million and contains the departments of Côte-d'Or (21), Nièvre (58), Saône-et-Loire (71) and Yonne (89). The region has few industries, which means that it's almost totally unspoiled and one of France's most beautiful and fertile areas (it has been dubbed the 'rural soul' of France). It's a timeless land where little has changed over the centuries – a haven of peace and serenity (particularly the Parc du Morvan at its heart).

The name Burgundy is synonymous with magnificent wines such as Nuits-Saint-Georges, Meursault, Beaune, Puligny-Montrachet, Gevrey-Chambertin and Pouilly-Fuissé, grown on the 60km (37mi) Côte d'Or hillside, as well as fine cuisine, including *boeuf bourguignon* (made with Charollais beef), *coq au vin* (with Bresse chicken), Morvan ham and snails, generally served with rich sauces, as well as *pain d'épices* ('spicy' bread) and *kir* (white wine with a dash of blackcurrant liqueur).

The region is also renowned for its many canals and canal boats, and has some 1,200km (750mi) of navigable waterways, including the Burgundy Canal and the rivers Saône and Yonne. Burgundy has a rich and colourful history (it was an independent kingdom for some 600 years), celebrated in numerous festivals and pageants, and a wealth of Romanesque churches, cathedrals, medieval villages and historic towns. Its most important towns include Autun, Auxerre, Beaune, Chalon-sur-Saône, Dijon (21), famous for its mustard and the regional capital, Fontenay, Mâcon, Nevers, Paray-le-Monial and Vézelay.

Somewhat surprisingly, Burgundy isn't popular with foreign property buyers, perhaps because of its relative isolation, and there are few holiday and retirement homes there. It rarely features in international property magazines and, although the region has a wealth of beautiful *châteaux*, manor houses and watermills, these (and vineyards) are rarely on the market. Prices tend to be higher than average for France, but inexpensive, habitable village houses and farmhouses in need of restoration can be found in most areas. Burgundy is located just 100km (around 65mi) south of Paris and 80km (50mi) north of Lyon, and has excellent connections with both the north and south of France via the A6 and A31 motorways and the *TGV* (see maps in **Appendix E**).

Brittany

Brittany (*Bretagne*), which has a population of 2.91 million, is the westernmost region of France (and Europe) and comprises the departments of Côtes-d'Armor (22), Finistère (29), Ille-et-Vilaine (35) and Morbihan (56). Brittany has some 3,000km (1,875mi) of Atlantic coast – over 25 per cent of the French coastline. The west coast is characterised by dramatic cliffs and rock formations, the north coast boasts attractive coves and tiny harbours,  and the south coast has wide estuaries and long, sandy beaches.

Brittany is popular with sailors, although the sea is not without its dangers – all those who die at sea are supposed to meet in the Baie des Trépassés ('Bay of the Departed') near Douarnenez, from where they're ferried to a mythical island of the blessed! More than a third of French lighthouses are in Brittany – most of them in Finistère. The inland region, known as the *Argoat* ('land of woods'), is almost flat; only two ridges and a solitary peak rise above 250m (800ft), although the Bretons call them mountains – the Montagnes Noires (Black Mountains), the Monts d'Arrée (Arée Mountains) and the Montagne de Locronan. Inland Brittany is also largely agricultural, unspoiled and scenic, with delightful wooded valleys, lakes and moors.

In contrast with Normandy (see page 76), Brittany is 55 per cent arable land and only 15 per cent grassland. Vegetables and fruit are the two main agricultural products, and the department of Ille-et-Villaine was France's biggest cider producer until the mid-20th century (when there were over 300 varieties of cider apples; today there are fewer than 100). The average Breton is reputed to drink over 300 litres of cider per year! Brittany is also a major producer of pork, poultry, milk and fish, as well as seaweed, which is used in food additives, fertilisers and cosmetics. Cancale is reputed to be a gastronomic Mecca, and the entire region is a paradise for seafood lovers. Local culinary specialities include *crêpes* and *galettes* (different types of pancake used for sweet and savoury fillings respectively), *cotriade,* a sort of paella without the rice (the Breton equivalent of *bouillabaisse*) and *cervoise,* a beer reputed to be the favourite drink of the Gauls (or Vikings, according to which history you read).

Brittany's population is just under 3 million, and the regional capital, Rennes, is its largest city, having just over 200,000 inhabitants. The next largest town is Brest with around 155,000. Other main towns in Brittany include Dinan, Dinard, Lorient, Quimper, Saint-Brieuc, Saint-Malo, Vannes and Vitré.

The local people (Bretons) are of Celtic origin with a rich maritime tradition and a unique culture (preserved mainly in the more isolated west). Proud and independent (they claim that Brittany is a country apart), they even have their own language which has been revived in recent years. Rennes University is a centre of Breton studies. Like Ireland, Brittany is a land of legend and folklore – the jagged coastline is said to have been carved out by the giant Gargantua, and the Forest of Broceliande is claimed to have been the hide-out of the Arthurian sorcerer Merlin. Traditional Breton costume is still worn on special occasions; one of the most colourful of these is the *Fête des Filets bleus* ('Festival of the Blue Nets'), which is held in the fishing village of Concarneau in August.

Brittany has long been a popular region for foreign buyers, particularly the British on account of its sea connections (via the ports of Roscoff and Saint-Malo, and the nearby Normandy ports of Caen and Cherbourg-Octeville) and similar climate and countryside, as well as their historical and cultural kinship. Britain in French is 'big Brittany' to distinguish it from the French region, which was founded by Cornish settlers fleeing Anglo-Saxon invaders in the fifth century. They took their language with them (curiously, Breton survives more successfully than   Cornish) and remain proudly Celtic. It wasn't until 1532 that Brittany officially became part of France. There are also more recent cultural ties between the region and the UK, with twinnings (e.g. Rennes with Exeter) and frequent cross-Channel exchanges. There's even the unlikely *hot dog Breton*, a sausage in a pancake, and Breton whisky, distilled at Lannion!

In fact, there has been an 'invasion' of British buyers in recent years, which has pushed up property prices but has also helped to regenerate many previously moribund rural areas. Property is expensive on the coast, particularly around Quimper and Bénodet (an area known as the Pays Bigouden), and very expensive on the islands (many of which are inhabited by rich Parisians and French celebrities). The triangle of land between Dinan, Dinard and Saint-Malo is also popular, which is reflected in relatively high prices. The interior is generally quieter and cheaper (nowhere in Brittany is more than an hour's drive from the coast), although the extreme west coast of Finistère is also good value if, obviously, the lease accessible part of the region.

In a wide-ranging survey of the 100 largest towns in France published in January 2002, *Le Point* magazine rated two Breton towns – Rennes (35) and Vannes (56) – among the country's 12 best places to live.

Centre-Val-De-Loire

The central region of France, known officially as Centre-Val-de-Loire but often called simply Centre (population 2.4 million), contains the departments of Cher (18), Eure-et-Loir (28), Indre (36), Indre-et-Loire (37), Loir-et-Cher (41) and Loiret (45), the Loire and its tributary, the Loir, giving their names to several of the departments.

The Loire is France's longest river (1,020km/628mi), with its source in the Vivarais mountains (south of Saint-Etienne) and its outlet at Saint-Nazaire in the Pays de la Loire. It's considered to be the dividing line between the colder regions of northern France and the warmer south, although the change is gradual.

The Loire valley is noted for its natural beauty and fertility, consisting of pleasant undulating woodland, lakes, rivers, orchards, and fields of maize and sunflowers (it's the market garden of France), as well as for its plethora of *châteaux*, widely considered to be among the most beautiful in the world. The principal *châteaux* are in Loir-et-Cher (Chambord, the largest; Chaumont; and Chéverny) and neighbouring Indre-et-Loire (Azay-le-Rideau; Chenonceaux, romantically built over the water; and Villandry, boasting magnificent gardens).

The region's main towns include Blois, Bourges, Chartres, Orléans and Tours (37), the regional capital. In fact, these last two towns were recently rated the second and third-best places to live in France by *Le Point* magazine. One of its most attractive areas is the old province of Berry (comprising the departments of Cher and Indre), whose ancient capital was the majestic city of Bourges.

The Loire valley is unspoiled by industry, mass tourism or a surfeit of holiday homes, although it's quite popular with retirees and second homeowners. Property prices vary considerably depending on the proximity to major towns, although they're generally well above the French average and bargains are rare. The region has excellent road connections via the A10, A11 and A71 motorways, which converge on Paris, as well as via the *TGV* from Paris to Poitiers and Bordeaux (see map in **Appendix E**).

Champagne-Ardenne

The Champagne-Ardenne region (population 1.34 million), which is often called simply Champagne, contains the departments of Ardennes

(08), Aube (10), Marne (51) and Haute-Marne (52). The region is celebrated for the sparkling wine after which it's named, and the production of champagne dominates most aspects of life in the region. Its main towns include Charleville-Mézières, Épernay, Reims, and Troyes (10), the regional capital. Reims is home to the *Grandes Marques* of champagne, such as Veuve Cliquot and Charles Heidsieck, although Épernay is the centre of champagne production. Reims cathedral is one of the most beautiful in France as well as historically the most important, being where the country's kings were crowned.

The region is highly cultivated and, although not one of France's most attractive areas, it's noted for its rolling landscape, immense forests (Verzy forest contains beech trees that are over 1,000 years old), deep gorges and vast rivers. Champagne-Ardenne also contains one of Europe's largest artificial lakes, the Lac du Der-Chantecoq near Saint-Dizier. Ardennes (which shares a border with Belgium) is the region's most picturesque department and its rolling, wooded landscape is dotted with ramparts, fortified castles and farmhouses. The Champagne-Ardenne region isn't popular with foreign homebuyers, despite property being relatively inexpensive, particularly in Ardennes. However, it becomes more expensive the nearer you get to Brussels in the north and Paris in the west (the western Aube is the most expensive area). The area has good road connections and is served by the A4 and A26 motorways.

Corsica (*Corse*)

Containing the departments of Corse-du-Sud (2A) and Haute-Corse (2B), the island of Corsica (*Corse*) has population of 260,00 and covers an area of 8,721km^2 (3,367mi^2) with a coastline of around 1,000km (620mi). It's situated 160km (99mi) from France and 80km (50mi) from Italy, with which it has strong historical ties, having been an Italian possession until 1768, when France purchased it from the Genoese. Corsica is quite different from mainland France, not only in its geography but in its people, culture and customs. (Corsican men are reputed to be among the most chauvinistic in France – which is saying something!) The island even has its own language, Corsican, spoken regularly by around 60 per cent of the people, although it has no official status and French is also universally spoken and understood.

There's a strong local identity (and independence movement) and Corsica enjoys a greater degree of autonomy than the mainland regions.

Corsica is sparsely populated with huge areas devoid of human life and has a stark, primitive beauty with superb beaches and picturesque hillside villages; it's considered by some to be the most beautiful Mediterranean island (it's known as the *Ile de Beauté*) and is a popular holiday destination (particularly the western coast). Mountains cover most of its surface, including some 200 peaks over 2,000m (6,500ft), the highest reaching over 2,700m (9,000ft) so that skiing is possible in the winter. Around half the island is covered in vegetation, including beech, chestnut and pine forests and the ubiquitous *maquis*, a dense growth of aromatic shrubs (heather and myrtle) and dark holm oak. Corsica also boasts some of Europe's most beautiful Romanesque art.

Tourism is the island's main industry (many French mainlanders holiday here), although it remains almost completely unspoiled and a haven for outdoor-lovers (hikers and bikers) and those seeking peace and serenity. Not surprisingly, Corsica has a slow pace of life, which is epitomised by its ancient and spectacular mountain railway. The main towns include Ajaccio (the regional capital and birthplace of Napoleon), Bastia, Bonifacio, Calvi and Porto-Vecchio, all situated on the coast. It's popular with holiday homeowners, particularly Italians, and prices have risen in recent years following increased interest. It has, however, avoided the devastation wrought in many other Mediterranean islands by high-rise developments; buildings are restricted to two storeys and construction is forbidden close to beaches. Corsica has good air connections with France and most other European countries. Sardinia is only a short boat ride away.

Franche-Comté

Franche-Comté (population 1.12 million), meaning literally 'free country', contains the departments of Doubs (25), Jura (39), Haute-Saône (70) and the Territoire-de-Belfort (90). It's a little-known region in eastern France bordering Switzerland, with which it shares much of its architecture, cuisine and culture. It's known for cheeses such as Comté and Morbier, Jura wines, and Morteau and Montbéliard sausages. Franche-Comté is acclaimed for its  beautiful, unspoiled scenery (more Swiss in appearance than French) and recalls a fairy-tale land where time has almost stood still. It's reputed to be the greenest region in France.

Sandwiched between the Vosges range to the north and the Jura mountains to the south, Franche-Comté boasts a landscape of rolling cultivated fields, dense pine forests and rampart-like mountains. Although not as majestic as the Alps, the Jura mountains are more accessible and are a Mecca for nature lovers and winter sports fans. The Doubs and Loue valleys (noted for their timbered houses perched on stilts in the river) and the high valley of Ain are popular areas. The region's main towns include Belfort and Besançon (25), the regional capital on the river Doubs.

Franche-Comté is largely ignored by foreign tourists and homebuyers, although it has many attractions. Property prices are higher than the French average, although bargains can be found, particularly if you're seeking a winter holiday home. Besançon is served by the A36 motorway and has good connections with the centre and south of France, Germany and Switzerland via *TGV* (see map in **Appendix E**).

Ile-De-France

The region of Ile-de-France (population 11 million), in northern central France, comprises eight departments. The city of Paris, a department unto itself (see below), is the heart and soul of the Ile-de-France, which is sometimes referred to as the *région Parisienne*. The three departments immediately adjacent to Paris, which make up the so-called *petit couronne* ('small crown' or 'small wreath') are Hauts-de-Seine (92), Seine-Saint-Denis (93) and Val-de-Marne (94). The outer circle of departments is called the *grand couronne* ('large crown' or 'large wreath') and consists of Seine-et-Marne (77), Yvelines (78), Essonne (91) and Val-d'Oise (95). Ile-de France means 'island of France' and, although the region isn't literally an island, it's more or less surrounded by rivers and was therefore considered an island through much of French history.

The Ile-de-France covers 12,070km^2 (around 4,700mi^2), a little over 2 per cent of France's land mass, but houses over 15 per cent of France's population. (Those who live in the Ile-de-France are called *Franciliens* or *Franciliennes*.) As these figures indicate, the Ile-de-France is the most densely populated region in France, with an average of around 900 inhabitants per km^2 overall. Paris is Europe's most crowded capital, with over 20,000 people per km^2 (over 50,000 per mi^2), almost five times the population density of London, compared with a mere 200 inhabitants per km² (around 500 per mi²) in relatively rural Seine-et-Marne. Overall (and obviously there are wide variations), the region is 20 per cent woodland, 20 per cent grassland, 50 per cent arable land and 30 per cent other uses (including urban areas).

The Ile-de-France is also, not surprisingly, the wealthiest region in the country in terms of the number of people with high incomes. Of the 100 main cities and towns in France, the Ile-de-France contains six of the seven wealthiest – Saint-Germain-en-Laye and Versailles (78), Boulogne-Billancourt, Neuilly-sur-Seine and Rueil-Malmaison (92) and Paris itself (the other is Cannes in Alpes-Maritimes). Together, these are home to almost 37 per cent of the country's richest people (almost 17 per cent of French people liable to wealth tax live in Neuilly!).

The Ile-de-France region offers a wide range of living environments and types of accommodation, as do the various districts (*arrondissements*) and neighbourhoods of the city of Paris. Each department and each district has a general character and reputation, although there are exceptions and 'atypical' towns and districts in each area.

Paris

The 'City of Light' is the most popular tourist destination in the world, having many of the world's great museums and galleries, as well as world renowned restaurants, cafés and *bistrots*, and enjoys a deserved reputation for fashion, romance and passion.

The city is divided into 20 *arrondissements*, each of which is a distinct political unit with its own town hall (*mairie*), mayor (*maire*) and police headquarters (*préfecture*) handling day-to-day administrative matters for local residents, including marriages, birth records, death certificates and voting. (The Mairie de Paris is an administrative centre for the 20 district governments and not normally open to the public.)

The numbering system for the *arrondissements* starts at the Palais du Louvre, formerly the French king's primary residence located roughly at the centre of the city, and proceeds in a clockwise spiral out to the city limits. Almost all addresses and directions in Paris include the relevant *arrondissement* number (as well as the name of the nearest underground station). For example, the post code 75016 indicates an address in the 16th *arrondissement*.

In an effort to lessen dependence on Paris, the government established five satellite towns in the mid-'60s, with the intention of making these 'new towns' (*villes nouvelles*) self-sufficient in terms of employment, local commerce and public services. The *villes nouvelles* are Cergy-Pontoise in Val-d'Oise to the north, Saint-Quentin-en-Yvelines to the west, Evry in Essonne to the south, and Marne-la-Vallée and Sénart in Seine-et-Marne to the east. Although the experiment wasn't entirely successful, the *villes nouvelles* have managed to dilute the concentration of jobs, people and services in the capital to a certain extent and offer a less frenetic alternative to the urban intensity of Paris itself.

Languedoc-Roussillon

The Mediterranean coast of France is one of the most popular areas for foreign (and French) homebuyers. The western part of the coast is in the region of Languedoc-Roussillon (population 2.3 million), which comprises the departments of Aude (11), Gard (30), Hérault (34), Lozère (48) and Pyrénées-Orientales (66). The popularity and spiralling prices of Provence-Alpes-Côte d'Azur (see page 82) has prompted many to look instead towards  Languedoc-Roussillon, which currently has only half as many British residents, for example, as PACA.

Languedoc-Roussillon, often referred to simply as 'the Languedoc' (after one of the two ancient languages of France, the *langue d'Oc*, the Roussillon part corresponding approximately to the Pyrénées-Orientales department) or by the French, confusingly, as *le Midi*, has an area of 27,376km² (17,010mi²) and a population of 2.3 million. It contains the coastal departments (from east to west) of Gard, Hérault, Aude and Pyrénées-Orientales, as well as Lozère, which is inland. The region resembles a hammock stretched between Mount Lozère 1,700m (5,580ft) in the north and Mount Canigou 2,784m (9,135ft) in the south. Lozère has the highest average altitude in France of 1,000m (3,280ft). Bordered by the Pyrenees, Andorra and Spain in the south, Languedoc-Roussillon extends north as far as the Massif Central (where Lozère is France's most sparsely populated department). It has a long Mediterranean coastline of virtually uninterrupted sandy beaches, stretching some 180km (110mi) from the Petite Camargue nature reserve in Gard, through Hérault, Aude and Pyrénées-Orientales, with its beautiful beaches and cliff inlets (*calanques*) of pink rock, to the Spanish border. Overall, the region is 30 per cent woodland, 15 per cent grassland, 10 per cent arable land and 45 per cent other uses (including urban areas – the second-highest proportion in France).

Few French regions are more steeped in history than Languedoc (home of the heretical Cathars), which also offers an abundance of excellent (but under-rated) wines such as Corbières, Minervois and Côtes du Roussillon. It encompasses the largest wine production area in

Europe (Béziers claims to be France's wine capital!). The region has a vast range of scenery and landscape, including the beautiful Cévennes national park and Tarn valley areas (famously written about by Robert Louis Stevenson in his *Travels with a Donkey*), the tranquil Canal du Midi, the gentle rolling hills of the Pyrenees, home to a handful of protected bears living in the wild, and the dramatic beauty (not always appreciated by the Tour de France cyclists) of the high Pyrenees peaks.

Languedoc is noted for its relaxed pace of life and is a popular hideaway for those seeking peace and tranquillity. It has its own ancient language (*Occitan*) and many towns close to the Spanish border have a Catalan feel (Catalan is also spoken here).

A number of purpose-built resorts have been created on the *Côte vermeille* (Vermillion Coast) in the last few decades, including Argelès-sur-Mer, Gruissan, Saint-Cyprien, Port Bacarès, Port Leucate and Cap d'Agde, where apartment blocks are mostly unattractive if you're looking for a home with character. Collioure, on the other hand, known as the 'jewel of the Vermilion Coast', is a most attractive (and expensive) port.

Limousin

Situated south-west of the centre of France, Limousin (population 710,000) is the name of the old province surrounding the town of Limoges. It covers an area of 16,942km² (10,600mi²) and has a population of less than 725,000. It's composed of just three departments: Corrèze (19 – the department of President Jacques Chirac and his wife, who is a town councillor), Creuse (23) and Haute-Vienne (87). The main towns are Brive-la-Gaillarde (19), Guéret (23) and Limoges (87). The region is world-renowned for Limoges porcelain and enamels and the tapestries of Aubusson. The region has also given its name to a school of painting known as the Crozant school, after the place where Monet painted his first series, and is home to the Centre for Contemporary Art at Vassivière.

Limousin is predominantly agricultural with very little heavy industry, which makes it largely unpolluted and unspoilt by modern industrial buildings. Being in the foothills of the Massif Central, the region features rolling hills and valleys (the lowest point, around Brive-la-Gaillarde, is almost 200m/655ft above sea level and the highest is

978m/3,200ft) without the bleakness of some mountainous areas, and almost 35 per cent of the area is forested (compared with 27 per cent nationally). Its mountains and forests, coupled with the many lakes, rivers and streams that flow into either the Loire or the Garonne, make Limousin a rural holiday paradise, and it's also becoming increasingly popular with foreign homebuyers. Limousin also boasts a vast man-made lake, the Lac de Vassivière (1,100ha/2,700 acres), the largest used for water-sports in the country and featuring beaches and adjoining holiday complexes, and is noted for its chocolate and Golden Delicious apples (reputed to be the best in the world).

Limousin is also 25 per cent woodland, but only 30 per cent grassland and 10 per cent arable land, with 35 per cent of its land unused or built on. Economically, Limousin is a relatively poor area, Creuse in particular suffering from the decline of agriculture and an ageing population.

Lorraine

Lorraine (population 2.31 million), or Lorraine-Vosges as it's also called, is situated in the north-eastern corner of France bordering Germany, Belgium and Luxembourg, and contains the departments of Meuse (55), Meurthe-et-Moselle (54), Moselle (57) and Vosges (88).

Like Alsace (see page 58), Lorraine has been fought over for centuries by France and Germany, between whom it has frequently swapped ownership (the region retains a strong Germanic influence). Although mainly an industrial area, Lorraine is largely unspoiled and is popular with nature lovers and hikers. It's noted for its meandering rivers, rolling hills, wooded valleys, and delightful medieval towns and villages.

Lorraine is famous for its Moselle wines and *quiche*, but regional cuisine also includes mouthwatering tarts, *clafoutis*, soufflés and gratins, and the local beer is highly regarded. Glass and crystal making are ancient traditions. Lorraine's main towns include Nancy (54), the regional capital, and Metz, and there's a wealth of picturesque villages, including Bussang, Ferrette, Le Hohwald, Saint-Amerin and Schirmeck, plus resort towns such as Masevaux and Plimbières-les-Bains. Lorraine has few foreign residents and is largely ignored by tourists and second homebuyers despite the relatively low cost of living and reasonable property prices. The region has good road access via the A4 and A31 motorways.

Midi-Pyrénées

France's largest region (bigger than Switzerland!), Midi-Pyrénées (population 2.55 million) comprises Ariège (09), Aveyron (12), Haute-Garonne (31), Gers (32), Lot (46), Hautes-Pyrénées (65), Tarn (81) and Tarn-et-Garonne (82). The Midi-Pyrénées borders Spain in the south, Languedoc-Roussillon to the east and Aquitaine to the west, and encompasses the French Pyrenees with Toulouse, its capital, at the centre. The Midi-Pyrénées boasts a wide  variety of stunning, unspoilt scenery ranging from the majestic snow-capped peaks of the Pyrenees in the south to the pastoral tranquillity of the Aveyron, Lot and Garonne valleys in the north. The region as a whole is 25 per cent woodland, 25 per cent grassland, 35 per cent arable land and 15 per cent other uses, including urban areas.

The department of Gers is widely regarded as the heart of the ancient province of Gascony (sometimes called 'Guyenne' by the French), which is often described as France's 'Tuscany' on account of its rolling green countryside and numerous pretty villages. Neighbouring Haute-Garonne is dominated by Toulouse but reaches right down to the Pyrenees, while Hautes-Pyrénées is a largely mountainous department boasting many ski resorts.

In the north-east of the region, Aveyron offers a variety of landscapes, including the wild, rocky area known as Les Causses, south of Millau, the town being regarded as the gateway to the Tarn Gorges – spectacular cuts through the lower Massif Central and a Mecca for hikers, canoeists, climbers and campers (the viewpoint at the top is appropriately called the Point Sublime!). The departments of Tarn and Tarn-et-Garonne in the east of the region have recently become extremely popular with foreign homebuyers, particularly the British (in many parts, you're almost certain to have British neighbours), and prices have risen accordingly.

In the south-east corner of Midi-Pyrénées, the department of Ariège has stunning scenery and is popular with a number of British and European notables, including Tony Blair, who has spent part of his summer holidays here for the past several years. (Perhaps he has been trying to strike it lucky: around 50kg (110lb) of gold is panned every year from the department's rivers!) The decline of agriculture means that there are plenty of inexpensive properties to be found, and the department has the dual advantages of being near the Pyrenees and close to Toulouse. On the Spanish border is the principality of Andorra, which offers its own ski resorts as well as tax-free shopping.

The Pyrenees are popular for year-round outdoor activities, including cycling, hiking and, of course, skiing. There are more than 30 ski resorts in the area, which are generally much less expensive than the Alpine resorts, although less challenging for advanced skiers. There are also numerous spa towns in the Midi-Pyrénées, owing to the region's many thermal springs. Lourdes, in Hautes-Pyrénées, is probably the most visited place in the region, millions of people flocking to the Roman Catholic holy shrine each year, many in search of miracle cures.

Named after its principal river, Lot (the 't' is pronounced) is geographically diverse, which contributes to its climatic variations. The altitude rises from west to east as you approach the Massif Central, and the highest point in the department is 780m (2,550ft) above sea level. Two major rivers cross the department: the Dordogne in the north and the Lot, with its many tributaries, in the south. The Dordogne basin is lush with small valleys, bubbling streams and tall cliffs (on which are perched many dramatic *châteaux*). In the southern half of the department are the *causses*, rocky plateaux and hills full of caves, and *Quercy blanc* ('White Quercy') – so called because of the white limestone used in the area's distinctive buildings. These plateaux are mainly hot and dry with little cultivation. In the extreme south, hemmed in by cliffs, are the plains of the Lot valley, covered with the vines of Cahors.

The department is rich in history and boasts many ancient and picturesque towns, including Souillac, 'where culture and history meet' (according to the tourist guides) and Rocamadour, a town built into the cliffs and France's second-most visited place outside Paris (after the Mont Saint-Michel in Brittany) and Like many other departments in central France, Lot is experiencing the decline of agriculture and ageing of the population, and parts of Lot are relatively poor, although in the area around Cahors, with its wine industry, the economy is booming. However, according to the last census in 1999, Lot's population has risen back to the level of 1936. This can in part be accounted for by the migration of both French and foreigners (mainly British) to the area. Tourism has contributed greatly to the economy of the department, as it has a lot to offer to both tourists and the many people who have second homes here (one in five houses is a second home). Surprisingly, a recent survey concluded that properties for sale in Lot were on average the second-most expensive in France outside Paris!

The people of the Midi-Pyrénées have long regarded themselves as a breed apart – brave and free-spirited, typified by the statue of D'Artagnan (famous as one of the 'Three Musketeers' in the novel of that name by Alexandre Dumas) in the shadow of the cathedral at Auch (32). In fact, D'Artagnan is reputed to have been modelled on Charles de Batz, Captain of the King's Musketeers and a native of Auch. Examples of the earliest forms of human art, 30,000-year old cave paintings depicting deer, bison and other animals, can be found in the grottoes of the Ariège department, and the region also retains influences of the Celts, who settled here in pre-Christian times, Romans and Moors (Arabs), who occupied the area for some 800 years. The local culture and especially the cuisine have therefore developed from both Roman and Arab roots and are celebrated in the region's many festivals

Several classic French dishes originate in this region, including *cassoulet*, made from Toulouse sausage, *magret de canard* (duck cutlet) and that most politically incorrect (but most typically French) of foods, *pâté de fois gras* (goose-liver pâté). Roquefort cheese is made here (in the town of Roquefort-sur-Soulzon in Aveyron) and another famous Gascon product is armagnac, a grape brandy similar to (but subtly different from) cognac, which is made in neighbouring Poitou-Charentes. (Many connoisseurs rate armagnac above cognac, claiming that is has a richer flavour thanks to its single distillation and oak casking.) Many armagnac producers also make a fine aperitif called Floc de Gascoigne, which is a blend of armagnac and wine, along with a number of armagnac-based liqueurs.

Normandy

Normandy (*Normandie*) has long been popular with foreign buyers, particularly the British on account of its proximity and similar climate and countryside, as well as its historical and cultural kinship. Like Britain, Normandy was invaded by the Vikings – 200 years before the Normans themselves invaded Britain – and it was part of England in the early Middle Ages (the Queen is still 'Duke of Normandy'!). There are also more recent cultural ties between the two regions and the UK, with twinnings (e.g. Honfleur with Sandwich in Kent, and the department of Calvados with Devon) and frequent cross-Channel exchanges.

Despite a widespread movement to reunite Normandy, it's currently divided into two official regions: Lower Normandy and Upper Normandy (see below). This relatively recent (1972) administrative division, however, has neither a historical nor a geographical basis. Historically, Upper and Lower Normandy were separated by the Seine, which now runs roughly along the dividing line between the departments of Eure and Seine-Maritime in Upper Normandy.

Geographically, Normandy can be said to be divided into three areas: the eastern 'plains' (roughly corresponding to Upper Normandy), interrupted by the Seine valley; the western *bocage*, a landscape of fields and hedges resulting from 19th century methods of dairy farming; and a central area divided vertically between plains to the west of the river Orne and *bocage* to the east. (Confusingly, the word *bocage* is used to describe both the area south-west of Caen and any similar landscape in Normandy or France as a whole.) Within the central area, south of Caen, is 'Swiss Normandy' (*La Suisse Normande*), so called because of its similarity to the Swiss landscape, with deep gorges and rocky peaks, although the highest point, Mont Pinçon, is only 365m (120ft) above sea level.

Normandy was originally divided into 'lands' (*pays*), many of which are still referred to and even marked on maps (although they often straddle departments and even the division between Upper and Lower Normandy), e.g. the Pays d'Argentan, Pays du Houlme and Pays du Perche in Orne, the Pays d'Auge (around Caen), the Pays de Bray (near the border with Picardy), the Pays de Caux (a largely rural and agricultural area between Rouen and Dieppe), the Pays d'Ouche (between Bernay and Verneuil-sur-Avre) and the Pays du Vexin normand in north-east Eure.

Normandy is noted for its lovely countryside and wide variety of scenery, including lush meadows, orchards, rivers and brooks, quiet country lanes, and over 600km (370mi) of coastline (100km/60mi of which were the scene of the D-Day landings in June 1944).

Normandy is a rich agricultural region, producing meat, milk, butter, cheese (most famously Camembert, but also numerous other cheeses, including Livarot, Neufchâtel and Pont l'Evêque), apples, cider and calvados – a spirit distilled from apple juice (Upper Normandy is sometimes referred to as 'calvaland'). It's also renowned for its cuisine, with local specialities including shellfish dishes (Calvados is a major shellfish producer) and apple tart.

Normandy is an important maritime centre, with no fewer than 50 ports along its coast, including Cherbourg-Octeville, Dieppe, Fécamp, Granville, Le Havre, Honfleur, Port-en-Bessin and Tréport, as well as the major inland ports of Rouen and Caen.

Normandy has four regional *parcs naturels* – Boucles de la Seine Normande (between Rouen and Le Havre), Marais du Cotentin et du Bessin (north of Saint-Lô on the Cotentin peninsula), Perche (east of Alençon, in Orne, stretching into Eure-et-Loir), Normandie-Maine (west of Alençon) – and three areas of marshland: around the mouth of the Vire in Manche (where the Parc régional du Cotentin et du Bessin is Europe's largest 'wetland'), around the mouth of the Orne in Calvados and around the mouth of the Seine in Seine-Maritime.

Normandy has long been popular with the British for holidays and second homes, particularly in and around the Channel ports and resorts. Two-thirds of foreign buyers are British. With the exception of Nord-Pas-de-Calais and Picardy, it's the most accessible region from the UK via the ports of Caen, Cherbourg-Octeville, Dieppe and Le Havre.

Coastal property is relatively expensive (homes with a sea view command a steep premium) and prices increase the closer you get to Paris (Parisians weekend on the Normandy coast). Honfleur has a surfeit of British residents and Deauville is packed with chic Parisians, and both are very expensive. On the other hand, there are still bargains to be found (particularly for British buyers) and relatively undiscovered parts, especially in the department of Orne. Prices generally are expected to increase annually by up to 20 per cent in the next few years.

Lower Normandy

Lower Normandy (*Basse-Normandie*) is the western 'half' of Normandy (population 1.42 million) and contains the departments of Calvados (14), Manche (50) and Orne (61), covering a total area of 17,600km² (7,000mi²). Demographically, Lower Normandy is more rural and 'traditional' than Upper Normandy. The largest city by far is Caen (117,000), the administrative capital, other major towns including Alençon, Lisieux, Mortagne-sur-Perche and Verneuil-sur-Avre. Some 50 per cent of Lower Normandy is grassland (the highest percentage in France); the north-west of Calvados is known as the Bessin – land of grass, milk and marshes. A further 30 per cent is arable land.

Upper Normandy

Upper Normandy (*Haute-Normandie*) comprises the departments of Eure (27) and Seine-Maritime (61). It covers an area of around 12,500km² (5,000mi²) and has a population of around 1.78 million. Upper Normandy is more urbanised and Paris-influenced than Lower Normandy (the department of Eure in particular is said to be in the shadow of the capital). Its largest cities are Rouen (population around 400,000), the administrative capital of Upper Normandy and Le Havre (193,000), other major towns including Dieppe, Evreux, Les Andelys, Louviers, Pont-Audemer and Yvetot. Some 30 per cent of Upper Normandy is grassland; a further 45 per cent is arable land.

Pays-De-La-Loire

The Pays-de-la-Loire (population 3.22 million), which covers an area of 32,082km² (12,512mi²) on the Atlantic coast, comprises five departments: Loire-Atlantique (44), Maine-et-Loire (49), Mayenne (53), Sarthe (72) and Vendée (85).  The Loire is France's longest river (1,020km/628mi), with its source in the Vivarais mountains (south of Saint-Etienne in the department of Loire) and its outlet at Saint-Nazaire in Loire-Atlantique. It flows through the middle of the Pays-de-la-Loire, dividing the departments of Maine-et-Loire and Loire-Atlantique horizontally, and is fed by a number of important tributaries in the area, notably the Vienne (which flows through the department of the same name), the Thouet (which joins the Loire at Saumur), the Mayenne (which joins it at Angers and is a favourite among watersports enthusiasts), and the Sèvre Nantaise (which joins it at the great coastal port of Nantes).

Along the coast to the west is the industrial town of Saint-Nazaire and beyond it several attractive and fashionable seaside resorts. Inland are the vineyards which produce the famous Muscadet and Rosé d'Anjou wines, and to the north the department of Mayenne, named after the river that runs into the Loire – an attractive area for boating as well as for walking and cycling.

The most easterly part of the region is Sarthe, which centres on Le Mans, notable not only for its 24-hour motor races but also for its spectacular cathedral. This part of the region is less than an hour from Paris by *TGV* or under two hours' drive by car and, with its fields, hedges and beech woodlands, is popular with Parisians, many of whom have second homes in the country.

On the southern part of the coast, much of Vendée is flat and windy (its symbol is a windmill). Inland parts of Vendée feature gently rolling countryside with small fields, hedges, trees and woodlands called *le bocage* and similar to that found in parts of Normandy. The department has a dark history of mass slaughter during the religious and revolutionary wars, but now the land is smiling, with its almost endless beaches, seaside resorts and fishing villages and a soft and sunny climate which encourages mimosa.

In the last few thousand years, the sea has been receding along the west coast leaving a flat plain. Along the border between the Pays-de-la-Loire and Poitou-Charentes (see below) is land which has been reclaimed from the sea, known as the *Marais Poitevin* (Poitevin Marsh).

Part of the Marsh hasn't been drained, however, and consists of a pattern of tree-lined canals between small fields used for market gardening and cattle rearing – an area known as '*la Venise verte*' ('Green Venice') and one of the most unusual landscapes in France.

Coastal areas benefit from tourism but are also attracting an increasing number of retired people, as well as foreigners. The department of Vendée in particular is attracting an increasing number of foreign homebuyers, and property prices are rising fast.

The Pays-de-la-Loire is 10 per cent woodland and 25 per cent grassland; the remaining 20 per cent of the land is put to other uses, including urban areas. The region is noted for heavy industry, with shipyards at Saint-Nazaire, and factories near La Rochelle.

In a survey of the 100 largest towns in France published in January 2002, *Le Point* magazine rated three towns in this area – Nantes (44), Angers (49) and La Roche-sur-Yon (85) – among the ten best to live in.

Picardy

The region of Picardy (*Picardie*) with a population of 1.86 million contains the departments of Aisne (02), Oise (60) and Somme (80) and is one of the least known regions of France. It's mainly famous for its battlegrounds from the first and second world wars, particularly the Somme, although the region is rich in earlier history and architecture. Picardy has a generally flat and uninteresting agricultural landscape, with just a 37km (23mi)  coastal strip around the mouth of the river Somme near Abbeville, although this is one of a number of attractive areas, including the valleys of the Aisne, Oise and Somme rivers. The region's main towns include the regional capital Amiens (80), Beauvais, Compiègne, Chantilly, Saint-Omer and Saint-Quentin. Picardy has some of the lowest property prices in France, although it isn't popular with foreign buyers. The Oise department is the most expensive of the three on account of its proximity to Paris. Picardy is crossed by the *TGV* line from Paris to Lille (see map in **Appendix E**) as well as by the A1, A16, A28 and A29 motorways and is within easy reach of England, via the Channel Tunnel or Calais ferries.

Poitou-Charentes

Poitou-Charentes (population 1.64 million), covering an area of 25,809km² (10,066mi²), is made up of four departments: Charente (16),

Charente-Maritime (17), Deux-Sèvres (79) and Vienne (86). The Poitou-Charentes region is almost completely unspoiled with virtually no industry and is one of the most tranquil in France. Its long Atlantic coastline is noted for long, sandy beaches, marinas, golf courses and islands, which make it an ideal summer holiday destination. Two large islands, the Ile de Ré and the Ile d'Oléron, with their pine-shaded beaches and superb shellfish, were connected by road  bridges to the mainland a generation ago and have seen their populations grow rapidly as a result; camp sites have also proliferated. No cars are allowed on the smaller island of Aix, where Napoleon spent his last night in France before leaving for Saint-Helena. The marshes along the estuary of the Seudre have been converted into oyster beds with lines of thick wooden posts, on which mussels are also farmed. In fact, the region is France's biggest centre for the production of oysters and other shellfish. Elsewhere, the flat shore is used for drying out sea water in shallow pans to make salt.

Inland, the landscape is flat, particularly in Charente, and the land is used for mixed farming and livestock breeding. The gently rolling chalk hills of Charente and Charente-Maritime are covered with white wine and cognac vines, poultry farms and grazing for dairy herds, the wooded hilltops rising to over 160m (500ft).

The region is crossed by the medieval routes used by pilgrims on their way to the shrine of Saint James at Compostella in Spain, a practice which is currently being revived. These routes were also used by the stone masons who built the region's many Romanesque churches, such as Saint Pierre at Aulnay (17). Other notable monuments include the 15th century church tower built by the English at Marennes (79), the fourth century baptistery in Poitiers (86)and the collection of 11th century frescos in the church at Saint-Savin (86), and there are numerous places of historical interest, including the fortified town of Brouage, abandoned as a port when the sea receded, the 17th century naval port of Rochefort which replaced it, and the Vieux Port at La Rochelle (all in 17). In contrast, present-day attractions include Futuroscope near Poitiers and what is reputed to be France's best zoo at La Palmyre.

Poitou-Charentes is 15 per cent woodland and 20 per cent grassland, the remaining 20 per cent of the land being put to other uses, including urban areas.

Poitou-Charentes is a popular region with tourists, holiday homeowners and retirees, particularly British property buyers, many of whom favour the area around Cognac (16) and Saintes (17). There's a huge difference between the cost of property on the coast and inland, where homes are good value.

Provence-Alpes-Côte D'Azur

For many people, both French and foreign, the jewel in France's crown is the eastern Mediterranean coastal region known officially as Provence-Alpes-Côte d'Azur (population 4.51 million), abbreviated to PACA but simply referred to as Provence by most people, which comprises the departments of Alpes-de-Haute-Provence (4), Hautes-Alpes (05), Alpes-Maritimes (6), Bouches-du-Rhône (13), Var (83) and Vaucluse (84). The magazine *Le Point* has  more than once elected Aix-en-Provence (13), the 'capital' of Provence, the best French town to live in, and *The Riviera Times* recently wrote with reference to the Côte d'Azur: "Sun, blue skies, warm sea, delicious food and tasty wines, idyllic villages and an allure of luxury. Surely that's the life we are all looking for?"

Slightly larger than its Mediterranean neighbour, Languedoc-Roussillon (see page 71), the PACA region occupies an area of 31,400km² (19,510mi²) and has a population approaching 4.6 million. Economically, it's the second most important region in France after the Ile-de-France. Overall, the region is 40 per cent woodland (the second-highest proportion in France), 15 per cent grassland, 10 per cent arable land and 35 per cent other uses (including urban areas).

The Provence area comprises the Alpes-de-Haute-Provence, Bouches-du-Rhône and Vaucluse departments and part of the Var, although opinions differ as to exactly where Provence ends and the Côte d'Azur (Azure Coast) begins. The Côte d'Azur was 'discovered' by the British, who dubbed it the 'French Riviera' and helped to create the world's first coastal playground for the rich and famous. At the end of the 19th century, Queen Victoria was influential in developing the area's popularity through her visits to Hyères (just east of Toulon), which was then considered the western extremity of the Côte d'Azur. Today, many people regard Saint-Tropez, 45km (28mi) further east along the coast, as the limit of Provence and the start of the Côte d'Azur (known locally as *la Côte*).

Another school of thought (whose members understandably include many local estate agents) believes that the Côte d'Azur lies between Hyères and the conurbation of Fréjus-Saint-Raphaël (east of Saint-Tropez). There are also those who consider the French Riviera as the stretch of coastline from Menton, close to the Italian border, to just beyond Cannes, the Côte d'Azur encompassing the French Riviera and extending to Saint-Tropez. (Note that Monaco, although geographically part of the Riviera/Côte d'Azur, is a separate principality and not part of France.)

Wherever it exactly begins and ends, Provence is a fascinating land of romance, history (it has its own ancient language, Provençal, now spoken only in Italy) and great beauty and is celebrated for its excellent climate, attractive scenery, fine beaches, superb cuisine and fashionable resorts. It's one of the most exclusive areas of France, and few places in Europe can compete with its ambience and allure, glamorous resorts and beautiful people. However, it's also a region of stark contrasts, with a huge variety of landscape and scenery encompassing extensive woodlands, rugged mountains, rolling hills, spectacular gorges (the Grand Canyon du Verdon is the deepest cleft in the surface of Europe), dramatic rock formations, lush and fertile valleys carpeted with lavender, extensive vineyards (which stretch to the foot of the Alps in Vaucluse), and a ravishing coastline dotted with quaint fishing villages and fine beaches.

A journey through Provence is an indulgence of the senses, and its diverse vegetation includes cypresses, gnarled olive trees, almond groves, umbrella pines, lavender, wild rosemary and thyme, all of which add to its unique and seductive sights and smells. Provence produces a number of excellent wines and includes the prestigious vineyards of Châteauneuf-du-Pape, Gigondas (mostly red) plus popular and drinkable wines such as Côtes du Lubéron and Côtes de Provence.

The region contains many naturally beautiful areas, notably the Lubéron National Park (Parc naturel régional du Lubéron), the heart of the provençal countryside and still a fashionable area for holiday homes and visitors, in spite of or perhaps because of Peter Mayle. The Camargue, between Arles and the sea (from which it was reclaimed), is one of the most spectacular nature reserves in France and famous for its wild horses.

Provence also contains a wealth of beautiful historic Roman towns and dramatically sited medieval villages, and both Marseille and Nice provide sea links to Corsica and North Africa, where the holiday resorts of Morocco and Tunisia are popular with the French (being former protectorates where French is still widely spoken).

Although the Alpes-Maritimes and Bouches-du-Rhône departments have very little coastline which isn't built-up, Var has perhaps the most attractive, unspoilt coastline in the PACA region, between Hyères and Fréjus-Saint-Raphaël.

Not surprisingly, Provence-Alpes-Côte d'Azur is the most popular region in France for holiday and retirement homes and has a large foreign community, the British, Germans and Italians being among the largest buyers of second homes. In 2001 there were around 8,000 official British residents (Peter Mayle's televised book, *A Year in Provence*, caused countless Brits to pack up and head south). Popularity, of course, has its price, notably in respect of property costs, which have risen beyond the reach of many, who may look instead towards Languedoc-Roussillon (see page 71), which currently has only half as many British residents as Provence.

Rhône-Alpes

The Rhône-Alpes region (population 5.65 million) runs from Lac Léman ('Lake Geneva'), the largest lake in western Europe, southwards towards the Mediterranean and is bounded by the Italian border to the east and the Rhône to the west. It includes the departments of Ain (01), Ardèche (07), Drôme (26), Isère (38), Loire (42), Savoie (73), Rhône (69) and Haute-Savoie (74). (The former province of Dauphiné corresponds approximately to the north-eastern part of Drôme and the Isère and Hautes-Alpes departments.) It's the most mountainous area of France, the Alps being Europe's biggest mountain range, 'shared' between France, Italy and Switzerland. The average altitude of the mountains in the Alps is 1,150m (3,772ft); the eastern area of the Alps has the highest peaks and forms a natural barrier with Italy. The most mountainous department is Isère, followed by Hautes-Alpes, Savoie, Haute-Savoie and Drôme. Mont Blanc, altitude 4,807m (15,767ft) in Haute-Savoie is the highest peak in Europe (excluding the mountains of Georgia). The Mont Blanc road tunnel and the Tunnel du Fréjus road and rail tunnel cut through the Alps, from Haute-Savoie and Savoie respectively, linking France to Italy.

The Alps area is of course noted for its majestic mountain scenery, which is unrivalled at most times of the year, and it's probably France's most picturesque region with its dense forests, lush pasture land, fast-flowing rivers, huge lakes and deep gorges. It's a paradise for sports fans and nature lovers with superb summer sports, such as rock-climbing and canyoning (abseiling and water-chute descents), hiking and walking, all-terrain cycling, hang-gliding and paragliding, and white-water sports, while winter sports and ski resorts offer some of the best facilities in Europe for downhill (Alpine) and cross-country (Nordic) skiing and snowboarding. Albertville (73), Chamonix (74) and Grenoble (38) have all been venues for the Winter Olympic Games. Top ski resorts include Chamonix, France's mountaineering capital, Courchevel, Megève, Méribel and Val d'Isère. The Alps therefore have two high seasons: the usual summer period, and the winter skiing season (December to April), the two peaks within the latter being the school holidays at Christmas and Easter.

The Alps is the third most popular tourist area in France, after Paris and the Côte-d'Azur, and Annecy is one of the most popular tourist towns in France after Paris, but property prices are well below those of Paris and prestigious towns on the Riviera. Lower property prices than neighbouring Switzerland attract many Swiss who live in the area and commute to work in Geneva and other Swiss cities.

Although largely unspoiled by development, the Rhône valley is one of France's major industrial regions. Lyon (69), which is the regional capital and France's second-largest city (the French spell it *Lyon*) as well as its gastronomic capital, has a beautiful medieval quarter. The Rhône river (whose source is high in the Swiss Alps) is a vital artery for river, road and rail traffic between the north and south of France. Rhône's other major towns include Bourg-en-Bresse, Privas and Saint-Etienne.

The price of property in the Rhône-Alpes region is well above the average, although the most expensive areas are mostly in the Alps. Ardèche with its spectacular gorge is increasingly popular with foreign buyers and is consequently becoming more expensive. Like Franche-Comté, Rhône-Alpes is popular with the Swiss, many of whom live in the region and commute to their workplaces in Geneva and other Swiss cities. The region is noted for its extremes of temperature and is usually freezing in winter and hot in summer, and most pleasant in spring and autumn. The Rhône-Alpes has excellent road, rail and air connections and Lyon is just two hours from Paris by *TGV* (see map in **Appendix E**).

LOCATION

The most important consideration when buying a home anywhere is usually its location – or, as the old adage goes, the three most important considerations are location, location and location! If you're looking for a good investment, a property in reasonable condition in a popular area is likely to be greatly preferable to an exceptional property in an out-of-the-way location. Even if you aren't concerned with making money from your property, there's little point in buying a 'dream home' if it's right next to a motorway or a rubbish dump or is so inaccessible that a trip to the baker is a major expedition. France offers almost everything that anyone could want, but you must choose the right property in the right spot.

⚠️ **The wrong decision regarding location is one of the main causes of disenchantment among foreigners who have purchased property in France.**

Many people's choice of location is based on previous holidays, friends' recommendations, accessibility or simply an area's reputation. However, if you're likely to be spending the rest of your life in your new home, and even if you will only be spending the occasional holiday there, it's worth taking the time and trouble to consider every aspect of its location first hand. When choosing a permanent home, don't be too influenced by where you've spent an enjoyable holiday or two. A place that was acceptable for a few weeks' holiday may be far from suitable for year-round living.

The 'best' place to live in France obviously depends on your preferences and it's impossible to specify a best location for everyone. The important thing is to identify the positive and possible negative aspects of each of your selected locations in order to help you to choose the one that suits you and your family best. If you want to live in (or avoid) one of France's most beautiful villages, contact Les Plus Beaux Villages de France, 19500 Collonges-la-Rouge (☎ 05 55 84 08 50, 🖳 www.villagesdefrance.free.fr), which has selected around 150 villages of fewer than 2,000 inhabitants for this accolade.

If you have a job in France, the location of a home will probably be determined by its proximity to your place of employment. Obtain a map of the area and decide the maximum distance you're prepared to travel to work, then draw a circle of the appropriate radius with your workplace in the middle. If you intend to look for employment or start a business, you must live in an area that allows you the maximum scope. Unless you have reason to believe otherwise, you would be foolish to rely on finding employment in a particular area. If, on the other hand, you're seeking a holiday or retirement home, you will have a huge choice of areas.

If you have little idea about where you wish to live, read as much as you can about the different regions of France (see **Regions** on page 58 and *The Best Places to Live in France* by Survival Books) and spend some time looking around your areas of interest. Note that the climate, lifestyle and cost of living can vary considerably from region to region (and even within a particular region). Before looking at properties, it's important to have a good idea of the kind of home that you're looking for and the price you wish to pay, and to draw up a shortlist of the areas or towns of interest. If you don't do this, you're likely to be overwhelmed by the number of properties to be viewed. Estate agents usually expect serious buyers to know where they want to buy within a 30 to 40km (20 to 25mi) radius and some even expect clients to narrow it down to specific towns and villages.

Don't, however, believe the times and distances stated in adverts and by estate agents. According to some agents' magical mystery maps, everywhere in the north is handy for Paris or a Channel port and all homes in the south are a stone's throw from Lyon or Nice. Check distances and ease of access yourself.

If possible, you should visit an area a number of times over a period of a few weeks, both on weekdays and at weekends, in order to get a feel for the neighbourhood (don't just drive around, but walk!). A property seen on a balmy summer's day after a delicious lunch and a few glasses of *vin rouge* may not be nearly so attractive on a subsequent visit *sans* sunshine and the warm inner glow.

You should also try to visit an area at different times of the year, e.g. in both summer and winter, as somewhere that's wonderful in summer can be forbidding and inhospitable in winter (or vice versa). If you're planning to buy a winter holiday home, you should also view it in the summer, as snow can hide a multitude of sins! In any case, you should view a property a number of times before making up your mind to buy it. If you're unfamiliar with an area, most experts recommend that you rent for a period before deciding to buy (see **Renting Before Buying** on page 108). This is particularly important if you're planning to buy a permanent or retirement home in an unfamiliar area. Many people change their minds after a period and it isn't unusual for families to move once or twice before settling down permanently.

When house hunting, obtain large scale maps of the area where you're looking. The best maps are the Institut Géographique National (IGN) green series of 74 maps with a scale of 1cm = 1km, *cartes de promenade* (1cm = 1km) and town and local maps (various scales), both of which series are blue. These maps show every building, track and waterway as well as contour lines, so it's easy to mark off the places that you've seen. You could do this using a grading system to denote your impressions. If you use an estate agent, he will usually drive you around and you can return later to those that you like most at your leisure (provided you've marked them on your map!).

You should also check the medium-term infrastructure plans for the area, with both the regional and national authorities, particularly with regard to planned road and railway construction. Although a rural plot may seem miles from anywhere today, there could be plans for a motorway passing along the boundaries within the next five or ten years. See *The Best Places to Buy a Home in France* (Survival Books) for details of planned developments in the most popular regions.

Bear in mind that foreign buyers aren't welcome everywhere, particularly when they 'colonise' a town or area (see **Community** below). There has been some resistance to foreigners buying property in certain areas and a few towns have even blocked sales to foreigners to deter speculators. Understandably, the French don't want property prices driven up by foreigners with more money than sense (particularly second homeowners) to levels they can no longer afford. However, foreigners are generally welcomed by the local populace (and in most areas are infinitely preferable to Parisians!), not least because they boost the local economy and in rural areas often buy derelict properties that the French won't touch. Permanent residents in rural areas who take the time and trouble to integrate with the local community are invariably warmly welcomed.

The 'best' place to live in France depends on a range of considerations, including the following:

Accessibility

Is the proximity to public transport, e.g. an international airport, port or railway station, or access to a motorway important? Note that the motorway network is continually being expanded and will eventually cover the whole country, and the expansion of the *TGV* rail network also means that many remote areas are now linked to Paris and other major cities in just a few hours (see maps in **Appendix E**). Don't, however, believe all you're told about the distance or travelling times to the nearest motorway, airport, railway station, port, beach or town, but check it for yourself.

SURVIVAL TIP
Although it isn't so important if you're buying a permanent home in France and planning to stay put, one of the major considerations when buying a holiday home is communications (road, rail and air links) with your home country.

If you buy a remote country property, the distance to local amenities and services could become a problem, particularly if you plan to retire to France. If you're buying a home with a view to retiring there later, check the local public transport, as you may not always be able (or wish) to drive. See also **Getting Around** on page 100 and **Retirement** on page 39.

Although budget airlines have recently made acessible previously remote parts of France, such services are notoriously fickle and it isn't wise to buy in a particular area purely because it's served by cheap flights; airlines create and cancel routes (and are bought and sold) at the drop of a hat and you could be left stranded – as many buyers discovered to their cost after the acquisition of Buzz by Ryanair and when Ryanair was subsequently 'forced' to withdraw from certain smaller airports.

Amenities

What local health and social services are provided? How far is the nearest hospital with an emergency department? What shopping facilities are provided in the neighbourhood? How far is it to the nearest town with good shopping facilities, e.g. a supermarket/hypermarket? How would you get there if your car was out of commission? If you live in a remote rural area you will need to be much more self-sufficient than if you live in a town.

Don't forget that France is a **BIG** country, and those living in remote areas need to use the car for everything. It has been calculated that it costs some €7,000 a year (including depreciation costs) to run a new small car doing 15,000km (9,300mi) a year (which is less than average). **The cost of motoring is high in France and is an important consideration when buying a home there.** Note also that many rural villages are dying and have few shops or facilities, and aren't usually a good choice for a retirement home.

Climate

For most people the climate (see page 25) is one of the most important factors when buying a home in France, particularly a holiday or retirement home. Bear in mind both the winter and summer climate as well as the position of the sun and the direction of the prevailing wind. The orientation or aspect of a building is vital and you must ensure that balconies, terraces and gardens face the right direction.

Community

When choosing the area, decide whether you want to live among your own countrymen and other foreigners in a largely expatriate community, such as those in Dordogne and parts of Provence, or whether you prefer (and are prepared) to integrate into an exclusively French environment.

However, unless you speak French fluently or intend to learn it, you should think twice before buying a property in a village. Note that the locals in some villages resent 'outsiders' moving in, particularly holiday homeowners, although those who take the time and trouble to integrate into the local community are usually warmly welcomed.

If you're buying a permanent home, it's important to check your prospective neighbours, particularly when buying an apartment. For example, are they noisy, sociable or absent for long periods? Do you think you will get on with them? **Good neighbours are invaluable, particularly when buying a second home in France.**

Crime

What is the local crime rate? In some areas the incidence of burglary is extremely high, which not only affects your security but also increases your insurance premiums. Is crime increasing or decreasing? Note that professional crooks like isolated houses, particularly those full of expensive furniture and other belongings, which they can strip bare at their leisure. You're much less likely to be a victim of theft if you live in a village, where strangers stand out like sore thumbs. See also **Crime** on page 296.

Employment

How secure is your job or business and are you likely to move to another area in the near future? Can you find other work in the same area, if necessary? If there's a possibility that you will need to move in some years' time, you should rent or at least buy a property that will be relatively easy to sell. What about your partner's and children's jobs?

Garden

If you're planning to buy a large country property with a big plot, bear in mind the high cost and amount of work involved in its upkeep. If it's to be a second home, who will look after the house and garden when you're away? Do you want to spend your holidays mowing the lawn and cutting back the undergrowth? Do you want a home with a lot of outbuildings? What are you going to do with them? Can you afford to convert them into extra rooms, guest accommodation or *gîtes*?

Hunting

Hunting is a jealously guarded 'right', and you should check whether hunting is permitted on your land if you don't want it invaded by armed men every Sunday between September and February. Note that it's possible to apply for your land to be designated a 'refuge' to the Association pour la Protection des Animaux Sauvages (☎ 04 75 25 10 00, 💻 www.aspas-nature.org), although this may not do much for your local popularity!

Local Council

Is the local council well run? Unfortunately, many are profligate and simply use any extra income to hire a few more of their cronies or spend it on grandiose schemes, and many local councillors abuse their positions to further their own ends. What are the views of other residents? If the municipality is efficiently run, you can usually rely on good local social and sports services and other facilities. In areas where there are many foreign residents, the town hall may have a foreign residents' department.

Natural Phenomena

Check whether an area is particularly susceptible to natural disasters, such as floods, storms, forest fires and lightning strikes (which are common in the south-east and Corsica). If a property is located near a waterway, it may be expensive to insure against floods, which are a constant threat in some areas. See also **Inspections & Surveys** on page 154.

Noise

Noise can be a problem in some cities, resorts and developments. Noisy neighbours account for around half of all police complaints in France, and 50 per cent of Parisians complain that their neighbours make too much noise. Although you cannot choose your neighbours, you can at least ensure that a property isn't located next to a busy road, industrial plant, commercial area, discotheque, night club, bar or restaurant (where revelries may continue into the early hours). Look out for objectionable neighbouring properties which may be too close to the one you're considering and check whether nearby vacant land has been 'zoned' for commercial use. In community developments (e.g. apartment blocks) many properties are second homes and are let short-term, which means you may need to tolerate boisterous holidaymakers as neighbours throughout the year (or at least during the summer months).

Don't assume, however, that rural life is necessarily tranquil. Other kinds of noise can disturb your peace and quiet, including chiming church bells, barking dogs, crowing cockerels and braying donkeys, and aircraft if you live near a civil or military airfield. On the other hand, those looking to buy a rural property should note that there may be times when noisy activities such as lawnmowing are prohibited (e.g. at lunchtime on Saturdays and all afternoon on Sundays).

Parking

If you're planning to buy in a town or city, is there adequate private or free on-street parking for your family and visitors? Is it safe to park in the street? In some areas it's important to have secure off-street parking if you value your car. Parking is a problem in many towns and most cities, where private garages or parking spaces can be very expensive (e.g. up to €5,000 in Provence!). Bear in mind that an apartment or townhouse in a town or community development may be some distance from the nearest road or car park. How do you feel about carrying heavy shopping hundreds of metres to your home and possibly up several flights of stairs? Traffic congestion is also a problem in many towns and tourist resorts, particularly during the high season.

Property Market

Do houses sell well in the area, e.g. in less than six months? Generally you should avoid neighbourhoods where desirable houses routinely remain on the market for six months or longer (unless the property market is in a slump and nothing is selling).

Radon

Radon (*radon*), a radioactive gas emitted by granite, is found in significant quantities in parts of Brittany, Corsica, and the Massif Central and Vosges mountains, and some 300,000 homes are reckoned to have dangerous levels of radon. Although there's evidence that exposure to high levels of radon can cause cancer, particularly among smokers, there's no proven danger in long exposure to low levels. If you're worried about radon levels and want a property checked, contact the Agence Nationale pour l'Amélioration de l'Habitat (ANAH), whose regional and departmental offices are listed on its website (🖳 www.anah.fr).

Schools

Consider your children's present and future schooling. What is the quality of local schools? Are there any bi-lingual or international schools nearby? Note that, even if your family has no need or plans to use local schools, the value of a home may be influenced by the quality and location of schools.

Sports & Leisure Facilities

What is the range and quality of local leisure, sports, community and cultural facilities? What is the proximity to sports facilities such as a beach, golf course, ski resort or waterway? Bear in mind that properties in or close to ski and coastal resorts are considerably more expensive, although they also have the best letting potential. If you're interested in a winter holiday home, which area should you choose?

Termites

Termites (*termites*) or white ants are found in over 50 departments – particularly in the south-west, the worst-affected departments being Landes (where there are termites in all departments), Gironde, Charente-Maritime and Lot-et-Garonne in that order. In certain communes, an inspection is required (known as *un état parasitaire*).

Details of areas affected can be obtained from the Observatoire de Lutte Xylophages (☎ 08 00 92 19 21, 🖥 www.olx.fr) and a list of recognised treatment companies from your local Direction Départementale de l'Equipement (DDE) or the Centre Technique de Bois et de l'Ameublement/CTBA (☎ 01 40 19 49 19, 🖥 www.termite.com.fr, where there's also a map showing affected areas).

Note that a certificat de non-infestation is valid only for three months, so in the average purchase procedure the inspection cannot be carried out until after you've signed the *compromis de vente*, in which case you must keep your fingers crossed that the result is positive. If it isn't, you can withdraw from the sale and have your deposit returned, negotiate a reduction in the selling price to allow for termite treatment (which can cost between €2,500 and €5,000) or ask the seller to have the treatment done before proceeding with the sale.

Tourists

Bear in mind that if you live in a popular tourist area, e.g. almost anywhere in the south of France, you will be inundated with tourists in summer. They won't only jam the roads and pack the public transport, but may even occupy your favourite table at your local café or restaurant!

Although a 'front-line' property on the beach or in a marina development may sound attractive and be ideal for short holidays, it isn't usually the best choice for permanent residents. Many beaches are hopelessly crowded in the high season, streets may be smelly from restaurants and fast food outlets, parking impossible, services stretched to breaking point, and the incessant noise may drive you crazy. You may also have to tolerate water restrictions in some areas.

Town Or Country?

Do you wish to be in a town or do you prefer the country? Bear in mind that if you buy a property in the country, you will probably have to put up with poor public transport (or none at all), long travelling distances to a town of any size, solitude and remoteness. You won't be able to pop along to the local *boulangerie* for a *baguette* and *croissants*, drop into the local bar for a glass of your favourite tipple with the locals, or have a choice of restaurants on your doorstep. In a town or large village, the weekly market will be just around the corner, the doctor and chemist close at hand, and if you need help or run into any problems, your neighbours will be close by.

On the other hand, in the country you will be closer to nature, will have more freedom (e.g. to make as much noise as you wish) and possibly complete privacy, e.g. to sunbathe or swim *au naturel*. Living in a remote area in the country will suit nature lovers looking for solitude who don't want to involve themselves in the 'hustle and bustle' of town life (not that there's much of this in French rural towns). If you're after peace and quiet, make sure that there isn't a busy road or railway line nearby or a local church within 'donging' distance (see **Noise** above).

Note, however, that many people who buy a remote country home find that the peace of the countryside palls after a time and they yearn for the more exciting night-life of a city or tourist resort. If you've never lived in the country, it's wise to rent first before buying. Note also that, while it's cheaper to buy in a remote or unpopular location, it's usually much more difficult to find a buyer when you want to sell.

GETTING THERE

Although it isn't so important if you're planning to live permanently in France and stay put, one of the major considerations when buying a holiday home is the cost of getting to and from France, and you should ask yourself the following questions:

- How long will it take to get to a home in France, taking into account journeys to and from airports, ports and railway stations?
- How frequent are flights, ferries or trains at the time(s) of year when you plan to travel?
- Are direct flights or trains available?
- Is it feasible to travel by car?
- What is the cost of travel from my home country to the region where I'm planning to buy a home in France?
- Are off-season discounts or inexpensive charter flights available?

If a long journey is involved, you should bear in mind that it may take you a day or two to recover, especially if you suffer jet-lag. Obviously, the travelling time and cost of travel to a home in France will be more significant if you're planning to spend frequent weekends there rather than a few long visits a year. When comparing costs between flying or taking the train or bus and driving via the Channel tunnel or ferry, take into account the price of motorway tolls (see page 104) and fuel.

SURVIVAL TIP
Allow plenty of time to get to and from airports,
ports and railway stations, particularly when travelling
during peak hours, when traffic congestion can be
horrendous, and also to take into account the
extra time that security checks may take.

Airline Services

All major international airlines provide scheduled services to Paris, and many also fly to other main French cities such as Bordeaux, Lyon, Marseille, Nice and Toulouse. The French state-owned national airline, Air France, is France's major international carrier, flying to over 30 French, 65 European and 120 non-European destinations in over 70 countries. Air France and its various subsidiaries (known collectively as Groupe Air France) has a fleet of over 200 aircraft and carries some 16 million passengers annually. It provides a high standard of service and, as you would expect, provides excellent in-flight cuisine.

Air France shares its monopoly on many international routes with just one foreign carrier and is thus able to charge high fares. The lack of competition means that international flights to and from most French airports, and French domestic flights, are among the world's most expensive. However, some opposition is starting to appear and high fares on some transatlantic flights have been reduced in recent years by travel agents such as Nouvelles Frontières. There are regular scheduled flights to Paris CDG from many North American cities, including Atlanta, Boston, Chicago, Dallas, Detroit, Houston, Los Angeles, Miami, Montreal, Newark, New York, Philadelphia, San Diego, San Francisco, Seattle, Toronto and Washington, to Lyon from Montreal and to Nice from Montreal, New York and Toronto. There are also transatlantic charter flights to other French airports (e.g. to Toulouse from Montreal and Toronto).

In recent years, British and Irish visitors have been particularly well served by cheap flights (as well as less inexpensive services) from a number of airports – especially London Stansted – to many regional French destinations. The major budget carrier is Ryanair), but low-cost flights are also offered by a number of other British operators. For a summary of services current in July 2004, see **Appendix F**. Note, however, that the low-cost airlines are notoriously fickle and frequently change services according to 'demand' (i.e. profitability), so you should check current services with the airline **and** the airport (who may well provide you with different information!). Take into account also any seasonal charter flights (e.g. to Nice in the summer and Lyon in the winter).

Airports

The main French airports handling intercontinental flights are Paris Roissy-Charles de Gaulle, Paris Orly, Lyon-Saint-Exupéry (formerly Satolas), Nice-Côte-d'Azur and Marseille-Provence. (A controversial third 'Paris' airport – actually over 120km/75mi from the city in the Somme! – is planned but wouldn't open before 2015 even if the many objections are overcome.) Charles de Gaulle (CDG) is the country's busiest airport, followed by Nice, which offers direct scheduled flights to around 80 cities worldwide, and Marseille, which serves around 70 international destinations.

Airports handling flights from the UK and Ireland are shown on the map in **Appendix F**. Other French airports served by other international as well as domestic flights include Brive-La-Gaillarde, Caen, Cherbourg, Dijon, Le Havre, Lille, Mulhouse/Basel, Nancy/Metz, Quimper, Rennes and Rouen. There are also flights to Ajaccio, Bastia, Calvi and Figari in Corsica. Depending on your destination, it's sometimes cheaper or quicker to fly to an international airport outside France, such as Luxembourg for north-eastern France and Geneva for eastern France.

Long and short-term parking is available at major airports, including reserved parking for the disabled, and car hire is also available at Paris and principal provincial airports.

The Aéroports de Paris website (🖥 www.adp.fr) has information on both CDG and Orly with maps and even pre-ordering from the airport duty-free shops! Details of all French airports and their current services can be found on 🖥 www.aeroport.fr. Airline websites are listed in **Appendix F**.

International Rail Services

There are direct trains to France from most major European cities, including Amsterdam, Barcelona, Basle, Berlin, Brussels, Cologne, Florence, Frankfurt, Geneva, Hamburg, London (see **Eurostar** below), Madrid, Milan, Munich, Rome, Rotterdam, Venice, Vienna and Zurich. Some international services run at night only and daytime journeys may involve a change of train. The high-speed *Thalys* service links Paris with Brussels and Amsterdam (see page 102). Some non-*TGV* international trains such as *Trans-Europ-Express* (*TEE*) and *Trans-Europ-Nuit* (*TEN*) are first class only.

Eurostar

The Channel Tunnel (the world's most expensive hole in the ground) joins France with England by rail and runs from Sangatte (near Calais) in France to Folkestone. Trains are operated exclusively by Eurostar and, since the opening of a separate, high-speed line from Folkestone to London Waterloo in October 2003, link London and Paris in just 2h35m. Speed and convenience comes at a cost: a standard return fare costs over €400, although a return trip including a weekend booked at least three weeks in advance can save you €250 and return tickets for under €100 can be had from London to other French cities. (In April 2003, Eurostar announced that it would be offering cheap fares to British commuters living in Pas-de-Calais.)

The 'hub' of the Eurostar network is Lille, Paris being the 'end of the line' for most trains, although a direct London to Avignon route, taking six hours, was inaugurated in summer 2003.

You can obtain train information in English or make a booking by calling ☎ 08705-186186 in the UK or ☎ 08 92 35 35 39 in France or by going to the Eurostar website (🖳 www.eurostar.com). Note that a £5 booking fee is made for telephone reservations. For car-train services through the Channel Tunnel, see **Eurotunnel** on page 100.

Motorail

Motorail is a European network of special trains (known as *auto-trains*), generally running overnight, carrying passengers and their cars or motorbikes over distances of up to 1,500km (900mi). Caravans cannot be taken on Motorail trains. The SNCF provides an extensive motorail network of some 130 routes linking most regions of France. The principal Motorail services from the UK operate from Calais and Dieppe to Avignon, Biarritz, Bordeaux, Brive-la-Gaillarde, Narbonne, Nice and Toulouse. Trains don't run every day and on most routes operate during peak months only.

Motorail journeys are expensive (e.g. a minimum or £230 for a family to travel from London to Brive-la-Gaillarde one way) and it's cheaper for most people to drive, although it's usually slower and not as relaxing (trains are now equipped with a 'bar car'!). The main advantage of Motorail is that you travel overnight and (with luck) arrive feeling refreshed after a good night's sleep. Note that there's a big difference between fares during off-peak and peak periods.

A comprehensive timetable (*Guide Trains Autos et Motos accompagnées*) is published for bookings made through a railway station or travel agent in France, containing routes, tariffs, general information and access maps for motorail stations. Passengers in the UK can obtain a brochure,

Motorail for Motorists – the Expressway into Europe. Further information can be found on the French Motorail website (💻 www.raileurope.co.uk/frenchmotorail) or by calling ☎ 0870-502 4000 in the UK.

International Bus Services

Eurolines (💻 www.eurolines.com or www.eurolines.fr) operate regular services from the UK to over 50 French cities, including Bordeaux, Cannes, Lyon, Montpellier, Nice, Orléans, Paris, Perpignan, Reims, Saint-Malo and Strasbourg.

International Ferry Services

Ferry services operate year round between France and the UK/Ireland. There's a wide choice of routes for travellers between France and the UK, depending on where you live and your intended route, but only one for Irish travellers. These are (from east to west):

● Dover/Dunkerque (Norfolk Line, 💻 www.norfolkline.com, which recently added a third ferry to its fleet; its two existing ferries will be replaced by new vessels in 2005 and 2006);

● Dover/Calais (Hoverspeed, 💻 www.hoverspeed.co.uk, P&O Ferries, 💻 www.poferries.com, and Sea France, 💻 www.seafrance.co.uk);

● Dover/Boulogne (Speed Ferries, 💻 www.speedferries.com) – a five-times daily fast ferry service with a crossing time of 50 minutes;

● Newhaven/Dieppe (Hoverspeed and Transmanche Ferries, 💻 www.transmancheferries.com);

● Portsmouth/Le Havre (Brittany Ferries, 💻 www.brittany-ferries.co.uk);

● Portsmouth/Caen (Brittany Ferries);

● Portsmouth/Saint-Malo (Brittany Ferries);

● Poole/Cherbourg (Brittany Ferries);

● Poole/Saint-Malo via Guernsey and Jersey (Condor Ferries, 💻 www.condorferries.co.uk);

● Weymouth/Saint-Malo via Guernsey and Jersey (Condor Ferries);

● Plymouth/Roscoff (Brittany Ferries);

● Cork/Roscoff (Brittany Ferries).

Note that the cross-Channel ferry companies rarely advertise contact telephone numbers in France and French residents may find the following numbers useful: Brittany Ferries (☎ 02 98 29 28 00);

Hoverspeed (☎ 03 21 46 14 54 for Calais and ☎ 02 32 14 42 80 for Dieppe); P&O Ferries (☎ 01 55 69 82 28); Sea France (☎ 03 21 46 80 00).

Some services operate during the summer months only, and the frequency of services varies from dozens a day on the busiest Calais-Dover route during the summer peak period to one a week on longer routes. Services are less frequent during the winter months, when bad weather can also cause cancellations. On the longer routes (i.e. Portsmouth/Le Havre and further west), there are overnight services.

Fares

With the end of duty-free shopping (see page 313) in 1999, cross-Channel fares were increased to compensate for the huge loss in revenue (although, miraculously, the ferry companies still manage to offer significant discounts on alcohol and tobacco products!). Peak fares are especially high, e.g. a standard Calais-Dover return with P&O for a vehicle up to 5m (16ft) in length costs around €540 (€270 single) including only the driver and one passenger. Nevertheless, increased competition has (finally) started to drive prices down and most ferry companies offer deals for short periods (e.g. one, three and five-day returns). Whenever you travel, always check for special offers. If you're able to book several months in advance, you can often earn up to 50 per cent discounts.

It's worthwhile shopping around for the best deal, which is probably best done by a travel agent who has access to fares from all companies or by using a company specialising in discount Channel crossings. These include Channelcrossings.net (🖳 www.channelcrossings.net), Cross-Channel Ferry Tickets (🖳 www.cross-channel-ferry-tickets.co.uk), Ferrybooker.com (🖳 www.ferrybooker.co.uk), International Life Leisure 2000 (🖳 www.ferrysavers.com) and Into Ferries (🖳 www.into ferries.co.uk). Note that it's difficult to consult ferry company fares online, as you don't have access to the full range of fares and can only find the price by using the (time-consuming) booking form or quote facility. Brochures rarely include the range of fares.

P&O shareholders who own at least GB£600 worth of P&O concessionary stock receive a 50 per cent discount on Calais-Dover crossings and 40 per cent off Cherbourg-Portsmouth and Le Havre-Portsmouth crossings. Some ferry lines have clubs for frequent travellers, e.g. Brittany Ferries' Property Owners' Travel Club (☎ 0870-908 1282), offering savings of up to 30 per cent on single and standard return fares, and Hoverspeed's Frequent Traveller scheme (☎ 0870-460 7333), offering 20 per cent off all fares without a membership fee. In some cases, it's cheaper to book a short break including ferry crossing and accommodation than the crossing alone!

Children under four years old usually travel free and those aged 4 to 14 travel for half fare. Students may be entitled to a small discount during off-peak periods. Bicycles are transported free on most services.

Eurotunnel

Eurotunnel (formerly Le Shuttle) operates a shuttle car train service between Coquelles (near Calais) and Folkestone via the Channel Tunnel. There are three trains per hour during peak periods, and the crossing takes just 35 minutes. Each train can carry around 180 cars. Fares are similar to ferries, e.g. a peak (summer) club class return costs around €600 and an off-peak (January to March) return around €280 for a vehicle and all passengers. It's wise to book in advance, and you shouldn't expect to get a place in summer on a 'turn up and go' basis, particularly on Fridays, Saturdays and Sundays.

Trains carry all types of vehicle, including cycles, motorcycles, cars, trucks, buses, caravans and motor-homes, although you pay more for vehicles over 1.85m (6ft 1in). Note also that caravans and motor-homes must have their gas supplies disconnected and gas bottles must be shut off (gas bottles are routinely inspected, so make sure they're accessible).

Eurotunnel operates a Points Plus scheme, offering discounts of up to 10 per cent to regular users. There's an annual 'membership' fee of around GB£15 and each time you travel you collect points, which can eventually be redeemed against the cost of a crossing. Further information is obtainable by telephone (☎ 0870-840 0026 in the UK or ☎ 03 21 00 61 00 in France) or from the Eurotunnel website (🖥 www. eurotunnel.com). There's also a Property Owners' Club, offering savings on a minimum of five crossings per year for a registration fee of £30 and an annual membership fee of £35 (UK ☎ 0870-243 0892). For general information ☎ 0870-535 3535 or 0800-096 9992 in the UK or ☎ 03 21 00 61 00 in France.

GETTING AROUND

Public transport (*transport public*) services in France vary considerably according to where you live. They're generally excellent in French cities, most of which have efficient local bus and rail services, many supplemented by underground railway and/or tram networks. French railways provide an excellent and fast rail service, particularly between cities served by the *TGV*, one of the world's fastest trains. France is also served by excellent domestic airline services. On the negative side, bus and rail services are poor or non-existent in rural areas and it's generally essential to have a car if you live in the country.

Paris in particular has one of the most efficient, best integrated and cheapest public transport systems of any major city in the world. In addition to its world-famous *métro*, public transport services include the *RER* express rail system, an extensive suburban rail network and comprehensive bus services. Other cities have similar systems, and several have reintroduced trams in recent years. (In fact, a tram system is also planned for Paris, and the first lines could be open in 2006.)

Thanks to government subsidies, public transport is generally inexpensive in France, although this doesn't stop the French from complaining about the cost. Various commuter and visitor discount tickets are also available.

For further details of domestic transport services in France, refer to *Living and Working in France* and *The Best Places to Live in France* (Survival Books – see page 389).

Domestic Flights

Sadly, most of France's regional airlines have been swallowed by Air France (☎ 08 20 32 08 20 for bookings, 💻 www.airfrance.fr), which now dominates the domestic flight market, although there are still a few regional services, e.g. Air Littoral and Airlinair, which operate flights on various routes, the Compagnie aérienne Corse Mediterranée and Corsair, which operate flights to Corsica, and Air Outre-Mer, which offers daily flights to Réunion. (Air Liberté went bankrupt in February 2003.) Note also that the American company Delta Airlines operates a number of internal French flights.

Air France offers domestic services between major cities such as Paris, Bordeaux, Lyon, Marseille, Mulhouse/Basel, Nice, Strasbourg and Toulouse. Domestic services from smaller airports operate mainly to the capital, and many domestic flights are timed to connect (*correspondance*) with international arrivals.

Competition on major domestic routes from *TGV*s (see below), e.g. Paris-Lyon and the new three-hour Paris-Marseille route, has helped reduce air fares, and flying is sometimes cheaper than travelling by train and quicker on most routes. Any destination in mainland France or Corsica can be reached in less than 100 minutes by air, although stricter security now means that check-in times can be up to 45 minutes before departure.

Domestic Rail Services

French railways are operated by the state-owned Société Nationale des Chemins de Fer Français (SNCF), which operates one of the most efficient rail systems in Europe and both employees and the French public take great pride in their trains. French railways are operated as a public service and charge reasonable fares and offer a wide range of discounts and special fares, all of which help increase passenger numbers, thus reducing road congestion and environmental damage. French high-speed trains compete successfully with road and air travel over long distances, both in cost and speed. The French railway network extends to every corner of France, although most routes radiate from Paris, there are few cross-country routes and services in most rural areas are limited.

The SNCF operates high-speed trains (*train à grande vitesse*, abbreviated to *TGV*) on its main lines, which are among the world's fastest trains, capable of over 550kph (around 350mph). *TGV* services operate to over 50 French cities. It takes just three hours to travel from Paris to Marseille by *TGV*. Standard trains have either electric (*Corail*) or gas turbine (*Turbotrain*) locomotives, which, although not in the *TGV* league, are fast and comfortable. Some branch lines operate *express* and *rapide* diesel trains. The slowest trains are the suburban *omnibus* services (some with double-deck carriages), which stop at every station. A *direct* train is a through train, usually classified as an *express* or *train express régional* (*TER*), stopping only at main stations and second in speed to the *TGV* (see above). A *rapide* is faster than an *omnibus* but slower than a *direct* or *express*.

All SNCF telephone enquiries are now centralised on a premium-rate telephone number (☎ 08 36 35 35 35); information can also be obtained and bookings made via the SNCF website (💻 www.sncf.com and www.voyages-sncf.com), where special offers are available on Tuesdays! The SNCF has offices in many countries, including the UK (Rail Europe, 178 Piccadilly, London W1V 0BA, ☎ 0870-241 4243 or 0870-584 8848 for European tickets, 💻 www.raileurope.co.uk). Rail information is also available via Minitel (3615 SNCF). The SNCF publishes a free quarterly magazine in some countries, e.g. *Top Rail* in the UK, plus a wealth of free brochures and booklets detailing its services, including *Le Guide du Voyageur*, available from French stations.

Domestic Bus Services

There's a nationwide campaign for 'car-free' cities, and there are excellent bus services in Paris and other major cities, some of which (including Bordeaux, Caen, Le Mans, Lyon, Montpelier, Nancy, Nantes, Nice, Orléans, Rouen, Strasbourg, Toulon and Valenciennes) also have trams or trolley buses. The town of Châteauroux (in Indre) recently became the first in France to offer free bus travel in order to persuade citizens to abandon their cars, and in Lille commuters are offered half-price bus travel.

In rural areas, however, buses are few and far between, and the scant services that exist are usually designed to meet the needs of workers, schoolchildren, and housewives on market days. This means that buses usually run early and late in the day with little or nothing in between, and may cease altogether during the long summer school holiday period (July and August). A city bus is generally called an *autobus* and a country bus a *car* or *autocar*. Smoking isn't permitted on buses in France.

The best place to enquire about bus services is at a tourist office or railway station. In large towns and cities, buses run to and from bus stations (*gare d'autobus/routière*) usually located next to railway stations. In rural areas, bus services are often operated by the SNCF and run between local towns and the railway station. An SNCF bus, on which rail tickets and passes are valid, is shown as an *autocar* in rail timetables. The SNCF also provides bus tours throughout France. Private bus services are often confusing and uncoordinated and usually leave from different locations rather than a central bus station. Some towns provide free or discount bus passes to senior citizens (over 60) on production of an identity card, passport, or *carte de séjour* and proof of local residence.

There are no national bus companies in France operating scheduled services, although many long-distance buses are operated by foreign companies such as Euroways/Eurolines, Riviera Express, Europabus, Miracle Bus and Grey-Green Coaches. Eurolines (🖥 www.eurolines.com or www.eurolines.fr) operate regular services from the UK to over 50 French cities, including Bordeaux, Cannes, Lyon, Montpellier, Nice, Orléans, Paris, Perpignan, Reims, Saint-Malo and Strasbourg. Discounts are provided for students and youths on some routes.

French Roads

France has a good road system that includes everything from motorways to forest dirt tracks. The quality of roads varies enormously, however: while motorways are generally excellent and most other main roads are also very good, urban roads and minor roads in rural areas can be poorly maintained. Trunk roads vary from almost motorway standard dual-carriageways to narrow two-lane roads passing through a succession of villages where the speed limit is 50kph (30mph).

Motorways

France boasts one of the best motorway (*autoroute*) networks in Europe, totalling over 9,500km (6,000mi). Unfortunately they are also among the world's most expensive, being mostly toll roads built by private companies (see below). Because of this, driving on motorways is considered a luxury by many French people and they therefore have the lowest traffic density of any European motorways. Partly for this reason, motorways are also France's safest roads – with the notable exception of the Paris *Périphérique*, an eight-lane race track around the city centre on which there's an average of one fatal accident a day!

Because of the continuous expansion of the network (early 2003 saw the completion of a motorway route from Calais to Spain via Bordeaux), you shouldn't use a motoring atlas that's more than a few years out of date.

Tolls: Most French motorways are toll roads (*à péage*) and are among the most expensive in Europe, although there are plans to privatise half the motorways in the south, which could reduce charges by up to 30 per cent. Rates aren't standardised throughout France and vary with the age of the motorway and the services provided. There are no tolls on the sections of motorways around cities. A new system of tolls has been introduced in some areas with higher tolls during peak periods. On average, however, motorway travel costs an average of €0.07 per kilometre for a car. There are five vehicle categories on most motorways, and motor-homes and cars towing trailers or caravans are more expensive than cars alone.

The approximate costs of driving a standard car from Calais or Le Havre to various French towns are shown below.

Biarritz	€65	Nancy	€28
Bordeaux	€62	Nantes	€56
Cahors	€38	Nice	€77
Clermont-Ferrand	€47	Paris	€16
Dijon	€36	Perpignan	€54
Grenoble	€52	Poitiers	€44
Lyon	€67	Strasbourg	€38
Marseille	€63		

An *Autoroute Tarifs* leaflet and other traffic information is available from the Association des Sociétés Françaises d'Autoroutes, 3 rue Edmond Valentin, 75007 Paris (☎ 08 92 68 10 77, 🖳 www.autoroutes.fr).

Tolls are also levied to use the Mont Blanc (Chamonix-Entrèves, Italy, 11.6km/7.2mi) tunnel, now in service again, the Fréjus (Modane-Bardonecchia, Italy, 12.8km/8mi) and Bielsa (Aragnouet-Bielsa, Spain, 3km/1.86mi) tunnels, and the Tancarville, Saint-Nazaire and Pont de Normandie bridges.

If you're travelling long distances, it may be cheaper to fly or take a *TGV* and will almost certainly be quicker, safer and less stressful.

Other Roads

Unlike French motorways, main trunk roads (*route nationale*) are jammed by drivers (including those of heavy goods vehicles) who are reluctant to pay or cannot afford the high motorway tolls. If you must get from A to B in the shortest possible time, there's no alternative to the motorway (apart from taking a plane or train). However, if you aren't in too much of a hurry, want to save money **and** wish to see something of France, you should avoid motorways. The money saved on tolls can pay for a good meal or an (inexpensive) hotel room. *Routes nationales* and other secondary roads are often straight and many are dual carriageways, on which you can usually make good time at (legal) speeds of between 80 and 110kph (50 to 70mph). On the other hand, many trunk roads pass through towns and villages, where the limit is reduced to 50kph (30mph), which can make for slow progress.

Information

In June each year, the French Ministry of Transport issues a 'wily bison' map (*Carte de Bison futé*) showing areas of congestion and providing information about alternative routes (*itinéraire bis*), indicated by yellow or green signs. The map is available free from petrol stations and tourist offices in France and from French Government Tourist Offices abroad as well as via the internet (🖳 www.bison-fute.equipement.gouv.fr). There are around 90 information rest areas throughout France, indicated by a black 'i' and an *Information Bison futé* sign. Green-arrowed holiday routes (*flèches vertes*) avoiding large towns and cities are also recommended. Colour-coded traffic days and traffic jams (*orange* for bad, *rouge* for very bad and *noir* for appalling) are announced on the radio and television.

Even if you don't have in-car GPS, route planning is simple thanks to the internet, where several sites can help you find the quickest and most economical route to your French home, including 🖳 www.mappy.com and www.viamichelin.fr (in French), and www.rac.co.uk, www.theaa.com and www.viamichelin.co.uk (in English).

Up-to-date information about French roads can be obtained from the Ministère de l'Equipement, des Transports et du Logement, Direction des Routes, Service du Contrôle des Autoroutes, La Défense, 92055 Paris Cedex (☎ 01 40 81 21 22) or by phoning *Information routière* (☎ 08 26 02 20 22). Details of current roadworks can be found on 🖳 www.trafic.asf.fr (southern France only) or by tuning in to *Autoroute Info* on 107.7FM. Information about motorways, tolls and driving in France can also be obtained from French Government Tourist Offices abroad. Details of planned new roads are provided in **The Best Places to Buy a Home in France** (Survival Books – see page 389).

3.

YOUR DREAM HOME

Once you've considered possible locations for your dream home in France, you must decide on the type of property that will best suit your requirements, weigh up the purchase options and assess the fees associated with buying.

There's an overwhelming choice of property for sale and a buyers' market in most areas, although less so than a decade ago. As when buying property anywhere, it's never wise to be in too much of a hurry. Have a good look around in your chosen region and obtain an accurate picture of the types of property available, their relative values and what you can expect to get for your money. However, before doing this you should make a comprehensive list of what you want (and don't want) from a home, so that you can narrow the field and save time on wild goose chases.

Although property in France is inexpensive compared with many other European countries, the fees associated with the purchase of properties more than five years old are the highest in Europe and add 10 to 15 per cent to the cost. To reduce the chances of making an expensive error when buying in an unfamiliar region, it's often prudent to rent a house for a period (see **Renting Before Buying** below), taking in the worst part of the year (weather-wise). This allows you to become familiar with the region and the weather, and gives you plenty of time to look around for a home at your leisure.

Wait until you find something you fall head over heels in love with and then think about it for a week or two before rushing headlong to the altar! One of the advantages of buying property in France is that there's usually another 'dream' home around the next corner – and the second or third dream home is often even better than the first. **However, don't dally endlessly, as good properties at the right price don't remain on the market for ever.**

RENTING BEFORE BUYING

As when making all major financial decisions, give yourself time to think.

> **SURVIVAL TIP**
> Unless you know exactly what you're looking for and where, it's best to rent a property for a period to reduce the risk of making a costly mistake, particularly when you're planning to buy in an unfamiliar area.

This is even more important for those planning to set up a business in France, when it isn't advisable to buy a home until you're sure that your business will be a success. Renting long-term before buying is particularly prudent for anyone planning to live in France permanently.

If possible, you should rent a similar property to the one you're planning to buy, during the time(s) of year when you plan to occupy it. The advantages of renting include the following:

- It allows you to become familiar with the weather, the amenities and the local people, to meet other foreigners who've made their homes in France and share their experiences, and to discover the cost of living for yourself.
- It 'buys' you time to find your dream home at your leisure.
- It saves tying up your capital and can be surprisingly inexpensive in many regions. You may even wish to consider renting a home in France long-term (or 'permanently'). Some people let their family homes abroad and rent one in France for a period (you may even make a profit!).

On the other hand, the disadvantages of renting should be taken into consideration, including the following:

- Annual property price increases in most areas are higher than interest rates, which means that you may be better of tying up your money in a property than investing it while you rent.
- Taking a long-term rental before buying means in effect moving house twice within a year or two; remember that moving is one of life's most stressful experiences!
- You may not find the type of rental property you want, which will colour your experience of living in a particular area and possibly in France generally. For example, most rental properties are apartments, and rural homes are rarely available for rent.

If you're looking for a rental property for a few months, you may need to rent a holiday apartment for a week or two to allow yourself time to find one that suits you.

Long-Term Rentals

If you're looking for a home for less than a year, you're usually better off looking for a furnished (*meublé*) apartment or house. However, most long-term rental properties are unfurnished (*non-meublé*), and long-term furnished properties are difficult to find, although tax incentives are encouraging owners to let furnished property long-term and a growing number of foreign owners who are unable to sell their French homes are letting them long-term, particularly outside the peak summer period.

Note that in France, 'unfurnished' doesn't just mean without furniture. An unfurnished property usually has no light fittings, curtain rods or even an outdoor TV aerial. There's also no cooker, refrigerator or dishwasher and there may be no kitchen units, carpets or kitchen sink! Always ask before viewing, as you may save yourself a wasted trip.

If the previous tenant has fitted items such as carpets and kitchen cupboards, he may ask you for a rebate (*reprise*) to leave them behind. You should negotiate the rebate and ensure that you receive value for money. A *reprise* isn't enforceable, although if the tenant has the approval of the landlord it's difficult to avoid paying it, even though it may amount to little more than a bribe.

Short-Term Rentals

France has an abundance of furnished, self-catering accommodation and the widest imaginable choice. You can choose from literally thousands of cottages (*gîtes*), apartments, villas, bungalows, mobile homes, chalets, and even *châteaux* and manor houses. However, most property is available for holiday lets (i.e. one or two weeks) only, particularly during the peak summer season, and, when the rental period includes the peak letting months of July and August, the rent can be prohibitive. Seasonal lets are sometimes available, but generally only in low season.

Standards vary considerably, from dilapidated, ill-equipped cottages to luxury villas with every modern convenience. Many short-term lets are *gîtes*, which literally means a home or shelter but is nowadays used to refer to most furnished, self-catering holiday accommodation. A typical *gîte* is a small cottage or self-contained apartment with one or two bedrooms (sleeping four to eight and usually including a sofa bed in the living room), a large living room/kitchen with an open fire or stove, and a toilet and shower room. In certain parts of France, notably the overcrowded Côte d'Azur, *gîtes* may be concrete 'rabbit hutches', built to a basic standard with minimal facilities. Check whether a property is fully equipped (which should mean whatever you want it to mean!) and whether it has central heating if you're planning to rent in winter.

Finding A Rental Property

Your success or failure in finding a suitable rental property depends on many factors, not least the type of rental you're seeking (a one-bedroom apartment is easier to find than a four-bedroom detached house), how much you want to pay and the area. France has a strong rental market in most areas, although rural properties are rarely available for long-term rental.

When looking for rented accommodation, try to avoid the months of September and October, when French people return from their summer holidays and (in university towns and cities) students are looking for accommodation.

Ways of finding a property to rent include the following:

- Visit accommodation and letting agents. Most cities and large towns have estate agents (*agences immobilières*) who also act as letting agents. Look under *Agences de Location et de Propriétés* in the yellow pages. It's often better to deal with an agent than directly with owners, particularly with regard to contracts and legal matters. Builders and developers may also rent properties to potential buyers.

- Contact travel agents and French Government Tourist Offices (who are agents for Gîtes de France), who may deal with short-term rentals.

- Look in local newspapers and magazines, particularly expatriate publications, and foreign property publications (see **Appendix B** for a list).

- Check newsletters published by churches, clubs and expatriate organisations, and their notice boards.

- Look for advertisements in shop windows and on notice boards in shopping centres, supermarkets, universities and colleges, and company offices.

- Search the internet: useful sites include ⊑ www.appelimmo.fr, ⊑ www. avendrealouer.fr, ⊑ www.entreparticuliers.fr, ⊑ www.foncia.fr, ⊑ www.lacentrale.fr, ⊑ www.lesiteimmobilier.com, ⊑ www.pap.fr and ⊑ www.seloger.com).

- Contact owners directly via the publications listed in **Appendix B**.

Rental Costs

Rental costs vary considerably according to the size and quality of a property, its age and the facilities provided. Prices are calculated according to the number of rooms (*pièces*), **excluding** the kitchen, bathroom(s), toilet(s) and other 'utility' rooms, and the floor area (in square metres). A one-room apartment has a combined living and sleeping room (it may have a separate kitchen and bathroom) and is called a *studio*. A two-room (*deux-pièces*) apartment usually has one bedroom, a living room, kitchen and bathroom. A three-room (*trois-pièces*) apartment has two bedrooms, a four-room (*quatre-pièces*) apartment may have three bedrooms or two bedrooms and separate dining and living rooms, and so on. The average size of a two-room apartment is around 50m² (500ft²).

Rental prices are also based on the prevailing market value of a property (*indice*), and the most significant factor affecting rental prices is location: the region of France, the city and the neighbourhood. Like everywhere, rental prices in France are dictated by supply and demand and are higher in Cannes, Grenoble, Lyon and Nice than in Bordeaux, Marseille, Strasbourg and Toulouse, for example. Rental accommodation in Paris is in high demand and short supply, and the prices are among the highest in Europe and often double those in other French cities. In Paris, you should expect to pay at least €25 per m²; a tiny studio apartment of around 20m² (215ft²) in a reasonable area costs around €500 per month, while a two or three-bedroom apartment (125m²/1,345ft²) in a fashionable *arrondissement* can cost up to ten times as much.

The lowest prices are found in small towns and rural areas, though there is not so much choice. As a general rule, the further a property is from a large city or town (or town centre), public transport or other facilities, the cheaper it is. In the provinces you can rent a two-bedroom apartment or cottage for €300 or less per month. Houses can be rented in most rural areas and on the outskirts of some towns; for a three-bedroom house, you can expect to pay at least €500 per month – double that in parts of the Ile-de-France and the south-east, including the Alps.

Rental prices are often open to negotiation and you may be able to secure a 5 to 10 per cent reduction if there isn't a queue of customers behind you. For details of prices and availability of long-term lets in different regions, refer to **The Best Places to Buy a Home in France** (Survival Books – see page 389).

Rental prices for short-term lets, e.g. less than a year, are higher than for longer lets, particularly in popular holiday areas. For short-term lets the cost is calculated on a weekly basis (Saturday to Saturday) and depends on the standard, location, number of beds and the facilities provided. The rent for a *gîte* sleeping six is typically from €250 to €350 per week in June and September, and €350 to €500 in July and August. The rent is higher for a *gîte* with a pool. However, when renting long-term outside the high season, you can rent a two-bedroom property for around €500 per month in most regions.

Rental Contracts

A rental contract, whether for an unfurnished or a furnished property, must be signed by all parties involved, including the agent handling the contract, if applicable. Next to their signature each party must also write the words *lu et approuvé* (read and approved). A contract for a furnished property is called a *contrat de location de locaux meublés*, while a seasonal contract is an *engagement de location meublée saisonnière*. French rental

▼ *Auffay, Seine-Maritime*
  (© Latitudes)

▲ *Térenez, Finistère (© Roger Moss)*

▼ *Caussiniojouls, Hérault*
  (© Latitudes)

▲ *Donzy, Burgundy (© Roger Moss)*

▶
Fabras, Ardèche
  (© Roger Moss)

◀ *Menerbes, Vaucluse* (© *Roger Moss*)

▲ *Savigny, Côte d'O*
(© *Latitudes*

▲ *Gerberoy, Oise* (© *Roger Moss*)

▲ *Vire, Manche* (© *Latitudes*

◀ *La Roche-sur-le-Buis,
Drôme* (© *Roger Moss*)

Savigné, Vienne ▶
(© Roger Moss)

◀ *Lannion, Côtes D'Armor*
(© Latitudes)

Hoffen, Bas-Rhin
▼ *(© Roger Moss)*

▲ *Arçais, Deux-Sèvres (© Roger Moss)*

▲ *Oloron-Sainte-Marie,*
Pyrénées-Atlantiques
(© Latitudes)

▲ *Nyon, Drôme* (© Roger Moss)

▲ *Nice, Côte d'Azur*
(© Latitudes

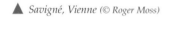

▲ *Savigné, Vienne* (© Roger Moss)

▲ *Riberac/Montpon,*
Dordogne (© Latitudes

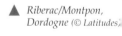

◀ *Verteuil, Charente*
(© Roger Moss)

laws (and protection for tenants) don't extend to holiday lettings or sub-lettings, however. For holiday letting, the parties are free to agree such terms as they see fit concerning the period, rent, deposit and the number of occupants permitted, and there's no legal obligation on the landlord to provide a written agreement. However, you should never rent a property without a written contract, which should be drawn up or checked by a notary for long-term rentals. This is important if you wish to get a deposit returned.

Hotels

French hotels are among the cheapest in the western world, including Parisian hotels, where you can still get an attractive double room for €60 to €75 per night. The same standard room in the country costs as little as €40, although rates vary according to the time of year, the location and the individual establishment. You may also be able to haggle over rates outside the high season and for long stays. Many hotels have rooms for three or four guests at reduced rates or provide extra beds for children in a double room free or for a small charge. A double room may contain one or two 'double' beds, although they may not be full-size double beds; often a room will have a double bed and one or two single beds.

Budget hotel chains include the following:

● Logis et Auberges de France, the world's largest hotel consortium with over 3,000 privately run hotel/restaurants in the provinces (none in Paris) with prices ranging from €25 to €65 per night for a double room. Contact the Fédération Nationale des Logis et Auberges de France, 83 avenue d'Italie, 75013 Paris (☎ 01 45 84 83 84, ▭ www.logis-de-france.fr) for further information. A *Logis de France* handbook is available from bookshops and FGTOs as well as via the Logis website.

● Formule 1 hotels (☎ 08 92 68 56 85, ▭ www.hotelformule1.com), which are common on the outskirts of towns and cities (often close to motorways). From around €25 per night, up to three people can share a room.

● Accor hotels (☎ 08 25 88 00 00, ▭ www.accorhotels.com), which are owned by the same company as Formule 1;

● Etap hotels (☎ 08 92 68 89 00, ▭ www.etaphotel.com), also owned by the same company as Formule 1;

● Ibis hotels (☎ 08 92 68 66 86, ▭ www.ibishotel.com), also owned by the same company as Formule 1;

● Mister Bed (☎ 01 46 14 38 00, ▭ www.misterbed.fr), a chain of 23 hotels in central and north-east France;

● Première Classe (☎ 08 25 00 30 03, or ☎ 01 64 62 46 46 from outside France, 💻 www.envergure.fr/pclassefr.html).

An even cheaper option is a *pension de famille*, which is similar to a bed and breakfast but normally for periods of at least a month. Charges, excluding meals, range from around €150 to around €250 per month, which works out at just €5 to €8 per night. Meals can often be provided and are correspondingly good value. *Pensions de famille*, which used to provide accommodation for factory workers and others, are becoming increasingly rare but can be found through tourist offices and local tourist boards.

An online guide to French hotels can be found at 💻 www.france-hotel-guide.com. Details of hotels and *pensions* can be obtained through the French Government Tourist Office (FGTO – also known as Maison de la France), which has offices in Austria, Belgium, Brazil, Canada, Denmark, Finland, Germany, Hungary, Ireland, Italy, Japan, Luxembourg, the Netherlands, Norway, Portugal, Spain, Sweden, Switzerland, the UK and the US as well as in France (20 avenue de l'Opéra, 75041 Paris Cedex 01, ☎ 01 42 96 70 00). Details of all offices can be found on the FGTO website (💻 www.franceguide.com/mieuxconnaitre/bureau.asp).

HOME EXCHANGE

An alternative to renting is to exchange your home abroad with one in France. This way you can experience home living in France for a relatively small cost and may save yourself the expense of a long-term rental. Although there's an element of risk involved in exchanging your home with another family, most agencies thoroughly vet clients and many have a track record of successful swaps.

There are home exchange agencies in most countries. Those in the US include Home Exchange.Com (or HomeExchange.com Inc.), PO Box 787, Hermose Beach, CA90254 (☎ 310-798-3864, 💻 www.homeexchange.com) and HomeLink International (☎ 305-294 7766 or 800-638 3841, 💻 www.homelink.org or www.swapnow.com), which has some 16,500 members in around 50 countries. HomeLink also has an office in the UK (7 St Nicholas Rise, Headbourne Worthy, Winchester SO23 7SY, ☎ 01962 8868822, 💻 www.homelink.org.uk), which publishes a *Directory* of homes and holiday homes for exchange. Other UK-based exhange agencies are Home Base Holidays, 7 Park Avenue, London N13 5PG, UK (☎ 020-8886 8752, 💻 www.homebase-hols.com) and Intervac Home Exchange, 24 The Causeway, Chippenham, Wilts SN15 3DB (☎ UK 01249 461101, 💻 www.intervac.com), which has representatives in some 30 countries. Green Theme International is a British agency based in France, at 9 rue des Insurgés, La Maillerie Ouest, 87130 Linards (☎ 05 55 08 47 04, 💻 www.gti-home-exchange.com).

HOUSE HUNTING

There are many ways of finding homes for sale in France, including the following:

- Newspapers and magazines, including the English-language publications listed in **Appendix B**, weekly French property newspapers such as *De Particulier à Particulier, Le Journal des Particuliers, La Centrale des Particuliers* and *La Semaine Immobilière*, national newspapers in your home country and France (if you're looking for an expensive property), local magazines, papers and newsheets (which may have private property advertisements), property magazines published by the French estate agent chains (e.g. ORPI), and general retail publications (e.g. *Daltons Weekly* and *Exchange & Mart* in the UK).

- Property exhibitions (see **Appendix A**);

- The internet, where there are many sites devoted to French property, including those run by French and foreign property agents (see **Appendix C**);

- Discovery tours, which are organised by a number of companies in various regions of France, allowing you to get a feel for an area and the type and prices of properties and maybe see a few properties that are available, although these tours aren't cheap and you may prefer to arrange your own itinerary (see below). For example, in the US there's International Living Discovery Tours (☎ 410-230-1253 or 866-381-8446 toll free, 🖳 www.ildiscoverytours.com), in the UK the KBM Consultancy, The Sycamores, 1 Bownham Mead, Rodborough Common, Stroud, Glos, GL5 5DZ. (☎ 08700-113141, 🖳 www.kbm consultancy.com), whose 'Immotours' currently cover Normandy and Brittany, and Bishop & Co. (☎ 01332-747474, 🖳 www.u2france.co.uk); in France there's The French Property Company t/a Moving to France (☎ 04 67 24 95 42, 🖳 www.moving-to-france.com).

- Visiting an area. Note that around half of French properties are sold privately and the only way to find out about them is to tour the area you're interested in, looking for FOR SALE (*A VENDRE* or sometimes simply *AV*) signs and asking locals or town hall officials if they know of properties for sale.

- Developers, some of whom sell direct, others via agents in France or abroad. Note that developers needn't be licensed to sell property.

- Property traders (*marchands de biens*) – see **Estate Agents** below;

- Estate agents (see below).

Make sure you avoid national holidays when visiting France on a house hunting trip. These include 1st January, Easter Monday, 1st and 8th May, Ascension Day (sixth Thursday after Easter), 14th July, 15th August, 1st and 11th November, and 25th December, and usually the day before/after a holiday if it falls on a Tuesday/Thursday.

If you go house hunting in France, remember to take a calculator (to work out how few euros you will get for your money), a mobile phone that works in France (and a charger and plug adapter), a camera and/or video camera, and instructions for remotely accessing your home answerphone, as well as a notepad, maps and contact numbers.

ESTATE AGENTS

Only some 50 per cent of property sales in France are handled by estate agents (*agent immobilier*). However, where foreign buyers are concerned, the vast majority of sales are made through agents or handled by *notaires* (see below). It's common for foreigners in many countries, particularly the UK, to use an agent in their own country who works with one or more French agents. A number of French agents also advertise abroad, particularly in the publications listed in **Appendix B**, and many have English-speaking staff (so don't be discouraged if you don't speak fluent French).

If you want to find an agent in a particular town or area, look under *Agences Immobilières* in the relevant French yellow pages (*pages jaunes*) available at main libraries in many countries. If using a local estate agent, it's best to go in person. **French estate agents generally don't post or fax you property details but expect you to be there, on the spot, and to go and visit houses immediately.**

Qualifications

French estate agents are regulated by law and must be professionally qualified and licensed and hold indemnity insurance. To work in his own right in France, an agent must possess a *carte professionnelle*, which is granted only to those with certain professional qualifications or considerable experience. The *carte* must be renewed annually and its number and place of issue should be shown on the agent's letterhead.

Estate agents should also provide a financial guarantee for at least €75,000; without this, they aren't entitled to handle clients' money. If an agent provides a guarantee for more than this amount, the name and address of the guarantor (i.e. bank) will also be shown on his letterhead.

If an agent has a lower guarantee, you should pay your deposit to the notary or another legal professional involved in the sale.

> **SURVIVAL TIP**
> Ensure that you're dealing with an agent who fulfils these requirements and, if in doubt, ask to see his qualifications and confirmation of the guarantees he offers.

Most French estate agents are members of a professional body, the three main ones being the Fédération Nationale de l'Immobilier (FNAIM, 🖥 www.fnaim.fr), the leading French association of estate agents, the Syndicat National des Professionnels Immobiliers (SNPI, 🖥 www.snpi.com) and the Union Nationale de la Propriété Immobilière (🖥 www.unpi.org).

Foreign Agents

Very few foreign agents in France possess the coveted *carte professionnelle*, and many are self-employed 'sales representatives' (*agents commerciaux*) of French-registered agents, who require no particular qualifications. If you're dealing with an *agent commercial*, you should check that he's listed on the local *registre du commerce* (he should have a registration number and a *SIRET* number) and, preferably, that the agent he represents is a member of the FNAIM (see page 160). **You shouldn't view properties with anyone who cannot produce a *carte professionnelle* (or who isn't employed by someone with one)**; if you have an accident while visiting a property you won't be able to claim unless an agent is legal and registered. The Federation of Overseas Property Developers, Agents and Consultants (FOPDAC), First Floor, 618 Newmarket Road, Cambridge CB5 8LP (☎ 0870-350 1223, 🖥 www.fopdac.com) can provide a list of its members, who are required to meet certain standards.

There may be advantages in using a foreign agent, particularly an English-speaking one who is experienced in selling to foreign buyers and is familiar with the problems they can encounter. Some foreign agents share their commission with a French agent, while others charge extra for their services – in some cases a great deal extra – and you should always check what's included in any prices quoted by foreign agents.

Marchands De Biens

A *marchand de biens* is a property 'trader' who is permitted to sell only property that he has owned for at least three months. Like developers, traders don't need a licence to sell property and you should take legal advice before buying from a *marchand de biens*. In fact, this is no longer a recognised profession in France. Note, however, that some licensed estate agents are also *marchands de biens*.

Fees

There are no government controls on agents' fees, although they're obliged to post a list (*barème*) in their offices. Fees are usually levied on a sliding scale between 5 and 10 per cent: the cheaper the property, the higher the percentage, e.g. 10 per cent on properties priced at €20,000 reducing to 5 per cent on properties costing €150,000 or more. On expensive properties an agent's fee may be negotiable. An agent's fees may be paid by the vendor, the buyer or be shared, although it's normal for the vendor to pay (i.e. the fee is 'included' in the purchase price). A price quoted as *net vendeur* excludes the selling agent's fees; *commission comprise* (written as C/C) indicates that the price includes the agent's commission. **Make sure when discussing the price that it's C/C and not *net vendeur*.**

Many foreign agents work with French agents and share the standard commission, so you usually pay no more by using a foreign agent. The agent's fee is usually payable on completion, but may be payable sooner.

SURVIVAL TIP
When buying, check in advance whether you need to pay commission or any extras on top of the sale price (apart from the normal fees and taxes associated with buying a property in France – see page 127).

Notaires

Around 15 per cent of property sales in France are negotiated by *notaires* (a peculiarly French official, whose functions aren't the same as a notary or notary public), who also have a monopoly on conveyancing (see page 202) for all property sales in France. *Notaires* have a strict code of practice and aren't, for example, permitted to display property details in their offices, which means that most have a working relationship with a number of estate agents. When a *notaire* is the selling agent, his 'agency' commission **isn't** included in the asking price and is paid by the **buyer**, which should be taken into account when calculating the overall cost of the property. However, the 'agency' fees charged by a *notaire* are usually lower than those levied by estate agents (see above), e.g. 5 per cent up to

€50,000 and 2.5 per cent above this figure. Although there may appear to be a conflict of interest when a *notaire* is instructed by the seller but receives his fee from the buyer, in practice there are usually no problems. VAT (*TVA*) at 19.6 per cent must be added to all fees.

Viewing

If possible, you should decide where you want to live, what sort of property you want and your budget **before** visiting France. Obtain details of as many properties as possible in your chosen area and make a shortlist of those you wish to view (it's also wise to mark them on a map). Most French agents expect customers to know where they want to buy within a 30 to 40km (20 to 25mi) radius and some even expect them to narrow their choice down to certain towns or villages. If you cannot define where and what you're looking for, at least tell the agent, so that he knows that you're undecided. If you're 'window shopping', say so. Many agents will still be pleased to show you properties, as they're well aware that many people fall in love with (and buy) a property on the spot.

The details provided by French estate agents are usually sparse; often there's no photograph and, even when there is, it usually doesn't do a property justice. In the case of many old properties in need of renovation, there isn't a lot that can be said apart from stating the land area and the number and size of buildings. French agents who advertise in foreign journals or who work closely with overseas agents, on the other hand, usually supply colour photographs and a full description, particularly for more expensive properties. The best agents provide an abundance of information.

Agents vary enormously in their efficiency, enthusiasm and professionalism. If an agent shows little interest in finding out exactly what you want, you should go elsewhere. Note that there are no national property listings in France, where agents jealously guard their lists of properties, although many work with overseas agents in areas popular with foreign buyers.

If you've made an appointment with an agent in your home country to see properties in France, make a note of their reference numbers in case the French agent hasn't been informed (or has lost them), it isn't unusual for a French agent's reference numbers not to match those you're given abroad! Some agents, particularly outside France, don't update their records frequently and their lists may be way out of date. If you're using a foreign agent, confirm (and reconfirm) the price and that a particular property is still available before travelling to France to view it.

It's common practice for agents to lure potential buyers with idyllic properties that are no longer for sale (or don't even exist!) and then try to sell them other properties, which may not even match their requirements.

In France you're usually shown properties personally by agents and won't be given the keys (especially to furnished properties) or be expected to deal with tenants or vendors directly. One reason is that many properties are almost impossible to find if you don't know the area, and it isn't unknown even for agents to get hopelessly lost when looking for properties! Many rural properties have no numbers, and street name signs are virtually non-existent (if someone invites you to dinner in rural France, make sure you have their telephone number for when you get lost).

You should make an appointment to see properties, as agents don't like people simply turning up. If you make an appointment, you should keep it or call and cancel it. If you're on holiday, it's acceptable to drop in unannounced to have a look at what's on offer, but don't expect an agent to show you properties without an appointment. If you view properties during a holiday, it's best to do so at the beginning so that you can return later to inspect any you particularly like a second or third time. Note that French agents and *notaires* don't usually work during lunch hours and most close on Saturday afternoons and Sundays and some also on Mondays.

A French agent may ask you to sign a document (*bon de visite*) before showing you any properties, which is simply to protect his commission should you obtain details from another source or try to do a deal with the owner behind his back.

You should try to view as many properties as possible during the time available, but allow sufficient time to view each property thoroughly, to travel and get lost between houses, and for breaks for sustenance (it's **mandatory** to have a good lunch in France). Although it's important to see enough properties to form an accurate opinion of price and quality, don't see too many in one day (between four and six is usually enough), as it's easy to become confused as to the merits of each property. If you're shown properties that don't meet your specifications, tell the agent immediately. You can also help the agent narrow the field by telling him exactly what's wrong with the properties you reject.

It's wise to make notes of both the good **and** bad features and take lots of photographs of the properties you like, so that you're able to compare them later at your leisure (but keep a record of which photos are of which house!). It's also shrewd to mark each property on a map so that, should you wish to return, you can find them without getting lost (too often). The more a property appeals to you, the more you should look for faults and negative points; if you still like it after stressing all the negative points, it must have special appeal.

PROPERTY PRICES

Apart from obvious points such as size, quality and land area, the most important factor influencing the price of a house is its location. A restored or modernised two-bedroom house might cost €75,000 in a remote or unpopular area but sell for double or treble that price in a popular location. The closer you are to the coast (or Paris), the more expensive a property will be, with properties on the Côte d'Azur the most expensive of all. A Charente farmhouse with a barn and land costs around the same as a tiny studio apartment in Paris or on the Côte d'Azur.

Note that when people talk about 'inexpensive' homes, they invariably mean something that needs restoring, which usually necessitates spending as much as the purchase price (or much more) to make it habitable. The French think that the British are particularly insane for buying up their tumbled down farmhouses and crumbling *châteaux*. Few Frenchmen (although it's becoming more common) share the British passion for spending their holidays and weekends up to their elbows in bricks and mortar! They do, however, have a grudging admiration for the British for their painstaking and sensitive restorations (see **Renovation & Restoration** on page 167).

Despite the recent increase in property prices, a slice of *la bonne vie* needn't cost the earth, with habitable cottages and terraced village homes available from around €50,000 and detached homes from as little as €75,000. In some rural areas it's still possible to buy an old property for as little as €25,000, although you usually need to carry out major restoration work. Modern studio and one-bedroom apartments in small towns cost from around €30,000 and two-bedroom apartments from €40,000. A modern two-bedroom bungalow costs from around €50,000 and a rural two-bedroom renovated cottage from around €60,000. However, if you're seeking a home with several bedrooms, a large plot and a swimming pool, you will need to spend at least €100,000 (depending on the area), and luxury apartments in Paris and villas in the south of France can cost many hundreds of thousands of euros.

Property in ski resorts varies considerably in price according to the resort and the location of the property. A two-bedroom apartment in a less popular purpose-built resort costs from around €100,000, while a similar property close to the ski lifts in a top resort can cost as much as such as €500,000. Courchevel is one of the most expensive resorts anywhere in the Alps, property costing around €9,000 per m² (Val d'Isère isn't far behind at €7,500 per m², Méribel costs around €6,000 and Les

Arcs is a snip at a mere €4,500 per m²). You can easily spend €1 million to buy a family-sized chalet in an average resort.

When property is advertised in France, the total living area in square metres (*mètres carrés*) is usually stated (written as m²) and the number of rooms (*pièces*), including bedrooms and reception rooms (such as a lounge) but not the kitchen, bathroom(s) or toilet(s). A two-room (*deux pièces*) apartment has one bedroom and a three-room (*trois pièces*) house has two bedrooms. Prices in Paris are similar to other international cities (e.g London). In central Paris, €200,000 barely buys a one-bedroom apartment in some areas and it isn't unusual to pay €2 million for a luxury apartment in a fashionable area. Prices are calculated per m², ranging from around €2,500 in the cheaper areas to €8,000 or more for a luxury property in the chic 8th and 16th districts (*arrondissement*). The average price of apartments in most other cities is between €1,000 and €1,500 per m².

To get an idea of property prices in different regions of France, see **The Best Places to Buy a Home in France** (Survival Books) and check the prices of properties advertised in French and English-language property magazines and newspapers (see **Appendix B**). Property price indexes for different areas are published by some French property magazines, although these should be taken as a guide only.

The table below is designed to give you a **rough** idea of what you can expect to receive for your money in France. Cheaper properties, say under €50,000, requiring restoration are rare in major cities and popular areas. Inexpensive properties (e.g. for restoration) are also difficult to find in certain regions, including Alsace, Franche-Comté and Rhône-Alpes. Unless otherwise stated, the prices listed below refer to property in all regions. Note also that rural properties such as farmhouses invariably come with a large plot (one or two acres is common).

Price (€)	Will Buy
25,000–50,000	A rural cottage or farmhouse requiring extensive restoration and modernisation; a large stone barn for conversion; a tiny studio apartment (e.g. 30m²) on the Côte d'Azur.
50,000–75,000	A restored or partly restored two or three-bedroom rural property with some land; a farmhouse requiring renovation in the Dordogne; a one-bedroom apartment in a popular resort (excluding the Côte d'Azur); a village house for restoration in some western parts of Provence.
75,000–100,000	A restored farmhouse or village house in good condition; a three or four-bedroom rural detached house in good condition; a small two-bedroom modern house.
100,000–150,000	A large three or four-bedroom rural property in good condition with a large plot (possibly with a pool); a one or two-bedroom apartment in a popular resort; a rural village house or farmhouse for restoration in Provence.

150,000–300,000	A restored four-bedroom rural property with a swimming pool and a substantial plot; a modern four-bedroom rural property; a two or three-bedroom apartment in most resorts; a studio or one-bedroom apartment in a good area of Paris; a modest village or rural home in an unfashionable area of Provence or the Alps; a one-bedroom apartment on the Côte d'Azur.
300,000–500,000	A small chalet in the Alps off the beaten track; a restored or partly restored manor house or small run-down *château*; a large restored rural property with a pool and a large plot; a large modern rural house or villa; a two-bedroom apartment in a fashionable resort on the Côte d'Azur; a small restored village house in a fashionable part of Provence; a one or two-bedroom apartment in central Paris.
500,000–1 million	A family-sized chalet in the Alps (excluding the most popular resorts); a large manor house in good condition; a small habitable *château* or a large *château* requiring restoration; a restored farmhouse (*mas*) or modern villa (with pool) in rural Provence; a large luxury apartment in a fashionable resort on the Côte d'Azur; a good-sized apartment in a fashionable Paris suburb; a small vineyard.
1 million plus	A habitable or restored *château* or large manor house; a large restored farmhouse in Provence; a large villa on the Côte d'Azur; a large chalet in a fashionable Alpine resort; a luxury Parisian three or four-bedroom apartment.

In addition to the purchase price, you must allow for various costs associated with buying a house in France, which are higher than in most other countries (see **Fees** on page 127). Note that prices may be quoted inclusive or exclusive of agency fees (see **Fees** on page 118). Make sure you know whether **all** agents' fees are included in the price quoted and **who must pay them**. If you negotiate a reduction, check that the agent or vendor hasn't excluded some fees from the price (to be added later).

Finally, note that it isn't unusual for French vendors to strip a house bare and take everything, including internal doors and the kitchen sink, so when comparing prices make sure you know and allow for what's included (and what isn't) – see **Contracts** on page 204.

Negotiating The Price

When buying a property, it usually pays to haggle over the price, even if you think it's a bargain. Prices in the south of France are usually more negotiable than in the north, but they're also higher. Don't be put off by a high asking price, as most sellers are willing to negotiate. In fact, sellers generally presume buyers will bargain and rarely expect to receive the asking price for a property (although some vendors ask an unrealistic price and won't budge a *centime*!). In popular areas (e.g. Paris and

Provence), asking prices may be unrealistically high (up to double the real market price), particularly to snare the unsuspecting and ignorant foreign buyer.

Although there has been evidence of dual pricing in the past, the practice of quoting higher prices to foreigners is rare. The prices advertised abroad are usually identical to those advertised in France. Nevertheless, the French drive a much harder bargain than most foreigners when buying a property, particularly an old one. French owners are sometimes astonished at the prices foreign buyers are prepared to pay for nondescript homes in uninspiring areas (although they **never** complain about foreigners pushing up prices when they're on the receiving end!). In recent years, many properties have sold for much less than their original asking prices, particularly properties priced at over €100,000.

It's a good idea for your peace of mind to obtain an independent valuation (appraisal) to determine a property's market value. If you're using an agent, it's worth asking him what to offer, although he may not tell you, as he's acting for the seller. If a property has been realistically priced, you shouldn't expect to obtain more than a 5 or 10 per cent reduction.

Timing is of the essence in the bargaining process. Generally the longer a property has been for sale and the more desperate the vendor is to sell, the more likely a lower offer will be accepted. Some people will tell you outright that they must sell by a certain date and that they will accept any reasonable offer. You may be able to find out from neighbours why someone is selling, which may help you decide whether an offer would be accepted. If a property has been on the market for a long time, e.g. longer than six months in a popular area, it may be overpriced (unless it has obvious defects). If there are many desirable properties for sale in a particular area or developments that have been on the market a long time, you should find out why, there may be a new road, railway or airport planned.

Before making an offer, you should find out as much as possible about a property, such as the following:

- When it was built;
- Whether it has been used as a permanent or a holiday home;
- How long the owners have lived there;
- Why they're selling (they may not tell you outright, but may offer clues);
- How keen they are to sell;
- How long it has been on the market;
- The condition of the property;

- The neighbours and neighbourhood;
- Local property tax rates (see page 247);
- Whether the asking price is realistic.

For your part, you must ensure that you keep any sensitive information from a seller and give the impression that you have all the time in the world (even if you must buy immediately). All this 'cloak and dagger' stuff may seem unethical, but you can be assured that if you were selling and a prospective buyer knew you were desperate and would accept a low offer, he certainly wouldn't be in a hurry to pay you any more!

If you make an offer that's too low you can always raise it, but it's impossible to lower an offer once it has been accepted (if your first offer is accepted without haggling, you will never know how low you could have gone!). If an offer is rejected, it may be worth waiting a week or two before making a higher offer, depending on the market and how keen you are to buy a particular property.

If you make a low offer, it's wise to indicate to the owner a few negative points (without being too critical) that merit a reduction in price. Note, however, that if you make a very low offer, an owner may feel insulted and refuse to do business with you!

SURVIVAL TIP
Be prepared to walk away from a deal rather than
pay too high a price.

If you want to buy a property at the best possible price as an investment, shopping around and buying a 'distress sale' from an owner who simply must sell is likely to result in the best deal. Obviously you will be in a better position if you're a cash buyer and able to close quickly. Cash buyers in some areas may be able to negotiate a considerable price reduction for a quick sale, depending on the state of the local property market and how urgent the sale is. However, if you're seeking an investment property it's wise to buy in an area that's in high demand, preferably with both buyers and renters. For the best resale prospects, it's usually best to buy in an area or community (and style) that's attractive to French buyers.

An offer should be made in writing, as it's likely to be taken more seriously than a verbal offer.

Declared Value

Don't be tempted by the French 'custom' of tax evasion, where the sale price declared to the tax authorities (*prix déclaré*) is reduced by an 'under the table' (*sous la table*) cash payment. It's possible when buying a property direct from the vendor that he may suggest this, particularly if he's selling a second home and must pay capital gains tax on the profit. Obviously if the vendor can show a smaller profit, he pays less tax. You will also save money on taxes and fees, but will have a higher capital gains tax bill when you sell if it's a second home.

You should steer well clear of this practice, which is strictly illegal (although widespread). If you under-declare the price, the authorities can revalue the property and demand that you pay the shortfall in tax plus interest and fines. They can even prosecute you for fraud, in which case you can receive a prison sentence! The authorities can also decide to buy a property at the under-declared price plus 10 per cent within three months of the date of purchase. If you're selling a property, you should bear in mind that, if the buyer refuses to make the under-the-table payment after the contract has been signed, there's nothing you can do about it (legally!).

Buying At Auction

The best property bargains are generally to be found at auctions (*ventes aux enchères*). There are two types of property auction in France: voluntary auctions run by *notaires* (*marché immobilier des notaires*), at which they sell properties that vendors wish to auction (e.g. for a quick sale), and judicial auctions (*ventes judiciares*), at which you can bid for properties that have been repossessed by mortgage lenders or over which there have been inheritance disputes, for example. The second type of auction is more common than the first.

Properties due to be sold at auction are advertised in local papers by the Tribunal de Grande Instance (local county court) responsible for the auction, and details are published around six weeks in advance by the person (e.g. the notary or lawyer) responsible for the sale. The form (*fiche*) contains the date and place of the sale, a description of the property, land details with *cadastre* references, the name and address of the person handling the sale, details regarding inspections, and the reserve price.

Properties usually have a reserve price, which is often as little as half the market price. When a property is sold by a bank, the reserve price is usually the amount owed to them, above which they aren't interested. Somewhat surprisingly, there often isn't a lot of competition for properties sold at auction, particularly as many are old properties in rural areas which aren't of much interest to French buyers.

SURVIVAL TIP
Before making a bid, it's imperative to accurately assess the market value of a property and (if applicable) what it will cost to bring it to habitable condition.

To make a bid, you need to appoint a *notaire* or lawyer (*avocat*) who is registered with the Tribunal de Grande Instance, as they're the only people permitted to make bids. Instructions regarding the maximum price that you're prepared to pay must be provided in writing and bids are delivered in sealed envelopes. You must deposit a (returnable) bidding entry fee via a cheque drawn on a French bank or a banker's draft (certified cheque) in euros, the amount of which is decided by the auctioneer. If you're successful, you will be required to pay a deposit equal to 10 per cent of the purchase price immediately after the bid (it may be requested before the bidding) and the balance of the sale price within 45 days. It isn't necessary to attend an auction in person, as you can appoint a lawyer to act on your behalf.

In addition to normal fees (see below), you must pay for the publication of the judgement, court expenses and lawyer's fees. Court expenses are between 1 and 2 per cent of the sale price. Fees must be paid within a month and the purchase price usually within two months. It's possible to arrange a mortgage after a successful bid, although if you fail to raise a loan you will lose your deposit.

A judge presides over the auction proceedings and bids, which start at the reserve price and increase in small increments. The sale usually takes place *à la bougie* (by candle). When no more bids are forthcoming, the court usher lights a candle, which burns for 10 to 15 seconds, and then a second candle. When this has been extinguished, the sale is concluded. However, if a new bid is made while the candles are burning, the sequence must be restarted.

The successful bidder must wait ten days, during which time someone can make a higher bid provided it's at least 10 per cent above the auction price (*surenchère*). If a higher bid is made, the property must be re-auctioned, usually within two months, starting at the price bid by the person who intervened. Such interventions are rare and are permitted once only. You can, of course, make no bid at the auction itself but wait until a successful bid has been made. Then, if you decide that it's worth more, you can make a higher bid and force a re-auction, although this may force the price up even higher!

Details of properties for sale by auction can be found via the internet (e.g. 🖳 www.66france.com and www.bidshares.com).

FEES

A variety of fees (also called closing or completion costs) are payable when you buy a property in France, which vary considerably according to the price, the age of the property, whether you're buying via an agent (as opposed to buying direct from the vendor), whether you've employed a lawyer and surveyor, and whether you have a French or foreign mortgage. They can amount to almost 40 per cent of the purchase price of a new property and almost 25 per cent for an property over five years old (see **Example** below).

Most property fees are based on the 'declared' value of the property, which may be less than the purchase price or its 'market' value.

 You should never be tempted to under-declare the price in order to pay lower fees as it can have serious consequences if it's discovered (see page 20).

The fees associated with buying a property in France are listed below, although not all will apply to all sales. Fees are payable on the completion of a sale if not before. Before signing a preliminary contract, check exactly what fees are payable and how much they are, and have them confirmed in writing.

Registration Taxes

Registration taxes (*taxes de publicité foncière/TPF*) vary according to whether you're buying a new or an 'old' (i.e. over five years old) property. On an old property registration taxes (known in this case as *droits de mutation*) total 4.89 per cent, which comprises 3.6 per cent departmental tax (*taxe départmentale*), which is itself subject to 2.5 per cent *frais de recouvrement* making an effective tax of 3.69 per cent, and 1.2 per cent communal tax (*taxe communale* or *taxe additionnelle*). The same rates apply to building plots and commercial property. On a property less than five years old that's being sold for the first time, *TPF* is at just 0.6 per cent of the price excluding VAT, which must also be paid (see below). Regional tax (*taxe régionale*) was abolished on residential property in 1999.

Stamp Duty

Stamp duty varies according to the extent of the deed of sale but is usually between around €150 and €250, except on newly built properties, which are exempt from stamp duty.

Land Registry Fees

Expenses associated with land registration depend on the size of the mortgage and the number of searches made by the notary in order to draft the deed of sale but usually total around 0.6 per cent of the property's value.

Notaire's Fees

The *notaire* handling the sale collects all the fees associated with a purchase (except a selling agent's commission), which are sometimes confusingly referred to as the *frais de notaire*, although only a small part of them are made by the *notaire* himself for his services; these are known as *honoraires* or *émoluments*) and are levied on a sliding scale as shown below:

Portion Of Purchase Price (€)	Rate (%)	Cumulative Fee (€)
Up to 3,333	5	166.50
3,334 – 6,666	3.3	276.46
6,667 – 18,333	1.65	468.95
Over 18,333	0.825	

This means that the *notaire*'s fees for a property costing €100,000, for example, would be €1,142.70. In addition, you will be charged around €250 for the preparation of a preliminary contract. Note, however, that *notaires* charge an estimated fee at the time of purchase, which can be considerably more than the actual amount due (allegedly in case of unforeseen expenses), and you can wait up to six months to receive a reimbursement of the amount overpaid. The English-language section of the *notaires*' association's website (🖳 www.immonot.com) may help you to calculate your total costs (click on 'Conveyancing).

Mortgage Fees

Mortgage arrangement fees may amount to around 1 per cent of the purchase price (see **Costs** on page 197). There's also a fee payable to the notary for registration of the mortgage at the *bureau des hypothèques*, which is around two-thirds of the conveyance fees listed above.

Selling Agent's Commission

The advertised price of a property in France normally includes a selling agent's commission (if an agent is being used); this is indicated by the terms *commission compris* or *frais d'agence inclus*. The words *net vendeur* indicate that commission isn't included. An estate agent's fees, which can be as high as 10 per cent of the purchase price, may be paid by the vendor or the buyer or they may be shared, although it's usual for the vendor to pay. However, when the selling 'agent' is a *notaire*, his commission is **always** paid by the buyer. Before signing a contract, check who must pay the selling agent's fees and what they will be.

Other Fees

Other fees may include the following:

- Lawyer's fees (see **Conveyancing** on page 202);
- Surveyor's or architect's fees (see **Inspections & Surveys** on page 154);
- Utility connection and registration fees (see page 327 and following pages).

Value Added Tax

VAT at 19.6 per cent must be paid on properties less than five years old when they're sold for the first time. If you sell a new property within five years, you must pay VAT on any profit (plus capital gains tax – see page 251). Since 1998, there has been no VAT on building plots purchased by individuals. Note also that most of the other fees associated with buying property (listed above) are subject to VAT at 19.6 per cent.

Example

The following example of fees is based on a property costing €100,000 purchased with a €50,000 mortgage. A new home is one less than five years old sold for the first time; an old home is one more than five years old or one less than five years old sold for the second (or subsequent) time. For details of utility connection fees, see page 327 and following.

	Fees (€)	
	New Home	**Old Home**
Registration Taxes	600	4,890
Stamp Duty	200	200
Land Registry Fees	600	600
Notary's Fees	1,400	1,400
Mortgage Fees	2,250	2,250
Agent's Commission	Up to 10,000	Up to 10,000
Lawyer's Fees	1,000	1,000
Surveyor's Fee	200–1,500	200–1,500
VAT	20,725	1,125
TOTAL	**Up to 39,275**	**Up to 23,965**

Running Costs

In addition to the fees associated with buying a property you must also take into account running costs. These include local property taxes (see page 247), building and contents insurance (see page 268), standing charges for utilities (see page 327 and following pages), community fees for a community property (see page 141), maintenance (e.g. garden and pool), plus a caretaker's or management fees if you leave a home empty or let it. Annual running costs usually average around 2 to 3 per cent of the cost of a property.

TYPES OF PROPERTY

For many foreign buyers, France provides the opportunity to buy a size or style of home that they could never afford in their home countries. In most areas, properties range from derelict farmhouses and barns to modern townhouses and apartments with all modern conveniences, from crumbling *châteaux* and manor houses requiring complete restoration to new luxury chalets and villas.

French homes are built to high structural standards and, whether you buy a new or an old home, it will usually be extremely sturdy. Older homes often have thick walls and contain numerous rooms. Most have a wealth of interesting period features, including vast fireplaces, wooden staircases, attics, cellars (*caves*), and a profusion of alcoves and annexes. Many houses have a basement (*sous-sol* or *cave*), used as a garage and cellar. In most old houses, open fireplaces remain a principal feature even when central heating is installed. In warmer regions floors are often tiled and walls are painted rather than papered, while elsewhere floors are carpeted or bare wood, and walls are more likely to be papered. When wallpaper is used, it's often garish and may cover everything, including walls, doors and ceilings! Properties throughout France tend to be built in a distinct local (often unique) style using local materials. There are stringent regulations in most areas concerning the style and design of new homes and the restoration of old buildings.

In older rural properties, the kitchen (*cuisine*) is the most important room in the house. It's usually huge with a large wood-burning stove for cooking, hot water and heating, a huge solid wood dining table and possibly a bread oven. French country kitchens are worlds apart from modern fitted kitchens and are devoid of shiny formica and plastic laminates. They're often comparatively stark, with stone or tiled floors and a predominance of wood, tiles and marble. Kitchens in older apartments in Paris and other cities may be very basic, although modern fitted kitchens (with dishwashers, cookers and refrigerators) are usually found in new properties, and 'American kitchens' (i.e. open plan kitchens separated from the living or dining room by a bar or counter) are increasingly common. New homes usually also contain many 'luxury' features, e.g. deluxe bathroom suites, fitted cupboards, smoke and security alarms, and coordinated interior colour schemes. New homes are usually sold *décorée*, which means not only that they're decorated but also that they have a fitted kitchen.

Refrigerators (*frigidaire* or *frigo*) and cookers (*cuisinière*) are generally quite small. Cookers in rural homes are usually run on bottled gas or a combination of bottled gas and electricity (see pages 334 and 327). Many homes have a gas water heater (*chaudière*) that heats the water for the bathroom and kitchen. Most houses don't have a separate utility room and the washing machine and drier are kept in the kitchen. A separate toilet (*toilette* or *WC/water*) is popular, and the bathroom (*salle de bains*) often has a toilet, a *bidet*, a bath (*baignoire*) and/or a shower (*douche*). Baths are more common than showers in older homes, although showers are found in most modern homes. Note that many old, unmodernised homes don't have a bath, shower room or an inside toilet.

Many rural properties have shutters (*volets*), both for security and as a means of insulation. External shutters are often supplemented by internal shutters that are fixed directly to the window frames. In France, windows open inwards rather than outwards, as in most other countries. In the south and south-west, many rural homes have outdoor swimming pools, and homes throughout France have a paved patio or terrace, which is often covered. Old farmhouses invariably have a number of outbuildings such as barns, which can usually be converted into additional accommodation.

A huge variety of new properties is available in France, including city apartments and individually-designed, detached houses. Many new properties are part of purpose-built developments (see **Community Properties** on page 138). Note, however, that many of these developments are planned as holiday homes and they may not be attractive as permanent homes (they're also generally expensive). If you're buying an apartment or house that's part of a development, check whether your neighbours will be mainly French or other foreigners. Some people don't wish to live in a *commune* of their fellow countrymen and this will also deter French buyers if you want to sell. Prices of new properties vary considerably according to their location and quality (see **Cost Of Property** on page 29).

France's bold and innovative architecture, as portrayed in its many striking public buildings, doesn't often extend to private dwellings, many of which seem to have been designed by the same architect. However, although new properties are often lacking in character, they're usually spacious and well endowed with modern conveniences and services, which certainly cannot be taken for granted in older rural properties. Standard fixtures and fittings in modern houses are more comprehensive and of better quality than those found in old houses. The French generally prefer modern homes to older houses with 'charm and character' (which to the locals mean 'expensive to maintain and in danger of falling down'!), although new homes often have pseudo period features such as beams and open fireplaces in new homes. Central heating, double glazing and good insulation are common in new houses, particularly in northern France, where they're essential. Central heating may be electric, gas or oil-fired. However, on the Côte d'Azur, where winter temperatures are higher, expensive insulation and heating may be considered unnecessary (don't you believe it!). Air-conditioning is rare, even in the south of France.

Note that most French families live in apartments or detached homes, and semi-detached and terraced properties are relatively rare . Some 45 per cent of the population lives in apartments (although less than 10 per cent in tower blocks), which are more common in France than in most other European countries. In cities and suburbs, most people have little choice, as houses are in short supply and prohibitively expensive. In the major cities there are many *bourgeois* apartments, built in the 19th or early 20th century, with large rooms, high ceilings and huge windows. Unless modernised, they have old fashioned bathrooms and kitchens and are expensive to decorate, furnish and maintain. Many apartments don't have their own source of hot water and heating, which is shared with other apartments in the same building. See also **Community Properties** on page 138.

For details of typical homes in the most popular regions of France, see *The Best Places to Buy a Home in France* (Survival Books).

You can also buy a plot and have an individual, architect-designed house built to your own specifications (see page 174).

BUYING A NEW HOME

A 'new' house is generally defined as one built in the last five years, which is also the legal definition. Although new properties may lack the charm and character of older buildings (see above), they offer attractive financial and other advantages (see below).

● A lower deposit (5 per cent rather than 10 per cent);

● Lower registration taxes (see page 128);

● Two years' exemption from property tax (see page 248);

● A ten-year guarantee (see below);

- Higher construction standards and therefore lower maintenance costs (see below);

- Better insulation and therefore lower heating bills (see below);

- Modern plumbing and electrics (including plenty of sockets), etc.;

- Better security (see below);

- No costs or problems associated with renovation or modernisation;

- Greater resale potential, especially to French buyers, who generally prefer modern homes.

The standard of new buildings in France is strictly regulated and houses are built to official quality standards. They're built to higher specifications than old houses and usually include roof, cavity and under-floor insulation, double-glazing, central heating, and ventilation and dehumidifying systems – it can cost up to three times as much to heat an old home without proper insulation as to heat a modern home. New properties are also covered by a ten-year guarantee (*garantie décennale*) against structural defects and it's against the law to sell a new house without a warranty. Other systems and equipment are covered by a minimum two-year warranty.

It's often cheaper to buy a new home than to restore a derelict property, as the price is fixed, unlike the cost of renovation which can soar way beyond original estimates (see **Renovation & Restoration** on page 167).

Most new buildings use low maintenance materials and must (by law) have good insulation and ventilation, keeping them warmer in winter and cooler in summer. The French government encourages the building of energy-efficient homes, and France builds more new homes than most other European countries (some 60 per cent of French homes have been built since 1945). Security is a priority for most new developments (which usually have security gates) and homes often have security blinds and other security features.

On the other hand, there are a few disadvantages to buying a new home, including the following:

- VAT at 19.6 per cent must be paid on all homes under five years old sold for the first time (see page 130); this can amount to several thousand euros.

- New homes are usually smaller than old properties and rarely come with a large plot.

- The garden may lack mature trees and shrubs.

- There may be 'teething troubles' with a very new building, such as cracking plaster.

- Unless you've chosen the decor, you may wish to change it.
- It may have less letting potential than an older building.

Most new properties are sold by developers (*promoteurs*) and builders, although they're also marketed by estate agents. All new developments and builders must be underwritten by a bank (*garantie extrinsèque*) or the developer himself (*garantie intrinsèque*), who must meet certain liquidity and other requirements. These guarantees (known as *garanties d'achèvement*) protect buyers from defaulting builders and developers. Where applicable, the deposit is made out to the underwriting bank and cannot be used by the developer. It's possible to check a developer's financial status, although your best insurance when buying a new property is the reputation of the developer or builder. Most new developments have a sales office (*bureau de vente*) and a show house or apartment (*maison/appartement témoin*).

Buying Off Plan

When buying a new property in a development, you're usually obliged to commit to a purchase before it's completed (or even before it's begun!) – a process known in English as buying off plan (also confusingly called 'on plan') and in French as *une vente en état futur d'achèvement/VEFA* ('a sale in a future state of completion'). In fact, if a development is built and largely unsold, particularly a quality development in a popular area, it usually means that there's something wrong with it!

Buying a home that hasn't yet been built may seem a risky business, but the procedure is usually safe and there can be several advantages. Off-plan properties are generally cheaper than built homes. You can usually choose your bathroom suite, kitchen, fireplace, wallpaper, paint, wall and floor tiles, and carpet in bedrooms, all of which may be included in the price. You may also be able to alter the interior room layout, although this will increase the price, but you won't be able to make major structural alterations or changes of material or design. Most developers will negotiate over the price or include 'free' extras (such as a fitted kitchen when it isn't included in the price), particularly if a development isn't selling well. Note that any changes or additions to a property, such as including an American kitchen, a chimney or an additional shower room, should be made during the design stage, as they will cost much more to install later. See also **Building Your Own Home** on page 174. All fixtures and fittings will, of course, be brand new, and you will benefit from modern insulation, ventilation, heating and other materials and systems. And, of course, the building will have a ten-year guarantee (see page 172). You will also pay a lower deposit and lower registration fees on an off-plan home (see **Fees** on page 118), which will be exempt from property tax for two years from 1st January following the completion date (see **Exemptions** on page 242).

Disadvantages of buying off plan include the fact that you must pay VAT at 19.6 per cent on building costs, although this is usually included in the price quoted to you, and you must start paying for your home long before you can actually live in it.

Note that the purchase procedure for a property yet to be built is different from that for a finished home (see **Buying Off Plan** on page 206).

Resale Homes

Buying 'new' doesn't necessarily mean buying a brand new home where you're the first occupant. There can be many advantages in buying a modern resale home rather than a brand new one, including better value, an established development with a range of local services and facilities in place, more individual design and style, no 'teething troubles', furniture and other extras included in the price, a mature garden and trees, and a larger plot. With a resale property you can see exactly what you will get for your money and the previous owners may have made improvements or added extras such as a swimming pool that may not be fully reflected in the asking price. The disadvantages of buying a resale home depend on its age and how well it has been maintained. They can include a poor state of repair and the need for refurbishment, redecoration or new carpets; inferior build quality and design, no warranty (i.e. with a home that's more than ten years old), termite or other infestations, and (in the case of a community property) the possibility of incurring high assessments for repairs.

BUYING AN OLD HOME

In terms of the fees associated with buying a property (see page 127), an 'old' property is one that's over five years old that has already had at least one owner. However, the term 'old home' usually refers to a building that's pre-second world war and possibly hundreds of years old and which is either in need of restoration and modernisation or has already been restored. If you want a property with abundant charm and character, a building for renovation or conversion, outbuildings, or a large plot, you must usually buy an old property. The advantages and disadvantages of buying a new home (see page 133) apply in reverse to an old home.

Many old properties purchased by foreigners in France are in need of restoration, renovation or modernisation. The most common examples are the many old farmhouses that have been neglected since they were built in the 18th or 19th centuries or even abandoned many years ago. In general, the French attitude to old buildings is one of almost total neglect until they're literally in danger of falling down, when complete rebuilding is often necessary. In many rural areas it's still possible to buy such a property for as little as €25,000.

When considering old properties that might be suitable, you should take vendors' (and particularly agents') descriptions with liberal amounts of salt: '*à finir*' usually means there's still plenty of work to be done; '*habitable*' can mean 'derelict'; '*à rénover*' implies that major reconstruction is required; and, if anything is described as a '*ruine*', you should be pleasantly surprised to find any walls still standing. Before spending time and money investigating old properties, you ask a lot of questions as to their condition. 'Partly renovated' usually means that part of a building is habitable, i.e. at least has sanitation, but the rest is in dire need of restoration. Bear in mind also that some rural properties lack basic services such as electricity, a reliable water supply and sanitation. See **Renovation & Restoration** on page 167.

Before buying a property requiring restoration or modernisation, you should consider the alternatives. An extra €20,000 or €30,000 spent on a purchase is usually better value than spending a similar amount on building work. It's often cheaper to buy a restored or partly restored property than a ruin in need of total restoration, unless you're going to do most of the work yourself.

The price of most restored properties doesn't reflect the cost and amount of work that went into them, and many people who have restored a ruin would never do it again and advise others against it.

If you're planning to buy a property that needs restoration or renovation, obtain an **accurate** estimate of the costs **before** signing a contract. Many foreign buyers are tempted by the low cost of old homes and believe they're getting a wonderful bargain, without fully investigating the renovation costs. Don't buy a derelict property unless you have the courage, determination and money to overcome the many problems you will certainly face.

Bear in mind that renovation or modernisation costs will invariably be higher than you imagined or planned! Taking on too large a task in terms of restoration is a common mistake among foreign buyers in all price ranges.

Unless you're prepared to wait until you can occupy it or are willing to live in a caravan for a long time while you work on it, it's better to spend a bit more and buy something habitable but untidy than buy a property that needs completely gutting before you can live in it.

Bear in mind also that, if you buy and restore a property with the intention of selling it for a profit, you must take into account not only the initial price and the restoration costs, but also the fees and taxes included in the purchase, plus capital gains tax if it's a second home (see page 251). It's difficult to sell an old renovated property at a higher than average market price, irrespective of the amount you've spent on it. The French have little interest in old restored properties, which is an important point if you need to sell an old home in a hurry in an area that isn't popular with foreign buyers. If you want to make a profit, you're better off buying a new home.

Nevertheless, old properties can be better value than new homes and there are still some good bargains around, although you must carefully check their quality and condition. Note also that work on a property over five years old attracts VAT at just 5.5 per cent instead of the standard 19.6 per cent. As with most things in life, you generally get what you pay for, so you shouldn't expect a fully restored property for €25,000. Note that, if you want a restored home, you should buy one from someone who has lovingly and sensitively restored it, rather than from someone who has transformed it out of all recognition.

At the other end of the scale, for those who can afford them, there's a wealth of beautiful *châteaux*, manor houses (*manoir*) and water mills (*moulin*), many costing no more than an average four-bedroom house in many other countries. However, if you aspire to live the life of the landed gentry in your own *château*, bear in mind that the reason there are so many on the market (and the relatively low prices) is that the cost of upkeep is **astronomical!**

COMMUNITY PROPERTIES

In France, properties with common elements (whether a building, amenities or land) shared with other properties are owned outright through a system called 'co-ownership' (*copropriété*), similar to owning a condominium in the US, but are referred to here as community properties to avoid confusion with part-ownership schemes such as timeshare (see page 145). Community properties include apartments, townhouses, and detached homes on a private estate with communal areas and facilities. Almost all French properties that are part of a development are owned *en copropriété*. In general, the only properties that aren't community properties are detached houses on individual plots in public streets or on rural land. Under the system of *copropriété*, owners of community properties own not only their homes (*parties privatives*) but also a share (*quote-part* or *tantième*) of the common elements (*parties communes*) of a building or development, including foyers, hallways, lifts, patios, gardens, roads, and leisure and sports facilities, according to the size or value of your property.

Some 45 per cent of the French population live in apartments in cities and towns. Many modern community developments are located near coastal or mountain resorts and they may offer a wide range of communal facilities, including a golf course, swimming pools, tennis and squash courts, a gymnasium or fitness club, and a restaurant. Most also have landscaped gardens, high security and a full-time caretaker (*gardien/gardienne*), and some even have their own 'village' and shops. At the other extreme, some developments consist merely of numerous cramped, tiny studio apartments. Note that community developments planned as holiday homes may not be attractive as permanent homes. Other advantages and disadvantages of community properties are listed below. Further information about community properties can be obtained from the Association des Responsables de Copropriété (ARC), 29 rue Joseph-Python, 75020 Paris (☎ 01 40 30 12 82, 🖳 www.unarc.asso.fr).

Advantages

The advantages of owning a community property may include the following:

- Increased security;
- Lower property taxes than detached homes;
- A range of community sports and leisure facilities;
- Community living with lots of social contacts and the companionship of close neighbours;
- No garden, lawn or pool maintenance;
- Fewer of the responsibilities of individual home ownership.

Community properties are also often in locations where owning a single-family home would be prohibitively expensive, e.g. a beach-front or town centre.

Disadvantages

The disadvantages of community properties may include the following:

- Restrictive rules and regulations;

- Excessively high community fees (owners may have no control over increases);
- A confining living and social environment and lack of privacy;
- Noisy neighbours (particularly if neighbouring apartments are rented to holidaymakers);
- Limited living and storage space;
- Expensive covered or secure parking;
- Acrimonious owners' meetings, where management and factions may try to push through unpopular proposals.

Note also that communal facilities in a large development may be inundated during peak periods; for example, a large swimming pool won't look so big when 100 people are using it, and getting a game of tennis or using a fitness room may be difficult.

Checks

Before buying a *copropriété* property, it's wise to ask current owners about the community. For example:

- Do they like living there?
- What are the fees and restrictions?
- Which is your parking space (if any)?
- Are owners required to pay part of the *taxe foncière* as well as the *taxe d'habitation* (see **Property Taxes** on page 247)?
- How noisy are other residents?
- Are the recreational facilities readily accessible?
- Would they buy there again (why or why not)?
- Is the community well managed?

You may also wish to check on your prospective neighbours. Permanent residents should avoid buying in a development with a high percentage of rental units, i.e. units that aren't owner-occupied. If you're planning to buy an apartment above the ground floor, you may wish to ensure that the building has an efficient lift. Note that upper floor apartments are both colder in winter and warmer in summer and may incur extra charges for the use of lifts. They do, however, offer more security than ground floor apartments. Note that an apartment that has apartments above and below it will generally be more noisy than a ground or top floor apartment.

Cost

Prices vary considerably with the location, for example from around €50,000 for a studio or one-bedroom apartment in an average location to hundreds of thousands of euros for a luxury apartment in a prime location. Garages and parking spaces must often be purchased separately in developments, a lock-up garage usually costing between €10,000 and €150,000 and a parking space from €3,000 to €5,000 (see **Garages & Parking** on page 143).

If you're buying a resale property, check the price paid for similar properties in the same area or development in recent months, but bear in mind that the price you pay may have more to do with the seller's circumstances than the price fetched by other properties. Find out how many properties are for sale in a particular development; if there are many on offer, you should investigate why, as there could be management or structural problems. If you're still keen to buy, you can use any negative aspects to drive a hard bargain. Under the Carrez law, the exact surface area (excluding cellars, garages, parking areas or anything less than 8m²) must be stated in the preliminary contract.

Community Fees

Owners must pay service charges for the upkeep of communal areas and for communal services. Charges are calculated according to each owner's share of the development and not whether they're temporary or permanent residents. For example, 20 apartments of equal size in an apartment block would each pay 5 per cent of the community fees. General charges cover such services as caretaking, upkeep of the garden and surrounds, swimming pool maintenance and refuse collection. In addition to general charges, there may also be special charges for collective services and common equipment such as lifts, central heating and hot water, which may be divided according to the share of the utility allocated to each apartment.

Check the level of general and special charges before buying an apartment. If you're buying a resale apartment, ask to see a copy of the service charges for previous years and the minutes of the last annual general meeting, as owners may be 'economical with the truth' when stating service charges, particularly if they're high. If you're buying a holiday apartment that will be vacant for long periods (particularly in winter), don't buy in an apartment block where heating and/or hot water charges are shared, or you will be subsidising your co-owners' heating and hot water.

If necessary, owners can be assessed an additional amount to make up any shortfall of funds for maintenance or repairs. You should check the condition of the common areas (including all amenities) in an old development and whether any major maintenance or capital expense is planned for which you could be assessed. Beware of bargain apartments in buildings requiring a lot of maintenance work or refurbishment (note that properties in ski resorts usually require more maintenance than those in coastal areas). However, under French law, disclosure of impending expenditure must be made to prospective buyers before they sign a contract. Owners' meetings can become rather heated when finances are discussed, particularly when assessments are being made to finance capital expenditure.

Fees vary considerably and can be high for luxury developments with a range of amenities such as a swimming pool and tennis courts, e.g. €1,000 per year for a two-room apartment and double this for a four-room property. However, high fees aren't necessarily a negative point (assuming you can afford them), provided the community is well managed and maintained. The value of a community property depends to a large extent on how well the development is maintained and managed. Since January 2002, all *copropriétaires* have been required to pay service charges quarterly, the amount being adjusted at the end of the year when the annual accounts have been approved by the committee. Owners also have the right to make payments from a separate bank account.

The managing agent of a *copropriété* should send the notary handling the sale a statement of the seller's account regarding the payment of community fees and any work in progress but not yet completed (for which owners are liable). The vendor should obtain a *Certificat de l'Article 20* stating that he doesn't owe any money to the *copropriété*; otherwise the notary must withhold payment to cover any fees due.

Management

The management of a *copropriété* is regulated by French law, and the rules and regulations are contained in a document called the *Règlement de Copropriété*. If you don't understand it, you should have it explained or get it translated. All decisions relating to the management and upkeep of a community development are decided by a general committee (*syndicat des copropriétaires*) presided over by a manager (*gérant/syndic*). He's responsible for the management, efficient daily running and the apportioning of charges relating to the building, e.g. insurance, repairs and maintenance. The manager bills individual owners for service charges and management fees. The committee must hold a meeting at least once a year to approve a budget, discuss other matters of importance such as capital expenditure and, if necessary, appoint a new manager. Owners must be given 15 days' notice by registered letter of the annual meeting or a special meeting and the opportunity to add items to the agenda no later than six days before the meeting. All decisions are made by a majority vote. Owners who are unable to attend may vote by proxy.

SURVIVAL TIP

If you're planning to buy a community property, it's important to ensure that it's well managed and that there aren't any outstanding major problems. If there are, you could be liable to contribute towards the cost of repairs, which could run into many thousands of euros.

Restrictions

The rules and regulations (*règlement de copropriété*) governing a community development allow owners to run their community in accordance with the wishes of the majority, while at the same time safeguarding the rights of the minority. Restrictions usually include such things as noise levels, the keeping of pets, renting, exterior decoration and plants (e.g. the placement of shrubs), rubbish disposal, the use of swimming pools and other recreational facilities, parking, business or professional use, and the hanging of laundry. Note that French law doesn't allow anything to be forbidden without good reason (for example, pets may be forbidden only if they cause a nuisance to other owners), so any such restrictions may be unenforceable. You should also check whether there are any rules regarding short or long-term rentals or leaving a property unoccupied for any length of time. If necessary, discuss any restrictions with residents.

Garages & Parking

A garage or private parking space isn't usually included in the price when you buy a new apartment or townhouse in France, although secure parking is usually available at an additional cost, possibly in an underground garage. Modern detached homes usually have a basement (*sous-sol*) that can be used as a garage and cellar. Smaller homes usually have a single garage, while larger properties may have garaging for up to four cars. Parking isn't usually a problem when buying an old home in a rural area, although there may not be a purpose-built garage.

When buying an apartment or townhouse in a new development, a lock-up garage usually costs an additional €10,000 or €15,000 and even a reserved parking space can cost €3,000 to €5,000. Note that the cost of a garage or parking space isn't usually recouped when selling, although it makes a property more attractive. The cost of parking is an important consideration when buying in a town or resort in France, particularly if you have a number of cars. It may be possible to rent a garage or parking space, although this can be prohibitively expensive in cities. Bear in mind that in a large development the nearest parking area may be some distance from your home. This may be an important factor, particularly if you aren't up to carrying heavy shopping hundreds of metres to your home and possibly up several flights of stairs.

SURVIVAL TIP
Without a private garage or parking space, parking can be a nightmare, especially in cities or during the peak season in busy resorts or developments. Free on-street parking may be difficult or impossible to find in cities and large towns, and in any case be suitable only for a wreck.

A lock-up garage is important in areas with a high incidence of car theft and theft from cars (e.g. most cities and popular resorts) and is also useful to protect your car from climatic extremes such as ice, snow and intense heat.

RETIREMENT HOMES

There are around 5,000 retirement homes (*résidence pour retraités/seniors*), which are becoming more common in France, although they're still relatively rare, as the French prefer to live among their family and friends in their twilight years.   There are several types of home: conventional retirement homes (*maison de retraite*), with or without specialist care facilities (*avec section de cure médicale*); sheltered apartments for those on low incomes (*foyer logement* and *foyer soleil* – the former being in blocks occupied entirely by elderly people, the latter in mixed occupancy blocks); serviced apartments (*résidence avec services pour personnes âgées* or simply *résidence services*, some of which are unfurnished); and retirement villages (*village retraite*).

Retirement villages have many advantages, including security, on-site amenities and services, and a ready-made community. Amenities may include a communal swimming pool, lounge, library, exercise and music rooms and a restaurant, and services can include caretaking, cleaning, administrative help, pet-sitting, meal delivery, hairdressing, physiotherapy and excursions, lectures, games, shows and films.

Most villages are in the south of France (e.g. the six operated by Séniorales, www.ramos.fr), but there are others elsewhere (e.g. the Village Séniors du Grand Logis near Saintes in Charente-Maritime and the Doyenné de la Risle near Rugles in Normandy). Developments usually consist of 50 to 60 one and two-bedroom villas (*pavilion*). Villas can be rented (for between around €300 and €600 per month) or purchased. A villa at the Grand Logis costs between €70,000 and €105,000 depending on size; a two-bedroom villa in the south of France can cost around €120,000, although the cost depends on which of three purchase options is chosen: outright freehold purchase, fixed term leasehold or lifetime leasehold.

Note that most retirement developments levy monthly service charges (usually between €150 and €500), which may include a certain number of weeks' nursing care per illness per year in a residents' nursing home. Service charges usually cover heating and air-conditioning, hot and cold water, satellite TV, and the other amenities and services listed above.

Information

Websites providing information about retirement and lists of retirement homes in France include www.maisons-de-retraite.net, www.maisons-retraite.com and www.plan-retraite.fr (the site of the Association Française de Protection et d'Assistance aux Personnes Agées).

TIMESHARE & PART-OWNERSHIP SCHEMES

If you're looking for a holiday home abroad, you may wish to investigate a scheme that provides sole occupancy of a property for a number of weeks each year. These include co-ownership, leaseback and timeshare (or timesharing).

Don't rush into any of these schemes without fully researching the market and before you're absolutely clear what you want and what you can realistically expect to get for your money.

Part-Ownership

Part-ownership (*bi-propriété*) – also known as co-ownership – includes schemes such as a consortium of buyers owning shares in a property-owning company and joint ownership between family, friends or even strangers. Some developers offer a turn-key deal whereby a home is sold fully furnished and equipped. Part-ownership allows you to recoup your investment in savings on holiday costs while retaining equity in a property. A common deal is a four-owner scheme (which many consider to be the optimum number of co-owners), where you buy a quarter of a property and can occupy it for up to three months a year. However, there's no reason why there cannot be as many as 12 part-owners, with a month's occupancy each per year (usually shared between high, medium and low seasons).

Part-ownership provides access to a size and quality of property that would otherwise be unimaginable, and it's even possible to have a share in a substantial *château*, where a number of families could live together simultaneously and hardly ever see each other if they didn't want to. Part-ownership can be a good choice for a family seeking a holiday home for a few weeks or months a year and has the added advantage that (because of the lower cost) a mortgage may be unnecessary. Note that it's cheaper to buy a property privately with friends than through a developer, when you may pay well above the market price for a share of a property (check the market value of a property to establish whether it's good value). Part-ownership is much better value than a timeshare (see below) and needn't cost much more.

A purchase should be treated like a business venture, even (or especially!) if you're buying with friends or relatives. In particular, you should do the following:

- Agree on occupancy periods for each co-owner (e.g. a share of high-, mid- and low-season weeks).
- Agree on any restrictions that will apply to users (e.g. regarding smoking, children and pets).
- Decide on the decor and furnishing of the property, who is to do it and how it will be paid for.
- Decide whether or not the property is to be let when not being used by any of the co-owners and, if so, how the letting is to be managed and the income apportioned and paid.
- Decide on notice periods and procedures if one party wishes to withdraw from the arrangement.
- Set annual maintenance fees for each co-owner (which should be on the high side to allow for unforeseen expenses).
- Establish a procedure for dealing with problems.
- Finally, have a water-tight contract drawn up by an experienced lawyer to protect the co-owners' interests.

One of the best ways to get into part-ownership, if you can afford it, is to buy a house yourself and offer shares to others. This overcomes the problem of getting together a consortium of would-be owners and trying to agree on a purchase in advance, which is difficult unless it's just a few friends or family members. You can form a French company (*société civile immobilière*) to buy and manage the property that can in turn be owned by a company in the part-owners' home country, thus allowing for any disputes to be dealt with under local law. Each part-owner is given a number of shares according to how much he has paid, entitling him to so many weeks' occupancy a year. Owners don't need to have equal shares and can all be made direct title holders. If a part-owner wishes to sell his shares, he must give first refusal to other part-owners. However, if they don't wish to buy them and a new part-owner cannot be found (which is unlikely), the property must be sold.

A number of companies specialise in part-ownership schemes, including OwnerGroups Company (UK ☎ 01628-486350, 🖥 www. ownergroups.com).

Leaseback

Leaseback (*propriété allégée* or *leaseback*) schemes (also known as 'tourism residencies') are a French innovation which has since been adopted in other countries and are designed for those seeking a holiday home for a few weeks each year. There has recently been a considerable increase in leaseback purchases and a corresponding increase in development schemes to meet demand, but prospective buyers should be aware of the disadvantages and possible problems of the scheme as well as the advantages that are promoted by developers.

Properties sold under a leaseback scheme are always located in popular resort areas, e.g. golf, ski or coastal resorts, where self-catering accommodation is in high demand, and are either new or totally rebuilt properties. Leaseback schemes are available in many parts of France, including the Alps and Pyrénées, Brittany, Côte d'Azur and the Atlantic coast, Normandy and Paris. Most estate agents – foreign as well as French – can provide details of properties available on a leaseback basis.

A leaseback scheme allows you to buy a new property at less than its true cost, e.g. 30 per cent less than the list price. In return for the discount the property must be leased back to the developer, usually for 9 to 11 years, so that he can let it as self-catering holiday accommodation. The buyer (in effect) becomes the landlord and qualifies for a refund of the VAT (19.6 per cent) that was included in the purchase price, although it can take up to five months for the refund to be made. In addition, the developer usually (but not always) 'guarantees' the buyer a fixed annual return (usually around 2 or 3 per cent of the property's value, adjusted annually for inflation according to the Index of Construction Costs published by INSEE), irrespective of his actual rental income, so that the buyer is effectively given a discount (e.g. 25 or 30 per cent) off the purchase price. The buyer owns the freehold of the property and the full price is shown in the title deed. During the period of the lease, the developer therefore takes all the risks associated with letting and you have a guaranteed income.

The buyer is also given the right to occupy the property for a period each year, usually between two and four weeks, spread over high, medium and low seasons. These weeks can usually be let to provide income or possibly even exchanged with accommodation in another resort (as with a timeshare scheme). The developer furnishes (usually with a standard furnishing 'pack') and manages the property and pays all the maintenance and bills (e.g. for utilities) during the term of the lease (even when the owner is in occupation).

What happens when the lease expires depends on the agreement you make with the developer: in some cases, the property is yours – unless you wish to extend the agreement, which you can usually do for a further three, six or nine years and with a longer usage period (e.g. eight weeks per year); in other cases, the lease must be renewed indefinitely.

 Unless you're happy with a 'permanent leaseback', ensure that you will have full and vacant possession at the end of the initial lease period, as with some leaseback agreements you NEVER actually own the property.

Note also that, if you sell a property within 20 years of purchase, you must pay a proportion of the VAT you saved to the government. Owners are also responsible for paying property taxes (see page 247) and income tax on the rent they receive from the developer (see page 242). The amount of tax you pay and the allowances to which you're entitled depend on the letting scheme you adopt: as a leaseback owner, you're normally eligible for the *BIC*, *LMNP* or *LMP* scheme, depending on your circumstances (see **Letting Schemes** on page 279).

Although the leaseback scheme is generally problem-free, you should beware of developers offering high annual returns (e.g. 6 or 7 per cent), as there is no guarantee that these will be achieved or maintained in the long term.

SURVIVAL TIP
Check the standing of the developer and ask for
references before committing to a scheme.

You should also check the penalties for opting out of the scheme should you wish or need to, as these can be high (the developer may have a right to claim 'commercial compensation'), and whether the developer has the right to renew the leaseback period automatically, as he is permitted to by law. The developer may also charge management fees, and you should check what these are and what they cover. Finally, check what happens to the property if the developer goes bankrupt.

```
SURVIVAL TIP
It's important to have a leaseback contract checked
by a legal expert.
```

Timesharing

Timesharing (*multipropriété*, but also called *interpropriété, polypropriété, pluripropriété, multijouissance* and *multivacances*) isn't as popular in France as in some other countries, e.g. Spain and the US. In France, timeshare owners purchase a right to occupy a property (*jouissance*) at designated times. Since 1986, timeshare properties have been owned by a limited company such as a *société civile immobilière*, in which owners hold voting shares intended to give them a say in how a property is managed. However, this is impractical when owners are spread around France or further afield, and management is generally performed independently (sometimes arbitrarily) by a developer or agent.

Timesharing (also called 'holiday ownership', 'vacation ownership' and 'holidays for life') has earned a poor reputation in the last few decades, although things are slowly improving. In recent years the Organisation for Timeshare in Europe (OTE) has been trying to restore respectability to timesharing, and its members (which include France) are bound by a code of conduct. This includes a requirement that buyers have secure occupancy rights and that their money is properly protected prior to the completion of a new property. A recent EU Directive requires timeshare companies to disclose information about the vendor and the property and to allow prospective buyers a ten-day 'cooling off period', during which they may cancel any sales agreement they've signed without penalty. However, although the directive technically binds timeshare companies, if they flout it you'll need to seek redress in a court of law, which may not be something you want (or can afford) to do!

The best timeshare developments are on a par with luxury hotels and offer a wide range of facilities, including bars, restaurants, entertainment, shops, swimming pools, tennis courts, health clubs and other leisure and sports facilities. If you don't wish to take a holiday in the same place each year, choose a timeshare development that's a member of an international organisation such as Resort Condominium International (RCI) or Interval International (II), which allow you (usually for a fee) to exchange your timeshare with one in another area or country. The highest rated RCI timeshares are classified as Gold Crown Resorts and allow you to exchange with any timeshare anywhere in the world (RCI has over 2,000 member resorts in some 70 countries).

France isn't plagued by the timeshare touts common in some other countries (such as Spain). However, you may be 'invited' to a presentation in a popular resort and should know what to expect. If you're tempted to attend a sales pitch (usually lasting at least two hours), you should be aware that you may be subjected to some of the most persuasive, high-pressure sales methods employed anywhere on earth. If you do attend, don't take any cash, credit cards or cheque books with you so that you won't be pressured into paying a deposit without thinking it over. Although it's illegal for a timeshare company to accept a deposit during the cooling-off period, many companies will try to get you to pay one. Don't rely on being able to get your money back if you pay by credit card. If you pay a deposit, your chance of getting it back is slim; if it's repaid, it's likely to take a long time. Bear in mind that of those who agree to buy a timeshare, around half cancel within the cooling-off period.

A personal guarantee must be provided by a timeshare company that the property is as advertised and, where applicable, the contract must be in the language of the EU country where the buyer is resident or the language of the buyer's choice (you cannot sign away any of your rights irrespective of what's written in the contract). If you're an EU citizen and get into a dispute, you can take legal action in your home country for a sale made in France. There have been so many scams associated with timeshares that it would take a dedicated book to recount them all. **Suffice to say that many people bitterly regret the day they signed up for a timeshare!**

Top-quality timeshares in a top-rated resort can cost up to €12,000 for a week in a one or two-bedroom apartment during a peak period, to which must be added annual management fees, e.g. €200 to €300 per week, plus other miscellaneous charges. Most experts believe that there's little or no advantage in a timeshare over a normal holiday rental and that you're better off putting your money into a long-term investment, where you retain your capital and may even earn sufficient interest to pay for a few weeks' holiday each year.

If you wish to buy a timeshare, it's best to buy a resale privately from an existing owner or from a timeshare resale broker, which sell for a fraction of their original cost. It's possible to buy a week for as little as €1,000. When buying privately, you can usually drive a hard bargain and may even get a timeshare 'free' simply by assuming the current owner's maintenance contract. Advertisements for resale timeshares can be found in retail publications such as *Daltons Weekly* and *Exchange & Mart* in the UK, and in local newspapers and on noticeboards.

Often timeshares are difficult or impossible to sell at any price and 'pledges' from timeshare companies to sell them for you or buy them back at the market price are usually just a sales ploy, as timeshare companies aren't interested once they've made a sale. Further information about timesharing can be obtained from the Timeshare Council (🖳 www.timesharecouncil.co.uk) in the UK. The Timeshare Consumers Association (Hodsock, Worksop, Notts S81 0TF, UK, ☎ 01909-591100, 🖳 www.timeshare.org.uk) publishes a useful booklet entitled *Timeshare: Guide to Buying, Owning and Selling*.

BUYING A BUSINESS PROPERTY

A large number of residential properties are sold with a business such as a farm, vineyard, hotel, restaurant or bar. For the purpose of this section a business property doesn't include a secondary or 'part-time' business such as *gîtes* or bed and breakfast, which are discussed in our sister publication, **Making Money From Your French Home** (see page 389), to be published in spring 2005.

There are usually separate prices for the business as a 'going concern' (*fonds* or *fonds de commerce*) and for the business premises (*murs* meaning literally 'walls'). If you don't buy the premises, a separate rental contract (lease) must be negotiated. If possible, you should purchase a business with the premises, particularly if you need to raise a loan. You can obtain a mortgage of up to 80 per cent on the premises, but you must fund the business yourself. Note that the protection afforded to domestic tenants doesn't extend to business rentals. Therefore, if you rent business premises, it's essential to take legal advice regarding a lease, which *must* contain a right to rent clause to ensure the future value of the business.

Before buying any property-based business, you must do your homework thoroughly, particularly regarding the history and viability of the business. You must also be certain that you have or can acquire the skills necessary to run the business successfully. When taking over an existing and operating company, French labour law requires new owners to respect existing employment contracts, which isn't a bad thing if you require help, as experienced staff are priceless. However, you aren't compelled to employ staff if you cannot afford them.

As when buying any property, many people wear (thick) rose-tinted spectacles when seeking a business property in France and only really investigate the pros and cons **after** they've committed themselves.

Buying a business in France is a complicated undertaking that should be concluded only after taking expert legal and professional advice.

A number of companies are only too willing to help you through the jungle, but you should bear in mind that they're usually trying to sell you a business and aren't necessarily interested in whether you get a good deal or can make a success of it.

Duty, Fees & Taxes

It's important to check the duty, fees and taxes payable when buying a business. Taking over the assets of a company such as the stock, the client list, business name, premises (etc.) can be expensive with regard to taxes. Registration duty of around 18 per cent is payable on the transfer of most elements of a business (*fonds de commerce*) such as the leasehold rights, furniture, fittings and equipment, business name, client list and licences. Stock is subject to 19.6 per cent VAT. Note that the authorities can reassess the value of a business and impose fines if they consider that it has been undervalued. The *notaire's* fees when buying a business property are usually around 20 per cent of the purchase price.

Farms

In recent years, an increasing number of foreigners have purchased farms in France. The price of farming land varies considerably: it's prohibitively expensive in some areas, while in others it's practically given away with farmhouses. In general, farmland is cheaper in France than in any other western European country. However, it isn't easy for foreigners to raise loans from French banks to buy farms and it's common to buy the farm buildings and rent the land. If you're seriously under-capitalised, as many farmers are, your chances of success are remote.

Information and advice on any aspect of farming can be obtained from departmental Sociétés d'Aménagement foncier et d'Etablissement rural (SAFER), which advise and control all transactions of agricultural land in France. For details of local offices contact the Fédération Nationale des Sociétés d'Aménagement Foncier et d'Etablissement Rural (FNSAFER), 3 rue de Turin, 75008 Paris (☎ 01 44 69 86 00, 🖳 www.safer-fr.com).

Farmers under 35 years of age with recognised farming qualifications may qualify for financial incentives to buy farms in France, including government grants and low interest loans, depending on their resources. Information about grants can be obtained from the relevant regional office of the Centre National pour l'Aménagement des Structures des

Exploitations Agricoles (CNASEA) by contacting its head office, 7 rue Ernest Renan, BP 1, 92136 Issy-les-Moulineaux Cedex (☎ 01 46 48 40 00, 🖳 www.cnasea.fr).

 More foreigners have had their fingers burnt buying farms or farming land than any other property-based business venture in France.

As in all countries, farming in France is fraught with problems, particularly the vagaries of the weather (e.g. droughts, floods, frosts, etc.), declining food prices and under-capitalisation. Many foreign farmers have fled with their tails between their legs within a few years, having learnt the reality of French farming the hard way (it isn't for nothing that the French are deserting their farms in droves).

 You should also be aware that there's open hostility to foreign farmers in some regions and there have been a number of reports of foreigners being sold substandard stock and land, and some have even had their crops sabotaged!

Problems are more likely in remote regions where the locals are unused to foreigners and are often insular or even xenophobic.

Vineyards

There are usually vineyards for sale in most wine-producing regions and there have been a number of bargains around in recent years, although you're unlikely to find a *premier cru* Bordeaux or *grand cru* Burgundy property for sale (and, if you did, you would need a king's ransom to buy it!). Buying and operating a vineyard isn't something to be taken lightly, as it requires a lot of hard work and resources. It's essential to hire experienced staff if you're inexperienced, as it take years to become a viticulture expert. Nevertheless, if you're successful, the financial rewards can be enormous as a number of Australian, British and Swiss owners can testify.

There are restrictions or prohibitions on planting new vines in many areas because of over-production, so if you wish to expand production it's essential to buy a vineyard which already has the necessary permits.

As with all farming, the weather is the biggest threat to your livelihood: a frost in late spring can destroy your entire grape crop overnight, and heavy rain in September can ruin the wine.

Vineyard prices vary enormously, e.g. from around €15,000 per hectare (2.5 acres) for an *appellation* red wine vineyard in an average area, e.g. Bergerac in the Dordogne, to over €60,000 per hectare for a top quality vineyard in a good area, and experts recommend that you look to invest between €300,000 and €500,000. White wine vineyards are generally cheaper than red wine vineyards. A vineyard may cover between 10 and 100 hectares, and the price may include a house and winery, although not current wine stocks, which must usually be purchased separately.

A commercial property is likely to be owned by a company, which is cheaper to buy in terms of transaction fees. The FNSAFER (see above) also assists foreigners seeking to buy a vineyard in France. See also **Working** on page 37.

INSPECTIONS & SURVEYS

When you've found a property that you like, you should not only make a close inspection of its condition, even if it's a fairly new building, but also ensure that 'what you see is what you get'. In many rural areas, boundaries aren't always clearly drawn – often because title deeds haven't been changed to match recent changes in local topography, e.g. the growth or clearance of woodland. If you're shown a property with a large amount of land included, the vendor or agent may wave his arms and declare airily: 'This is all yours; it's included in the price'. The truth may be rather more complicated!

There are various ways you can carry out an inspection, and which one you choose will depend largely on whether the property is a ruin in need of complete restoration, partly or totally renovated, or a modern home.

You should ensure that a property over ten years old is structurally sound, as it will no longer be covered by a warranty (warranties are transferable if a property is sold within ten years of construction). Although France is noted for its high building standards, you should never assume that a building is sound, as even relatively new buildings can have serious faults (although rare).

Although a vendor must certify that a property is free from 'hidden defects', this provides little assurance, as he can usually plead ignorance and it's usually difficult or expensive to prove otherwise if a defect is discovered after purchase.

Doing Your Own Checks

There are a number of checks you can carry out yourself, including the following. For further details, see *Renovating & Maintaining Your French Home* (Survival Books – see page 389)

- Visit the local town hall and check the development plan (*plan local d'urbanisme* or *plan d'occupation des sols/POS*) of the land on which the property stands. To obtain details of the local development plan, you can complete a form (available from the town hall) called *renseignements d'urbanisme*, which will tell you whether the property you wish to buy is subject to a *droit de préemption urbain* or the *loi d'alignement* or is situated in a 'restricted development zone' (*zone d'aménagement différé* or *ZAD*) or an area due to become a *ZAD* or a regional conservation area (*zone de préemption 'espaces naturels sensibles des départements'*). A completed form must be accompanied by three copies of a scale plan (1:5,000 to 1:25,000) of the property and surrounding area and three copies of a scale plan (1:500 to 1:5,000) of the plot.

- While you're at the town hall, ask if the property is in a termite-contaminated zone; they're obliged to let you consult any documents pertaining to contamination in the commune. If the property is in a contaminated zone, the vendor is obliged to pay for a termite survey within three months of the sale.

- Also at the town hall, ask for details of any areas that are liable to flooding (*zones inondables*) and, if the property is in or near one, ask to see the local flood prevention plan (*plan de prévention des risques d'inondation/PPRI*), which is now required by law, and check that it's adequate. Boards (*batardeaux*) across the doors of neighbouring properties or signs nearby including the words *inondable* or *submersible* should be a warning to you! You can also check local weather patterns and historical data on the websites of Météo-France (🖳 www.meteo.fr), the Direction Régionale de l'Environnement (🖳 www.environnement.gouv.fr) and the local Préfecture.

- Ask the vendor or agent to see a copy of the title deeds, which should contain a copy of the relevant section of the local land registry plan (*un extrait du plan/relevé cadastral*); better still, visit the local office of *le cadastre* to obtain a copy and use it to check the boundaries of the property. This is a check that will be made by the *notaire* handling the sale (see **Conveyancing** on page 202), but it's worth anticipating any doubts or disputes by checking at this stage. Land in France is divided into plots or 'parcels' (*une parcelle*), which are marked on the cadastral plan, with each plot numbered (and in some cases named); an accompanying register lists the owner of each plot. It's possible that the land you're buying consists of more than one plot and you may need to negotiate the purchase with several owners! If the boundaries of the property you've been shown don't correspond to the plan, you will need to consult a *géomètre-expert* (see page 160).

- While considering boundaries, check the condition of any walls, fences or hedges and find out who they belong to and therefore who is responsible for their upkeep.

- Check whether there are any rights of way or use (e.g. hunting or fishing) on the land you plan to buy. If a right of way impinges on the property, check whether it can be moved, which is sometimes possible, although it may cost €1,500 or more.

 If the current owner allows a farmer to use his land (e.g. to graze animals), this can create a tenancy in law, which lasts for a minimum of nine years.

- If you're planning to make extensions or alterations (e.g. the addition of a swimming pool or stables) that may require planning permission, you should make enquiries whether such permission is likely to be granted (see **Planning Permission** on page 168).

- When it comes to examining the building itself, check the outside first, where they may be signs of damage and decay, such as bulging or cracked walls, damp, missing roof tiles and rusty or insecure gutters and drainpipes, dry or wet-rot in beams and other woodwork, and doors and windows that no longer hinge, lock or fit properly. Plants growing up or against walls can cause damp, and the roots of trees or shrubs close to a building can damage foundations (look for telltale cracks). Use binoculars to inspect the roof and a torch to investigate the loft, noting any cracks or damp patches using a camera and notepad. If you see a damp patch on the outside, check whether it runs right through the wall when you go inside.

- In the case of a property that has been restored, if work has been carried out by registered local builders, ask to see the bills, as all building work in France is guaranteed for ten years (*garantie décennale*). If the current (or a previous) owner did the work himself, it's essential to consult an expert (see **Professionals** on page 158). I

- If the property has a swimming pool, check that planning permission was granted for its construction, as it isn't unusual for owners to construct pools without permission, in which case you could be obliged to demolish it or fill it in. Check also the type of pool structure, which is rarely specified in purchase documents, and its condition, that the filtration and other cleaning systems work as they should. If you know little or nothing about swimming pools, it's worthwhile getting an expert to make the checks for you. The small cost of an inspection should be set against the potentially astronomical cost of repairing an unsound pool and, if repairs are required, these may be paid for by the vendor or covered by a reduction in the price of the property.

Make sure that a pool has an approved safety system, especially if you plan to let the property (see **Swimming Pools** on page 166); if there isn't a safety system, take into account the cost of installation.

More generally, consider the location of the pool, the local climate and your inclinations, and ask yourself (honestly) how often you're likely to use it and whether its maintenance will be more trouble and expense than it's worth.

● Test the electrical system, plumbing, mains water, hot water boiler and central heating systems as applicable. **Don't take someone's word that these work, but check for yourself and, at the same time, find out how these systems work.**

● If the property doesn't have electricity or mains water, check the nearest connection point and the cost of extending the service to the property, as it can be very expensive in remote rural areas (see **Utilities** on page 327). If a property has a well or septic tank, you should have them tested (see **Septic Tanks** on page 164).

● Check also whether the property is due to be connected to mains drainage (if it isn't already) – see **Sewerage** on page 337.

● Check the quality of the water in the area of the property; for example, is it hard or soft and what is the nitrate content? (See **Water** on page 335.)

● Locate the stop cock for the mains water supply, if there is one, and test the pressure (preferably in summer during a dry spell). Ask where the meter is and check it.

● If a building has a 'ventilation space' (*vide sanitaire*) beneath the ground floor, check that this hasn't become blocked by plants or been filled with debris; if it has, this could have caused ground-level wooden floors to rot and damp to rise up walls.

● In an area that's liable to flooding, storms and subsidence, it's wise to check an old property after heavy rainfall, when any leaks should come to light.

● If you buy a waterside property, you should ensure that it has been designed with floods in mind, e.g. with electrical installations above flood level and solid tiled floors.

● If the soil consists of clay (*argile*), the ground surrounding a house can 'shrink' after a long dry period. Large trees can create the same effect by drawing water out of the soil. This shrinkage can cause cracks in walls and, in extreme cases, subsidence. Shrinkage is a problem in around 33 departments, including Dordogne, but detailed maps showing 'danger areas' aren't yet available (these have been commissioned by the Department of the Environment for the end of 2005) and, if there's a chance that a house is built on 'shrinkable clay', check with the Direction Départementale de l'Equipement (DDE).

● Find out if there are any airfields nearby – public or private; you don't want your rural idyll spoiled by droning light aircraft or, worse, buzzing microlights.

● Check the local crime rate by asking neighbours and contacting the nearest gendarmerie in order to assess whether any existing security measures, such as shutters and locks, are likely to be adequate or whether you will need to install additional systems, such as an alarm or window bars, which will affect not only your budget but also the appearance of your property. Take into account that neighbours may be reluctant to tell you if burglary and vandalism is prevalent, and the local police may have different standards of comparison from your own!

It's strongly recommended that, if possible, you visit your prospective home at least once in winter; not only do many house prices drop substantially when the tourist season ends, but media images rarely hint at how cold and daunting January can be, even in the south of France. Such a visit may also reveal problems that weren't apparent at another time (e.g. that the DIY shop you were banking on for materials and tools is closed until the spring, which can be the case in remote areas). Winter visits also let you decide on your accommodation during work time, if the house is uninhabitable.

Although you can make such obvious checks yourself, the cost of a professional inspection is a small price to pay for the peace of mind it affords. In any case, some lenders insist on a 'survey' before approving a loan, although in France this usually consists of a perfunctory valuation to confirm that a property is worth the purchase price.

> **SURVIVAL TIP**
> **If you would have a survey carried out if you**
> **were buying the same property in your home country,**
> **you should have one done in France.**

Professionals

Although a survey isn't legally required as part of the purchasing process, except for mandatory termite, lead and asbestos inspections, it's strongly recommended before committing to a purchase. Many French buyers simply ask a builder friend to come along with them when visiting a property, or ask a local builder for a quote before buying (perhaps the cheapest and easiest way), but as a foreigner you're recommended to commission at least a valuation and preferably a full survey, especially if you're contemplating buying an old building.

There's a widely held belief that the French don't have professional valuers and surveyors. In fact, there are various types of professional in France, each qualified and experienced in different areas, as described below.

If you decide that you will need a survey before buying a property, it's worthwhile making enquiries at an early stage to ascertain who's best qualified to help you, what type of survey reports they offer and how much they charge. You can expect that a competent surveyor won't be immediately available.

Estate Agents

An estate agent (*agent immobilier*) can carry out a 'survey', but this is usually little more than a valuation and can cost as much as €300. Rather than ask the agent handling the sale to do a valuation, it may be preferable to pay another agent to do so in order to obtain a less biased opinion.

Notaires

Notaires will often be able to provide assistance and sometimes will have on their staff someone qualified to give valuations. However, *notaires* tend to provide valuations for legal rather than for information purposes.

Experts Immobilier

Not to be confused with an *agent immobilier* (see **Estate Agents** above), an *expert immobilier* generally works for banks, loss adjustors and members of the legal profession, including *notaires*, and is called upon to produce valuation and survey reports for submission to the courts (e.g. in the case of a divorce settlement or inheritance dispute or an investigation by the tax authorities). Each *agent immobilier* tends to specialise in a particular area of the property market, such as private housing, commercial property, farmland or forestry. He (most *experts* are male) is bound by the Civil Code to use 'prudence and due attention' and will have professional indemnity insurance.

In the case of a private property purchase, an *expert immobilier* will provide *une expertise amiable et privée*, costing around €200, which is a 'rough' appraisal containing essential information about a property and drawing conclusions appropriate to the buyer's needs, notably regarding the property's condition and value, or, for at least €500, *un bilan de santé immobilier* (literally 'a property health report').

You can find an *expert immobilier* through local estate agents, architects or the yellow pages (where they're listed under *Experts en Estimation Immobilière, Industrielle et Fonds de Commerce*), or contact the Chambres des Experts Immobiliers, c/o FNAIM, 129 rue du Faubourg Saint-Honoré, 75008 Paris (🖳 www.fnaim.fr), stating the department in which you're thinking of buying.

Géomètre-Experts

If you want to verify the boundaries of a property or check the area of an apartment, you should employ a *géomètre-expert*, who will charge from around €150 to €1,500 depending on the size and complexity of the job. *Géomètres-experts* are listed under that heading in the yellow pages.

Experts En Techniques Du Bâtiment

Another kind of expert is an *expert en techniques du bâtiment* (listed under that heading in the yellow pages), who normally carries out inspections for termites, asbestos, lead and other possible problems, such as damp.

Foreign Surveyors

You may prefer to employ a British or other Anglophone surveyor practising in France, who will write a report in English and in a style to which you're accustomed. However, a French surveyor (or other local expert) usually has a more intimate knowledge of local properties and building methods. If you employ a foreign surveyor, you must ensure that he's experienced in the idiosyncrasies of French properties and that he has professional indemnity insurance covering France (which means you can happily sue him if he does a bad job!).

English-speaking surveyors advertise in the expatriate press and Francophile magazines (see **Appendix B**).

Architects

An architect (*architecte*) is usually best qualified to check a modern house (unless he designed it himself!). Look under *Architectes* in the yellow pages or contact the Conseil National de l'Ordre des Architectes, 9 rue Borromée, 75015 Paris (🖳 www.architectes.org), which keeps a register.

Master Builders

A master builder (*maître d'oeuvres*) can be employed to check an older (i.e. pre-1945) property for soundness and will also be able to tell you whether the price is too high, given any work that needs to be done, for which he can be asked to quote. If you have work done by him, you may pay nothing for the inspection, although you should obtain at least one other quote for comparison. Master builders are listed under *Maîtres d'oeuvre en bâtiment* in the yellow pages.

Maisons Paysannes De France

For a 'free' survey of an old property (*visite conseil*) you can join Maisons Paysannes de France, 8 passage des Deux Soeurs, 75009 Paris (☎ 01 44 83 63 63, ✉ maisons-paysannes.org), who will send an expert in traditional restoration to assess whether previous restoration work has been done well or badly, what work remains to be done and how to do it. They will also put you in touch with a local architect with the appropriate expertise if required. Membership costs from €25 for an individual and from €28 for a couple.

 Not having a property assessed by an expert when there is any suspicion of structural problems could jeopardise any future insurance claims.

Safety Checks

A number of safety checks may be desirable or even compulsory in certain cases. These include the following.

Asbestos

Since January 2003, an asbestos test is required before any building can be sold. It must be carried out by an expert en techniques du bâtiment and be paid for by the vendor (it costs around €500). A test for the presence of asbestos can be done at the same time as a termite inspection (see below). The report is around ten pages long and contains detailed plans of the property and any areas where asbestos is present. You should keep the report in a safe place, as you may be required to show it to contractors and tradesmen before they will undertake any work on the property. **If there's asbestos on the premises, its removal must be carried out by a specialist (and certified) company.**

Lead

Lead (*plomb*) was present in paint until the mid-20th century and a lead check (by the Direction Régionale ou Départementale des Affaires Sanitaires et Sociales or the Direction Régionale ou Départementale de l'Equipement) is required by law in certain communes and for all properties built before 1st January 1948.

Radon

Radon (*radon*), a radioactive gas emitted by granite, is found in significant quantities in parts of Brittany, Corsica, and the Massif Central and Vosges mountains, and some 300,000 homes are reckoned to have dangerous levels of radon. A radon test isn't compulsory but, if you're worried about radon levels and want a property checked, contact the Agence Nationale Pour L'Amélioration de l'Habitat (ANAH), whose regional and departmental offices are listed on ▣ www.anah.fr.

Termites

Termites (*termite*) or white ants are found in over 50 departments – particularly in the south-west, the worst-affected departments being Landes (where there are termites in all departments), Gironde, Charente-Maritime and Lot-et-Garonne in that order. In certain communes, an inspection is required (known as *un état parasitaire*).

Details of areas affected can be obtained from the Observatoire de Lutte Xylophages (☎ 08 00 92 19 21, ▣ www.olx.fr) and a list of recognised treatment companies from your local Direction Départementale de l'Equipement (DDE) or the Centre Technique de Bois et de l'Ameublement/CTBA (☎ 01 40 19 49 19, ▣ www.termite.com.fr, where there's also a map showing affected areas).

Termite treatment costs around €4,500 to €5,250 and, even if a property is only mildly affected, you must usually pay for a complete treatment.

Note that a *certificat de non-infestation* is valid only for three months, so in the average purchase procedure the inspection cannot be carried out until after you've signed the *compromis de vente*, in which case you must keep your fingers crossed that the result is positive. If it isn't, you can withdraw from the sale and have your deposit returned, negotiate a reduction in the selling price to allow for termite treatment, or ask the seller to have the treatment done before proceeding with the sale.

Other Checks

You should also check whether a property is a listed building (*monument historique*) or within 500m of a listed building or in a conservation area (*zone de protection du patrimoine architectural urbain et paysage*). If it is, find what restrictions exist, particularly regarding renovation. In neither case are you likely to be able to make significant alterations to the facade, for example, and you may be severely limited in your choice of materials, finishes and even colours, which may affect not only your concept but also your budget. On the other hand, grants or tax relief may be available to reduce the cost of restoration (although you may have to wait a LONG time before receiving a grant!).

If a property is close to a listed historical monument or site, an organisation called Bâtiments de France may restrict the extent to which it can be renovated or altered, in some cases specifying materials and colours to be used. If there's an old church nearby, it's likely that this is the case and you should check with the town hall.

If you're considering buying a property covering more than a hectare (2.47 acres), note that the purchase can be opposed and even blocked by the Société d'Amenagément Foncier et d'Establissement Rural (SAFER), which has a right of pre-emption in order to preserve land which it feels should remain in agricultural use. Although SAFER rarely exercises this right, the notaire handling the sale is obliged to notify the organisation of the impending sale. Should SAFER object, any agreement is null and void and your only consolation is that you're entitled to the return of your deposit.

Survey Report

You should receive a written report (within ten days of the survey) on the condition of a property, including anything that could affect its value or your enjoyment of it in the future, and an estimate of its current and possibly future value. Some surveyors will allow you to accompany them and they may produce a video of their findings in addition to a written report.

You may be able to make a 'satisfactory' survey a condition (une clause suspensive) of the preliminary purchase contract, although this isn't usual in France and a vendor may refuse or insist that you carry out a survey before signing the contract. If serious faults are revealed by the survey, a clause suspensive should allow you to withdraw from the purchase and have your deposit returned. You may, however, be able to negotiate a satisfactory compromise with the vendor.

Discuss with your surveyor in advance exactly what will be included in his report and, more importantly, what will be excluded (you may need to pay extra to include certain checks and tests). A home inspection can be limited to a few items or even a single system only, such as the wiring or plumbing in an old house.

The report should first identify and establish that the property and land being offered for sale are, in fact, in the vendor's name and that the land 'for sale' matches the land registry plan; it isn't unusual for the area of land stated in an agent's details to be substantially different from what's set out in the *relevé cadastral*. Although this is normally the role of the notaire, your valuer or surveyor has a duty to check it carefully, as a greater or lesser amount of land can affect a valuation. The surveyor should also check the cadastral plan on the ground.

Second, the surveyor should also check the location of the property in relation to the local *plan local d'urbanisme*. Both steps in the checking process should be made by the *notaire* handling the sale, but invariably by this stage you will be well down the road to concluding a purchase and will have almost certainly agreed a price.

The surveyor should then consider any rights of way (*servitude*) over the property. Having this information at the valuation stage can have a significant bearing on the price before your pen is poised in the *notaire*'s office! You should also ask your surveyor to check that there aren't other restrictions such as buried electricity lines or water pipes that may affect renovation or building work.

In the case of an old property, perhaps the most important part of a valuation and survey is to ensure that, once any necessary repairs have been done, you won't be spending more than the property will be worth if you need or want to sell it. This involves determining what essential work needs to be carried out, the likely cost of such work and the estimated value of the property once it has been done; the difference between the two figures is the correct purchase price for the unrenovated property. (If no essential work is necessary, the valuation is made on the property as it stands.)

Needless to say, unless you use an English-speaking builder or surveyor, the report will be in (technical) French and you may need to have it translated, although some architects and surveyors in popular parts of France will provide bi-lingual reports.

SEPTIC TANKS

If the property is connected to a mains sewerage system, you're fortunate! Most rural properties and many in small towns aren't on mains drainage (*tout à l'égout*) and therefore have individual sewerage systems (officially termed *une filière d'assainissement non collectif* or *autonome* or a 'non-collective or autonomous sanitary system'), which normally consist of a septic tank (*une fosse septique toutes eaux* or *fosse toutes eaux* or most commonly simply *fosse septique*).

Before committing yourself to a purchase, have an existing septic tank checked or, if there isn't a tank, ask a specialist to assess your requirements and the likely cost of installing a system. Contact your departmental or regional Direction de l'Environnement (ask at your town hall for the telephone number) and obtain a list of approved specialists (*bureau d'études*) authorised to carry out an inspection or a feasibility study (*étude de filière*); the cost of either is between around €300 and €350.

If you're contemplating buying a house with a septic tank, bear in mind that recent legislation means that certain properties must be connected to mains drainage by the end of 2005. The new rules will generally affect homes in the centre of villages. If the property is within this area or on the edge of it, ask at the town hall whether it's due to be connected to the mains. Even if it's on the outskirts of a village, it's worth checking, as each commune has the discretion to decide which outlying properties are to be connected and which left with their *fosses septiques*, although it may be possible to refuse connection provided you have a system that meets current standards.

Although all this might sound like good news if the idea of having a septic tank in your garden is less than appealing, there's a slight *inconvénient* to be taken into consideration – namely cost: there will be a charge for connection to the mains drainage system, which must be paid within two years of connection, plus a hefty annual 'service' charge added to your water bill.

Another bit of bad news is that properties that aren't considered worthy of connection to the main drainage system will have their tanks inspected before the end of 2005 (and thereafter every four years or so) to make sure they meet the latest standards, which in many cases will be more exacting than those that applied when the tank was installed. In other words, you could be faced with a hefty bill for a new system. Note in particular that cesspits will be illegal.

Even if they don't need replacing, old septic tanks may be in need of drainage, repair, or new pipes. Modern regulations demand, for example, considerably lengthened overflow pipes, which may need to be extended by up to 10m. This may not be possible within the property's boundaries, and you may need to enter negotiations with neighbours.

There are essentially two types of septic tank: older tanks (*fosse traditionnelle*) take bathroom waste only, which is allowed to soak into the ground through gravel, while newer tanks (*fosse à toutes eaux*) take all household waste water and treat it before it's discharged through a system of filters. Note that some older *fosses toutes eaux* have an aerator (*brouilleur* or *batteur*) to help break down the solid matter and allow it to settle while clear water overflows into an underground drainage system.

These are now more or less obsolete, so it may be difficult to obtain spare parts if required.

 Individual sewage systems are subject to strict regulations, which are currently in the process of being updated to meet EU standards, and inspections will become routine.

If the property has neither mains drainage nor a septic tank, you must check that one can be installed. If you need to install a septic tank, you should check the following:

- That there's enough available land, bearing in mind that the drains for a septic tank must be installed a certain minimum distance from the boundaries of a property (e.g. 3 to 5m), and must cover a certain area depending on the size of the tank (generally at least 85m^2);
- Whether there are rivers, canals or other water courses (including underground springs and waterways) that might affect the siting of the tank and soak-away and the type of soak-away – for example, a septic tank mustn't be less than 35m from a well;
- Whether the ground is marshy or rocky, in which case installation could be difficult and/or expensive;
- Whether the land slopes upwards away from the house, which may mean that waste water must be pumped up to the soak-away – another additional expense;
- Whether there's access to the site for a lorry (delivering the tank and subsequently emptying it) and a digger to install the soak-away.

The cost of installation, which can be between €2,000 and €5,000 depending on the size of tank and the type of installation, must be taken into account in your budget. Make sure that a tank is large enough for the property in question, e.g. 2,500 litres for two bedrooms and up to 4,000 litres for five bedrooms. **It's essential to check these things before purchasing a property.**

SWIMMING POOLS

It's common for foreign buyers to install a swimming pool at a home in France, which will greatly increase your rental prospects and the rent you can charge if you plan to let. Note that many self-catering holiday companies won't take on properties without a pool. There are many swimming pool installation companies in France or you can even buy and install one yourself.

There are various types of pool, each with advantages and disadvantages. Above-ground pools are the cheapest but can be unsightly. A 15m long oval pool can be installed for as little as €2,500, and smaller 'splasher' pools can cost less than €500, although more elaborate fibreglass or wooden pools can cost €6,000 or more.

In-ground pools come in three general types: moulded fibreglass (or 'one-piece') pools, which can simply be 'dropped' into a hole in the ground and cost around €10,000 for a reasonable size moulding; panelled pools, which can be bought in kit form and put together without professional help and cost from around €5,000; and concrete block pools, which normally require professional installation and are therefore usually the most expensive option, costing from around €18,000 for a 10m x 5m pool.

Note that you need planning permission to install a pool of more than 20m^2 and should apply a few months in advance (see page 168). Note also that regulations introduced in January 2003 mean that all new pools and all existing pools in rented properties must have an approved safety systems (i.e. an alarm, fencing, safety cover or enclosure) and all other pools will have to be fitted with similar systems by January 2006. Failure to comply with regulations can lead to fines of up to €45,000. Details of requirements can be obtained from any recognised pool installation company.

Pools require regular maintenance and cleaning, which is also expensive (heating a pool, particularly an outdoor one, can cost a fortune, especially in cooler regions). If you have a holiday home in France or let a property, you will need to employ someone to maintain your pool (you may be able to get a local family to look after it in return for using it).

RENOVATION & RESTORATION

Once you've decided to buy a property requiring renovation or restoration – a decision not to be taken lightly (see **Buying An Old Home** on page 136) – there are a number of important checks to be made before committing yourself to a purchase (see below). These should be made in addition to those listed on page 154.

Land & Boundaries

If a property will need extensive restoration or renovation, you should check that there's access to the site for the necessary machinery and materials. Ask yourself whether vehicles can pass safely under overhead cables and whether they will be able to turn round or reverse out, for example. It also means checking that there's room for the storage of demolished and new materials.

The condition of a garden should be taken into consideration. A badly overgrown garden can take years to restore to an acceptable state, let alone turn into an orderly and attractive garden, especially if most of your time is taken up with renovating the house. Bear in mind that grass, plants, trees and weeds grow quickly in most parts of France.

Planning Permission

If modernisation of an old building involves making external alterations, such as building an extension or installing larger windows or new doorways, you will need planning permission (*permis de construire*) from your local town hall. If you plan to do major restoration or building work, you should ensure that a conditional clause (*clause suspensive*) is included in the preliminary contract stating that the purchase is dependent on obtaining planning and building permission (copies of the applications must be sent to the *notaire* handling the sale). It usually takes a number of months to obtain planning permission and, once it's issued and published, the public usually have two months in which to lodge an appeal if they have an objection.

If the built area is less than 170m² (1,829ft²), you can make the planning application yourself, but if it exceeds this an architect must make it. **Never start any building work before you have official permission.**

It's also wise to obtain permission from your local town hall before demolishing buildings on your land, irrespective of how dilapidated they are. Note also that you may be able to sell the building materials or get a builder to demolish them free of charge in exchange for the materials.

Once work is completed, a *certificat de conformité* is required to confirm that it has been carried out according to the planning application and building regulations. Further details of the intricacies of French planning permission can be found in **Renovating & Maintaining Your French Home** (Survival Books – see page 389).

DIY Or Builders?

One of the first decisions you need to make regarding restoration or modernisation is whether to do all or most of the work yourself or have it done by professional builders or specialist tradesmen. A working knowledge of French is essential for DIY, especially the words associated with building materials and measurements (renovating a house in France will also greatly improve your ability to swear in French!).

When restoring a period property, it's important to have an informed and sensitive approach. You shouldn't tackle jobs yourself or with friends unless you're sure that you're capable. In general you should aim to retain as many of a property's original features as possible and use local building materials in keeping with the style of the property. When renovations and 'improvements' have been botched, there's often little that can be done except to start again from scratch.

Even if you do much of the work yourself, you will still need to hire specialists for certain jobs.

SURVIVAL TIP
You must have third party insurance
for anyone working on your property and you're advised
to pay casual workers using the *chèque emploi service*
system (ask at your French bank for details).

There's a wide choice of DIY equipment and building supplies in France, although they can be more expensive than in some other countries, e.g. French paint and varnish are expensive and not always good, although imported paint is also available. There are many DIY (*bricolage*) shops and supermarkets in France, which in addition to stocking most DIY materials also have a wide range of tools and machinery for hire. Most DIY stores accept credit cards and have plenty of knowledgeable staff. Look out for promotions; even if something appears not to be on offer, it's worthwhile asking, as offers aren't always advertised.

DIY stores are relatively expensive for some items, so it's also worth checking trade suppliers. Most towns have a hardware store (*quincaillerie*) that's handy for tools and small items. Second-hand stores such as the ubiquitous *trocs* are good for plumbing parts and porcelain, doors and mantelpieces. There are also specialists in reclaimed materials, such as old floor tiles, doors and windows. Ask your neighbours about where to buy fittings and materials, as they usually know the best places locally. Lists of suppliers of reclaimed materials and details of DIY supermarkets in France can be found in *Renovating & Maintaining Your French Home* (Survival Books – see page 389).

When it's a choice between French and foreign builders, most experts recommend using local labour for a number of excellent reasons. French tradesmen (*artisans*) understand the materials and the traditional style of building, are familiar with local planning and building regulations, and usually do excellent work. There are few jacks of all trades in France, where all tradesmen have a specialist trade, such as bricklayer, stonemason, joiner, roofer, plasterer, plumber or electrician. If you employ local builders, you can virtually guarantee that the result will be *authentique* and it could also save you money. French builders' quotations are binding and their prices are usually reasonable. Finally, bringing in foreign labour won't endear you to the local populace and may even create friction.

Nevertheless, finding a French builder who is available can be difficult, finding one who will give you a quote for anything other than a major restoration project even more so, and getting a job done within a set time next to impossible. Communication may also be a problem. There are many excellent foreign builders who have built up a good local reputation and can be relied upon to do a good job within a set period for a competitive price.

 Note that you should only employ registered tradesmen and never employ 'black' labour (French or foreign): apart from the fact that he won't be insured, there are stiff penalties for avoiding tax, VAT and social security contributions.

Cost

All building work, including electrical work, masonry and plumbing, is costed by the metre or square metre. The cost of total restoration by professional builders varies, but you should expect to pay a minimum of €600 per m² and as much as €1,000 per m² to bring a ruin to a habitable condition (or around half this for outbuildings), although the exact cost depends on the type of work involved, the quality of materials used and the region.

 You should expect the cost of renovating an old *'habitable'* building to be at least equal to its purchase price and possibly much more.

How much you spend on restoring a property depends on your purpose and the depth of your pockets. If you're restoring a property as a holiday or permanent home, money may be no object. On the other hand, if you're restoring a property as an investment, it's easy to spend more than you can ever hope to recoup when you sell it. Keep an eye on your budget (which will usually be at least 50 per cent below the actual cost!) and don't be in too much of a hurry. Some people take many years to restore a holiday home, particularly when they're doing most of the work themselves. However, it isn't unusual for buyers to embark on a grandiose renovation scheme and run out of money before it's completed and be forced to sell at a huge loss.

It's possible to obtain a mortgage that includes the cost of renovation work, but you must obtain detailed written quotations for a lender. It's also possible to obtain a grant to restore a historic property in some regions (contact the Conseil Régional) or in return for providing low/medium rent apartments for a period of years. Note also that VAT on renovation work (i.e. work on a house more than five years old) is at 5.5 per cent instead of the standard rate of 19.6 per cent until at least the end of 2005.

If you're renovating a property for a business, e.g. as *gîtes*, it may be advantageous to buy it through a French company, which will enable you to recover your VAT. Note that, if you buy an old house and completely renovate it, e.g. retaining only the roof and external walls, thus transforming it into a 'new' house, you may be liable for VAT. Therefore you should, if possible, retain a small part of the existing internal structure.

Quotations

Before you buy a property that needs renovation or restoration, it's vital to obtain accurate estimates of the work involved from one or more reliable local builders. Builders' quotations may be binding, but extras added or alterations made to the plan after work starts will escalate costs wildly, even up to 100 per cent. You should obtain written quotations (*devis*) from at least two builders before employing anyone, although obtaining quotes from French builders and tradesmen is sometimes almost impossible. It helps if you offer to pay a fee, e.g. €75, which should be reimbursed by the builder who gets the job.

Note that for quotations to be accurate, you must detail exactly the work that's required, e.g. for electrical work this would include the number of lights, points and switches, their exact location and the quality of materials to be used. If you have only a vague idea of what you want, you will receive a vague and unreliable quotation. Make sure that a quotation includes everything you want done and that you fully understand it (if you don't get it translated). Look out for any terms in a quotation allowing for the price to be increased for inflation or a general rise in prices, and check whether it's definitive or provisional, i.e. dependent on further exploratory work.

When you accept a quotation, you should sign a copy of the *devis* with the builder, which then becomes a fixed price contract if work is started within three months. You should fix a date for completion (*fin de travaux*) and, if you can get a builder to agree to it, include a penalty for failing to meet it. It's difficult to get French builders to agree to this, but it's worth persevering; otherwise, he may take on other jobs and string the work out for ever. After signing a contract, it's usual to pay a deposit, e.g. 10 to 25 per cent, depending on the size of the job.

Supervision

If you aren't on the spot and able to supervise work, you should hire a 'clerk of works' such as a master builder (*maître d'oeuvres*) or an architect to oversee a job; otherwise it could drag on for months (or years) or be left half-finished. This will add around 10 per cent to the bill but is usually worth every penny. Many unsupervised French workmen are about as disciplined as French drivers and it isn't uncommon for tradesmen to work a few hours or a few days and then disappear for weeks or months on end! Be extremely careful whom you employ if you have work done in your absence and ensure that your instructions are accurate in every detail. Make absolutely certain that you understand what has been agreed and if necessary get it in writing (with drawings). It pays to keep everything connected with a job, from the first letters, including old drawings and even bits of paper with scribbles on. It isn't unusual for foreign owners to receive huge bills for work done in their absence that shouldn't have been done at all!

SURVIVAL TIP

If you don't speak French, it's even more important to employ someone to oversee building work. Progressing on sign language is a recipe for disaster!

Make sure that a job is completely finished (including repairing any damage done by workmen) before paying bills. Never pay a builder in advance, particularly a large sum, as it's possible that he will disappear with your money (particularly if he's a foreign, non-registered builder). It's best to pay a month in arrears, which most builders will agree to. On the other hand, if you want a job doing while you're away, you will need to pay a builder a sum in advance or get someone local to supervise his work and pay him regularly, or he's unlikely to finish the job. You may be able to pay in cash without VAT, although you should bear in mind that this is illegal and, if you don't have a legitimate bill, you won't be able to offset the cost of work against rental income or capital gains tax when you sell, and you also won't have a guarantee against faulty workmanship.

Guarantees

All work done by French and foreign builders registered in France is covered by insurance, which guarantees work for one to ten years, even if a builder goes out of business before the guarantee period has expired. A ten-year guarantee (*garantie décennale*) is provided for building work such as brick and stone work. A two-year guarantee of 'perfect functioning' is provided for all systems (such as plumbing and electrical installations) and a one-year guarantee is given against minor defects that may appear after completion of building work, such as cracking due to shrinkage after concrete or plaster dries out.

Information

No one attempting DIY in France should be without the *Oxford-Duden Pictorial French-English Dictionary* or the *Harraps French Visual Dictionary*. A good French/English architecture and building dictionary is the *Dictionnaire d'Architecture et de Construction* by J. R. Forbes (Lavoisier). There are also a number of books on the market for those brave enough to attempt their own renovations, such as **Renovating & Maintaining Your French Home** (Survival Books – see page 389). If your French is up to it, there are many excellent French DIY and home improvements magazines.

See also **Buying An Old Home** on page 136, **Inspections & Surveys** on page 154, **Wiring Standards** on page 329, **Water** on page 335 and **Heating & Air-Conditioning** on page 297.

MOBILE HOMES

An increasing number of people – both French and non-French – are buying a mobile home (*mobile-home*), permanently installed on a French campsite, which can be an inexpensive way of obtaining a holiday home in France. On a well-run site, pitches (*emplacement*) are sheltered by trees and hedges and mobile homes have permanent patios as well as storage areas, where you can keep valuables while 'your' home is rented out to other users, as well as pitched roofs, porches and shutters to make them more like houses than caravans.

There are essentially two options when it comes to buying a mobile home: buy an existing home and take over the rental from the previous owner, or find a site which accepts mobile homes and install your own.

Finding a home to buy in situ isn't easy, and you may need to go to your chosen area and ask whether any are for sale. Finding sites that accept homes is simpler. The French magazine *le Caravanier* (12 rue Rouget-de-Lisle, 92442 Issy-les-Moulineaux Cedex, ☎ 01 41 33 47 47, 🖳 www.lecaravanier.com) publishes a supplement about mobile homes, *Maisons, Mobiles et Chalets*, which includes a list of sites that accept mobiles. Mobile home dealers will often help you to find a suitable site and arrange transport and installation, as well as purchase plans allowing you to pay for a home in instalments even though it's in another country. Specialist mobile home transport companies may also be able to recommend sites. Note, however, that many sites insist that you buy from selected local dealers and that prices in France may be considerably higher than those in the UK, for example.

Some companies (e.g. Haven Europe, UK ☎ 0870-242 8888, 🖳 www.haveneurope.com or 🖳 www.havenfrance.com) offer a 'turnkey' package, including a pitch on one of their own sites and a choice of new or second-hand homes; you may be able to bring in your own home (for a fee), provided it's of an approved design and style. Other companies (e.g. Breakaway Homes, UK ☎ 01903-741010) offer a similar service using French-owned sites, although Breakaway is now also acquiring its own sites in France.

A new mobile home can cost €30,000 or more. Manufacturers, who will put you in touch with your nearest dealer, are listed on 🖳 www. martex.co.uk/leisure-and-living/malphafr.htm. If you're looking for a second-hand bargain, contact the major camping companies (e.g. Eurocamp, UK ☎ 01606-787000, and Eurosites, UK ☎ 01254-300612) and ask about their annual sale of used homes; five- or six-year-old homes start at around €6,000, and you can be sure that they've been well maintained.

Pitch rental rates vary between around €1,200 and €3,000 per year, although you may pay only a proportion of this if you allow your home to be let to other users when you aren't using it. Maintenance costs on a mobile home can be significantly lower than those on a 'proper' home, and your pitch is maintained for you by the campsite owners. Although a mobile home normally depreciates more rapidly than a house, you can find that your property increases in value over the years.

As when buying a house or apartment, it pays to rent before buying, so spend a holiday in a mobile home on or near the site you're looking to buy into before making a final decision. Haven, for example, offer a free three-night 'inspection visit' in one of their homes.

BUILDING YOUR OWN HOME

If you want to be far from the madd(en)ing crowd, you can buy a plot and have a house built to your own design or to a standard design provided by a nationwide building company such as Maison Bouygues Immobilier (🖳 www.bouygues-immobilier.com) or a small local builder (*constructeur*). You can even buy a 'kit' house, offered by a number of firms for installation in France. Although French builders have a range of standard designs, they will accommodate almost any interior or exterior variations (for a price), provided they're permitted under the local building regulations. If you literally want to build your own home (known as *auto-construction*), you might want to join an association called Savoir Faire et Découverte (La Caillère, 61100 La Carneille, ☎ 02 33 66 74 67, 🖳 www.lesavoirfaire.com), which organises 'hands-on' days, weekends and courses with expert tradesmen, although it currently covers only Champagne-Ardenne, Nord-Pas-de-Calais and Normandy. Building your own home is becoming an increasingly attractive option as the price of property and of renovation increases. It allows you not only to choose the design of your home, but to ensure that the quality of materials and workmanship are first class, but it isn't a project to be undertaken lightly. (see **CCMI** on page 207).

Finding A Plot

Building plots (*terrains à bâtir or terrains constructibles*) are available in most areas of France. Plots range from around 400m² to several hectares, the average plot being between 1,000 and 3,000m² (around half an acre to an acre). They can be bought through estate agents (see page 116) or directly from the owner (e.g. a farmer). Builders usually also have a selection of plots for sale or know of plots that are available. Most builders offer package deals that include the land and the cost of building a home. However, it isn't always advisable to buy the plot from the builder who's going to build your home and you should shop around and compare separate land and building costs. If you do decide to buy a package deal from a builder, you must insist on separate contracts for the land and the building and obtain the title deed for the land before signing a building contract. Sometimes a batch of plots (*lotissements*) are released by a communal authority, although priority is often given to local people. In these cases, there are often specific restrictions as to the type and size of property that can be built. There are a number of websites listing plots for sale, including 🖳 www.allobat.fr and 🖳 www.terrain.fr.

Checks

You must take the same care when buying land as you would when buying a home (see page 154), particularly regarding local development plans and planning permission (see page 168). You can apply for your own *certificat d'urbanisme*, which should provide the necessary information. The application form (*demande de certificat d'urbanisme*) must be accompanied by four copies of plans as described above as well as a description of the property. Approval (or refusal) should be granted within two months and, once approval has been granted, you should be able to obtain a building permit, depending on the type of construction you propose, provided you apply within a year. Note, however, that a *certificat d'urbanisme* merely confirms that land may be built on and doesn't in itself entitle you to build anything, for which you must obtain the necessary planning permission (see page 168).

Never assume that you will be able to build the same sort of house as your neighbours, as regulations vary according to the situation and type of plot or the rules may have changed since other homes were built. Don't rely on the builder or developer to check for you, but do so yourself or have your lawyer do it. **If a mistake is made, a building may need to be demolished!**

Also check the maximum permitted size of a building on the plot; all too often, foreign buyers have found themselves the proud owners of a rustic plot on they cannot build anything larger than a shed!

Before you buy land, particularly in rural areas, you should take advice from a professional (preferably a lawyer) who should thoroughly investigate the conditions and regulations affecting the land.

 Never believe an owner or estate agent keen to sell you a plot who says there will be 'no problem' getting planning permission, but check with the local town hall and make it a condition of the purchase of a building plot.

Some plots are unsuitable for building as they're too steep, rocky or sandy and therefore require prohibitively expensive foundations (it's wise to take a soil sample). It's wise to consider the access to a plot if this isn't via a surfaced road. Rainfall in some areas can be torrential and many tracks turn into impassable mud baths and some are even washed away. It's a good idea to consult an architect, who will be able to tell you whether the plot is suitable for construction. You should also have a land survey of the plot before you commit yourself to a purchase (see **Inspections & Surveys** on page 154).

Note also that the cost of providing services to a property in a remote rural area may be prohibitive (see **Utilities** on page 327), and it must have a reliable water supply. If you don't have mains water and have to rely on other sources such as wells, you should make sure that the supply will be adequate for your needs.

Finally, if you yearn for a cottage by the sea, note that the 'Coastal Law' (*Loi littoral*) of 1986 prohibits building within 100m (330ft) of the French coast.

Cost

Prices vary enormously according to location and whether main services are connected. A plot with mains connections (e.g. electricity, gas, telephone, water and sewerage) is said to be *viabilisé* and you should check which services, if any, are available, as it can be **very** expensive to have a plot connected to the mains (see **Utilities** on page 327). Land in or near a small village, where there's no mains drainage, can be bought for less than €5 per m², whereas land with connections to all services, including water and telephone, near a town can cost as much as €100 per m² but you should be able to find a good plot for around €50 per m². The average plots (between 1,000 and 3,000m²) costs between €10,000 and €40,000. If you have school-age children, you may even qualify for a grant, as many small communes are keen to boost local school numbers!

Building costs range from around €500 per m² in an average area to €1,500 (or more) per m² in resorts, depending on the design and the quality of construction. Note, however, that you should add an extra 10 to 15 per cent to the estimated price, as the actual cost is **always** higher than the original budget. Note also that labour costs may be considerably higher if your plot is situated in a remote area, where you will also have to pay extra for transporting materials. Value added tax at 19.6 per cent is payable on new buildings and in some communes you must pay a *taxe locale d'équipement* (*TLE*). Shop around and compare prices, which can vary considerably (small family builders often provide the best value).

Before accepting a quotation, it's wise to have it checked by a building consultant to confirm that it's a fair deal. You should also check whether the quotation (which must include VAT) is an estimate or a fixed price, as sometimes the cost can escalate wildly due to contract clauses and changes made during building work.

Finding An Architect & Builder

When looking for an architect or builder, it's wise to obtain recommendations from local people you can trust, e.g. a *notaire*, local mayor or neighbours. Professionals aren't always the best people to ask, as they may receive a commission. Always obtain references (e.g. from previous customers) before employing either.

All qualified tradesmen living in France must be registered at the local town hall (*mairie*) and have a *SIRET* number. Note that it's usually better to use a local building consortium or contractor (*entrepreneur*) rather than a number of independent tradesmen, particularly if you won't be around to supervise them, although it will cost you a bit more. On the other hand, if you do it 'yourself' using local hand-picked tradesmen, you can save money and learn a great deal into the bargain.

A good architect should be able to recommend a number of reliable builders, but you should also do your own research, as the most important consideration when choosing a new home is the reputation (and financial standing) of the builder. You should be wary of an architect with his 'own' builder (or a builder with his own architect): as it's the architect's job to ensure that the builder does his work according to the plans and specifications, you don't want their relationship to be too cosy! Inspect other homes the builder has built and check with the owners as to what problems they've had and whether they're satisfied. Note that building standards in France vary considerably and you shouldn't assume that the lowest offer is the best value.

SURVIVAL TIP
Your best insurance when building a property is the reputation of the builder and his liquidity.

Details of French builders can be obtained from the Association Maisons de Qualité (💻 www.maisons-qualite.com). A register of architects is kept by the Conseil national de l'Ordre des Architectes, 9 rue Borromée, 75015 Paris (💻 www.architectes.org). A nationwide franchised network of registered builders is MIKIT, which has a UK partner firm, Capital Mover (💻 www.capitalmover.com).

Contracts

If you're buying land for building, you should make it a condition of the purchase that a building permit is granted; otherwise, you could be forced to buy land on which you cannot build. If you're having a home built to your specifications, you should ensure that the building contract includes the following:

● A detailed description and a list of the materials to be used (with references to the architect's plans);

● The exact location of the building on the plot;

● The building and payment schedule, which must be made in stages according to building progress;

● It is worth trying to get a penalty clause for late completion included in the contract, though few builders will agree to this.

● The retention of a percentage (e.g. 5 to 10 per cent) of the building costs as a guarantee against defects;

● An explanation of how disputes will be settled.

Ensure that the contract includes all costs including the architect's fees (unless contracted separately), landscaping (if applicable), all permits and licences (including the costs of land segregation, the declaration of new building, and the horizontal division for a community property), and the connection of utilities (e.g. electricity) to the house, not just to the building site. The only extra is usually the cost of electricity and water meters.

> **SURVIVAL TIP**
> It isn't uncommon to have problems during construction, particularly regarding material defects, so it's vital to have a contract checked by a lawyer, as building contracts are often heavily biased in the builder's favour and give clients very few rights.

If you're buying a property in a development off plan (*en état futur d'achèvement*), the developer should provide a standard contract (see **Buying Off Plan** on page 206).

Guarantees

French law requires a builder to guarantee his work against structural defects for ten years (*garantie décenniale*). An architect is also responsible for ten years for defects due to poor supervision, incorrect instructions given to the builder, or problems caused by poor foundations, e.g. subsidence. On completion, a builder must provide a 'perfect completion guarantee' (*garantie de parfait achèvement*) covering minor defects that may appear during the year after completion, such as cracks in plaster, and a 'good functioning guarantee' (*garantie de bon fonctionnement*), valid for two years, covering systems such as plumbing and electrical installations. You should have a completed building checked by a structural surveyor for defects and a report drawn up. If there are any defects, he should determine exactly who was responsible for them.

It's also important that the builder provides a 'termination' guarantee (backed by a bank or insurance company) to cover you in the event that he goes bust before completing the property and its infrastructure, which must be specified in the contract (see **Buying Off Plan** on page 206).

Avoiding & Resolving Problems

If you want a house built in France exactly to your specifications, you will need to personally supervise it every step of the way or employ an architect or engineer to do it for you. (See also **Supervision** on page 172.) Without close supervision it's highly likely that your instructions won't be followed. Note that it isn't uncommon to have problems during construction, particularly regarding material defects. You must usually be extremely patient when trying to resolve problems and should keep a record of every conversation and take relevant photographs as evidence.

4.

MONEY MATTERS

One of the most important aspects of buying a home in France is finance, including transferring and changing money, opening a bank account and obtaining a mortgage, all of which are dealt with in this chapter. Whether or not you plan to live in France, you may also incur French taxes, which are covered in **Chapter 7**.

If you're planning to invest in property or a business in France that's financed with funds in a non-euro currency (e.g. GB£ or US$), it's important to consider both the present and possible future exchange rates. If you need to borrow money to buy property or for a business venture in France, you should carefully consider where and in what currency to raise finance.

 Bear in mind that if your income is paid in a currency other than euros it can be exposed to risks beyond your control when you live in France, particularly regarding inflation and exchange rate fluctuations.

On the other hand, if you live and work in France and are paid in euros, this may affect your financial commitments abroad.

If you own a home in France, you can employ a French accountant or tax adviser to look after your financial affairs there and declare and pay your local taxes. You can also have your financial representative receive your bank statements, ensure that your bank is paying your standing orders (e.g. for utilities and property taxes) and that you have sufficient funds to pay them. If you let a home in France through a French company, they may perform the above tasks as part of their services. A 26-page booklet providing advice on financing a property in France is available free from independent financial advisers Siddalls (UK ☎ 01329-288641).

SURVIVAL TIP
You should ensure that your income is (and will remain) sufficient to live on, bearing in mind devaluations (if your income isn't paid in euros), rises in the cost of living (see page 31), unforeseen expenses such as medical bills and anything else that may reduce your income (such as stock market crashes and recessions!).

Foreigners, particularly retirees, often under-estimate the cost of living and many are forced to return to their home countries after a year or two.

Although the French prefer to pay in cash or by cheque or debit card rather than use credit or charge cards, it's wise to have at least one credit card when visiting or living in France (Visa and MasterCard are the most widely accepted). Even if you don't like credit cards and shun any form of credit, they do have their uses, for example no-deposit car rentals, no pre-paying hotel bills (plus guaranteed bookings), obtaining cash 24 hours a day, simple telephone and mail-order payments, greater security than cash and, above all, convenience. Note, however, that not all French businesses accept credit cards, particularly those without a microchip.

FRENCH CURRENCY

The euro replaced the franc as France's official currency (*monnaie*) on 1st January 2002. The franc, which is worth €0.15 and continues to be the official currency of Monaco, French overseas territories, such as Guadeloupe and Martinique, and many former French colonies, is, however still used by most French people (even bank managers!), who automatically think and talk in francs (which they usually call *balles*). In fact, many French people, and not just the elderly, talk in old francs (a hundred times smaller than a 'new' franc), which were abolished in 1958, particularly when discussing large numbers such as house prices; you may, for example, hear the word *brique*, which is a million old francs or 10,000 new francs or approximately €665 . . . When house buying in France, it pays to have a calculator handy!

The euro (€) is divided into 100 cents (nostalgically called *centimes* by the French) and coins are minted in values of 1, 2, 5, 10, 20, 50 *centimes*, €1 and €2. The 1, 2 and 5 *centimes* coins are brass-coloured, the 10, 20 and 50 *centimes* copper-coloured. The €1 coin is silver-coloured in the centre with a brass-coloured rim, and the €2 coin has a brass-coloured centre and silver-coloured rim. The reverse ('tail' showing the value) of euro coins is the same in all euro-zone countries, but the obverse ('head') is different in each country.

Euro banknotes (*billets*) are identical throughout the euro-zone and depict a map of Europe and stylised designs of buildings (as the 12 countries couldn't agree which actual buildings should be shown!). Notes are printed in denominations of €10, €20, €50, €100, €200 and €500 (worth over £300 or $500!). The size of notes increases with their value (who said size doesn't matter?). Euro notes have been produced using all the latest anti-counterfeiting devices. Nevertheless, you should be wary of €200 and €500 notes – if only because of the risk of losing them! Note that money is *argent* in French and *monnaie* means currency or change (*change* means exchange, as in *bureau de change*). To pay 'in cash' is either *en espèces* or *en liquide*.

The euro symbol may appear before the amount (as in this book), after it (commonly used by the French, who have been used to putting F after the amount) or even between the euros and centimes, e.g. 16€50. Values below one euro are invariably written using the euro symbol, e.g.

€0,75 (the French put a comma, rather than a point, before decimals), rather than with an American-style cent symbol.

It's wise to obtain some euro coins and banknotes before arriving in France and to familiarise yourself with them. You should have some euros in cash, e.g. €75 to €150 in small notes, when you arrive. This will save you having to change money on arrival at a French airport, although you shouldn't carry a lot of cash and should avoid high value notes, which sometimes aren't accepted, particularly for small purchases or on public transport.

IMPORTING & EXPORTING MONEY

Shop around for the best exchange rate and the lowest costs when transferring money to France. Banks are often willing to negotiate on fees and exchange rates when you're transferring a large amount of cash.

 Don't be too optimistic about the exchange rate, which can change at short notice and can cost you tens of thousands of euros (or pounds or dollars) more than you planned.

For example, if you're buying a home in France costing €300,000 and are paying in pounds sterling, this would be equal to £193,548 at an exchange rate of £1 = €1.55. However, if the £/€ exchange rate 'falls' to €1.45 between the time your purchase offer is accepted and the time you come to pay, it will cost you £206,896 – an increase of £13,348!

It's possible to 'fix' the exchange rate to guard against unexpected devaluations by buying a Forward Time Option or Limit Order from your bank or through a specialised currency exchange firm (e.g. Currencies For Less in the UK, ☎ 020-7228 7667, 💻 www.currencies4less.com); the further in advance you buy, the more you pay. The downside is that you may regret doing so if there's a big swing in your favour!

Declaration

Exchange controls in France were abolished on 1st January 1990 and there are no restrictions on the import or export of funds. A French resident is permitted to open a bank account in any country and to export an unlimited amount of money from France. However, if you're a French resident, you must inform the French tax authorities of any new foreign account in your annual tax return. Sums in excess of €7,500 deposited abroad, other than by regular bank transfers, must be reported to the Banque de France. If you send or receive any amount above €1,500 by post, it must be declared to customs. Similarly if you enter or leave France with €7,500 or more in French or foreign banknotes or securities (e.g. traveller's cheques, letters of credit, bills of exchange, bearer bonds, giro cheques, stock and share certificates, bullion, and gold or silver coins quoted on the official exchange), you must declare it to French customs. **If you exceed the €7,500 limit, you can be fined over €1,500.**

Transfers

When transferring or sending money to (or from) France you should be aware of the alternatives available:

- **Bank Draft** (*chèque de banque*) – A bank draft should be sent by registered post but, if it's lost or stolen, it's impossible to stop payment and you must wait six months before a new draft can be issued. In France, bank drafts must be cleared, like personal cheques.

- **Bank Transfer** (*virement*) – A 'normal' transfer should take three to seven days, but usually takes much longer, and an international bank transfer between non-affiliated banks can take weeks! (It's usually quicker and cheaper to transfer funds between branches of the same bank than between non-affiliated banks.) In fact, the larger the amount the longer it often takes, which can be particularly awkward when you're transferring money to buy a property.

- **SWIFT Transfer** – One of the safest and fastest methods of transferring money is via the Society of Worldwide Interbank Financial Telecommunications (SWIFT) system. A SWIFT transfer **should** be completed in a few hours, funds being available within 24 hours, although even SWIFT transfers can take five working days, especially from small branches that are unused to dealing with foreign transfers. Australian and UK members of the SWIFT system are listed on the Society's website (🖳 www.swift.com). The cost of transfers varies considerably – not only commission and exchange rates, but also transfer charges – but is usually between around €30 and €50. Britons should note that one of the cheapest ways to transfer money to France is via the Co-Operative Bank's TIPANET service.

- **Currency Dealer** – It may be quicker to use a specialist currency dealer (e.g. Currencies For Less in the UK, ☎ 020-7228 7667, 🖳 www. currencies4less.com) to carry out the transfer for you, and you may get a better exchange rate than from a bank.

When you have money transferred to a bank in France, ensure that you give the name, account number, branch number (*code agence*) and the bank code (*clé*) – known as a bank's IBANK number. Otherwise, your money can be 'lost' while being transferred to or from a French bank account and it can take weeks to locate it.

SURVIVAL TIP
If you plan to send a large amount of money to France or abroad for a business transaction such as buying property, you should ensure you receive the commercial rate of exchange rather than the tourist rate.

Always check bank charges and exchange rates in advance and agree them with your bank (you may be able to negotiate a lower charge or a better exchange rate).

Note that it isn't wise to close your bank accounts abroad, unless you're certain that you won't need them in the future. Even when resident in France, it's cheaper to keep money in local currency in an account in a country that you visit regularly than to pay commission to convert euros. Many foreigners living in France maintain at least two accounts, a foreign bank account for international transactions and a local account with a French bank for day-to-day business.

Obtaining Cash

There are various methods of obtaining smaller amounts of money for everyday use. These include the following:

● **Banks & Post Offices** – Most banks in major cities have foreign exchange windows, where you can buy and sell foreign currencies, buy and cash travellers' cheques, and obtain a cash advance on credit and charge cards. The Post Office also offers an exchange service. Rates vary little, and neither banks nor the post office normally charge commission.

● **Bureaux De Change** – Bureaux de change often have longer business hours than banks, particularly at weekends. Most offer competitive exchange rates and low or no commission (but check). They're easier to deal with than banks but banks generally offer better rates. There are many private exchange bureaux at airports, main railway stations and major cities. At airports and in tourist areas in major cities, there are automatic change machines accepting up to 15 currencies, including US$, £sterling and Swiss francs. **However, airport bureaux de change and change machines usually offer the worst exchange rates and charge the highest fees (e.g. handling charges).** Never use unofficial money changers, who are likely to short change you.

The exchange rates (*cours de change*) against the euro for most major currencies are listed in banks and daily newspapers and can be obtained via the internet (e.g. 🖳 www.x-rates.com).

● **Cards** – If you need instant cash, you can draw on debit, credit or charge cards (but there's usually a daily limit). Many foreigners living in France (particularly retirees) keep the bulk of their money in a foreign account (perhaps with an offshore bank – see page 192) and draw on it with a cash or credit card. This is an ideal solution for holidaymakers and holiday homeowners (although homeowners will still need a French bank account to pay their bills). Exchange rates are better when obtaining cash with a credit or debit card as you're given the wholesale rate, although there's a 1.5 per cent charge on cash advances and ATM transactions in foreign currencies. Some ATMs may reject foreign cards – if this happens try again and if necessary try another ATM.

● **Postcheques** – Giro postcheques issued by European post offices (Eurogiros) can be cashed (with a postcheque guarantee card) at main post offices in France. The maximum value per cheque depends on the country where it's issued, e.g. €250 if issued in the UK. There's a standard charge for each cheque of €3.80 plus 0.7 per cent of the amount. You can also send money to France via the Girobank Eurogiro system from post offices in Europe and the US to some French banks.

● **Telegraphic Transfer** – One of the quickest (it takes around ten minutes) and safest methods of transferring cash is via a telegraphic transfer, e.g. Moneygram (☎ UK 0800-666 3947, 🖳 www.money gram.com) or Western Union (☎ UK 0800-833 833, 🖳 www.western union.com), but it's also one of the most expensive, e.g. commission of 7 to 10 per cent of the amount sent! Western Union transfers can be picked up from a post office in France (and 100 other countries) just 15 minutes after being paid into an office abroad. Money can be sent via American Express offices by Amex cardholders.

● **Travellers' Cheques** – If you're visiting France, it's safer to carry travellers' cheques (*chèque de voyage*) than cash. It's best to buy euro travellers' cheques when visiting France, although they aren't as easy to cash as in some other countries, e.g. the US. They aren't usually accepted as cash by businesses, except perhaps in Parisian hotels, restaurants and shops, most of which offer a poor exchange rate.

You can buy travellers' cheques from any French bank, usually for a service charge of 1 per cent of the face value. There should be no commission charge when cashing euro travellers' cheques at any bank in France (you must show your passport) and exchange rates are generally similar to those for cash.

Always keep a separate record of cheque numbers and note where and when they were cashed. American Express provides a free, 24-hour replacement service for lost or stolen travellers' cheques at any of their offices world-wide, provided you know the serial numbers of the lost cheques. Without the serial numbers, replacement can take three days or longer. All companies provide local numbers for reporting lost or stolen travellers' cheques.

 One thing to bear in mind when travelling in France, or anywhere for that matter, is not to rely on one source of funds only.

BANKS

There are two main types of bank in France: commercial and co-operative. The largest commercial banks have branches in most large towns and cities and include the Banque Nationale de Paris (BNP Paribas), Crédit Lyonnais and Société Générale. All three have now been privatised and, in order to compete with other larger European banks, are intent on merging, the latest proposal being a union between BNP and Société Générale. Village banks are rare, although in many villages there are bank offices (*permanence*), which usually open one morning a week only.

The largest co-operative banks are Crédit Agricole, Crédit Mutuel and BRED Banque Populaire. They began life as regional, community-based institutions working for the mutual benefit of their clients, although most are now represented nationally and offer a full range of banking services. Unlike commercial banks, each branch office of a co-operative bank is independent and issues its own shares. Anyone can become a member and invest in their shares, which is usually mandatory if you wish to take out a mortgage or loan but isn't necessary to open a current account.

Crédit Agricole is the largest co-operative bank (and the biggest landholder) in France. It's the largest retail bank in Europe with around 10,000 branches and some 17 million customers and has an English-language service (see **Foreign Banks** below). The top four French banks (Crédit Agricole, Crédit Lyonnais, Société Générale and BNP Paribas) are among the world's top ten banks. (In 2003, Crédit Agricole bought Crédit Lyonnais, which has, however, continued to trade as Crédit Lyonnais, albeit with around 85 fewer branches, which have closed or are due to close as a result of the take-over.)

Note that the Banque de France is the authority which sets interest rates and regulates other banks; you cannot open an account with the Banque de France.

All banks, including foreign banks, are listed in the yellow pages under *Banques*. For further information about French banks, see *Living and Working in France* (Survival Books – see page 389).

Post Office Banking

As in many other countries, the most popular banking facility in France is operated by the post office (*La Poste*), which also offers some of the 'cheapest' banking. In terms of the amount of money handled, *La Poste* is the country's third-largest bank (after Crédit Agricole and Caisse d'Epargne). In rural areas, where the nearest bank is often many kilometres away, many people use the post office as their local bank. Another advantage of the post office is that many branches are open for longer hours than banks, although many aren't. Post office accounts provide the same services as bank accounts, including international money transfers (by post and telegraph to many countries) and payment of bills. Post office account holders are issued with a (free) cash card for withdrawals from cash machines (ATMs) located outside main post offices. Every transaction is confirmed with a receipt by post.

Savings Banks

There are also savings banks in France, the major bank being Caisse d'Epargne with a network of over 400 regional institutions. Savings banks are similar to British building societies and American savings and loan organisations and offer savings schemes and loans for property and other purchases, although general banking services are limited compared with commercial and co-operative banks.

Foreign Banks

Foreign-owned banks in France number some 175, more than in any other European country except the UK, although they have a small market share. However, competition from foreign banks is set to increase, as EU regulations allow any bank trading legitimately in one EU country to trade in another. Among foreigners in France, the British are best served by their national banks, both in Paris and in the provinces, particularly the Côte d'Azur. The most prominent British bank is Barclays with around 100 branches, including at least one in all major cities. National Westminster has branches in most major cities, the Abbey National has around 12 branches, and Lloyds and HSBC one each (in Paris).

If you do a lot of travelling abroad or carry out international business transactions, you may find that the services provided by a foreign bank are more suited to your needs. They're also more likely to have staff who speak English and other foreign languages. Note, however, that many foreign banks (and some French banks) handle mainly corporate clients and don't provide banking services for individuals. Most major foreign banks are present in Paris, but branches are rare in the provinces.

Note that the Crédit Agricole has an English-language service, called 'Britline', based at its Caen branch, 15 esplanade Brillaud de Laujardière, 14050 Caen Cedex (☎ 02 31 55 67 89, 🖳 www.britline.com). Only some of its forms are printed in English, but an English-speaker always answers the telephone. Note, however, that branches of Crédit Agricole in other parts of France aren't familiar with dealing with Britline and, if you have an account in Caen, you cannot pay cheques into any branch outside Calvados.

Some other French banks have English-language helplines, including the Charente-Périgord branch of Crédit Agricole (☎ 05 45 20 49 60).

'Virtual' Banking

Banking has become highly automated in recent years, and French banks now offer an efficient and wide-ranging service, including online banking (for which there's usually a charge, e.g. €3 per month). Internet banking has been slow to catch on in France, but organisations such as Egg have recently set up operations and aim to attract customers away from traditional banks.

Opening Hours

Normal bank opening hours are from 09.00 to 17.30 or 17.45, Mondays to Fridays, although banks may open any time between 08.30 and 09.30 and some close between 16.00 and 17.00. Larger branches may stay open until 18.30 or 19.00 on certain days or every day in cities. Banks at main railway stations in Paris are open from 09.00 until between 20.00 and 23.00, although they usually have long queues.

In small towns, banks close for lunch from 12.00 or 12.30 until 13.30 or 14.00. Many banks open on Saturdays (e.g. 09.00 to 16.00), particularly in market towns, although when a bank in a rural area opens on Saturdays it may close on Mondays. Banks are closed on public holidays; when a public holiday falls on a Tuesday or Thursday, banks usually also close on the preceding Monday or the following Friday respectively.

At major airports such as Paris' Charles de Gaulle and Orly airports, *bureaux de change* are open from 07.00 to 23.00 daily. In Paris and other cities, private *bureaux de change* are usually open from 09.00 to 18.00, Mondays to Saturdays.

Opening An Account

You can open a bank account in France whether you're a resident or a non-resident (see below). It's best to open a French bank account in person, rather than by correspondence from abroad. Ask your friends, neighbours or colleagues for their recommendations and just go to the bank of your choice and introduce yourself. You must be aged at least 18 and provide proof of identity, e.g. a passport (be prepared to produce other forms of identification), and of your address in France if applicable (an electricity bill usually suffices).

If you wish to open an account with a French bank while you're abroad, you must first obtain an application form, available from overseas branches of French banks (e.g. the Crédit Lyonnais in London, ☎ 020-7758 4000, 🖥 www.creditlyonnais.fr). You need to select a branch from the list provided, which should be close to where you will be living in France. If you open an account by correspondence, you must provide a reference from your current bank, including a certificate of signature or a signature witnessed by a solicitor. You also need a photocopy of the relevant pages of your passport and a euro draft to open the account.

Any account holder can create a joint account by giving his spouse (or anyone else) signatory authority. A joint account can be for two or more people. If applicable, you must state that cheques or withdrawal slips can be signed by any partner and don't require all signatures. Note that in the event of the death of a partner, a joint account is blocked until the will has been proven.

Non-Residents

If you're a non-resident (i.e. spend at least six months per year outside France), you're only entitled to open a non-resident account (*compte non-résident*). There's little difference between non-resident and resident accounts and you can deposit and withdraw funds in any currency without limit, although there may be limits on the amount you can transfer between accounts (an anti-money-laundering measure). Non-resident accounts have a ban on ordinary overdrafts (*découverts*), although loans for a car or house purchase are often possible. Note, however, that banks are increasingly imposing minimum deposit levels on non-resident accounts and you may need €3,000 or more to open one, although it's unlikely that a bank will close an account if your balance subsequently falls below the opening level.

If you're a non-resident with a second home in France it's possible to survive without a French account by using travellers' cheques and credit cards, although this isn't wise and is an expensive option. If you're a non-resident, you can have documentation (e.g. cheque books, statements, etc.) sent to an address abroad.

Residents

You're considered to be a resident of France if you have your main centre of interest there, i.e. you live or work there more or less permanently. To open a resident account you must usually have a residence permit (*carte de séjour*) or evidence that you have a job in France.

Offshore Banking

If you have a sum of money to invest or wish to protect your inheritance from the tax man, it may be worthwhile looking into the accounts and services (such as pensions and trusts) provided by offshore banking centres in 'tax havens' such as the Channel Islands (Guernsey and Jersey), Gibraltar and the Isle of Man (around 50 locations worldwide are officially classified as tax havens). A large number of American, British and other European banks and financial institutions provide offshore banking facilities in one or more locations. Most institutions offer high-interest deposit accounts for long-term savings and investment portfolios, in which funds can be deposited in any major currency. Many people living abroad keep a local account for everyday business and maintain an offshore account for international transactions and investment purposes. Money can be deposited in a variety of currencies, many accounts offer a debit card (e.g. MasterCard or Visa), which can be used to obtain cash via ATMs throughout the world, and most offshore banks also offer telephone banking (usually seven days a week) and internet banking.

SURVIVAL TIP
Most financial experts advise investors not to
rush into the expatriate life and invest their life savings
in an offshore tax haven until they know what their
long-term plans are.

Offshore banking is not 'tax-free' (i.e. you can no longer hide from the taxman by depositing your money in an offshore bank). You must declare your worldwide income to the relevant tax authority (i.e. in France if you're resident there, in another country if you aren't), and a recent EU directive, which comes into force on 1st July 2005, allows governments to exchange personal banking information in an attempt to track down tax evaders, although those of Austria, Belgium and Luxembourg have so far been granted an exemption from this requirement.

Accounts have minimum deposits levels which usually range from £500 to £10,000 ($750 to $15,000), with some as high as £100,000 ($150,000). In addition to large minimum balances, accounts may also have stringent terms and conditions, such as restrictions on withdrawals or high early withdrawal penalties. You can deposit funds on call (instant access) or for a fixed period, e.g. from 90 days to one year (usually for larger sums). Interest is usually paid monthly or annually. Monthly interest payments are slightly lower than annual payments, although they have the advantage of providing a regular income. There are usually no charges provided a specified minimum balance is maintained, but some banks (e.g. those in Andorra, Guernsey, the Isle of Man, Jersey, Liechtenstein, Monaco, San Marino and Switzerland) impose a 15 per cent withholding tax on interest earnings, which is due to be increased to 20 per cent in 2008 and to 35 per cent in 2011.

The new EU measures mean that offshore banking is no longer an effective method of (legally) reducing your tax bill, and you may be better advised to investigate other investment options, such as offshore tursts or insurance bonds.

When selecting any financial institution, your first priority should be for the safety of your money. In some offshore banking centres all bank deposits are guaranteed up to a maximum amount under a deposit protection scheme (the Isle of Man, Guernsey and Jersey all have such schemes). Unless you're planning to bank with a major international bank (which is only likely to fold the day after the end of the world!), you should always check the credit rating of a financial institution before depositing any money, particularly if it doesn't provide deposit insurance. All banks have a credit rating (the highest is 'AAA') and a bank with a high rating will be happy to tell you (but get it in writing). You can also check the rating of an international bank or financial organisation with Moody's Investor Service. You should be wary of institutions offering higher than average interest rates, as if it looks too good to be true it probably will be. Further information about offshore banking can be found via the internet (e.g. 🖳 www.ifap.org.uk, www.lowtax.net, www.moneyfacts. co.uk and www.worldoffshorebanks.com).

MORTGAGES

Mortgages or home loans (*hypothèque*) are available from all major French banks (for both residents and non-residents) and many foreign banks; the French post office will start offering mortgages some time in 2005. It's possible to obtain a foreign currency mortgage, other than in euros, e.g. GB£, Swiss francs or US$.

SURVIVAL TIP
**If you need to obtain a mortgage to buy a home
in France, you should shop around and compare interest
rates, terms and fees (which can be very high) from a
number of banks and financial institutions – not just in
France but also in your home country. Bear in mind that
mortgages in France are generally for a shorter period
than in the UK and US, and therefore your
repayments may be much higher.**

It's generally recognised that you should take out a loan in the currency in which you're paid or in the currency of the country where a property is situated. In this case, if the foreign currency is devalued you will have the consolation of knowing that the value of your French property will have increased by the same percentage when converted back into the foreign currency. When choosing between a euro loan and a foreign currency loan, be sure to take into account all costs, fees, interest rates and possible currency fluctuations.

 You should be extremely wary before taking out a foreign currency mortgage, as interest rate gains can be wiped out overnight by currency swings and devaluations.

However you finance the purchase of a second home in France, you should obtain professional advice from your bank manager and accountant. Most French banks offer euro mortgages on French property through foreign branches in EU and other countries. Most financial advisers recommend borrowing from a large reputable bank rather than a small one. Crédit Agricole is the largest French lender, with a 25 per cent share of the French mortgage market.

Both French and foreign lenders have tightened their lending criteria in the last few years as a result of the repayment problems experienced by many recession-hit borrowers in the early '90s. Some foreign lenders apply stricter rules than French lenders regarding income, employment and the type of property on which they will lend, although some are willing to lend more than a French lender. It can take some foreigners a long time to obtain a mortgage in France, particularly if they have neither a regular income nor assets there. Note also that it can be particularly difficult for a single woman to obtain a mortgage in France. If you have difficulty, you should try a bank that's experienced in dealing with foreigners, such as the Banque Transatlantique (🖥 www.transat.tm.fr).

It's also possible to remortgage or take out a second mortgage on an existing property (see page 198).

Types Of Mortgage

All French mortgages are repaid using the capital and interest method (repayment); endowment and pension-linked mortgages aren't offered.

Interest rates can be fixed or variable, the fixed rate being higher than the variable rate to reflect the increased risk to the lender. The advantage of a fixed rate is that you know exactly how much you must pay over the whole term. Variable rate loans may be fixed for the first two or more years, after which they're adjusted up or down on an annual basis in line with prevailing interest rates, but usually within preset limits, e.g. within 3 per cent of the original rate.

You can usually convert a variable rate mortgage to a fixed rate mortgage at any time. There's normally a redemption penalty, e.g. 3 per cent of the outstanding capital, for early repayment of a fixed rate mortgage, although that isn't usual for variable rate mortgages. If you think you may want to repay early, you should try to have the redemption penalty waived or reduced before signing the agreement.

An alternative to a *hypothèque* is a *privilège de prêteur de deniers* (*PDD*), which is marginally cheaper but has certain restrictions (e.g. you can only take out a *PDD* at the time of purchase and may not take out a *PDD* for more than the purchase price of a property).

Terms & Conditions

It's customary in France for a property to be held as security for a loan taken out on it; in other words, the lender takes a charge on the property. Note, however, that some foreign banks won't lend on the security of a French property.

French law doesn't permit French banks to offer mortgages or other loans where repayments are more than 30 per cent of your net income. Joint incomes and liabilities are included when assessing a couple's borrowing limit (usually a French bank will lend to up to three joint borrowers). Note that the 30 per cent limit includes existing mortgage or rental payments, both in France and abroad. If your total repayments exceed 30 per cent of your income, French banks aren't permitted to extend further credit. Should they attempt to do so, the law allows a borrower to avoid liability for payment.

To calculate how much you can borrow in France, multiply your total net monthly income by 30 per cent and deduct your monthly mortgage, rent and other regular payments. Note that earned income isn't included if you're aged over 65. As a rough guide, repayments on a €60,000 mortgage are around €600 per month at 6 per cent over 15 years. There are special low mortgage rates for low-income property buyers in some departments. In October 2004, the maximum interest rate for a fixed rate mortgage was 7.37 per cent and maximum variable rate interest was 6.89 per cent.

As a condition of a French mortgage, you must take out a life (usually plus health and disability) insurance policy equal to 120 per cent of the amount borrowed. The premiums are included in mortgage payments. An existing insurance policy may be accepted, although it must be assigned to the lender. A medical examination may be required, although this isn't usual if you're under 50 years of age and borrowing less than €150,000.

Note that in France, a borrower is responsible for obtaining building insurance (see page 269) on a property and must provide the lender with a certificate of insurance.

French mortgages are usually limited to 70 or 80 per cent of a property's value (although some lenders limit loans to just 50 per cent). A mortgage can include renovation work, when written quotations must be provided with a mortgage application. Note that you must add expenses and fees, totalling around 10 to 15 per cent of the purchase price on an 'old' property, i.e. one over five years old. For example, if you're buying a property for €75,000 and obtain an 80 per cent mortgage, you must pay a 20 per cent deposit (€15,000) plus 10 to 15 per cent fees (€7,500 to €11,250), making a total of €22,500 to €26,250.

Mortgages can be obtained for any period from 2 to 20 years, although the usual term in France is 15 years (some banks won't lend for longer than this). In certain cases mortgages can be arranged over terms of up to 25 years, although interest rates are higher and a mortgage must usually be paid off before you reach the age of 70 (in some cases 65). Generally the shorter the period of a loan, the lower the interest rate.

All lenders set minimum loans, e.g. €15,000 to €30,000, and some set minimum purchase prices. Usually there's no maximum loan amount, which is subject to status and possibly valuation (usually required by non-French lenders).

In France, a mortgage cannot be transferred from one person to another, as is possible in some countries, but can usually be transferred to another property.

If you fail to maintain your mortgage repayments, your property can be repossessed and sold at auction. However, this rarely happens, as most lenders are willing to arrange lower repayments when borrowers get into financial difficulties.

Procedure

To obtain a mortgage from a French bank, you must produce your passport (or a copy) and those of any joint applicants and provide proof of your monthly income and all out goings such as mortgage payments, rent and other loans or commitments. Proof of income includes three months' pay slips for employees, confirmation of income from your employer and tax returns. If you're self-employed, you require an audited copy of your balance sheets and trading accounts for the past three years, plus your last tax return. French banks aren't particularly impressed with accountants' letters. If you want a French mortgage to buy a property for commercial purposes, you must provide a detailed business plan (in French).

It's possible to obtain agreement in principle to a mortgage, and most lenders will supply a guarantee or certificate valid for two to four months (in some cases subject to valuation of the property), which you can present to the vendor of a property you intend to buy. There may be a commitment fee of around €150, but the deposit paid when signing a preliminary property purchase contract (*compromis de vente*) is protected under French law should you fail to obtain a mortgage.

Once a loan has been agreed, a French bank will send you a conditional offer (*offre préalable*), outlining the terms. In accordance with French law, the offer cannot be accepted until after a 'cooling off' period of ten days. The borrower usually has 30 days to accept the loan and return the signed agreement to the lender. The loan is then held available for four months in the case of a normal purchase; it can be used over a longer period if it's for a building project.

Fees

There are various fees associated with mortgages. All lenders charge an administration fee (*frais de dossier*) for setting up a loan, usually 1 per cent of the loan amount. There's usually a minimum fee, e.g. €350 plus VAT (*TVA*), and there may also be a maximum.

Although it's unusual for buyers to have a survey in France, foreign lenders usually insist on a 'valuation survey' (costing around €250) for French properties before they grant a loan (see **Inspections & Surveys** on page 154).

If a loan is obtained using a French property as security, additional fees and registration costs are payable to the notary (*notaire*) for registering the charge against the property at the *bureau des hypothèques*, which amounts to around 2.5 per cent of the amount borrowed (see **Fees** on page 127).

If you borrow from a co-operative bank (see **Banks** on page 188), you're obliged to subscribe to the capital of the local bank. The amount (number of shares) is decided by the board of directors and you will be sent share certificates (*certificat nominatif de parts sociales*) for that value. The payment (e.g. €75) is usually deducted from your account at the same time as the first mortgage repayment. When the loan has been repaid, the shares are reimbursed (if required).

Note that if you have a foreign currency mortgage or are a non-resident with a euro mortgage, you must usually pay commission charges each time you make a mortgage payment or remit money to France. However, some lenders will transfer mortgage payments to France each month free of charge or for a nominal amount.

If you're buying a new property off plan, when payments are made in stages, a bank will provide a 'staggered' loan, where the loan amount is advanced in instalments as required by the *contrat de réservation*. During the period before completion (*période d'anticipation*), interest is payable on a monthly basis on the amount advanced by the bank (plus insurance). When the final payment has been made and the loan is fully drawn, the mortgage enters its amortisation period (*période d'amortissement*).

Remortgaging

If you have spare equity in an existing property, either in France or abroad, it may be more cost-effective to remortgage (or take out a second mortgage) on that property than to take out a new mortgage for a second home. Depending on the equity in your existing property and the cost of a French property, this may enable you to pay cash for a second home. There may be several advantages to remortgaging, including the following:

● Remortgaging involves less paperwork and therefore lower legal fees.

● You may not require additional life insurance.

● All documentation will be in English.

- You can take advantage of any types of mortgage not available in France (e.g. endowment or pension mortgage) if appropriate.

The disadvantages of remortgaging or taking out a second mortgage on an existing property include the following:

- You may have to pay higher interest rates (e.g. in the UK) than in France.
- If you plan to let the property, you may not be eligible for tax relief on mortgage interest payments in France.
- You reduce the amount of equity available in the property.
- If your mortgage payments are in a non-euro currency and your income is in euros, you put yourself at the mercy of a devaluation in the euro against the foreign currency (although the reverse is true if you take out a euro mortgage and your income is in another currency – see **Importing & Exporting Money** on page 184).

Note also that French lenders are usually reluctant to remortgage.

5.

THE PURCHASE PROCEDURE

This chapter details the purchase procedure for buying a home in France, which is relatively straightforward. Nevertheless, there are pitfalls, and it's wise to employ a lawyer before paying any money or signing a contract and, if necessary, have him check anything you're concerned about regarding a property you're planning to buy (see **Avoiding Problems** on page 20).

CONVEYANCING

Conveyancing (the legal term is conveyance, but conveyancing is more commonly used) is the processing of paperwork involved in buying and selling property and transferring the deeds of ownership. In France, conveyancing is strictly governed by French law and can be performed only by a *notaire* (roughly equivalent to a notary public) authorised by the Ministry of Justice and controlled by the Chambre des Notaires. There are around 5,000 *notaires'* offices (*études*) in France and some 7,500 *notaires*.

A *notaire* can act for a client anywhere in France. He (there are few women *notaires*) must follow a strict code of conduct and have personal insurance covering his professional responsibility and guaranteeing clients against any errors he may make. He also has a financial guarantee covering money temporarily in his safekeeping (such as deposits). A *notaire* represents neither the seller nor the buyer, but the French government, one of his main tasks being to ensure that all state taxes are paid on a sale.

 A *notaire* won't necessarily protect or act in your interests, and you should engage your own lawyer to ensure that everything is carried out to your satisfaction.

Conveyancing includes the following:

● Checking whether the land is registered at the land registry;

● Verifying the identity of the vendor(s) and buyer(s) – see **Civil Status** on page 211;

● Verifying that the property belongs to the vendor or that he has legal authority from the owner to sell it;

● Verfiying that the details of the property match those on the registration documents (see **Registration** on page 217);

● Checking that there aren't any restrictions on the transfer of ownership, e.g. an outstanding mortgage larger than the selling price;

● Verifying that there are no pre-emption rights (*droits de préemption*) or restrictive covenants over a property, such as rights of way, and informing anyone who may have such rights, who has two months in which to claim them (see **Pre-Emption & Business Use** on page 214).

 The local commune may have the right to intervene and prevent the purchase, irrespective of the wishes of the seller or the buyer, and the return of your legal fees and other expenses can be a laborious procedure;

● Obtaining a copy of the local planning rules relating to the property;

● Checking that there are no plans to construct anything which would greatly affect the enjoyment or use of the property (see notes below);

● Checking that the property isn't in a flood zone (the attached *certificat d'urbanisme* should state this);

● Registering the transfer of ownership (and the mortgage if applicable) – see **Registration** on page 217.

A *notaire* **checks only planned developments directly affecting a property itself and not those that may affect its value, such as a new railway line or motorway in the vicinity.** Obviously a new motorway or railway that disturbs the peace of your home would be something of a disaster; on the other hand, a motorway junction or *TGV* station within a few kilometres may enhance its value. Unfortunately, there's no public service in France where you can find out this information, although you can contact the relevant departmental public works department (Direction Départementale de l'Equipement/DDE) and check building projects planned for the area (you may need to speak to people in several departments to find out about different kinds of project!). You could also ask the local residents, particularly the mayor, who usually know of anything planned that would adversely affect a property.

 Even if you make all these checks, a local council may still 'expropriate' your property in order to build a road, school or new houses that will be 'of benefit' to the community!

In France, the vendor's *notaire* traditionally acts for both the vendor and buyer, although a buyer can insist on using his own *notaire*. It doesn't cost a buyer any more to engage his own *notaire*, as the two *notaires* work together and share the same fee. This is misleadingly called a 'competition' (*concurrence*) sale, and only one (the vendor's) can execute the deed. Although some people consider that you should instruct your own *notaire*, this is rarely done, as a *notaire* must remain strictly impartial. One case where it would be prudent to engage your own *notaire* is when the vendor's *notaire* is also the selling agent.

Don't expect a *notaire* to speak English (few do) or any language other than French or to explain the intricacies of French property law, for which you will need to engage a lawyer (see **Legal Advice** on page 208). It's also possible to take out insurance against unforeseen problems arising during a purchase (see **Avoiding Problems** on page 20).

CONTRACTS

The first stage in buying a home in France is the signing of a preliminary contract. The *notaire* is responsible for ensuring that the contract is drawn up correctly and that the purchase price is paid to the vendor.

 The *notaire* doesn't verify or guarantee the accuracy of statements made by the vendor in a contract or protect you against fraud.

There are a number of different types of preliminary contract depending on whether you're buying an existing (built) property or a new property off-plan, i.e. yet to be built or under construction.

Buying An Existing Property

There are various types of preliminary contract (generally called a *contrat de vente* or *contrat de vente sous clauses suspensives* if there are conditional clauses – see page 204) used to buy an existing property:

- *Compromis de Vente* – The most common, most comprehensive and most binding contract, which commits both parties to the sale. With a *compromis de vente*, a buyer is committed from the start and can legally be forced to go through with a purchase. The contract includes full details of the property, the price to be paid, how the purchase is to be financed, details of the vendor and buyer, the agent's commission and who must pay it (if applicable) and the date of completion – usually two months after the signing of the *compromis*. It also states what will happen if either party breaks the contract and includes any conditional clauses (see page 210).

- *Promesse de Vente* – A commitment on the part of the vendor to sell the property at an agreed price allowing the buyer a period (usually up to three months) during which he can withdraw and forfeit his 10 per cent deposit. If you're obliged to use this type of contract, you should ensure that it is carefully worded and includes conditional clauses allowing you to reclaim your deposit if, for example, you're unable to obtain a mortgage (see **Conditional Clauses** on page 210).

- *Promesse d'Achat* – A commitment on the part of the buyer to purchase a property.
- *Offre de Vente* **and** *Offre d'Achat* – An offer to sell and to buy respectively, neither of which is binding on either party unless accepted.

Contracts other than a *compromis de vente* offer little protection to the buyer and should generally be avoided. Note, however, that you may not be able to dictate the type of contract used, which may vary according to the agent or *notaire* handling the sale. Agents and *notaires* usually have their own pre-printed contracts, although all contracts should follow a standard design. Some French agents or *notaires* provide an English translation of a contract, although translations are often so bad as to be meaningless or misleading. You should ensure that you understand **every** clause in the preliminary contract.

You should be given or sent a copy of a preliminary contract signed by you and the vendor, with a notice advising you that a 'cooling-off' period of seven days applies; in other words, you may cancel your agreement within that period without penalty. Should you wish to cancel, you must write to the *notaire* handling the sale, using registered post (*lettre recommandée*) – your cancellation is valid provided you post the letter within the cooling-off period, irrespective of when (or whether!) it arrives. You don't need to give a reason for the cancellation.

If you've paid a deposit, it must be returned to you within 21 days of the date of your cancellation. Note that the right to cancel doesn't apply to the purchase of land for building.

Buying Off Plan

The most common preliminary contract when buying off-plan is a *contrat de réservation* (more correctly called a *contrat préliminaire*). The contract, which must be in writing, contains full details of the property to be built (including a copy of the plans and drawings showing its exact location within a development and whether it's part of a *co-propriété*, the number of rooms and the estimated total habitable area, and the materials to be used in its construction), any services to be provided, the timetable for construction, the price (including any possible variations or additions), a schedule of payments and completion, details of penalties for non-completion and circumstances under which the deposit is to be refunded, and details of any guarantees applicable (see below). The *contrat de réservation* should also confirm that a draft title deed will be given to the buyer at least a month before completion.

The floor plan and technical specifications are signed by both parties to ensure that the standard and size of construction is adhered to. The vendor is referred to as the *réservant* and the buyer as the *réservataire*. Like a *compromis de vente*, a *contrat de réservation* is subject to a cooling-off period of seven days from the date of receipt of a registered letter of notification, which usually accompanies a copy of the signed contract.

The developer should provide one of two types of 'termination' guarantee: a *garantie extrinsèque* or a *garantee intrinsèque*. Both assure you that you'll be provided with any funds necessary to complete the building on time, but in the case of a *garantie extrinsèque* the funds are provided by a bank or other financial institution, whereas with a *garantee intrinsèque* (which is more common) it's the developer himself who must provide them. As the latter provides less security, you shouldn't sign the definitive purchase contract (*acte de vente*) until at least the foundations of the building are finished, whereas with a *garantie extrinsèque* it's usually safe to sign as soon as building permission has been granted.

The definitive contract may be a *contrat à terme*, whereby you undertake to pay for the property once it's finished, or (more commonly) a *contrat en l'état futur d'achèvement*, which transfers ownership progressively as the property is constructed. If the property is to be a *co-propriété*, you should also be given a copy of the rules of the owners' association. See also **Payment** on page 216.

You should, of course, make regular checks (if possible in person) to ensure that everything is going according to plan, although it's unlikely that you will be allowed onto the construction site itself for safety reasons (accompanied site visits are sometimes permitted). When the property is finished, you will have a site meeting to check its condition; you may wish to engage a surveyor or architect to accompany you (see **Inspections & Surveys** on page 154), although this isn't normally necessary, as an independent inspector will already have approved each stage of the construction (you can ask for copies of the inspector's *attestations*).

If you aren't happy with anything, you should make your complaints in writing (known as a *procès-verbal*) and send it to the developer by registered post (*lettre recommandée*); you have 30 days in which to do so. In extreme circumstances, you can refuse to go through with the purchase, in which case a new completion date must be agreed by the developer; failing this, you can take him to court, although this is obviously a last resort.

Various guarantees apply to the finished building and installations such as plumbing and electrical systems (see **Guarantees** on page 172).

CCMI

If you're buying a plot and engaging a builder, you should take out a contract known as a *contrat de construction d'une maison individuelle* (*CCMI*). There are two types of *CCMI*: with and without plans (*fourniture*

du plan). The former might apply when you have plans drawn up by an architect or design the home yourself; the latter applies when the builder draws up his own plans.

As with a *vente en état futur d'achèvement* (see above), the builder must provide a financial guarantee but in this case it must be a *garantie extrinsèque* (i.e. backed by a bank or other financial institution). Stage payments are similar to those made when buying off plan (see page 206).

Legal Advice

The preliminary contract is usually binding on both parties, so it's important to obtain legal advice before signing it. Although it isn't necessary to employ a *notaire* when signing a preliminary contract, it's recommended, as he lends extra legal weight to a deal. Note, however, that a *notaire* won't necessarily protect your rights or interests. A *notaire* will rarely point out possible pitfalls in a contract, proffer advice or volunteer any information (as an estate agent might). If you need additional legal advice, you should employ an experienced lawyer, either locally or in your home country (who must naturally be fluent in French and be an expert in French property law). He must also speak English or a language that you both speak fluently. Employing a lawyer is wise in any case if you don't speak French fluently (even if you do, your understanding of French legal jargon may be limited!).

SURVIVAL TIP
Most experts advise that you have a preliminary contract
checked by a legal adviser before signing it.

One of the main reasons to engage a lawyer is to safeguard your interests through the insertion of any necessary conditional clauses (see page 210) in the preliminary contract, which are of little concern to a *notaire*, and you could employ a lawyer just to check the preliminary contract.

There are various other reasons to employ a lawyer: for example, the best way to buy a property in France is sometimes through a French company (see page 212), or you may wish to make special provisions regarding inheritance (see **Inheritance & Gift Tax** on page 252).

 The method used to buy French property has important consequences, particularly regarding French inheritance laws, and it can be difficult or expensive to correct any errors later.

Before hiring a lawyer, compare the fees charged by a number of practices and get quotations in writing. Check what's included in the fee and whether it's 'full and binding' or just an estimate (a low basic rate may be supplemented by much more expensive 'extras'). A lawyer's fees may be calculated as an hourly rate (e.g. €150 per hour) or a percentage of the purchase price of a property, e.g. 1 to 2 per cent, with a minimum fee of €600 to €1,200. In the case of an off-plan purchase, there may be a basic fee based on the value of the property plus an hourly charge for unforeseen extra work.

Deposit

When you sign the preliminary contract, you must pay a reservation fee (*réservation*) or deposit (*acompte/dépot de garantie*, also known as an *apport personnel*). This is usually 5 per cent when buying a property off-plan and 10 per cent for an existing property. The safest and fastest method of paying the deposit is usually to make a bank-to-bank transfer from your bank to the *notaire*'s or agent's bank account. Note that an estate agent must be bonded to hold clients' monies (see **Estate Agents** on page 116).

If the deposit is described as a *dédit*, the buyer will lose his deposit if he withdraws; similarly, if the vendor defaults, he must pay a penalty equal

to the amount of the deposit. If the deposit is described as *acompte*, neither party can withdraw and the sale can be legally enforced. The deposit is refundable under strict conditions only, notably relating to any conditional clauses such as failure to obtain a mortgage (see below), although it can also be forfeited if you don't complete the transaction within the period specified in the contract, e.g. 90 days. Note that, if you withdraw from a sale after all the conditions have been met, not only will you you lose your deposit but you must also pay the estate agent's commission.

```
                          SURVIVAL TIP
        Make sure you know exactly what the conditions are
          regarding the return or forfeiture of a deposit.
```

Conditional Clauses

All preliminary contracts, whether for old or new properties, contain a number of conditional clauses (*clauses/conditions suspensives*) that must be met to ensure the validity of the contract. Conditions usually apply to events out of control of the vendor or buyer, although almost anything the buyer agrees with the vendor can be included in a preliminary contract. If any of the conditions aren't met, the contract can be suspended or declared null and void, and the deposit returned. However, if you fail to go through with a purchase and aren't covered by a clause in the contract, you will forfeit your deposit or could even be compelled to go through with a purchase. If you're buying anything from the vendor such as carpets, curtains or furniture that are included in the purchase price, you should have them listed and attached as an addendum to the contract. Any fixtures and fittings present in a property when you view it (and agree to buy it) should still be there when you take possession, unless otherwise stated in the contract (see also **Completion** below).

There are many possible conditional clauses concerning a range of subjects, including the following:

● Being able to obtain a mortgage (see below);
● Obtaining planning permission, e.g. for a septic tank;
● Plans to construct anything (e.g. roads, railways, etc.) which would adversely affect the enjoyment or use of the property;
● Confirmation of the land area being purchased with a property;
● Pre-emption rights or restrictive covenants over a property (such as rights of way);
● Dependence on the sale of another property;
● A satisfactory building survey or inspection.

Mortgage Clause

The most common conditional clause states that a buyer is released from the contract should he be unable to obtain a mortgage. This condition is compulsory for all property purchases under the Scrivener Law (*Loi Scrivener*). If you don't intend to obtain a loan, you're expected to endorse the contract to this effect in your own handwriting, meaning that you give up your rights under the law. **This isn't always wise, even when you have no intention of obtaining a mortgage** (you don't have to obtain a mortgage, even if you state that you're going to). If you give up your right to obtain a mortgage and later find that you need one but fail to obtain it, you will lose your deposit.

The mortgage clause should state the amount, term and interest rate expected or already agreed with a lender, plus the lender's name (if known). If you cannot obtain a mortgage for the agreed amount and terms, you won't lose your deposit. You must make an application for the loan within a certain time after signing the contract and have a specified period in which to secure it (e.g. six weeks). **If you're unable to obtain a loan for reasons that could reasonably have been foreseen, you can still lose your deposit.**

Marital Status

Once you've signed the preliminary contract, the *notaire* will need to establish your marital status (*état civil*) before processing a sale. This isn't simply to verify your identity, but also to satisfy French inheritance law. To do this the *notaire* needs to see your passport, birth certificate, marriage or divorce certificate (or if widowed, a death certificate), and a copy of an electricity or telephone bill verifying your permanent residence. If you have a marriage contract, the *notaire* will require a copy or a certified French translation.

If you don't have a contract (e.g. if you were married in the UK), you should say so but specify that your marital status is similar to the French *séparation de biens*, which means that each of you is considered to own assets separately, rather than the French *communauté universelle*, whereby all assets acquired since your marriage are considered to belong to both of you (see **Avoiding Inheritance Tax** on page 254), and a 'transfer clause' (*clause d'attribution*) should be added to the contract.

SURVIVAL TIP
French inheritance law is complicated, and you're strongly advised to take legal advice before deciding in whose name to register a property.

Before registering the title deed of a home, you should carefully consider the tax and inheritance consequences for those in whose name the deed will be registered. Ownership of a French property can be registered in a single name, the joint names of a couple, their children only or in the names of the whole family. In the case of joint names, you must choose between ownership *en division* and ownership *en tontine*, which may have important consequences in the event of the death of one partner, particularly if you haven't made a will. Unmarried and previously married couples must take particular care with regard to inheritance when buying a property jointly in France. See **Avoiding Inheritance & Gift Tax** on page 254.

 However you decide to buy a property, it should be done at the time of purchase as it may be prohibitively expensive (or even impossible) to change it later.

Buying Through A Company

Buying a property through a limited company (which in turn could be owned by an offshore company) has certain advantages and may save you capital gains tax and inheritance tax. However, it may only be worthwhile when a large sum is being invested (e.g. €500,000 or more) or when the buyer has a complicated family or inheritance situation, e.g. an elderly person who's planning to leave a property to a non-relative.

Buying a property in France through a French company such as a *société civile immobilière* (*SCI*) can be beneficial, particularly when two or more people or families are buying jointly or when you wish to circumvent French forced inheritance laws (see page 254). An *SCI* is a fully incorporated company with a registered office in France, which can be the property itself. The *SCI* owns the property (the individuals), and the family members become shareholders in the company. The home owner(s) retain a majority share in the *SCI*, thus giving them control of the company, while the remaining shares can be divided up according to their wishes. As with any property registration, you should consider carefully how you want the shares allocated, as this can affect your tax situation and inheritance.

When a number of foreigners are buying a property together, the *SCI* can be owned by a company in their home country, thus allowing legal disputes to be dealt with under local law. However, an *SCI* is a property holding company and cannot trade, although you will be permitted to let the property, as letting isn't considered a commercial activity in France.

The principal advantages of an *SCI* are that its shares can be simply transferred to new owners and, after the company has been established for three years, stamp duty is lower than with direct transfers of property. On the death of an owner, shares in an *SCI* are treated as movable assets and can be bequeathed in accordance with the owner's domicile, thus avoiding the restrictions of French succession law. In the case of a purchase by a couple, the *SCI* should incorporate a *clause tontine* (see page 255). The use of an *SCI* requires minimal annual bookkeeping, although certain formalities (e.g. the holding of AGMs) must be observed. Owning French property through an *SCI* is of little or no benefit to owners resident in France, however, as many of the advantages don't apply.

There may also be disadvantages to buying through an *SCI*. French inheritance tax (see page 252) applies to the transfer of shares in an *SCI* upon death (assuming that the French property represents at least 50 per cent of the *SCI*'s assets). A property owned under an *SCI* is also subject to French capital gains tax and, if you're a UK citizen, the property may be regarded as a 'benefit in kind', irrespective of how long you spend in it, in which case you would be taxed in the UK at 7 per cent of its market value. Note also that if you let a property owned by an *SCI*, it may be necessary to pay a higher rate of tax on the rental income.

If you plan to own a property through an *SCI*, it should be done at the outset, as it will be much more expensive to do it later (e.g. attracting transfer tax at 4.89 per cent plus *notaire*'s fees). The costs of establishing an *SCI* are around €1,500 to €3,000 in addition to the normal fees. You should also ensure that you declare the company to the tax authorites immediately; otherwise, you could face a 3 per cent tax on foreign companies owning property in France.

Other options are to purchase a property through a French trading company (which may be advantageous if you plan to generate an income, although set-up costs are high) or a foreign or offshore company. Setting up an offshore company can cost around €1,000 plus a similar annual 'maintenance' fee. Buying a French property through a foreign or offshore company can result in being hit by various punitive French taxes and it may also incur high management fees. Yet another purchase option is to set up a trust, although these aren't recognised in France and it may be necessary for the trust to own the property through a limited company.

Further information and advice (in English) regarding house purchase through a company can be obtained from specialist financial advisers with experience of French regulations, such as Anthony & Cie, 06560 Valbonne (☎ 04 93 65 32 23, ⌨ www.antco.com) and, in the UK, Blake Lapthorn Linnell, Holbrook House, 14 Great Queen street, London WC2B 5DG (☎ 020-7421 1632, ⌨ www.bllaw.co.uk).

SURVIVAL TIP
Before buying through an *SCI* or any other company,
it's important to weigh up the long-term advantages and
disadvantages and to obtain expert legal advice.

Pre-Emption & Business Use

If the plot on which a property is built or the land which is sold with a property is over 2,500m² (0.25 hectares/around half an acre), the Fédération Nationale des Sociétés d'Aménagement Foncier et d'Etablissement Rural (FNSAFER – see page 152) must give permission for the sale according to the 'pre-emption' law (*loi de préemption*). This is usually a formality unless you're contemplating buying a farm, a large estate or a vineyard.

It's necessary to inform the *notaire* handling the sale if you're planning to operate a commercial business from a property within three years of its purchase, as this will increase the taxes payable on completion.

COMPLETION

Completion (or closing) is the name for the transfer of legal ownership to the purchaser, involving the signing of the final deed (*acte de vente* or *acte authentique*), the date of which is usually 10 to 12 weeks after the signing of the preliminary contract and is specified in the preliminary contract (although it may be 'moveable'). When all the necessary documents concerning a purchase have been returned to the *notaire*, he will contact the buyer and request the balance of the purchase price less the deposit and, if applicable, the amount of a mortgage. He will also send you a bill for his fees and all taxes, which must be paid on completion.

At the same time, the *notaire* should also send you a draft deed of sale (*projet de l'acte de vente*). If he doesn't, you should request one. This should be complete and shouldn't contain any blank spaces to be filled in later. If you don't understand the deed of sale, you should have it checked by your legal adviser. Note that it's a legal requirement in France that properties are insured against third party risks on completion and the *notaire* will ensure that this is done.

Final Checks

Property is sold on the condition that the buyer accepts it in the state it's in at the time of completion, so you should be aware of anything that occurs between the signing of the preliminary contract and completion. It isn't unknown for vendors to dig up the entire garden, for example.

 Before signing the deed of sale, it's imperative to check that the property hasn't fallen down or been damaged in any way, e.g. by a storm or the owners.

If you've employed a lawyer or are buying through an agent, he should accompany you on this visit. You should also do a final inventory immediately prior to completion (the previous owner should have already vacated the property) to ensure that the vendor hasn't absconded with anything that was included in the price.

You should have an inventory of the fixtures and fittings and anything that was included in the contract or purchased separately, e.g. carpets, light fittings, curtains or kitchen appliances, and check that they're present and in working order. This is particularly important if furniture and furnishings (and major appliances) were included in the price. You should also ensure that expensive items (e.g. kitchen apparatus) haven't been replaced by inferior ones. Any fixtures and fittings (and garden plants and shrubs) present in a property when you viewed it should still be there when you take possession, unless otherwise stated in the contract. It's quite common for French vendors to remove not only light bulbs, but the bulb-holders and ceiling roses as well (see **Electricity** on page 327)!

If you find that anything is missing, damaged or isn't in working order, you should make a note and insist on immediate restitution such as an appropriate reduction in the amount to be paid. In such cases it's normal for the *notaire* to withhold an appropriate amount in escrow from the vendor's proceeds to pay for repairs or replacements. **You should refuse to go through with the completion if you aren't completely satisfied, as it will be difficult or impossible to obtain redress later.** If it isn't possible to complete the sale, you should consult your lawyer about your rights and the return of your deposit and any other funds already paid.

Signing

The signing of the deed of sale (*acte de vente*) takes place in the *notaire*'s office. Before the deed of sale is signed, the *notaire* checks that all the conditions contained in the preliminary contract have been fulfilled. It's normal for both parties to be present when the deed of sale is read, signed and witnessed by the *notaire*, although either party can give a representative power of attorney (*procuration*). This is quite common among foreign buyers and sellers and can be arranged by your *notaire*. **If a power of attorney is arranged outside France, it must be signed and authenticated before a public notary abroad.**

The *notaire* reads through the *acte de vente* and both the vendor and buyer must initial each page and sign the last page after writing, in French, *bon pour accord*, which means that they've understood and accept the terms of the document. The *notaire* is supposed to seek the assistance of an English (or other) translator if either party doesn't understand sufficient French, although this is rare and you should be prepared to do so yourself.

Payment

The balance of the price after the deposit and any mortgages are subtracted must be paid on completion. The money can be transferred directly to the *notaire*'s bank account, which can be done by a bank-to-bank transfer. However, it's important to allow sufficient time for the funds to be transferred (see **Importing & Exporting Money** on page 184). Alternatively, you can pay by banker's draft, which is probably the best method, as you will have it in your possession (a bank cannot lose it!) and the *notaire* can confirm payment immediately. It also allows you to withhold payment if there's a last minute problem (see **Final Checks** above) that cannot be resolved.

Note that, when the vendor and buyer are of the same foreign nationality, they can agree that the balance is paid in a currency other than euros (e.g. £sterling), although the *notaire* must also agree to this. In this case, the money should be held by a lawyer in the vendor's and buyer's home country. After paying the money and receiving a receipt, the *notaire* gives you an *attestation de propriété*, which certifies that you're the owner of the property. You will also receive the keys!

Buying Off Plan

In an off-plan purchase, payments are spread over 12 to 18 months; payment schedules vary, although there are legal limits to the amount that can be requested at each stage. A typical schedule is shown below:

Stage	Payment
Initial deposit	5%
Completion of foundations	30%
Completion of roof (waterproofing)	30%
Connection of water and services	5%
Completion of internal walls	10%
Tiling and completion of wall surfaces	10%
Completion	5%
Delivery of keys	5%

If completion isn't planned for at least two years, the initial deposit (*dépôt de garantie*) is 2.5 per cent. The final 5 per cent may be retained by the buyer if there are any defects still to be rectified or there's a dispute over fulfilment of the contract. The *notaire*'s fees are usually paid on completion of the foundations.

Registration

There are no title deeds as such in France and proof of ownership is provided and guaranteed by registration of the property (*titre de propriétaire*) at the land registry (*cadastre*). The land registry's stamp is placed on the deed of sale, a certified copy (*expédition*) of which is given to the buyer by the *notaire* two to six months after completion of the sale along with a statement and final bill (usually a small refund!) for the *notaire*'s fees. If you have a mortgage, the deed is also registered at the *bureau des hypothèques* ('mortgage office'). The original deed is retained indefinitely by the *notaire*.

Note also that you will need to transfer services into your name as soon as possible after the deed is signed.

6.

MOVING HOUSE

Moving into your new French home is the culmination of your dreams; it can also be a highly stressful experience. However, it's possible to limit the strain on your mental and physical health by careful planning and preparation. This chapter contains checklists that should help to ensure that you don't forget anything important.

SHIPPING YOUR BELONGINGS

It usually takes just a few days to have your belongings shipped from other parts of continental Europe or the UK. From anywhere else the time varies considerably, e.g. around four weeks from the east coast of America, six weeks from the US west coast or the Far East, and around eight weeks from Australasia. Customs clearance is no longer necessary when shipping your household effects from one European Union (EU) country to another. However, when shipping your effects from a non-EU country to France, you should enquire about customs formalities in advance. If you fail to follow the correct procedure, you can encounter numerous problems and delays and may be charged duty or fined.

The relevant forms to be completed by non-EU citizens depend on whether your French home will be your main residence or a second home. Removal companies usually take care of the paperwork and ensure that the correct documents are provided and properly completed (see **Customs** on page 224). Major international moving companies usually also provide a wealth of information and can advise on a wide range of matters concerning an international relocation. Check (with a local embassy or consulate) the current procedure for shipping your belongings to France.

It's wise to use a major shipping company with a good reputation. For international moves it's best to use a company that's a member of the International Federation of Furniture Removers (FIDI) or the Overseas Moving Network International (OMNI), with experience in France. Members of FIDI and OMNI usually subscribe to an advance payment scheme providing a guarantee: if a member company fails to fulfil its commitments to a client, the removal is completed at the agreed cost by another company or your money is refunded. Some removal companies have subsidiaries or affiliates in France, which may be more convenient if you encounter problems or need to make an insurance claim.

You should obtain at least three written quotations before choosing a company, as costs vary considerably. Moving companies should send a representative to provide a detailed quotation. Most companies will pack your belongings and provide packing cases and special containers, although this is naturally more expensive than packing them yourself. Ask a company how fragile and valuable items are packed and whether the cost of packing cases, materials and insurance (see below) is included in a quotation. If you're doing your own packing, most shipping companies will provide packing crates and boxes. Shipments are charged by volume, e.g. the square metre in Europe and the square foot in the US. You should expect to pay from €4,000 to €7,000 to move the contents of a three to four-bedroom house within western Europe, e.g. from London to the south of France.

If you're flexible about the delivery date, shipping companies will quote a lower fee based on a 'part load', where the cost is shared with other deliveries. This can result in savings of 50 per cent or more compared with an individual delivery. Whether you have an individual or shared delivery, obtain the maximum transit period in writing, otherwise you may need to wait months for delivery!

Be sure to fully insure your belongings during removal with a well established insurance company. Don't insure with a shipping company that carries its own insurance, as its rates are usually high and it may fight every *centime* of a claim. Insurance premiums are usually 1 to 2 per cent of the declared value of your goods, depending on the type of cover chosen. It's prudent to make a photographic or video record of valuables for insurance purposes.

Most insurance policies provide cover for 'all risks' on a replacement value basis. Note that china, glass and other breakables can usually be included in an all-risks policy only when they're packed by the removal company. Insurance usually covers total loss or loss of a particular crate only, rather than individual items (unless they were packed by the shipping company). If there are any breakages or damaged items, they must be noted and listed before you sign the delivery bill (although it's obviously impractical to check everything on delivery).

If you need to make a claim, be sure to read the small print, as some companies require clients to make a claim within a few days, although seven is usual. Send a claim by registered post. Some insurance companies apply an 'excess' of around 1 per cent of the total shipment value when assessing claims. This means that if your shipment is valued at €30,000 and you make a claim for less than €300, you won't receive anything.

If you're unable to ship your belongings direct to France, most shipping companies will put them into storage and some allow a limited free storage period prior to shipment, e.g. 14 days, after which you may be charged between €40 and €80 per month for an average container, excluding insurance, although prices (and the quality of storage facilities) vary greatly.

 If you need to put your household effects into storage, it's imperative to have them fully insured, as warehouses have been known to burn down!

Make a complete list of everything to be moved and give a copy to the removal company. Don't include anything illegal (e.g. guns, bombs or drugs) with your belongings, as customs checks can be rigorous and penalties severe.

Provide the shipping company with **detailed** instructions of how to find your French address from the nearest main road and a telephone number where you can be contacted. If your French home has poor or impossible access for a large truck you must inform the shipping company (the ground must also be firm enough to support a heavy vehicle). Note also that, if furniture needs to be taken in through an upstairs window, you may need to pay extra. You should also make a simple floor plan of your new home with rooms numbered and mark corresponding numbers on furniture and boxes as they're packed, so that the removal company will know where everything is to go and you can leave them to it.

After considering the shipping costs, you may decide to ship only selected items of furniture and personal effects and buy new furniture in France. If you're importing household goods from another European country, you can rent a self-drive van or truck (but bear in mind that you may need to return the van to where you hired it from).

If you plan to transport your belongings to France personally, check the customs requirements in the countries you must pass through. Generally, it isn't wise to do your own move unless it's a simple job, e.g. a few items of furniture and personal effects only. It's no fun heaving beds and wardrobes up stairs and squeezing them into impossible spaces. If you're taking pets with you, you may need to ask your vet to tranquillise them, as many pets are frightened (even more than people) by the chaos and stress of moving house.

If you're moving permanently to France, take the opportunity to sell, give away or throw out at least half of your possessions. It will cut down your removal bill, clear your mind, and make life simpler, plus you will have the fun of buying new furniture that really suits your new house.

Bear in mind when moving home that everything that can go wrong often does, so allow plenty of time and try not to arrange your move from your old home on the same day as the new owner is moving in; that's just asking for fate to intervene! See also **Pets** on page 48, **Customs** on page 224 and the **Checklists** on page 232.

PRE-DEPARTURE HEALTH CHECK

If you're planning to take up residence in France, even for part of the year only, it's wise to have a health check (including general health, eyes, teeth, etc.) before your arrival, particularly if you have a record of poor health or are elderly. If you're already taking medicine regularly, you should note that the brand names of drugs and medicines vary from country to country, and should ask your doctor for the generic name (see page 47).

IMMIGRATION

France is a signatory to the Schengen agreement, which means that, if you arrive in France from another Schengen country (currently Austria, Belgium, France, Germany, Greece, Iceland, Italy, Luxembourg, the Netherlands, Portugal, Spain and Sweden), there are usually no immigration checks or passport controls (although France invoked a special 'safeguard' clause in the Schengen agreement to preserve frontier controls because of fears over illegal immigration and cross-border drug trafficking).

If you arrive from a non-Schengen country, you must go through immigration (*police des frontières*) for non-EU citizens. **If you require a visa to enter France and attempt to enter without one, you will be refused entry** (see page 32). If you have a single-entry visa, it will be cancelled by the immigration official. If you think you will need to prove your date of entry (e.g. if your visa is valid for a limited period), you should obtain a declaration of entry (*déclaration d'entrée sur le territoire*).

Immigration officials may ask non-EU visitors to produce a return ticket, proof of accommodation, health insurance and financial resources (e.g. cash, traveller's cheques and credit cards). If you're a non-EU national coming to France to work, study or live, you may be asked to show documentary evidence (see page 35). The onus is on visitors to show that they won't violate French law. Immigration officials aren't required to prove that you will breach the law and can refuse you entry on the grounds of suspicion only. Young people may be more susceptible to interrogation, especially ones with 'strange' attire, and should therefore carry international credit or charge cards, a return or onward travel ticket, a student identity card, and a letter from an employer or college stating that they're on holiday.

All foreigners intending to remain in France for longer than 90 days must register with the local authorities within a week of arrival and obtain a residence permit. EU nationals who visit France with the intention of finding employment or starting a business have 90 days in which to find a job. Once employment has been found, an application must be made for a residence permit. If you don't have a regular income or adequate financial resources, your application will be refused. Failure to apply for a residence permit within 90 days is a serious offence and may result in a fine. For further information see **Residence Permits** on page 36.

French immigration officials are usually polite and efficient, although they're occasionally a little over-zealous in their attempts to exclude illegal immigrants.

CUSTOMS

The shipment of personal (household) effects to France from another EU country isn't subject to customs formalities, although an inventory must be provided. Note, however, that those arriving in France from outside the EU (including EU citizens) are subject to customs checks and limitations on what may be imported duty-free. There are no restrictions on the import or export of French or foreign banknotes or securities, although if you enter or leave France with €10,000 or more in cash or 'negotiable instruments' (see page 184), you must make a declaration to French customs.

Information about duty-free allowances can be found on page 313 and pets on page 48. If you require general information about French customs regulations or have specific questions, contact the Centre des Renseignements Douaniers, 84 rue d'Hauteville, 75498 Paris Cedex 10 (☎ 08 25 30 82 63, 🖥 www.douane.gouv.fr – in English). Specific written questions should be addressed to your regional customs office. The website lists local and regional customs office addresses.

Visitors

Visitors' belongings aren't subject to duty or VAT (*TVA*) and may be imported without formality when they're visiting France for up to 90 days, provided their nature and quantity doesn't imply any commercial aim. This applies to the import of private cars, camping vehicles (including trailers or caravans), motorcycles, aircraft, boats (see below) and personal effects. All means of transport and personal effects imported duty-free mustn't be sold, loaned or given away in France and must be re-exported before the end of the 90-day period.

If you enter France by road you may drive (at a walking pace) through the border without stopping. However, any goods and pets that you're carrying mustn't be the subject of any prohibition or restriction (see page 226). Customs officials may stop anyone for a spot check, e.g. for drugs or illegal immigrants. If you enter France from Spain – particularly if you're a single male in an old car – your vehicle is likely to be searched and 'inspected' by a sniffer dog. Occasionally you will come across an obstructive customs officer who will insist on inspecting everything in your car, and unfortunately there's nothing you can do to prevent him.

If you arrive at a seaport by private boat, there are no particular customs formalities, although you must show the boat's registration papers if asked. If you arrive at a river port or land border with a boat, you may be asked to produce registration papers for the boat and its outboard motor(s). A foreign-registered boat may remain in France for a maximum of six months in a calendar year, after which it must be re-exported or permanently imported (and duty and tax paid).

Non-EU Nationals

If you're a non-EU national planning to take up permanent or temporary residence in France, you're permitted to import your furniture and personal effects free of duty. These include vehicles, mobile homes, pleasure boats and aircraft. However, to qualify for duty-free importation, articles must have been owned and used for at least six months. Value added tax must be paid on items owned for less than six months that weren't purchased within the EU. If goods were purchased within the EU, a VAT receipt must be produced.

To import personal effects, an application must be made to the Direction régionale des Douanes in the area where you will be resident. Customs clearance can be carried out by a customs office in an internal town in France, rather than at the border, in which case you should obtain a certificate (*carte de libre circulation*) proving that you've declared your belongings on entry into France and are entitled to travel with them.

All items should be imported within a year of the date of your change of residence, either in one or in a number of consignments, although it's best to have one consignment only. After a year's residence in France, you must pay French VAT on further imports from outside the EU, except in certain circumstances, such as property resulting from an inheritance. A complete inventory of items to be imported (even if they're imported in a number of consignments) must be provided for customs officials, together with proof of residence in your former country and proof of settlement in France. If there's more than one consignment, subsequent consignments should be cleared through the same customs office.

If you use a removal company to transport your belongings to France, they will usually provide the necessary forms and take care of the paperwork. Many of the forms are now available online, either through the Customs website (🖳 www.douane.gouv.fr) or by following the links on the Service Public site (🖳 www.service-public.fr). If the removal company packs your belongings, ask them to mark the containers 'Mover Packed'; this will speed the customs clearance process.

Always keep a copy of forms and communications with customs officials, both French customs officials and those in your previous or permanent country of residence. You should have an official record of the export of valuables from any country in case you wish to re-import them later.

Prohibited & Restricted Goods

Certain goods are subject to special regulations, and in some cases their import (and export) is prohibited or restricted. This applies in particular to animal products, plants (see below), wild fauna and flora and products derived from them, live animals, medicines and medical products (except for prescribed medicines), firearms and ammunition, certain goods and technologies with a dual civil/military purpose, and works of art and collectors' items. If you're unsure whether any goods you're importing fall into the above categories, you should check with French customs.

To import certain types of plant into France, you must obtain a phytosanitary health certificate (*certificat sanitaire*). Information can be obtained from the Service de la Protection des Végétaux, 175 rue du Chevaleret, 75646 Paris Cedex 13 (☎ 01 45 84 13 13) or your country's customs department.

If you make it through customs unscathed with your car loaded to the gunwales with illicit goods, don't be too quick to break out the champagne in celebration. France has 'flying' customs officials (*douane volante*) with the power to stop and search vehicles at random anywhere within its borders (they often stop vehicles at motorway toll stations and roundabouts on trunk roads).

REGISTRATION

All foreigners intending to remain in France for longer than 90 days must register with the local authorities within a week of arrival and obtain a residence permit. EU nationals who visit France with the intention of finding employment or starting a business have 90 days in which to find a job. Once employment has been found, an application must be made for a residence permit. **Failure to apply for a residence permit within 90 days is a serious offence and may result in a fine.** For further information see **Residence Permits** on page 36.

Nationals of some countries are recommended to register with their local embassy or consulate after taking up residence in France. Registration isn't usually compulsory, although most embassies like to keep a record of their country's citizens resident in France (it helps them to justify their existence).

FINDING HELP

One of the biggest difficulties facing new arrivals in France is how and where to find help with day-to-day problems, particularly as many administrative matters are handled at a regional, departmental or even local level rather than nationally. How successful you are at finding local information depends on your employer, the town or area where you live (e.g. residents of Paris are better served than those living in rural areas), your nationality, French proficiency (there's an abundance of information available in French, but little in English and other foreign languages) and to some extent your sex (women are better served than men through numerous women's clubs). An additional problem is that much of the available information isn't intended for foreigners and their particular needs. Nevertheless, you should exploit the following sources of local information.

Company

Some companies employ staff to help new arrivals or contract this job out to a relocation consultant. However, most French employers are totally unaware of (or uninterested in) the problems and difficulties faced by foreign employees and their families.

Colleagues & Friends

Note that in France it isn't what you know, but who you know that can make all the difference between success or failure. String-pulling or the use of contacts is widespread in France and is invaluable when it comes to breaking through the numerous layers of bureaucracy, when a telephone call on your behalf from a French neighbour or colleague can work wonders. In fact any contact can be of help, even a professional acquaintance, who may not even charge you for his time. **But take care!** Although work colleagues and friends (either existing or new) can often offer advice based on their own experiences and mistakes and invariably mean well, you're likely to receive as much false and conflicting information as accurate (it may not necessarily be wrong but may be invalid for your particular situation).

Local Community

Your local community is usually an excellent source of reliable information, but you usually need to speak French to benefit from it. Your town hall (*mairie*) is often the local registry of births, deaths and marriages, passport office, land registry, council office, citizens' advice bureau and tourist office.

Embassy Or Consulate

Most embassies and consulates provide their nationals with local information including details of lawyers, interpreters, doctors, dentists, schools, and social and expatriate organisations. The American Embassy also has a particularly good website (🖥 www.amb-usa.fr), which includes quite a bit of information (in English!) about practical living in France, including lists of English-speaking professionals, from doctors to private investigators. Much of the information comes from their popular *Blue Book*, which can be obtained directly from the US Embassy, 2 rue Saint Florentin, 75001 Paris (☎ 01 43 12 23 47).

Expatriate Organisations

There's usually at least one English-language expatriate organisation in French cities; in Paris foreigners are well served by English-speaking clubs and organisations and there are several Anglophone organisations in the Bordeaux area. Contacts can be found through many expatriate magazines and newspapers (see **Appendix B**). In Paris, the American Church (65 quai d'Orsay, 75007 Paris, ☎ 01 40 62 05 00, 🖥 www.acparis.org), runs an annual newcomer's orientation series in October called 'Bloom Where You Are Planted'. The programme is designed to help foreigners adjust to life in France and consists of seminars on topics such as overcoming culture shock, survival skills, personal and professional opportunities, networking, enjoying France, food, fashion, travel and wine.

WICE (20 boulevard du Montparnasse, 75015 Paris, ☎ 01 45 66 75 50, ▣ www.wice-paris.org), an anglophone expatriate organisation, also operates a 'Living in France' programme for newcomers, as do expatriate clubs and organisations throughout France. The British Community Committee publishes a free Digest of British and Franco-British Clubs, Societies and Institutions, available from British consulates in France (see **Appendix A**).

An organisation offering bespoke directories of local information is Purple Pages, Grosbout, 16240 La Forêt de Tessé, France (☎ 05 45 29 59 74) or Bridge Chambers, High Street, Welwyn, Herts AL6 9EQ, UK (☎ 0871-425 4305, ▣ www.purplepages.info). Directories covering the Poitou-Charentes region and the departments of Dordogne, Lot and Lot-et-Garonne are available in book form under the series title *Lifeline* (Survival Books – see page 389); other titles in the series, covering Brittany, Normandy and Provence, are planned. Further details of local and regional organisations are contained in *The Best Places to Buy a Home in France* (Survival Books – see page 389).

AVF

An organisation of particular interest to foreigners moving to France is the Union nationale des Accueils des Villes Françaises (AVF). The AVF is a national organisation comprising over 600 local volunteer associations who provide a welcome for individuals and families and help them to settle into their new environment. Each association operates an information centre where information and advice is available free of charge. The address of local associations in France can be found via Minitel (3615 AVF-ACCUEIL) terminals at any post office or on their website (▣ www.avf-accueil.com), where some information is available in English and there's a list of groups in each department as well as details such as whether information and services are available in English. Groups often have at least one fluent English-speaker. Foreigners planning to move to France can obtain information about particular areas from the Union Nationale des AVF, Relations Internationales, Secrétariat Administratif, 3 rue de Paradis, 75010 Paris (☎ 01 47 70 45 85, ▣ www.avf.asso.fr). Write to them indicating the town, department and region where you're planning to live and the reason for moving to France, e.g. work, retirement, study or training.

CIRA

If you don't know which administrative department to contact for particular information (which is often the case in France), you can ask your local Centre Interministériel de Renseignements Administratifs (CIRA). CIRA is a 'pan-governmental' organisation, which can answer questions on a range of subjects, including employment, finance, accommodation, health, consumer affairs, the environment and education. There are nine information centres, whose telephone numbers are listed under *Les infos administratives: justice* at the front of the yellow pages, on the Service Public website, 🖳 www.service-public.fr, and on Minitel (3615 VOSDROITS).

Publications

A useful reference book is the *Guide des Sources d'Information*, published by the Centre de Formation et de Perfectionnement des Journalistes (CFPJ), which will direct you to a variety of information sources.

The Disabled

Disabled people can obtain advice and help from the Association des Paralysés de France (☎ 01 40 78 69 00, 🖳 www.apf.asso.fr), which isn't only for those who are paralysed, the Association pour Adultes et Jeunes Handicappés (APAJH), 26 rue du Chemin vert, 75541 Paris Cedex 11 (☎ 01 48 07 25 88) and the Fédération Nationale des Accidentés de Travail et des Handicappés, 20 rue Tarentaize, BP 520, 42007 Saint-Etienne Cedex 1 (☎ 04 77 49 42 42, 🖳 www.fnath.org). Disabled people looking for work or employment-related information should contact the Association Gestion du Fonds d'Insertion Personnes Handicappées/ AGEFIPH (🖳 www.agefiph.asso.fr, which provides contact details for the 18 regional associations).

If you're seriously and permanently disabled, you should apply to the Commission Technique d'Orientation et de Reclassement professionel (COTOREP) for an invalidity card (*carte d'invalidité civile*), which entitles you to a number of benefits.

MOVING IN

One of the most important tasks to perform after moving into a new home is to make an inventory of the fixtures and fittings and, if applicable, the furniture and furnishings. When you've purchased a property, you should check that the previous owner hasn't absconded with any fixtures and fittings which were included in the price or anything that you specifically paid for, e.g. carpets, light fittings, curtains, furniture, kitchen appliances, garden ornaments, plants or doors (see **Completion** on page 214). It's common to do a final check or inventory when buying a new property, which is usually done a few weeks before completion.

When moving into a long-term rental property it's necessary to complete an inventory (*inventaire détaillé/état des lieux*) of its contents and a report on its condition. This includes the condition of fixtures and fittings, the state of furniture and furnishings, the cleanliness and state of the decoration, and anything that's damaged, missing or in need of repair. An inventory should be provided by your landlord or agent and may include every single item in a furnished property (even the number of teaspoons).

The inventory check should be carried out in your presence, both when taking over and when terminating a rental agreement. If an inventory isn't provided, you should insist on one being prepared and annexed to the lease. If you find a serious fault after signing the inventory, send a registered letter to your landlord and ask for it to be attached to the inventory.

The inventory can be drawn up (for around €150) by a *huissier*, who's an official (similar to a bailiff) authorised to prepare factual legal documents. If the inventory is prepared by a *huissier*, you have a better chance of resolving any disputes, as his evidence is indisputable in a court of law. An inventory should be drawn up both when moving into (*état des lieux d'entrée*) and when vacating (*état des lieux de sortie*) a rented property. If the two inventories don't correspond, you must make good any damages or deficiencies or the landlord can do so and deduct the cost from your deposit. Although French landlords are generally no worse than those in most other countries, some will do almost anything to avoid repaying a deposit. Note the reading on your utility meters (e.g. electricity, gas, water) and check that you aren't overcharged on your first bill. The meters should be read by utility companies before you move in, although you may need to organise it yourself.

It's wise to obtain written instructions from the previous owner concerning the operation of appliances, heating and air-conditioning systems, maintenance of grounds, gardens and lawns and swimming pool, care of special surfaces such as wooden or marble floors, and the names of reliable local maintenance men who know the property and are familiar with its quirks. Check with your local town hall regarding local regulations of such things as rubbish collection, recycling and on-road parking.

Finally, don't expect your new neighbours to come round with a casserole! Remember that it takes time to get to know the French.

Nevertheless, you should introduce yourselves to neighbours at the earliest opportunity – even if your French is basic.

CHECKLISTS

When moving permanently to France, there are many things to be considered and a 'million' people to be informed. Even if you plan to spend just a few months a year in France, it may be necessary to inform a number of people and companies in your home country. The checklists below are designed to make the task easier and help prevent an ulcer or a nervous breakdown (provided, of course, you don't leave everything to the last minute). Note that not all points are applicable to non-residents or those who spend only a few weeks each year in France.

Before Arrival

The following are tasks that should be completed (if possible) before your arrival in France:

● Check that your and your family's passports are valid.

● Obtain a visa, if necessary, for you and your family members (see page 32). Obviously this **must** be done before arrival in France.

● Arrange inoculations and shipment for any pets that you're taking with you (see page 48).

● Visit France before your move to compare schools and to arrange schooling for your children.

● If you live in rented accommodation, give your landlord adequate notice (check your contract).

● Arrange to sell or dispose of anything you aren't taking with you, e.g. house, car and furniture. If you're selling a home or business, you should obtain expert legal advice, as you may be able to save tax by establishing a trust or other legal vehicle. Note that if you own more than one property, you may have to pay capital gains tax on any profits from the sale of second and subsequent homes.

● Arrange shipment of your furniture and belongings by booking a shipping company well in advance (see page 220).

● Before exporting a car to France, complete the relevant paperwork required by your current vehicle licensing authority (e.g. the DVLA in the UK).

- Arrange health insurance for yourself and your family (see page 263). This is essential if you aren't covered by a private insurance policy and won't be covered by French social security.

- Check whether you need an international driving licence or a translation of your national driving licence(s). Note that some foreigners are required to take a driving test before they can buy and register a car in France.

- Open a bank account in France (see page 191) and transfer funds (see page 184). Give the details to any companies that you plan to pay by standing order (e.g. utility companies).

- If you're exporting a car, you will need to complete the relevant paperwork in your home country and re-register it locally after your arrival. Contact your local French embassy or consulate for information.

- Check whether you're entitled to a rebate on your road tax, car and other insurance. Obtain a letter from your motor insurance company stating your no-claims discount.

- You may qualify for a rebate on your tax and social security contributions. If you're leaving a country permanently and have been a member of a company or state pension scheme, you may be entitled to a refund or be able to continue payments to qualify for a full (or larger) pension when you retire. Contact your company personnel office, local tax office or pension company for information.

- It's wise to arrange health, dental and optical check-ups for your family before you leave your home country. Also, obtain a copy of any health records and a statement from your private health insurance company stating your present level of cover.

- Terminate outstanding loan, lease or hire purchase contracts and pay all bills (allow plenty of time, as some companies are slow to respond).

- Return any library books and anything borrowed.

- If you don't already have one, it's wise to obtain an international credit or charge card, which may be useful during your first few months in France, particularly until you've opened a bank account. Note, however, that credit cards are not universally accepted in France.

- Don't forget to bring all your family's official documents, including birth certificates, driving licences, marriage certificate, divorce papers or death certificate (if a widow or widower), educational diplomas, professional certificates and job references, school records and student ID cards, employment references, copies of medical and dental records, bank account and credit card details, insurance policies and receipts for any valuables. You will also need the documents necessary to obtain a residence permit (see page 36) plus certified copies, official translations and numerous passport-size photographs (students should take at least a dozen).

- Inform the following people:

  - Your employer, e.g. give notice or arrange leave of absence, or clients if you're self-employed;

  - Your town hall or municipality (you may be entitled to a refund of your local property or income taxes);

  - The police, if it was necessary to register with them in your home country (or present country of residence);

  - Your electricity, gas, water and telephone companies (contact companies well in advance, particularly if you need to have a deposit refunded);

  - Your insurance companies (e.g. health, car, home contents and private pension), banks, post office (if you have a post office account), stockbroker and other financial institutions, credit card, charge card and hire purchase companies, lawyer and accountant, and local businesses where you have accounts;

  - Your family doctor, dentist and other health practitioners (health records should be transferred to your new doctor and dentist abroad, if applicable);

  - Your children's schools (try to give a term's notice and obtain a copy of any relevant school reports or records from your children's current schools);

  - All regular correspondents, social and sports clubs, professional and trade journals, friends and relatives (give them your new address and telephone number and arrange to have your mail redirected by the post office or a friend);

  - Your local or national vehicle registration office if you have a driving licence or car (return your registration plates if applicable);

- If you will be living in France for an extended period (but not permanently), you may wish to give someone 'power of attorney' over your financial affairs in your home country so that he can act for you in your absence. This can be for a fixed or unlimited period and can be for a specific purpose only. **You should take expert legal advice before giving someone power of attorney over any of your financial affairs!**

- Obtain some euros before arriving in France, as this will save you time on arrival and you may obtain a better exchange rate.

- Finally, allow plenty of time to get to the airport or ferry, register your luggage, and clear security and immigration.

After Arrival

The following tasks should be completed after arrival in France (if not done before):

- On arrival at a French airport or port, have your visa cancelled and your passport stamped, as applicable.

- If you've exported a vehicle, re-register it in France.

- If you aren't taking a car with you, you may wish to rent one for a week or two until buying one locally. Note that it's practically impossible to get around in rural areas without a car. If you purchase a car in France, register it and arrange insurance.

- Apply for a residence permit at your local town hall or *préfecture* within a week of your arrival (see page 36).

- Register with your local embassy or consulate (see page 226).

- Make sure that your employer has applied for a social security card as soon as you start working.

- Give the details of your bank account to your employer.

- Arrange schooling for your children.

- Find a local doctor and dentist.

- Arrange whatever insurance is necessary, including health (see page 263) car, household (see page 268) and third party liability insurance (see page 273).

- Make courtesy calls on your neighbours and the local mayor within a few weeks of your arrival. This is particularly important in villages and rural areas if you want to be accepted and become part of the community.

7.

TAXATION

An important consideration when you're buying a home in France, even if you don't plan to live there permanently, is taxation, which includes property tax, wealth tax, capital gains tax (CGT) and inheritance tax. You will also have to pay income tax if you live permanently in France or earn an income from a property there.

France is one of the highest taxed countries in the European Union when income tax, social security contributions, VAT (*TVA*) at 19.6 per cent and other indirect taxes are taken into consideration.

Before you decide to settle in France permanently, you should obtain expert advice regarding French taxes. This will (hopefully) ensure that you take maximum advantage of your current tax status and that you don't make any mistakes that you will regret later.

As you would expect in a country with millions of bureaucrats, the French tax system is inordinately complicated and most French people don't understand it. It's difficult to obtain accurate information from the tax authorities and, just when you think you have it cracked, (ho! ho!) the authorities change the rules or hit you with a new tax. Taxes are levied at both national and local levels, although even 'national' taxes such as income tax are usually calculated and paid locally. (It's even possible to meet your tax man, if you should so wish!) There's a five-year statute of limitations on the collection of back taxes in France: i.e. if no action has been taken during this period to collect unpaid tax, it cannot be collected. Late payment of any tax bill usually incurs a surcharge of 10 per cent.

INCOME TAX

Personal income tax (*impôt sur le revenu des personnes physiques/IRPP*) in France is below average for EU countries, particularly for large families, and accounts for some 20 per cent of government revenue only. The government has been reducing income tax levels for the past decade; in August 1999 a three-year, €6 billion income tax reduction programme was announced, and the present administration has pledged to reduce it by a further €30 billion over five years. (Corporation tax is also to be reduced by 10 per cent to 33.3 per cent.)

Employees' income tax **isn't** deducted at source by employers in France (although the government is considering introducing such a system, in line with those of other EU countries), and individuals are responsible for declaring and paying their own income tax. Most taxpayers pay their tax a year in arrears in three instalments, although it can be paid in ten monthly instalments (see **Payment** on page 246).

Tax is withheld at flat rates and at source only for non-residents who receive income from employment and professional activities in France;

they must file a statement with the Centre des Impôts de Non-Résidents (9 rue d'Uzès, 75094 Paris Cedex 02, ☎ 01 44 76 18 00) each year.
Families are taxed as a single entity, although you can elect for a dependent child's income to be taxed separately if this is advantageous (a dependant's income up to a certain amount is exempt from income tax). The French income tax system favours the family, as the amount of income tax paid is directly related to the number of dependent children. French tax rates are based on a system of coefficients or 'parts' (*parts*), reflecting the family status of the taxpayer and the number of dependent children. The number of parts is known as the *quotient familial* (*QF*).
Note that French law distinguishes between living with someone on an 'unofficial' basis (*en union libre*) and cohabiting with a spouse or 'official' partner (*en concubinage*). A partner can be made 'official' by entering into an agreement called a *pacte civil de solidarité* (*PACS*). If you live *en union libre*, you're treated for tax purposes as two single people, whereas if you live *en concubinage*, you're treated as a couple and are entitled to a number of tax advantages.
It's difficult to obtain accurate information from the tax authorities, and errors in tax assessments are commonplace. Unless your tax affairs are simple, it's prudent to employ an accountant (*expert comptable*) to complete your tax return and ensure that you're correctly assessed. In fact, a good accountant will help you (legally) to save more in taxes than you will pay him in fees.
The information below applies only to personal income tax (*Impôt sur le Revenu des Personnes physiques/IRPP*) and not to company tax. A list of registered tax consultants is available from the Conseil Supérieur de l'Ordre des Experts-Comptables (☎ 01 44 15 60 00, 🖳 www.experts-comptables.fr). Details of Franco-British tax consultants are available from the Franco-British Chamber of Commerce in Paris (☎ 01 53 30 81 30).
Many books are available to help you understand and save taxes, and income tax guides are published each January, including the *Guide Pratique du Contribuable*. The Service Public website (🖳 www.service-public.fr) also has extensive tax information under 'Impôts'. If your French isn't up to deciphering tax terminology, refer to *Taxation in France* by Charles Parkinson (PKF Publications). You can obtain tax information and calculate your tax using Minitel (3615 IR SERVICE).

Liability

Your liability for French taxes depends on where you're domiciled. Your domicile is normally the country you regard as your permanent home and where you live most of the year. A foreigner working in France for a French company who has taken up residence in France and has no income tax liability abroad is considered to have his tax domicile (*domicile fiscal*) in France. A person can be resident in more than one country at any given time, but can be domiciled only in one country. The domicile of a married woman isn't necessarily the same as her husband's but is determined using the same criteria as for anyone capable of having an independent domicile. Your country of domicile is particularly important regarding inheritance tax (see page 252).

Under the French tax code, domicile is decided under the 'tax home test' (*foyer fiscal*) or the 183-day rule. You're considered to be a French resident and liable to French tax if **any** of the following applies:

- Your permanent home, i.e. family or principal residence, is in France;
- You spend over 183 days in France during any calendar year;
- You carry out paid professional activities or employment in France, except when secondary to business activities conducted in another country;
- Your centre of economic interest, e.g. investments or business, is in France.

If you intend to live permanently in France, you should notify the tax authorities in your present country (you will be asked to complete a form, e.g. a form P85 in the UK). You may be entitled to a tax refund if you depart during the tax year. The tax authorities may require evidence that you're leaving the country, e.g. evidence of a job in France or of having bought or rented a property there. If you move to France to take up a job or start a business, you must register with the local tax authorities (Centre des Impôts) soon after your arrival.

Double Taxation

French residents are taxed on their world-wide income, subject to certain treaty exceptions (non-residents are taxed only on income arising in France). Citizens of most countries are exempt from paying taxes in their home country when they spend a minimum period abroad, e.g. a year. According to the Convention for the Avoidance of Double Taxation and the Prevention of Fiscal Evasion, France has double-taxation treaties with over 70 countries, including all members of the EU, Australia, Canada, China, India, Israel, Jamaica, Japan, New Zealand, Norway, Pakistan, the Philippines, Singapore, Sri Lanka, Switzerland and the US.

Treaties are designed to ensure that income that has already been taxed in one treaty country isn't taxed again in another treaty country. The treaty establishes a tax credit or exemption on certain kinds of income, either in the country of residence or the country where the income is earned. Where applicable, a double-taxation treaty prevails over domestic law. Many people living abroad switch their investments to offshore holdings to circumvent the often complicated double-taxation agreements (see **Offshore Banking** on page 192). If you're in doubt about your tax liability in your home country, contact your nearest embassy or consulate in France. The US is the only country that taxes its non-resident citizens on income earned abroad, although there are exclusions on foreign-earned income (around $76,000 per spouse).

UK citizens should note that a new British-French double-taxation treaty made in January 2004 and expected to come into force in 2005 or 2006 will affect the taxation of foreign property in certain cases. Whereas UK citizens resident in France are currently exempt – in both France and the UK – from CGT on the sale of UK property, they will now be liable for French CGT. UK property-owners resident in France should therefore consider selling their UK property before the new rules come into effect, unless they've owned it for more than 15 years, in which case they may be exempt from French tax (see **Capital Gains Tax** on page 251). The new treaty will, on the other hand, exempt property owned by UK citizens resident in France from inclusion in wealth tax liability for the first five years of their residence (see **Wealth Tax** on page 247). The new treaty also impinges on the taxation of UK companies conducting business in France. For details, consult a tax expert.

Leaving France

Before leaving France, foreigners must pay any tax due for the previous year and the year of departure by applying for a tax clearance (*quitus fiscal*). A tax return must be filed prior to departure and should include your income and deductions from 1st January of the departure year up to the date of departure. The local tax inspector will calculate the tax due and provide a written statement. When departure is made before 31st December, the previous year's taxes are applied. If this results in overpayment, a claim must be made for a refund. A French removal company isn't supposed to export your household belongings without a 'tax clearance statement' (*bordereau de situation*) from the tax authorities stating that all taxes have been paid.

Leaving (as well as moving to) France may offer you an opportunity for 'favourable tax planning' (i.e. tax avoidance rather than tax evasion). To take the maximum advantage of your situation, you should obtain professional advice from a tax adviser who is familiar with both the French tax system and that of your present or future country of residence.

Taxable Income & Exemptions

Income tax is calculated upon both earned income (*impôt sur le revenu*) and unearned income (*impôt des revenus de capitaux*). If you have an average income and receive interest on bank deposits only, tax on unearned income won't apply, as it's deducted from bank interest before you receive it.

Taxation Of Property Income

Income tax is payable in France on rental income (*revenu foncier*) from a French property, even if you live abroad and the money is paid there. All rental income must be declared to the French tax authorities, whether you let a property for a few weeks to a friend or 52 weeks a year on a commercial basis. For most letting income, you must complete Form 2044. Furnished property lettings are exempt from VAT, although you may need to charge clients VAT if you offer services such as bed and breakfast, a daily maid, linen or a reception service.

The amount of tax you pay and the allowances you're eligible for depend on the letting scheme you choose (see **Letting Schemes** on page 279), as well as on your residence, as detailed below.

Residents

Resident property owners are eligible for deductions such as repairs, maintenance, security and cleaning costs, mortgage interest (French loans only), management and letting expenses (e.g. advertising), local taxes, and an allowance to cover depreciation and insurance, depending on the letting scheme they're using (see **Letting Schemes** on page 279). You should seek professional advice to ensure that you're claiming everything to which you're entitled. An additional tax called the *contribution additionelle à la contribution représentative du droit de bail* (*CACRDB*) is charged at 2.5 per cent. You should contact your local tax office to clarify your position (don't rely on your accountant).

If your net letting income is over €23,000 or comprises more than half the income of your household, you're considered to be a landlord and must make a business registration. This will also mean that you will pay higher social security contributions.

If you run a *gîte* or B&B, you will also normally be liable for *taxe professionelle* (see page 250), although you may be granted exemption if you let for less than half the year and/or the property is also your principal residence.

Finally, if your property is over 15 years old, you may be liable for a letting tax called *contribution sur les revenus locatifs (CRL)*.

Non-Residents

Non-resident property owners who receive an income from a French source must file a tax return, *Déclaration des Revenus* (Cerfa 2042/2042C), available from local tax offices in France or French consulates abroad. Completed forms must be sent to the Centre des Impôts de Non-Résidents (9 rue d'Uzès, 75094 Paris Cedex 02, ☎ 01 44 76 18 00) before 30th April each year. It's wise to keep a copy of your return and send it by registered post (so that there's no dispute over whether it was received). Like residents, you can take advantage of various tax allowances, depending on the type of letting scheme you use (see **Letting Schemes** on page 279).

Some months after filing you will receive a tax assessment detailing the tax due. There are penalties for late filing and non-declaration, which can result in fines, high interest charges and even imprisonment. The tax authorities have many ways of detecting people letting homes and not paying tax and have been clamping down on tax evaders in recent years.

Non-residents must also declare any income received in France on their tax return in their country of residence, although tax on French letting income is normally paid only in France. However, if you pay less tax in France than you would have paid in your home country, you must usually pay the difference. On the other hand, if you pay more tax in France than you would have paid on the income in your home country, you aren't entitled to a refund.

Note that if you're a non-resident of France for tax purposes and own residential property there that's available for your use, you're liable for French income tax on the basis of a deemed rental income equal to three times the real rental value of the property (usually calculated to be 5 per cent of its capital value). There are, however, exceptions, e.g. if you have French source income that exceeds this level or when you're protected by a double-taxation treaty (see page 240). Consult a tax accountant to clarify your position.

 There are severe penalties for failing to declare property income to the French tax authorities, who can impose tax on 52 weeks' letting income and cancel your entitlement to tax deductions in future.

Allowances

Although the tax percentage rates in France are high, your taxable income is considerably reduced by allowances. These include social security payments, which **aren't** taxable and are deducted from the gross income of salaried employees, a 10 per cent allowance (*déduction forfaitaire*) for 'professional' or 'notional' expenses, to which all salaried taxpayers are entitled, unless such expenses are specified, and a further general deduction (*abattement général*) of 20 per cent, which is then applied to certain categories of income, including salary, pensions and life annuities.

Note that the self-employed don't qualify for the 10 per cent allowance or the 20 per cent general deduction. If you're self-employed, however, you can obtain a 20 per cent reduction on your taxable income by joining your regional Association Agréé des Professions Libérales (commonly known as a *centre de gestion*), a government-sponsored body that regulates the income tax declarations of self-employed people.

The figure you arrive at after deducting all allowances is your net taxable income (*revenu net imposable*).

Calculation

The tax year in France runs for the calendar year (i.e. from 1st January to 31st December). The income tax rates for a single person (1 part) for 2004 income (2005 tax return) are shown in the table below. To calculate the taxable income for a couple without children, double the figures in the left column.

Taxable Income (€)	Tax Rate (%)	Tax (€)	Aggregate Tax (€)
Up to 4,262	0	0.00	0.00
4,262 – 8,382	6.83	281.40	281.40
8,382 – 14,753	19.14	1,219.41	1,500.81
14,753 – 23,888	28.26	2,581.55	4,082.36
23,888 – 38,868	37.38	5,599.52	9,681.88
38,868 – 47,932	42.62	3,863.08	13,544.96
Over 47,932	48.09		

Reductions & Credits

Once you've calculated your tax 'base', you may be eligible for reductions (*réductions*) or credits (*crédits*) to this amount. For example, tax credits may apply to major expenditure on home improvements and VAT on major items of domestic equipment purchased from and installed by a VAT-registered company.

Self-Employed

Those who qualify as self-employed in France include artisans or craftsmen (*professions artisanales*) such as builders, plumbers and electricians. Others include those involved in trading activities such as shopkeepers, anyone buying and selling goods, agents, brokers and property dealers. If you're a professional (*profession libérale*) such as an accountant, doctor or lawyer or a freelance worker (*travailleur indépendent*) such as an artist or writer, you may complete a *déclaration contrôlée* (form 2035) requiring you to keep accounts of income and expenses, including all related receipts and documents, or, if your earnings are below €25,000, a *micro-entreprise* or *micro-BNC*, on which you declare all earnings and qualify for a 50 per cent tax reduction. Other self-employed people should complete a normal tax return, unless your earnings are below a certain level (€25,000 for service-related businesses, €76,000 for sales businesses), in which case you may complete a *micro-BIC*. If your income is from letting a property privately, you can complete a *micro-foncier*, provided you've earned less than €15,000; otherwise, you need to complete form 2044 (see **Letting Schemes** on page 279).

Note that the self-employed don't qualify for the 10 per cent allowance or the 20 per cent general deduction on taxable income, although they can obtain a 20 per cent reduction by joining their local Association agréé des Professions libérales, (commonly known as a Centre de Gestion); the joining fee is around €110 and you must pay an annual subscription of around €150, which means that membership is to your advantage if your income exceeds around €9,000. The self-employed can also claim against tax any payments made to a complementary health insurance scheme, provided the contract is drawn up according to the *loi Madelin* (named after the minister who introduced the legislation).

Note also that, if you run a business from home, you must also pay a *taxe professionelle*, although you can claim a reduction in property tax (see page 248).

Tax Return

You're sent an annual tax return (*déclaration des revenus*) by the tax authorities in late February or early March of each year. If you aren't sent a form, you can obtain one from your local town hall or tax office (look in the telephone book under '*Impôts, Trésor Public*').

French tax returns are complicated, despite attempts to simplify them in recent years. The language used is particularly difficult to understand for foreigners (and many French). You can make an appointment for a free consultation with your local tax inspector at your town hall. However, if your French isn't excellent you will need to take someone with you who's fluent. Local tax offices (Centre des Impôts) are usually helpful and will help you complete your tax return. The Centre des Impôts also offers assistance via telephone (☎ 08 20 32 42 52 – between 08.00 and 22.00 Mondays to Fridays and from 09.00 to 19.00 on Saturdays), Minitel (3615 IRSERVICE) and the internet (🖥 www.ir. dgi.minefi.gouv.fr). Alternatively, you can employ a tax accountant (*expert comptable/conseiller fiscal*).

Note that tax declarations can be made online, but not the first time you make a declaration in France; once you've been issued with a taxpayer number, you can use the online facility, which is free and allows you an extension of one to three weeks on the filing deadline.

If you pay income tax abroad, you must return the form uncompleted with evidence that you're domiciled abroad. Around a month later you should receive a statement from the French tax authorities stating that you have no tax to pay (*vous n'avez pas d'impôt à payer*). The French tax authorities may request copies of foreign tax returns. Americans who are going to be abroad on 15th April should ask for an Extension Form. Note that US income tax returns cannot be filed in with the IRS office in Paris but must be sent to the IRS in the US. IRS Publication 54, *Tax Guide for US Citizens and Resident Aliens Abroad*, can be downloaded from the IRS website (🖥 www.irs.gov/pub/irs-pdf/p54.pdf).

Tax returns must be filed by late March for employees and by late April for the self-employed. **Late filing, even by one day, attracts a penalty of 10 per cent of the amount due.**

Payment

Some time between August and December, you will receive a tax bill (*avis d'imposition*). There are two methods of paying your tax bill in France: in three instalments (*tiers provisionnels*) or in ten equal monthly instalments (*mensualisation*).

Note that you become liable for French tax as soon as you establish your principal residence in France (see page 239), which normally means the day you move into your French home. Therefore, if you arrive in France in September 2004, you won't make your first tax payment until September 2005, and then only for the last three or four months of the year 2004, so you won't need to pay any significant income tax until two years after your arrival, i.e. September 2006, although you may of course also be liable for tax in your previous country of residence for the first part of the year of your move.

WEALTH TAX

A wealth tax (*impôt sur la fortune/ISF*) was introduced on 1st January 1989 (since when billions of francs have disappeared into foreign banks!) and is payable by each 'fiscal unit' (*foyer fiscal*), e.g. couple or family, when its annual income exceeds €720,000. Wealth tax is assessed on the net value of your assets on 1st January each year and is payable by the following 15th June by French residents (15th July for other European residents and 15th August for all others). On 1st January 2003 the rates were increased to the following:

Assets (€'000)	Rate (%)	Cumulative Liability (€)
Up to 720	0	0
720 – 1,160	0.55	2,420
1,160 – 2,300	0.75	10,970
2,300 – 3,600	1.0	23,970
3,600 – 6,900	1.3	66,870
6,900 – 15,000	1.65	200,520
Over 15,000	1.8	

Certain exemptions apply, e.g. PERP and PERCO savings plans and income from long-term letting of rural property. If you're domiciled in France, the value of your estate is based on your worldwide assets. If you're resident in France but not domiciled there, the value of your estate is based on your assets in France only. Changes to wealth tax legislation introduced in January 2004 allow partial exemption in respect of company shares. Consult a tax expert for details.

PROPERTY TAXES

There are four types of local property tax (*impôt local*) in France: *taxe d'habitation* (referred to here as 'residential tax'), *taxe foncière* (referred to as 'property tax'), *taxe assimilée* ('sundry tax') and *taxe professionelle* ('professional tax'). Taxes pay for local services, including rubbish collection, street lighting and cleaning, local schools and other community services, and include a contribution to departmental and regional expenses. You may be billed separately for rubbish collection.

Both residential and property taxes are payable whether the property is a main or a second home and whether the owner is a French or foreign resident. Both taxes are calculated according to a property's notional 'cadastral' rental value (*valeur locative cadastrale*), which is reviewed every six years. If you think a valuation is too high, you can contest it.

Property and residential taxes vary from area to area and are generally higher in cities and towns than in rural areas and small villages, where few community services are provided. They also vary with the type and size of property and will be significantly higher for a luxury villa than for a small apartment. If you're renting a property, check whether you're required to pay part of the *taxe foncière* as well as the *taxe d'habitation*. Note that there's no reduction in either tax for a second home (*résidence secondaire*); in fact, your *taxe d'habitation* is likely to be higher, as there's a reduction for principal residences (*maison principale*).

Forms for the assessment of both residential and property tax are sent out by local councils and must be completed and returned to the regional tax office (Centre des Impôts) by a specified date, e.g. 15th November or 15th December for residential tax. They will calculate the tax due and send you a bill. You may be given up to two months to pay and a 10 per cent penalty is levied for late payment. It's possible to pay residential tax monthly (in ten equal instalments from January to October) by direct debit from a French bank account, which helps to soften the blow.

Property Tax

Property tax (*taxe foncière*) is paid by owners of property in France and is similar to the property tax (or rates) levied in most countries. It's payable even if a property isn't inhabited, provided it's furnished and habitable. Property tax is levied on all 'shelters' for people or goods, including warehouses and house boats (fixed mooring), as well as on certain land. The tax is split into two amounts: one for the building (*taxe foncière bâtie*) and a smaller one for the land (*taxe foncière non bâtie*). Tax is payable on land whether or not it's built on. Property tax isn't applicable to buildings and land used exclusively for agricultural or religious purposes, nor to government and public buildings.

The amount of property tax payable varies by up to 500 per cent with the region, and even between towns or villages within the same region, and may be as little as €300 or as much as €1,500 per year, although there are plans to make the application of the tax 'fairer'. Strangely, the Paris area has some of the country's lowest rates.

Note that many village properties are to be connected to mains drainage by December 2005 and owners will be charged a connection fee, which will be added to the *taxe foncière* (see **Sewerage** on page 337); you should therefore check whether this will affect the property you plan to buy and, if so, what will be the cost.

Note also that, if you move permanently to France, you should notify the local Service du Cadastre (part of the Tax Office) **and** the local Trésorerie; otherwise, you may find that your first property tax bill is sent to your previous address (even if this is abroad) and, when you fail to pay (because you haven't received it), you're charged for late payment!

Exemptions

New and restored buildings used as main or second homes are exempt from property tax for two years from 1st January following the completion date (new houses and apartments financed by certain types of government loan or purchased by an association for letting to people on low incomes may be exempt for 10 or 15 years). An application for a temporary exemption from property tax must be made to your local property tax office (Centre des Impôts Fonciers) or Bureau du Cadastre before 31st December for exemption the following year. Applications must be made within 90 days of the completion of building work.

Certain people (e.g. those aged over 75 and those receiving a disability pension below a certain level) are exempt from property tax, and others (e.g. those over 65 on low incomes) may qualify for a discount (*allégement*) of around €100.

You may claim a reduction in your *taxe foncière* if you work from home (see **Professional Tax** below).

If you sell a property part of the way through the year, the purchaser isn't legally required to reimburse you for a proportion of the property tax due (or paid) for that year. However, it's customary for property tax to be apportioned by the notary between the seller and buyer from the date of the sale (a clause to that effect should be included in the *promesse de vente*). Therefore, if you purchase a property in July, you will normally be asked 'reimburse' the vendor for half the annual property tax. Because you're not obliged to do so, you can negotiate the amount (or the purchase price of the property), although you may not make yourself popular with the vendor!

Residential Tax

Residential tax (*taxe d'habitation*) is payable by anyone who resides in a property with a rental value (*valeur locative*) of over €4,600 in France on 1st January, whether as an owner, tenant or rent-free.

 Note that, even if you vacate or sell a property on 2nd January, you must pay residential tax for the whole year and have no right to reclaim part of it from a new owner.

Residential tax is payable on residential properties (used as main or second homes), outbuildings (e.g. accommodation for servants, garages) located less than a kilometre from a residential property, and on business premises that are an indistinguishable part of a residential property. It's calculated on the living area of a property, including outbuildings, garages and amenities, and takes into account factors such as the quality of construction, location, renovations, services (e.g. mains water, electricity and gas) and amenities such as central heating, swimming pool, covered terrace and garage. Properties are placed in eight categories ranging from 'very poor' to 'luxurious'. Changes made to a building, such as improvements or enlargements, must be notified to the land registry within 90 days.

Residential tax is levied by the town where the property is located and varies by as much as 400 per cent from town to town. As with property tax (see above), the Paris area has some of the country's lowest rates. Generally, you should expect to pay around half the amount paid in *taxe foncière*. Residential tax is usually payable in autumn of the year to which it applies.

Exemptions

Premises used exclusively for business, farming and student lodging are exempt from residential tax. Residential tax isn't paid by residents whose income is below a certain level (e.g. €16,290 for a single person), nor by certain retirees whose income in the preceding year was below €7,165 (plus around €1,914 for each dependant).

Professional Tax

Professional tax (*taxe professionelle*) is payable on your business premises and is levied at between around 15 and 20 per cent (the exact percentage varies with the commune) of a 'base', which is currently 8 per cent of your annual income including VAT. For example, if you earn €30,000 per year, your tax base will be €2,400; if professional tax is levied at 20 per cent in your commune, you will pay €480 per year.

If you work from home, you're liable for professional tax **as well as** residential and property taxes (and sundry tax, if applicable), although you can claim a reduction on your property tax according to the proportion of your home that's used for business purposes. To calculate this, measure the total area of your living room, dining room, bedrooms and office (if separate). If your office occupies 10 per cent of the total area, for example, you may claim a 10 per cent reduction in *taxe foncière*. Certain types of workers are exempt from professional tax, including writers and artists and people letting holiday accommodation. You should check with an accountant.

Professional tax is assessed as follows: in your first year of French residence, you will pay nothing; in your second year, you will pay according to your earnings in Year 1 (pro rata if you moved to France part way through the year); in Year 3, your tax will again be based on your Year 1 earnings, in Year 4 on your Year 2 earnings, and so on.

Other Taxes

In some areas – especially popular tourist resorts, where the local authorities must spend more than usual on amenities and the upkeep of towns – a regional or sundry tax (*taxe assimilée*) is levied. 'Buildings tax' (*taxe sur les immeubles*) is levied at 3 per cent on property owned by certain businesses.

CAPITAL GAINS TAX

Capital gains tax (*impôt sur les plus-values*) is payable on the profit from sale of certain assets in France, including antiques, art and jewellery, securities and property. Gains net of capital gains tax (CGT) are added to other income and are liable to income tax (see page 239). Capital gains are also subject to social security contributions at 8 per cent. Changes to the capital gains regulations were made in the Finance Act, 2004, which also requires a *notaire* handling a property sale to calculate and pay CGT on behalf of the vendor.

Principal Residence

CGT isn't payable on a profit made on the sale of your principal residence in France, provided that you've occupied it since its purchase (or for at least five years if you didn't occupy it immediately after purchase). You're also exempt from CGT if you're forced to sell for family or professional reasons, e.g. you're transferred abroad by your employer. Income tax treaties usually provide that capital gains on property are taxable in the country where the property is located.

Note that, if you move to France permanently and retain a home abroad, this may affect your position regarding capital gains. If you sell your foreign home before moving to France, you will be exempt from CGT, as it's your principal residence. However, if you establish your principal residence in France, the foreign property becomes a second home and is thus liable to CGT when it's sold. **EU tax authorities co-operate in tracking down CGT dodgers.**

Second Homes

Capital gains on second homes in France worth over €15,000 (i.e. anything other than a caravan!) are payable by both residents and non-residents up to 15 years after purchase (until 2004, the period was 22 years). The basic rates of CGT are 26 per cent for residents, 16 per cent for non-resident EU citizens, and 33.3 per cent for non-resident non-EU citizens. Any inheritance or gift tax paid at the time of purchase is taken into account when determining the purchase price, and there are certain exemptions to the above tax rates, as follows:

● If you've owned a property for more than five years but less than 15, you're entitled to a 10 per cent reduction in CGT for every year of ownership over five (i.e. 10 per cent for six years' ownership, 20 per cent for seven years', etc.).

● If you've owned a property for at least five years and can produce proof of substantial expenditure on improving it (e.g. receipts for work done by professionals), you can claim a further deduction of 15 per cent of the property's purchase price against CGT (irrespective of the actual cost of the work), but you're no longer entitled to claim for work you've done yourself, nor any materials purchased for DIY improvements.

However, the purchase price of a property is no longer 'indexed' to increases in the cost of living. Note also that, if you make a loss on the sale of a second home, you cannot claim this against other CGT payments, nor against income tax!

Before a sale, the *notaire* prepares a form calculating the tax due and appoints an agent (*agent fiscal accrédité*) or guarantor to act on your behalf concerning tax. If the transaction is straightforward, the local tax office may grant a dispensation (*dispense*) of the need to appoint a guarantor, provided you apply **before** completion of the sale. If you obtain a dispensation, the proceeds of the sale can be released to you in full after CGT has been paid. The *notaire* handling the sale must apply for the dispensation and must declare and pay CGT on your behalf; you're no longer required to make a CGT declaration.

INHERITANCE & GIFT TAX

As in most other western countries, giving away your assets, either while you're living or when you die, doesn't free you (or your inheritors) from the clutches of French tax inspectors. France imposes both gift and inheritance taxes on its inhabitants, as detailed below. Note, however, that taxes are due to be reduced in January 2005, so you should check the latest figures with a French tax expert.

Inheritance Tax

Inheritance tax (*droits de succession*), called estate tax or death duty in some countries, is levied on the estate of a deceased person. Both residents and non-residents are subject to inheritance tax if they own property in France. The country where you pay inheritance tax is decided by your domicile (see **Liability** on page 239). If you're living permanently in France at the time of your death, you will be deemed to be domiciled there by the French tax authorities. If you're domiciled in France, inheritance tax applies to your world-wide estate (excluding property); otherwise it applies only to assets located in France.

SURVIVAL TIP

It's important to make your domicile clear, so that there's no misunderstanding on your death.

When a person dies in France, an estate tax return (*déclaration de succession*) must be filed within six months of the date of death (within 12 months if the death occurred outside France). The return is generally prepared in France by a notary.

Inheritance tax in France is paid by individual beneficiaries, irrespective of where they're domiciled, and not by the estate. Tax may be paid in instalments over five or, in certain cases, ten years or may be deferred.

The rate of tax and allowances varies according to the relationship between the beneficiary and the deceased. French succession laws are quite restrictive compared with the law in many other countries. The surviving spouse has an allowance (*abattement*) of €76,000 and the children and parents of the deceased an allowance of €46,000. After the allowance has been deducted, there's a sliding scale up to a maximum of 40 per cent on assets over €1.7 million, as shown in the table below:

Value (€) Above Allowance		Tax Rate (%)
Spouse	Children/Parents	
Up to 7,600	Up to 7,600	5
7,600 – 15,000	7,600 – 11,400	10
15,000 – 30,000	11,400 – 15,000	15
30,000 – 520,000	15,000 – 520,000	20

520,000 – 850,000	520,000 – 850,000	30
850,000 – 1.7 million	850,000 – 1.7 million	35
Above 1.7 million	Above 1.7 million	40

An unmarried couple with a *PACS* agreement (see page 239) qualifies for an allowance of €57,000 from the third year after making the agreement. Inheritances from the other partner above that amount are taxed at 40 per cent up to €15,000 and at 50 per cent above €15,000.

Note that, if you're resident in France and receive an inheritance from abroad, you're subject to French inheritance tax. However, if you've been resident for less than six years in France, you're exempt (or, if you paid the bill in another country, the amount is deducted from your French tax bill).

Gift Tax

You may make tax-free gifts every ten years to a spouse (up to €76,000), child (up to €46,000) or grandchild (up to €30,000). (Each of these figures is increased by €46,000 if the recipient is handicapped.) There are no allowances for gifts between brothers and sisters or between unrelated people.

Gift tax (*droits de donation*) is calculated in the same way as inheritance tax (see above), according to the relationship between the donor and the recipient and the size of the gift. On lifetime gifts, there's now a tax reduction of 50 per cent, irrespective of the age of the donor (this reduction previously applied only if the donor was under 65), but only on gifts made before 30th June 2005! Any gifts made within ten years of the death of the donor (*en avancement d'horie*) must be included in the inheritance tax return and are valued at the time of death rather than at the time of donation.

 Note that gift tax is payable on gifts made between spouses in France, so assets should be equally shared before you're domiciled there.

Payment of gift tax can be spread over a number of years, except in the case of the donation of a business.

Avoiding Inheritance Tax

It's important to understand French inheritance laws, which apply to both residents and non-residents with property in France.

First, property is divided into 'movable' and 'immovable' property: *meubles*, including not only furniture but all belongings except land and buildings, and *immeubles*, including land and buildings. Immovable property must be disposed of in accordance with French law, irrespective of whether you're resident or non-resident in France, whereas movable property is subject to French law only if you're resident (or spend the majority of your time) in France.

Second, all property subject to French law is divided into a 'disposable part' (*quotité disponible*) and a 'heritary part' (*réserve héréditaire*). Irrespective of your will(s), the hereditary part **must** be disposed of according to French law. The size of the hereditary part depends on how many children you have. If you have one child, half of your affected property must be left to him; if you have two children, they must inherit two-thirds; three or more children three-quarters. If you have no children but a living parent or grandparent, a quarter of the property must be left to them.

A couple's marital status is also of relevance to inheritance. French couples normally enter into a marriage contract, whereby their assets are either shared (*communauté universelle*) or owned separately (*séparation de biens*). Foreign couples who don't have a marriage contract will normally be regarded as having separate ownership unless they state otherwise in the property purchase contract (see page 204). This means that, if one spouse dies, the other retains ownership of his part of the property and only the deceased's part is disposed of as explained above. If, on the other hand, you've specified that your marital 'arrangement' is similar to the French *communauté universelle*, ownership of all property will pass to the surviving spouse on the death of the other.

In view of the above, couples considering buying property in France should decide **in advance** how they wish to dispose of it.

There are a number of ways of limiting or delaying the impact of French inheritance laws, including inserting a clause (such as a *clause tontine*) in a property purchase contract (*acte de vente*) – see below, officially changing your marital regime in France, e.g. to joint ownership or *communauté de biens*, and buying property through a company (see **Buying Through A Company** on page 212).

The *clause tontine* (or *pacte tontinier*) – an obscure law relating to an archaic finding system set up by an Italian banker in the 17th century and hardly used by French people – allows a property to be left entirely to a surviving spouse or partner and not shared among the children. Because it places the entire inheritance tax burden on the surviving partner, rather than sharing it among the partner and children, it's particularly advantageous for inexpensive properties; with more expensive property, it may be advantageous only for married couples, who are entitled to higher inheritance tax allowances (see above). Bear in mind also that recent changes to French inheritance laws allow a survivng spouse to inherit at least 25 per cent of a property. In any case, a *clause tontine* is likely to be valid only if both partners have a similar life expectancy (otherwise, it could be argued that it was used expressly as a way of disinheriting children). Another consideration to be made before using a *clause tontine* is that, if you want to sell the property but your spouse objects, there's nothing you can do to force a sale.

A surviving spouse can also be given a life interest (*usufruit*) in an estate in priority to children or parents through a gift between spouses (*donation entre époux*). This is also known as a 'cross-purchase' (*achat croisé*). This means that the spouse may occupy the property for life and take any income generated by it but may not sell or otherwise dispose of it; on the other hand, the property cannot be sold of disposed of without the spouse's consent. A gift between spouses therefore delays the inheritance of an estate by any surviving children, who will have a 'reversionary interest' (*nue-propriété*) in it, i.e. ownership reverts to them on the death of the spouse. A *donation* must be prepared by a *notaire* and signed in the presence of the donor and the beneficiary. You must take along your passports, marriage certificate, birth certificates, *titres de séjour* (if applicable) and evidence of your address and occupations; a *donation entre époux* costs around €160. Note, however, that it may not apply to non-residents, who will be governed by the law of their home country.

Note that French law doesn't recognise the rights to inheritance of an unmarried partner, unless a *PACS* agreement has been signed (see page 239), although there are a number of solutions to this problem, e.g. a life insurance policy.

Another way to reduce your inheritance liability is to make a *donation partage* to your children, although gift tax will be payable (see above).

Whatever your marital situation, it's important to make a French will (even if you already have a foreign will that's valid in France), which can help to reduce your French inheritance tax liability or delay its payment.

 French inheritance law is an extremely complicated subject, and professional advice should be sought from an experienced lawyer who understands both French law and that of any other country involved.

WILLS

It's an unfortunate fact of life that you're unable to take your hard-earned assets with you when you take your final bow (or come back and reclaim them in a later life!). All adults should make a will (*testament*), irrespective of how large or small their assets. The disposal of your estate depends on your country of domicile (see **Inheritance & Gift Tax** above). As a general rule, French law permits a foreigner who **isn't** domiciled in France to make a will in any language and under the law of any country, provided it's valid under the law of that country.

Note, however, that 'immovable' property (*immeubles*) in France, i.e. land and buildings, must be disposed of (on death) in accordance with French law. All other property in France or elsewhere (defined as 'movables' – *meubles*) may be disposed of in accordance with the law of your country of domicile. Therefore, it's extremely important to establish where you're domiciled under French law. A possibility for a non-resident who wishes to avoid French inheritance laws regarding immovable property located in France is to buy it through a French holding company, in which case the shares of the company are 'movable' assets and are therefore governed by the succession laws of the owner's country of domicile (see **Buying Through A Company** on page 212).

French law is restrictive regarding the distribution of property and the identity of heirs and gives priority to children, including illegitimate and adopted children, and the living parents of a deceased person. Under French law (*code Napoléon*) you cannot disinherit your children, who have first claim on your estate, even before a surviving spouse. However, since July 2002, a surviving spouse has the right to at least a quarter of an inheritance: if you die leaving one child, he must inherit half of your French estate, and two children must inherit at least two-thirds; if you have three or more children, they must inherit three-quarters of your estate. If a couple has no surviving children, the deceased's parents each inherit a quarter of the estate and the surviving spouse half (if only one parent is alive, the spouse inherits three-quarters). If there are neither children nor parents, the spouse inherits the whole estate apart from family possessions, half of which must go to any surviving brothers or sisters of the deceased. There are, however, many legal ways to safeguard the rights of a surviving spouse, some of which are mentioned above under **Avoiding Inheritance & Gift Tax.**

The part of a property that must be inherited by certain heirs (*héritiers réservataires*) is called the legal reserve (*réserve legale*). Once the reserved portion of your estate has been determined, the remaining portion is freely disposable (*quotité disponible*). Only when there are no descendants or ascendants is the whole estate freely disposable.

It's possible to make two wills, one relating to French property and the other to foreign property. Opinion differs on whether you should have separate wills for French and foreign property, or a foreign will with a codicil (appendix) dealing with your French property (or vice versa). However, most experts believe it's better to have a French will from the point of view of winding up your French estate (and a will for any country where you own immovable property). **If you have French and foreign wills, make sure that they don't contradict one another (or, worse, cancel each other out, e.g. when a will contains a clause revoking all other wills).**

Types Of Will

There are three kinds of will in France: holographic (*olographe*), authentic (*authentique*) and secret (*mystique*), described below.

Holographic Will

The most common form of will used in France. It must be written by hand by the person making the will and be signed and dated by him. No witnesses or other formalities are required. In fact it shouldn't be witnessed at all, as this may complicate matters. It can be written in English or another language, although it's preferable if it's written in French (you can ask a *notaire* to prepare a draft and write a copy). A holographic will must be handed to a *notaire* for filing. He sends a copy to the local district court, where the estate is administered. A holographic will can be registered in the central wills registry (*fichier de dernières volontés*). For anyone with a modest French estate, e.g. a small second home in France, a holographic will is sufficient.

Authentic Or Notarial Will

This is used by some 5 per cent of French people. It must be drawn up by a *notaire* in the form of a notarial document and can be handwritten or typed. It's dictated by the person making the will and must be witnessed by two *notaires* or a *notaire* and two other witnesses. Unlike a holographic will, an authentic will is automatically registered in the central wills registry. An authentic will costs around €80.

Secret Will

A secret will is rarely used and is a will written by or for the person making it and signed by him. It's sealed in an envelope in the presence of two witnesses. It's then given to a *notaire*, who records on the envelope that it has been handed to him and that the testator has affirmed that the envelope contains his will. The *notaire* then files the will and sends a copy to the local district court where the estate is administered.

General Information

Note the following information regarding wills in France:

- In France, marriage doesn't automatically revoke a will, as in some other countries, e.g. the UK.
- Wills aren't made public in France and aren't available for inspection.
- **Where applicable, the rules relating to witnesses are strict; if they aren't followed precisely, a will may be rendered null and void.**
- Under French law, the role of the executor is different from that in many other countries; his duties are supervisory only and last for a year and a day. He's responsible for paying your debts and distributing the balance of the inheritance in accordance with your will. The executor who's dealing with your affairs in France must file a *déclaration de succession* within a year of your death. At your death your property passes directly to your heirs and it's their responsibility to pay inheritance tax and any debts relating to that property. Winding up an estate takes much longer than in many other countries and usually isn't given priority by *notaires*.
- You should keep a copy of your will(s) in a safe place and another copy with your solicitor or the executor of your estate. Don't leave them in a bank safe deposit box, which in the event of your death is sealed for a period under French law. Keep information regarding bank accounts, pensions and benefits, investments and insurance policies with your will(s), but don't forget to tell someone where they are! You should also make a separate note of your last wishes (e.g. regarding funeral arrangements) where your next-of-kin can find it immediately after your death, along with your social security number, birth, marriage, divorce and spouse's death certificates (as applicable) and the names and whereabouts of any children.

 French inheritance law is a complicated subject and it's important to obtain professional legal advice when writing or altering a will.

8.

INSURANCE

An important aspect of owning a holiday home in France is insurance (*assurance*), not only for your home and its contents, but also for your family when visiting.

SURVIVAL TIP

It's vital to ensure that you have sufficient insurance when visiting your home abroad, which includes travel insurance, continental car insurance (including breakdown insurance), building and contents insurance, third party liability insurance and health insurance.

If you live in France permanently, you will require additional insurance, including third party car insurance, third party liability insurance for tenants/homeowners (see page 273), and life insurance if you have a mortgage, depending on the amount borrowed (see page 194) – all of which are compulsory. Voluntary insurance includes health, household and travel insurance, which are covered in this chapter, as well as car breakdown, dental, disability and life insurance and supplementary pensions – for details of which see *Living and Working in France* (Survival Books – see page 389).

 It's your responsibility to ensure that you and your family are legally insured, and French law is likely to differ from that in your home country or your previous country of residence, so never assume that it's the same.

It's unnecessary to spend half your income insuring yourself against every eventuality from the common cold to being sued for your last *centime*, but it's important to insure against any event that could precipitate a major financial disaster, such as a serious illness or accident or your house falling down.

When buying insurance, shop till you drop! Obtain recommendations from friends, colleagues and neighbours (but don't believe everything they tell you!). Compare the costs, terms and benefits provided by a number of companies before making a decision. **Simply collecting a few brochures from insurance agents or making a few telephone calls could save you a lot of money.** Note also that insurance premiums are often negotiable.

Further information about insurance in France can be found on the Service Public website (🖥 www.service-public.fr) or from the Centre de Documentation et d'Information de l'Assurance (CDIA), Fédération Française des Sociétés d'Assurances, 26 boulevard Haussmann, 75311 Paris Cedex 09 (☎ 01 42 47 90 00, 🖥 www.ffsa.fr – in English).

HEALTH INSURANCE

Whether you're visiting or living or working in France, it's extremely risky not to have health insurance for yourself and your family; if you're uninsured or under-insured, you could be faced with some very high medical bills. **When travelling in France, you should carry proof of your health insurance with you.**

Visitors

If you have a holiday home and come to France as a visitor (i.e. for less than 90 days at a time and less than 183 days in any year), you should check whether you qualify for free or subsidised health treatment in France as part of a reciprocal health agreement between your home country and France (see **Reciprocal Health Agreements** on page 264). If you don't, you must choose between a private international health insurance policy (see page 265), and holiday/travel insurance (see page 267).

Residents

If you're planning to take up residence in France and will be contributing to French social security (*sécurité sociale*) – e.g. if you will be working in France – you and your family will be entitled to subsidised or (in certain cases) free medical and dental treatment. Most residents also subscribe to a complementary health insurance fund (*assurance complémentaire maladie*, commonly called a *mutuelle*) that pays the portion of medical bills that isn't paid by social security. A *mutuelle* may also provide a supplementary pension.

You should nevertheless check the conditions under which you may become covered by the French state health scheme and when such cover might become effective.

> **SURVIVAL TIP**
> If you're planning to take up residence in France, you should ensure that you and your family have full health insurance during the interval between leaving your last country of residence and obtaining health insurance in France.

One way to cover yourself for this interim period is to take out a holiday/travel insurance policy (see page 267). If you already have private health insurance, however, it's better to extend your present health insurance policy to provide international cover (which is usually possible) than to take out a new policy. This is particularly important if you have an existing health problem that won't be covered by a new policy.

Residents who don't contribute to social security (e.g. retirees) and aren't covered by a reciprocal agreement (see **Reciprocal Agreements** above) must choose between a private international health insurance policy (see page 265), which is mandatory for non-EU residents when applying for a visa or residence permit (*carte de séjour*), and holiday/travel insurance (see page 267).

Reciprocal Health Agreements

If you're entitled to social security health benefits in another EU country or in a country with a reciprocal health agreement with France, you will receive free or subsidised medical treatment in France. **The US doesn't have a reciprocal health agreement with France, so Americans who aren't covered by French social security must have private health insurance or a holiday/travel policy that covers them in France.**

EU citizens should apply for a certificate of entitlement to treatment (form E111) from their local social security office (or a post office in the UK) at least three weeks before they plan to travel to France. An E111 covers you for a six-month period and must be renewed annually. However, you must continue to make social security contributions in the country where it was issued and, if you become a resident in another country (e.g. in France), it becomes invalid in that country. An E111 covers emergency hospital treatment but doesn't include prescribed medicines, special examinations, X-rays, laboratory tests, physiotherapy and dental treatment.

If you do incur any medical costs in France, you will need to go to the local CPAM, the authority which deals with health insurance, and apply for reimbursement, which will be sent to you or credited to your UK bank account. Details of the procedure are included in the booklet that comes with the E111 form. **Note that it can take months for medical expenses to be reimbursed.**

 Even with an E111, you can receive a large bill from a French hospital, as your local health authority assumes only the cost of equivalent treatment in your home country.

Form E112 is required by pregnant women instead of form E111. (Form E112 used to be required by people with existing medical conditions, who are now covered by an E111).

As soon as they have a permanent address in France, **even if this is within the six month period the E111 covers you for**, EU citizens must obtain an E121, which is available in the UK from the Overseas Payments Section of the Inland Revenue's Centre for Non-Residents (☎ 0191-218 7777). This form in effect transfers you out of your home country's system and into the French system, for which you will also need to obtain a French medical card (*Carte Vitale*). This means that you may no longer be entitled to 100 per cent reimbursement of treatment costs and may wish to take out a *mutuelle* (see above).

British visitors or Britons planning to live in France can obtain information about reciprocal health treatment in France from the Department of Social Security, Overseas Branch, Newcastle-upon-Tyne, NE98 1YX, UK (☎ 0191-218 7777).

International Health Insurance

If you already have private health insurance in another country, it may be possible to extend it to cover you in France. You should bear in mind, however, that in some countries, e.g. the UK, if you inform your insurance companies that you're moving abroad permanently they may automatically cancel your insurance policies without notifying you!

When changing health insurance companies, it's also wise to inform your old company if you have any outstanding bills for which they're liable.

 If you're planning to change your health insurance company, you should ensure that no important benefits are lost, e.g. existing medical conditions won't usually be covered by a new insurer.

If you don't already have an international policy, shop around for the one that best suits your requirements. Most international insurance companies offer health policies for different areas, e.g. Europe, world-wide excluding North America, and world-wide including North America. Most companies offer different levels of cover, e.g. basic, standard, comprehensive and prestige. There's always an annual limit on medical costs, which should be at least €500,000 (although many provide cover of up to €1.5 million), and some companies also limit the charges for specific treatment or care such as specialists' fees, operations and hospital accommodation.

Most private health insurance policies don't pay family doctors' fees or pay for medicines other than those provided in a hospital or they charge a high excess (deductible), e.g. you must pay the first €75 of a claim, which often exceeds the cost of treatment. Most will, however, pay 100 per cent of specialists' fees and hospital treatment.

A medical examination isn't usually required for international health policies, although 'pre-existing' health problems are excluded for a period, e.g. one or two years. Most international health policies include repatriation or evacuation, which may also cover shipment (by air) of the body of a person who dies abroad to his home country for burial. An international policy also allows you to have non-urgent medical treatment in the country of your choice.

Claims are usually settled in most major currencies, and large claims are usually settled directly by insurance companies (although your choice of hospitals may be limited). Check whether an insurance company will settle large medical bills directly; if you're required to pay bills and claim reimbursement from an insurance company, it can take several months before you receive your money (some companies are slow to pay). It isn't usually necessary to translate bills into English or another language, although you should check a company's policy. Most international health insurance companies provide emergency telephone assistance.

The cost of international health insurance varies considerably according to your age and the extent of cover. Note that with most international insurance policies, you must enrol before you reach a certain age, usually between 60 and 75, to be guaranteed continuous cover in your old age. Premiums can sometimes be paid monthly, quarterly or annually, although some companies insist on payment annually in advance. When comparing policies, carefully check the extent of cover and exactly what's included and excluded from a policy (often indicated only in the **very** small print), in addition to premiums and excess charges. In some countries, premium increases are limited by law, although this may apply only to residents in the country where a company is registered and not to overseas policyholders.

Although there may be significant differences in premiums, generally you get what you pay for and can tailor premiums to your requirements. The most important questions to ask yourself are: does the policy provide the cover required and is it good value? If you're in good health and are able to pay for your own out-patient treatment, such as visits to your family doctor and prescriptions, the best value is usually a policy covering specialist and hospital treatment only.

When deciding on the type and extent of private health insurance, make sure that it covers **all** your family's present and future health requirements in France **before** you receive a large bill. A health insurance policy should cover you for **all** essential health care whatever

▲ *Fortran, Vienne (© Roger Moss)*

▲ *Béarn, Pyrénées-Atlantiques*
(© Latitudes)

▲ *Sospel, Alpes-Maritimes (© Roger Moss)*

▲ *Gournay-Rouen,*
Seine-Maritime
(© Latitudes)

▶

Roussillon, Vaucluse
(© Roger Moss)

◀ *Gordes, Vaucluse*
  (© Roger Moss)

▲ *Ferrensac, Lot-et-Garonne*
  (© Latitudes)

▼ *Eymet, Dordogne*
  (© Latitudes)

▲ *Linazay, Vienne*
  (© Roger Moss)

◀ *Lavoute-Chilhac,*
  Haute-Loire
  (© Roger Moss)

Balluc, Vienne ►
(© *Roger Moss*)

▲ *Neuvic, Corrèze*
(© *Latitudes*)

▼ *Gournay en Bray,*
Oise (© *Latitudes*)

▲ *Roussillon, Vaucluse*
(© *Roger Moss*)

►

Bellevue, Ile d'Oléron,
Charente-Maritime
(© *Roger Moss*)

Vinsobres, Drôme
(© Roger Moss)

▲ *Lannion, Côtes D'Armor*
(© Latitudes)

▲ *Linazay, Vienne*
(© Roger Moss)

▲ *St Paul de Vence,*
Alpes-Maritimes
(© Latitudes)

◄ *Vallerargues, Gard*
(© Roger Moss)

the reason, including accidents (e.g. sports accidents) and injuries, whether they occur in your home or while travelling. Don't take anything for granted, but check in advance.

 Some foreign insurance companies don't provide sufficient cover to satisfy French regulations, and you should check the minimum cover necessary with a French consulate in your country of residence.

HOLIDAY & TRAVEL INSURANCE

Holiday and travel insurance (*assurance voyage*) is recommended for those whose health and possessions aren't covered by an existing policy while travelling. As you're no doubt already aware, innumerable things can (and often do) go wrong with a holiday, sometimes before you even reach the airport or port, particularly when you **don't** have insurance.

Travel insurance is available from many sources, including travel agents, insurance agents, motoring organisations, transport companies and direct from insurance companies. Package holiday companies also offer insurance policies, **most of which don't provide adequate cover.** It isn't wise to depend on travel insurance provided by charge and credit card companies, household or car insurance policies or private medical insurance, none of which usually provide adequate cover (although you should take advantage of what they offer). For example, car insurance may include personal accident and health insurance (e.g. through Mondial Assistance) even if you don't take your car but won't cover you for belongings or cancellation of flights.

Before taking out travel insurance, carefully consider the level of cover you require and compare policies. Most policies include cover for loss of deposit or holiday cancellation, missed flights, departure delay at both the start and the end of a holiday (a common occurrence), delayed baggage, lost or stolen money, luggage and other belongings, medical expenses and accidents (including repatriation if necessary), personal liability, legal expenses and a tour operator or airline going bankrupt.

Medical expenses are an important aspect of travel insurance and you shouldn't rely on reciprocal health arrangements (see **Reciprocal Health Agreements** on page 264). The minimum medical insurance recommended by experts is €500,000 in France and the rest of Europe and €1 million to €2 million in North America and some other destinations, e.g. Japan. If applicable, check whether pregnancy-related claims are covered and whether there are restrictions for those aged over 65 or 70. Third party liability cover should be around

€1.5 million in Europe and €3 million in North America. Always check any exclusion clauses in contracts by obtaining a copy of the full policy document (all relevant information isn't included in the insurance leaflet).

The cost of travel insurance varies considerably according to your destination and the duration of your trip. Usually the longer the period, the lower the daily or weekly cost. You should expect to pay around €25 for a week's insurance in Europe, €30 for two weeks and €50 for a month. Premiums are around double for travel to North America, where medical treatment costs an arm and a leg (although they also accept dollars!). Premiums may be higher for those aged over 65 or 70. Many insurance companies offer annual travel policies from around €150 that are good value for frequent travellers, although you should check exactly what's covered (or omitted), as these policies may not provide adequate cover. Note, however, that many French insurance companies don't offer annual policies.

Although travel insurance companies gladly take your money, they aren't usually so keen to honour claims and you may have to persevere before they pay up. Always be persistent and make a claim **irrespective** of any small print, as this may be unreasonable and therefore invalid in law. Insurance companies usually require you to report a loss (or any incident for which you intend to make a claim) to the local police (or carriers) within 24 hours and obtain a written report. Failure to do this usually means that a claim won't be considered.

HOUSEHOLD INSURANCE

Household insurance in France generally includes third party liability (*responsabilité civile* – see also page 273), building and contents insurance, all of which are usually contained in a multi-risk policy (*assurance multirisques habitation*). Nine out of ten French homeowners have a multi-risk policy, but not all policies cover the same risks: for example, while over 90 per cent of policies cover water damage, fewer than 90 per cent include third party liability, only around 75 per cent include theft, and just over half cover you for glass breakage.

All buildings under construction and major renovation or repair work on existing buildings must be covered by insurance for damages (*assurance dommages*) that guarantees the work for ten years after completion. It's the builder who is responsible for taking out this coverage, but during the first ten years of the building's life it passes automatically to a new owner and will pay for damage caused by faults in the original construction.

Building

Although it isn't compulsory for owners, it's wise to take out building (*bâtiment*) insurance covering damage due to fire, water, explosion, storm, freezing, snow, theft, malicious damage, acts of terrorism and natural catastrophes, which are usually covered by a multi-risk policy (see above).

Note that in certain cases, claims for certain kinds of property damage aren't considered unless the government declares the situation a natural catastrophe or 'act of God', as has happened with floods in southern France in recent years, where many people found after the floods that their household insurance didn't cover them for water coming in from ground level, only for water seeping in through the roof. Read the small print and, if floods are one of your concerns, make sure that you're covered. It's particularly important to have insurance for storm damage in France, which can be severe in some areas. Note, however, that if you live in an area that's hit by a succession of natural disasters (such as floods), your household insurance may be cancelled. You may need to take out additional cover for *catastrophes naturelles*, which should cost only a small amount (e.g. €10 per year).

Note also that theft is covered only under certain conditions (e.g. that doors and windows were locked and that thieves had to break in to a property.) Property insurance is based on the cost of rebuilding your home and is increased each year in line with an industry-agreed inflation figure.

SURVIVAL TIP
Make sure that you insure your property for the true
cost of rebuilding.

Apartments

If you're a *copropriétaire*, building insurance is included in your service charges, although you should check exactly what's covered. You must, however, still be insured against third party liability in the event that you cause damage to neighbouring apartments, e.g. through flooding or fire (see page 273).

Rented Accommodation

If your accommodation is rented, your landlord will usually insist that you have third party liability insurance (see page 273). A lease requires you to insure against 'tenant's risks' (*risques locatifs*), including damage you may make to a rental property and to other properties if you live in an apartment, e.g. due to floods, fire or explosion. You can choose your own insurance company and aren't required to use one recommended by your landlord but your landlord is entitled to void your lease if you don't provide him with proof of adequate cover within the time specified (usually a month or two after moving in).

Contents

Contents (*contenu*) are usually insured for the same risks as a building (see above) and are insured for their replacement value. Items of high value must usually be itemised and photographs and documentation (e.g. a valuation) provided. When claiming for contents, you should produce the original bills if possible (always keep receipts for expensive items) and bear in mind that replacing imported items may be much more expensive than buying them abroad. Note that contents policies usually contain security clauses and if you don't adhere to them a claim won't be considered.

Holiday Homes

Premiums are generally higher for holiday homes (*résidence secondaire*) than for main residences (*résidence principale*) because of their vulnerability, particularly to burglaries, and are usually based on the number of days per year a property is inhabited and the interval between periods of occupancy. Cover for theft, storm, flood and malicious damage may be suspended when a property is left empty for more than three weeks at a time (or if there's no visible forced entry). It's possible to negotiate cover for periods of absence for a hefty surcharge, although valuable items are usually excluded. If you're absent from your property for long periods, e.g. more than 60 days per year, you may also be required to pay an excess (e.g. €500) on a claim arising from an occurrence that takes place during your absence (and theft may be excluded). You should read all small print in policies.

SURVIVAL TIP
Where applicable, it's important to ensure that a policy specifies a holiday home and not a principal home.

In areas with a high risk of theft (e.g. some parts of Paris and the Côte d'Azur), you may be required to fit extra locks (e.g. two locks on external doors, one of a deadlock type) and internal-locking shutters or security bars on windows. A policy may specify that all forms of protection on doors must be employed whenever a property is unoccupied for two or more days and after 22.00. Some companies may not insure holiday homes in high risk areas. It's unwise to leave valuable or irreplaceable items in a holiday home or a home that will be vacant for long periods. **Some insurance companies will do their utmost to find a loophole which makes you negligent and relieves them of their liability.** Always carefully check that the details (*conditions particulières*) listed on a policy are correct; otherwise, your policy could be void.

Insuring Abroad

It's possible and legal to take out building and contents insurance in another country for a property in France, although the policy is usually written under French law. The advantage is that you will have a policy you can understand and you will be able to handle claims in your own language. This is usually a good option for the owner of a holiday home in France, although it can be much more expensive than insuring with a French company, so it pays to compare premiums. While it may be more convenient to take out contents insurance abroad, you should be aware that this can lead to conflicts when the building is insured with a French company, e.g. in France door locks are part of the contents and in the UK they constitute part of the building. British buyers should note that Norwich Union is currently the only major UK insurance company that will cover a second home abroad as part of an existing home insurance policy.

Premiums

Premiums are usually based on the size of a property – either the habitable area in square metres or the number of rooms – rather than its value. Usually the sum insured (house and contents) is unlimited, provided the property doesn't exceed a certain size, e.g. 1,200m^2 (12,900ft^2), and is under a certain age, e.g. 200 years. However, some companies restrict home insurance to properties with a maximum number of rooms (e.g. seven) and/or a maximum value of contents. e.g. €50,000. The cost of multi-risk property insurance in a low risk area is around €120 to €150 per year for a property with one or two bedrooms, €180 to €240 for three or four bedrooms and around €240 to €275 for five or six bedrooms. Premiums are much higher in high-risk areas (especially Paris and the Côte d'Azur) and increase annually. If you have an index-linked policy, your cover is increased each year in line with inflation.

French and foreign insurers may not charge an excess (deductible) unless a property is left unoccupied for long periods (e.g. more than a week), in which case you may have to pay the first €200 or more of a claim. Note also that French insurance premiums include a tax of over 25 per cent.

Claims

If you wish to make a claim, you must usually inform your insurance company in writing (by registered letter) within two to five days of the incident or 24 hours in the case of theft. Thefts should also be reported to the local police within 24 hours, as the police statement (*déclaration de vol/plainte*), of which you receive a copy for your insurance company, is required when submitting your claim. Check whether you're covered for damage or thefts that occur while you're away from the property and are therefore unable to inform the insurance company immediately.

Cancellation

Like other French insurance policies, a household policy is automatically renewed annually unless you cancel (*résilier*) in writing, in which case you must normally give at least two months' notice (i.e. cancel at least two months before the end of your annual insurance period), although the notice period is sometimes only a month and in a few cases three months, so you should check.

There are certain circumstances in which you're entitled to a refund for the unexpired period of the insurance contract, including the following:

● Moving home;

● Selling the property;

● Changing your marital status (e.g. becoming divorced);

● Changing your profession (if the change is relevant to your home ownership) or retiring;

● If the insurance company increases your premiums by more than the official index (*indice*), based on the Index of Construction Costs published by INSEE.

If you cancel a policy for any other reason, you won't get a refund. Standard cancellation letters (*lettre type de résiliation*) are usually provided by insurance companies and brokers.

THIRD PARTY LIABILITY INSURANCE

It's customary in France to have third party liability insurance (*assurance responsabilité civile*, sometimes called *responsabilité civile vie privée*) for all members of a family. This covers you for damage done or caused by you, your children and even your pets, e.g. if your dog bites someone, although where damage is due to negligence, benefits may be reduced. Check whether insurance covers you against accidental damage to your home's fixtures and fittings. Third party liability insurance is usually combined with household insurance (see above). The cost of third party liability insurance when not included in household insurance is around €160 per year and you may need to pay an excess, e.g. the first €75 to €150 of a claim.

If you're self-employed or run a business, you must also have third party liability insurance for 'managers' (*assurance responsabilité civile chef d'entreprise*), the cost of which depends on your line of work.

If you're letting a property, make sure that you're covered for third party liability in respect of your tenants, as most home insurance policies exclude such 'commercial' liability.

9.

LETTING

Many people planning to buy a holiday home in France are interested in owning a property that will provide them with an income to cover the running costs and help with mortgage payments (or to supplement a pension). The most common method of earning money from a property is to let all or part of it (see **Types Of Property** below).

Owning and operating a furnished cottage (e.g. a *gîte*) or B&B accommodation (*chambre d'hôtes*) isn't usually considered a commercial activity by the French authorities, provided you don't set up a trading company or register as a business. Operating on a self-employed basis rather than trading through a company usually means lower taxes and social security payments. However, a property with six or more rooms to let is classed as a commercial business and is more expensive to establish and operate. You must also notify your insurance company if a property is to be let. When letting an apartment, you may be required to notify the community's manager (see page 138). Check before buying an apartment that letting is permitted.

SURVIVAL TIP
Always obtain professional advice before buying a commercial property. See also Working on page 37 and Buying For Investment on page 24.

It's difficult to make a living providing holiday accommodation in most areas, as the season is too short and there's too much competition (the market is saturated in most of the popular places).

 If you're planning to let a property, it's important not to overestimate the income, particularly if you're relying on letting income to help pay the mortgage and running costs.

The letting season is longest in Paris, where you can let year-round and may achieve 35 weeks' rental. Southern France, particularly the Côte d'Azur, is the next most popular for letting and you may be able to let an apartment for 30 weeks or a villa for 25 during the spring, summer and early autumn. In other coastal areas, the summer season is limited to around 20 weeks. Inland properties are generally restricted to a maximum of 16 weeks and in some areas the letting season can be as short as ten weeks. However, you're unlikely to achieve this many weeks' occupancy in your first year and you should budget for around half these figures, even when letting full time. The Alps are a special case, as there are two letting seasons: summer and winter, although properties in ski resorts are astronomically expensive.

Note also that running a *gîte* or B&B is hard work and not suitable for those looking for an activity compatible with semi-retirement. In the early '90s many overseas buyers lost their French homes after they defaulted on their mortgage payments, often because rental income failed to meet expectations. In many areas, the rental market is now over provided, and many owners are unable to find enough customers to generate sufficient income. Buyers who over-stretch their financial resources often find themselves on the rental treadmill, constantly struggling to find sufficient income to cover their running costs and mortgage payments.

 If you have a mortgage on a property in France, you're highly unlikely to meet your mortgage payments and running costs from rental income alone. Most experts recommend that you don't purchase a home in France if you need to rely on rental income to pay for it.

This chapter contains a summary of the considerations to be made when buying a property for letting. Details of making money from a home in France can be found in *Making Money From Your French Home* (Survival Books – see page 389).

TYPES OF RENTAL PROPERTY

There are essentially two types of rental accommodation: self-catering units, which can be either outbuildings in a property you use as a principal residence, or your second home let as self-catering accommodation when you aren't occupying it yourself; and a permanent home in which you offer accommodation on a bed and breakfast basis. See also **Working** on page 37.

Self-Catering Accommodation

Self-catering accommodation in France is generally referred to as a *gîte* and can be anything from one or two converted outhouses to a large luxury property with a number of self-contained apartments and cottages. It makes sense to have a number of units, thus reducing the running cost per unit and spreading the cost of installing amenities such as a swimming pool. Note, however, that an established *gîte* business with a good income costs anything between €200,000 and €400,000.

Existing tax legislation in France favours anything to do with the tourist industry and in particular *gîtes*. *Gîtes* aren't considered a commercial activity, so it isn't necessary to register them as a business. Before establishing a *gîte*, however, it's wise to obtain legal advice and contact your town hall regarding local regulations. **If you're buying a property with the express intention of setting up *gîtes*, make sure that permission will be granted before you buy, or make it a condition of purchase** (see **Contracts** on page 204).

Grants are available to set up *gîtes* (and other types of holiday accommodation) in certain areas, e.g. from the Gîtes de France, La Maison des Gîtes de France et du Tourisme Vert, 59 rue Saint-Lazare, Paris 75439 Cedex 09 (☎ 01 49 70 75 75, 💻 gites-de-france.fr) but you must apply **before** starting work. There's a time limit of two years for the completion of work associated with a grant from Gîtes de France. Grants are conditional on the quality of restoration or conversion and the accommodation provided (properties are assessed annually). The basic grant is usually equal to around 30 per cent of the cost of work (up to a maximum of €5,000) excluding taxes, which may be paid only on completion, although 50 per cent is sometimes paid halfway through a project. Note that a grant from Gîtes de France is conditional on the property being available to rent by them for a period of ten years; if you sell within this period or the property isn't made available, you must repay the grant. You must also bear in mind that if you let your *gîte* under the banner of Gîtes de France or a similar organisation, you may need to wait a long time to get paid.

Note that properties suitable for conversion to *gîtes* (i.e. large farmhouses with plenty of outbuildings) are few and far between in the certain parts of France (e.g. Languedoc-Roussillon), where it may be preferable to buy a small village house, which is easier to maintain and service and can be sold at any time should the need arise.

Bed & Breakfast Accommodation

No authorisation is required to offer bed and breakfast accommodation (B&B), although it must be registered as a commercial activity with the local trade registry (*Registre du Commerce*). The most common B&B accommodation in France is a *chambre d'hôtes*, which provides the option of an evening meal, usually taken with the family. Note that, if alcohol is to be served with the evening meal (mandatory in France!), a licence is required from the local town hall and you should check in advance whether one will be available, as there's normally a limit on the number of licences permitted in each commune according to its population.

Grants are available from Gîtes de France (see above) for creating or renovating rooms as *chambres d'hôtes*. If you operate a Gîtes de France approved *chambre d'hôtes*, food must be French and include regional dishes. Running a *chambre d'hôtes* with a number of rooms isn't a part-time activity, at least not in the summer, and it's generally vital that one of the owners speaks good French, or you will have to rely on foreign guests.

RULES & REGULATIONS

Various rules and regulations apply to the letting of property in France and, if you're planning to buy a community property (see page 138), you must check whether there are any restrictions on short-term letting. The property must be registered with the local town hall and (if you're offering bed and breakfast accommodation or a hotel with more than seven rooms) the local *préfecture*, and it must meet appropriate standards and comply with local regulations. The local authority may charge you a *taxe de séjour* for each paying guest (e.g. €0.15 per person per night in July and August). You may also be required to notify your insurance company.

In general, short-term rentals are exempt from the *Loi Mermez* (1989), which is designed to protect long-term tenants, but the law is complicated and you should check with a lawyer. For example, there are regulations governing deposits, such as how much you can ask for (usually a maximum of 25 per cent of the total rental charge) and how far in advance you can request it. Information about rules and regulations can be obtained from tourist offices, offices of the FNAIM or UNPI (see page 116) and the Centre de Documentation et d'Information de l'Assurance (🖥 www.ffsa.fr).

Note also that, if you let a property in France, you're required to pay tax on your rental income in France and not in the country where the income is received (e.g. the UK), irrespective of any double taxation or other agreements. See **Taxation Of Property Income** on page 242.

Letting Schemes

A variety of letting schemes (*régime*) are available to property owners in France; the one that's most suitable for you will depend on a number of factors, including whether or not you are (or plan to be) resident in France and whether you intend to let furnished or unfurnished. It's possible to combine some schemes but not others. Before choosing a scheme or schemes, check the conditions or restrictions and ensure that you're eligible to use it.

Unfurnished Lettings

The following schemes apply to the letting of unfurnished property:

Micro-Foncier Scheme: If your annual rental income is less than €15,000, you qualify for the *régime micro-foncier*, unless you're letting a listed building or a property owned under the Malraux scheme or benefiting from the Robien scheme (see below). The *régime micro-foncier* entitles you to an income tax allowance of 40 per cent to cover your letting expenses; you aren't allowed to claim any additional expenses against tax, even major capital expenditure. Instead of the usual Form 2044, you should complete Form 2042, on which you must declare 60 per cent of your rental income.

Normal Scheme: If you don't qualify for the *régime micro-foncier* (see above) or will be spending more than around a quarter of your rental income on improving a property, the *régime réel* (or *régime réel simplifié*) will normally apply. Under this scheme, you may claim your actual expenses plus a discount (*déduction forfaitaire*) of 14 per cent to cover administrative costs, insurance and depreciation. Since January 2004, you're entitled to carry forward any deficit resulting from major improvement work for up to six years, offsetting up to €10,700 per year against your taxable income. If you adopt this scheme, you must let the property unfurnished for at least three years after the year you first claim the discount. The 'normal scheme' cannot be combined with the listed buildings, Malraux or *micro-foncier* schemes (see below).

Malraux Scheme: The Malraux Act allows the cost of improvement work to be offset against total income and not only against rental income but can be used only if the property is designated for renovation or restoration by the local authority and provided that the improvement work affects the whole property, which must then be let for at least six years.

Robien Scheme: The Robien Act allows you to offset against tax the cost of construction of a new building, a restored property or (under certain circumstances) existing buildings. Under the scheme, 8 per cent of the cost can be offset annually for the first five years and 2.5 per cent for the next ten years. In the case of an existing building, you qualify for a 40 per cent allowance, as with the *régime micro-foncier* (see above).

Listed Building Scheme: If you're buying a listed building, you can claim interest charged on a mortgage or loan as well as capital expenditure against tax. Your inheritors should also qualify for an inheritance tax exemption.

Furnished Lettings

The following schemes apply to furnished property lettings:

Micro-BIC Scheme: If you're letting as an individual and not a company, aren't liable for VAT (*TVA*) and have an annual gross rental income of less than €76,300, you may qualify for this scheme, which entitles you to a 72 per cent tax allowance. Leaseback properties don't qualify for this scheme.

BIC Scheme: If you don't qualify for the *micro-BIC* scheme or intend to undertake major improvement work, you can opt for the *BIC* scheme, whereby you claim actual expenses, including management costs, local taxes, mortgage interest and renovation costs (up to 10 per cent of the property's value) against letting income over five years.

LMNP Scheme: The *location meublée non-professionelle* scheme applies to individuals who aren't registered as landlords and whose annual rental income is below €23,000 **and** is less than half of their total taxable income. Owners of more than two properties may be ineligible for this scheme. The first €760 of rental income is exempt from tax but you cannot claim any losses against tax. Normal property taxes (see page 247) apply, as do standard capital gains tax regulations (see page 251).

LMP Scheme: The *location meublée professionelle* scheme applies to registered landlords whose letting income is over €23,000 **or** is more than half of their total income. It allows you to offset losses against income and to write off your investment over a number of years. If you let the property for at least five years and earn less than €152,000 per year in rental income, you're exempt from capital gains tax on resale. Other exemptions may apply to wealth tax and inheritance tax.

Contracts

It's a legal requirement to have a written contract for all rentals. Most people who let a property for holiday accommodation draw up a simple agreement form that includes a property description, the names of the clients, and the dates of arrival and departure. However, if you do regular letting, you may wish to check with a lawyer that your agreement is legal and contains all the necessary safeguards. For example, it should specify the types of damage for which the lessor is responsible. Strictly, all descriptions, contracts and payment terms must comply with French laws. If you're letting through an agent (who must be licensed in France – see **Estate Agents** on page 116), he will provide a standard contract. Note, however, that if you plan to let to non-English speaking clients you must have a letting agreement in French or other foreign languages.

If you offer longer lets (e.g. from one to six months) outside the high season, you need to ensure that you or your agent uses the appropriate contract (see **Rental Contracts** on page 112).

Insurance

For a property let unfurnished you can take out an 'unoccupied insurance' policy (*une assurance non-occupant*), which costs less than a normal household policy (between around €150 and €200 per year for an average house). If you're letting a property furnished, however, you must add the value of the furnishings.

LOCATION

If letting income is a priority, you should buy a property with this in mind, in which case location is paramount (see **Location** on page 85). Generally, no part of France is 'better' or 'worse' than any other for letting, although coastal areas tend to be more popular than inland departments – with the exception of Dordogne. In particular, you should consider the following.

Climate

Properties in an area with a pleasant year-round climate such as the Mediterranean Coast and Corsica have a greater rental potential, particularly outside the high season. This is also important should you wish to use the property yourself outside the high season; for example, you could let a property during the summer months, when rental rates are at their highest, and use it yourself in May or October and still enjoy fine weather.

Proximity To An Airport

A property should be situated within easy travelling distance of a major airport, as most holidaymakers won't consider travelling more than 30 to 45 minutes to their destination after arriving at the airport. Make sure you choose an airport with frequent flights from your home country (see page 95). It isn't wise to rely on an airport served only by budget airlines, as they may alter or cancel routes at short notice.

Accessibility

It's an advantage if a property is served by public transport (e.g. local buses) or is situated in a town where a car is unnecessary. If a property is located in a town or development with a maze of streets, you should provide a detailed map. On the other hand, if it's in the country where signposts are all but non-existent, you will not only need to provide a detailed map with plenty of landmarks, but you may also need to erect signs (for which permission might be necessary). Holidaymakers who spend hours driving around trying to find a holiday home are unlikely to return or recommend it! Maps are also helpful for taxi drivers, who may be unfamiliar with the area.

Attractions

The property should be as close as possible to a major attraction (or more than one), e.g. a beach, theme park, area of scenic beauty or tourist town, although this will depend on the sort of clientele you wish to attract. If you want to let to families, a property should be within easy distance of leisure activities such as theme parks, water parks, sports activities (e.g. tennis, golf, water sports, etc.) and night-life. If you're planning to let a property in a rural area, it should be somewhere with good hiking possibilities, preferably near one of France's many natural parks. Proximity to one or more golf courses is also an advantage to many holidaymakers and is an added attraction outside the high season, particularly in northern France, where there may otherwise be little to attract visitors in the winter.

SWIMMING POOL

A swimming pool is desirable, particularly in warmer regions, as properties with pools are much easier to let than those without (unless a property is situated near a beach, lake or river). It's usually necessary to have a private pool with a single-family home, but a shared pool is sufficient for an apartment or townhouse. You can also charge a higher rent for a property with a pool and you may be able to extend the season even further by installing a heated or indoor pool. Some private letting agencies won't handle properties without a pool. Note that there are new safety regulations regarding pools used by the public, which include pools at private homes that are let for holidays (see page 166).

LETTING RATES

Letting rates vary considerably according to the time of year, the area, and the size and quality of a property. A house sleeping six in an average area can be let for around €1,000 to €1,500 per week in high season. A luxury property in a popular area with a pool and accommodation for 8 to 12 can be let for between €4,000 and €6,000 per week in high season. High season generally includes the months of July and August and possibly the first two weeks of September. The mid-season usually comprises June, September and October (and possibly Easter), when rents are usually around 25 per cent lower than in high season; the rest of the year is low season. For long lets in low season, a house sleeping six usually rents for around €500 per week or €2,000 per month in most regions, the tenant paying for all services.

Most people who let year round have low, medium and high season rates. Rates are much lower for winter lets, when you shouldn't expect to earn more than around €500 per week or €2,000 per month in most regions for a *gîte* sleeping six. The tenant usually pays for the running costs, including utilities. Note that central heating is essential if you want to let in the winter. If you let a property long-term, you should be aware that there are separate laws governing unfurnished accommodation, furnished accommodation and holiday lettings, i.e. furnished lets of less than six months (see **Renting Before Buying** on page 108).

Bear in mind that you must pay tax on all income from property letting (see **Taxation Of Property Income** on page 242).

FURNISHINGS

If you let a property, don't fill it with expensive furnishings or valuable belongings. While theft is rare, items will be damaged or broken eventually. When furnishing a property that you plan to let, you should choose durable furniture and furnishings and hard-wearing, dark-coloured carpets that won't show the stains. Small, two-bedroom properties usually have a sofa-bed (*canapé-lit*) in the living room. Properties should be well-equipped with cooking utensils, crockery and cutlery, and it's also best to provide bed linen and towels. You may need a cot or high chair for young children. Depending on the price and quality of a property, your guests may also expect central heating, a washing machine, dishwasher, microwave, covered parking, a barbecue and garden furniture. Some owners provide bicycles and sports (e.g. badminton and table tennis) equipment. It isn't usual to have a telephone in rental homes, although you could install a credit card telephone or a phone that will receive incoming calls only.

KEYS

You will need several sets of spare keys, which will inevitably get lost at some time. If you employ a management company, their address should be on the key fob and not the address of the house. If you let a home yourself, you can use a 'keyfinder' service, whereby lost keys can be returned to the keyfinder company by anyone finding them. You should ensure that you get 'lost' keys returned, otherwise you may need to change the locks (in any case it's wise to change the external locks periodically if you let a home). You don't need to provide clients with keys to all the external doors, only the front door (the others can be left in your home). If you arrange your own lets, you can post keys to clients in your home country, or they can be collected from a caretaker in France. It's also possible to install a key-pad entry system, though small boys seem to be able to crack the code quite easily.

USING AN AGENT

If you're letting a second home, the most important decision is whether to let it yourself or use a letting agent (or agents). If you don't have much spare time, you're better off using an agent, who will take care of everything and save you the time and expense of advertising and finding clients. An agent will charge commission of between 20 and 40 per cent of gross rental income, although some of this can be recouped through higher rents. If you want your property to appear in an agent's catalogue, you must contact him the summer prior to the year in which you wish to let it (the deadline is usually September). Note that, although self-catering holiday companies may fall over themselves to take on a luxury property on the Côte d'Azur, the top letting agents turn down as many as 90 per cent of the properties they're offered.

Most agents don't permit owners to use a property during the peak letting season (July and August) and may also restrict its use at other times. Many French estate agents also act as letting agents for property owners and some specialise in long-term winter lets. French regional tourist agencies can put you in touch with French letting agents, who must be appropriately qualified (see **Estate Agents** on page 116).

There are numerous self-catering holiday companies, including Allez France (☎ UK 0870-160 5743, 🖳 www.allezfrance.com), Bowhills (☎ UK 0845-634 2727, 🖳 www.bowhills.co.uk), French Country Cottages (☎ UK 0870-197 5889, 🖳 www.french-country-cottages.co.uk) and Interhome (☎ UK 020-8891 1294, 🖳 www.interhome.co.uk) in the UK, and ferry companies such as Brittany Ferries.

Take care when selecting a letting agent, as a number have gone bust in recent years owing customers thousands of euros. Make sure that your income is kept in an escrow account and paid regularly, or even better, choose an agent with a bonding scheme who pays you the rent **before** the arrival of guests (some do). It's absolutely essential to employ an efficient, reliable and honest company, preferably long-established. Anyone can set up a holiday letting agency and there are many 'cowboy' operators. Ask a management company to substantiate rental income claims and occupancy rates by showing you examples of actual income received from other properties. Ask for the names of satisfied customers and check with them. It's also worthwhile inspecting properties managed by an agency to see whether they're well looked after.

Other things to ask a letting agent include the following:

- Who they let to;
- Where they advertise;
- What information they send to potential clients;
- Whether they have contracts with holiday and travel companies;
- Whether you're expected to contribute towards marketing costs;
- Whether you're free to let the property yourself and use it when you wish.

You should also check the type of contract you will have with the agency: whether, for example, you will receive a detailed analysis of income and expenditure and what notice you're required to give if you decide to terminate the agreement. Management contracts usually run for a year.

The larger companies market homes via newspapers, magazines, overseas agents, colour brochures and the internet, and have representatives in many countries. A management company's services should include the following:

- Arranging routine and emergency repairs;
- Reading meters (if electricity is charged extra);
- Routine maintenance of house and garden, including lawn cutting and pool cleaning;
- Arranging cleaning and linen changes between lets;
- Advising guests on the use of equipment;
- Providing guest information and advice (possibly 24-hours in the case of emergencies).

Agents may also provide someone to meet and greet clients, hand over the keys and check that everything is in order. The actual services provided will usually depend on whether a property is a basic *gîte* or a luxury villa. A letting agent's representative should also make periodic checks when a property is empty to ensure that it's secure and that everything is in order.

You may wish (or need) to make periodic checks on an agency to ensure that all bookings are being declared and that your property is being well managed and maintained.

DOING YOUR OWN LETTING

Some owners prefer to let a property to family, friends and colleagues, which allows them more control (and with luck the property will be better looked after). In fact, the best way to get a high volume of lets is usually to do it yourself, although many owners use a letting agency in addition to doing their own marketing in their home country.

Rental Rates & Deposits

To get an idea of the rent you should charge, simply ring a few letting agencies and ask them what it would cost to rent a property such as yours at the time of year you plan to let. They're likely to quote the highest possible rent you can charge. You should also check the advertisements in newspapers and magazines. Set a realistic rent, as there's a lot of competition. Add a returnable deposit (e.g. €150) as security against loss (e.g. of keys) or breakages, although this cannot be more than 25 per cent of the rental fee or be requested more than six months in advance. A deposit should be refundable only up to six weeks before a booking. It's normal to have a minimum two-week rental period in July and August. You will need to have a simple agreement form that includes the dates of arrival and departure and approximate times. Note that if you plan to let to non-English speaking clients, you must have a letting agreement in French or other foreign languages.

Advertising

You can advertise among friends and colleagues, in company and club magazines (which may even be free), and on notice boards in companies, stores and public places. The more marketing you do, the more income you're likely to earn. It also pays to work with other local people in the same business and send surplus guests to competitors (they will usually reciprocate). It isn't necessary to just advertise locally or stick to your home country; you can extend your marketing abroad. It's necessary to have an answerphone and a fax machine.

Publications

There's a wide range of French and foreign newspapers and magazines in which you can advertise, e.g. *Daltons Weekly* and newspapers such as the *Sunday Times* in the UK. Most of the English-language newspapers and magazines listed in **Appendix B** also include advertisements from property owners. You will need to experiment to find the best publications and days of the week or months to advertise.

There are also companies that produce directories of properties let directly by owners such as Bonnes Vacances (☎ UK 01306-876876, 🖳 www.bvdirect.co.uk) and Private Villas, part of *Daltons Weekly* (☎ UK

020-8329 0222, 💻 www.privatevillas.co.uk) in the UK. You pay for the advertisement but handle bookings yourself. Advertisements must be placed by September for publication in November.

Other companies, such as Brittany Ferries and Crystal Holidays, publish holiday rental brochures (also in the autumn) and will advertise your property, although they may handle the bookings, on which they take a commission. Note that Brittany Ferries offer a choice between their Holiday Homes (including letting) and Owners in France (advertising only) schemes.

Internet

Advertising on the internet is an increasingly popular option for property owners. There are two options: place an advertisement on an agent's site (e.g. 💻 www.abritel.fr, 💻 www.cheznous.com, 💻 www.french connections.co.uk, 💻 www.frenchcountry.co.uk, 💻 www.holidayrentals. co.uk or 💻 www.villarama.com), which will cost you between around €120 and 150 per year, or set up your own site.

Although more expensive to set up, a personalised website is virtually free thereafter and can include photographs, brochures, booking forms and maps of the area, as well as comprehensive information about your property. You can also provide information about flights, ferries, car rental, local attractions, sports facilities and links to other useful websites. A good website should be easy to navigate (don't include complicated page links or indexes) and must include contact details, preferably via e-mail. It's also advisable to subscribe to a company that will submit your website to all the popular search engines, such as Altavista, Google and Yahoo. You can also exchange links with other websites.

Brochures & Leaflets

It's wise to produce a coloured brochure or leaflet containing the following:

- External/internal pictures (or a single colour brochure with coloured photographs glued to it, although this doesn't look so professional);
- Important details;
- The exact location;
- Local attractions; details of how to get there (with a small map);
- The name, address and telephone number of your local caretaker or letting agent.

Handling Enquiries

If you plan to let a home yourself, you will need to decide how to handle enquiries about flights and car rentals. It's easier to let clients make their own bookings, but you should be able to offer advice and put them in touch with airlines, ferry companies, travel agents and car rental companies. You will also have to decide whether you want to let to smokers or accept pets or young children (some people don't let to families with children under five years of age because of the risk of bed-wetting). It's best to provide linen (some agents provide a linen hire service), which is usually expected; electricity may or may not be included in the rental fee.

You should enclose a stamped addressed envelope when sending out leaflets. It's necessary to make a home look as attractive as possible in a brochure without distorting the facts or misrepresentation (you can be fined heavily for this in France). Advertise honestly and don't over-sell your property. **Finally, keep detailed records and ensure that you never double book!**

INFORMATION PACKS

You should also provide information packs for clients who have booked: one to be sent to them before they leave home and another for them to use when they arrive.

Pre-Arrival

After accepting a booking, you should provide guests with a pre-arrival information pack containing the following:

- Information about local attractions and the local area (available free from tourist offices);

- A map of the local area and instructions how to find the property;

- Emergency contact numbers in your home country (e.g. the UK) and France if guests have any problems or plan to arrive late;

- The keys or instructions on where to collect them on arrival.

Post-Arrival

It's an advantage if you can arrange for someone to be on hand to welcome your guests when they arrive, explain how things work, and deal with any special requests or minor problems. You should also provide an information pack in your home for guests explaining the following:

- How things work, e.g. kitchen appliances, TV/video, heating and air-conditioning;
- Security measures (see **Security** on page 292 and **Home Security** on page 300);
- What not to do and possible dangers (for example, if you allow young children and pets, you should make a point of emphasising dangers such as falling into the pool);
- Local emergency numbers and health services such as a doctor, dentist and hospital/clinic;
- Emergency assistance such as a general repairman, plumber, electrician and pool maintenance (you may prefer to leave the telephone number of a local caretaker who can handle any problems);
- Recommended shops, restaurants and attractions.

Many people provide a visitor's book, in which guests can write their comments and recommendations regarding local restaurants and attractions, etc. Some owners also send out questionnaires.

If you really want to impress your guests, you may wish to arrange for fresh flowers, fruit, a bottle of wine and a grocery pack to greet them on their arrival. It's little personal touches like this that ensure repeat business and recommendations. If you go 'the extra mile', it will pay off and you may even find after the first year or two that you rarely need to advertise. Many people return to the same property each year and you should do an annual mail-shot to previous clients and send them some brochures. **Word-of-mouth advertising is the cheapest and always the best.**

MAINTENANCE

If you do your own letting, you will need to arrange for cleaning and maintenance, including pool cleaning and a gardener if applicable. You should also allow for the consumption of electricity, gas, water, etc. by your tenants and the cost of additional equipment (e.g. cots and highchairs for children).

 When letting a property, you should take care not to underestimate maintenance and running costs, which can be considerable.

Caretaker

If you have a second home in France, you will find it beneficial or even essential to employ a local caretaker, irrespective of whether you let it. You may also need to employ a gardener. You can have your caretaker prepare the house for your family and guests as well as looking after it when it isn't in use. If you have a holiday home in France, it's wise to have your caretaker check it periodically (e.g. fortnightly) and to give him authority to authorise minor repairs. If you let a property yourself, your caretaker can arrange for (or do) cleaning, linen changes, maintenance and repairs, gardening and the payment of bills. Ideally you should have someone on call seven days a week who can repair broken appliances or arrange any necessary maintenance.

 Properties are often damaged and occasionally ruined by holidaymakers, so make sure you have a good contract, take an adequate deposit and have your guests sign an inventory as well as having someone on call to repair the damage.

If you employ a caretaker or housekeeper (*femme de ménage*) you should expect to pay at least the minimum wage (€7.61 per hour in 2004), possibly plus social security costs.

Closing A Property For The Winter

Before closing a property for the winter, you should turn off the water at the mains and drain all pipes, remove the fuses (except the one for a dehumidifier if you leave it on while you're away), empty the food cupboards and the refrigerator/freezer, disconnect gas cylinders, bring in any outdoor furniture and empty dustbins. All exterior doors, large windows and shutters should of course be locked, but you should leave interior doors and a few small windows (with grilles or secure shutters), as well as wardrobes, open to provide ventilation. Many people keep their central heating on a low setting during the winter when they're absent to prevent pipes from freezing.

If you think vermin are likely to find a way into the property, put down suitable poison (but remember where you put it so that you can remove it when you return!) and put away or cover with plastic sheeting anything that can be nibbled (e.g. pillows, cushions, bedding and rugs).

If your property is in an area liable to flooding, move valuable and easily damaged items to an upper floor, raise the fridge, washing machine and other apparatus off the floor (e.g. on pallets) and, if necessary, fit flood boards (*batardeaux*) across external doors and lay sand bags against them.

Secure anything of value against theft or leave it with a neighbour. Check whether any essential work needs to be done before you leave and if necessary arrange for it to be done in your absence. Most importantly, leave a set of keys with a neighbour and have a caretaker check your home periodically (e.g. once a month). It's worth making yourself a checklist of things to be done each time you leave your property unattended.

SECURITY

Note that most people aren't security conscious when on holiday, and you should therefore provide detailed instructions for guests regarding security measures and emphasise the need to secure the property when they're out. It's also important for them to be security-conscious when in the property, particularly when having a party or in the garden, as it isn't unusual for valuables to be stolen while guests are outside.

SURVIVAL TIP

Security is of paramount importance when buying a home in France, particularly if it will be left empty for long periods. Obtain advice from local security companies and neighbours and take note of what they tell you. However, bear in mind that no matter how good your security, a property is rarely impregnable, so you should never leave valuables in an unattended home unless they're kept in a safe.

When leaving a property unattended, it's important to employ all the security measures available, including the following:

- Storing valuables in a safe (if applicable) – hiding them isn't a good idea, as thieves know ALL the hiding places;

- Closing and locking all doors and windows;

- Locking grilles on patio and other doors;

- Closing shutters and securing any bolts or locks;

- Setting the alarm (if applicable) and notifying the alarm company when absent for an extended period;

- Making it appear as if a property is occupied by the use of timers and leaving lights and a TV/radio on.

It's possible to employ a 'house-sitter' to look after your home while you're away. People looking for house-sitting work sometimes advertise in the English-language press (see **Appendix B**). See also **Caretaker** on page 291)

Bear in mind that prevention is always better than cure, as stolen property is rarely recovered. If you have a robbery, you should report it to your local police station, where you must make a statement. You will receive a copy, which is required by your insurance company if you make a claim (see **Household Insurance** on page 268). See also **Home Security** on page 300.

INCREASING RENTAL INCOME

It's possible to increase rental income outside the high season by offering special interest or package holidays, which can be done in conjunction with other local businesses in order to broaden the appeal and cater for larger parties. These may include the following:

- Activity holidays, such as golf, tennis, cycling or hiking;

- Cooking, gastronomy and wine tours/tasting;

- Arts and crafts such as painting, sculpture, photography and writing courses.

You don't need to be an expert or conduct courses yourself, but can employ someone to do it for you.

10.

MISCELLANEOUS MATTERS

This chapter contains miscellaneous – but nevertheless important – information for homeowners in France, including facts about crime, heating and air-conditioning, home security, postal and telephone services, shopping, television and radio, utilities and waste disposal, selling a home and wills (arranged in alphabetical order).

CRIME

France has a similar crime rate to most other European countries and in common with them crime has increased considerably in recent years. (There has been a 75 per cent increase in illegal gun possession since 1996.) Stiffer sentences have failed to stem the spiralling crime rate and the prison population in France doubled to some 60,000 in the decade between 1988 and 1998, creating a crisis in the overcrowded jails, although it has since fallen to around 44,000, around 95 per cent male. (The death penalty was abolished in 1981.) The incidence of crime has almost doubled in a decade and the number of reported crimes rose by almost 8 per cent to over 4 million between 2000 and 2001.

Although most crimes are against property, violent crime is increasing, particularly in Paris and the Ile-de-France, where there was a mass protest of policemen demanding increased protection against criminals in 2001. Mugging is on the increase throughout France, although it's still relatively rare in most cities. In some towns in southern France pensioners have been the target of muggers and even truffle hunters have been robbed of their harvest at gunpoint. Sexual harassment (or worse) is common in France, where women should take particular care late at night and never hitchhike alone.

Thefts are soaring (around half of crimes involve theft) and burglary has reached epidemic proportions in some areas ('holiday' or second homes are a popular target). Many people keep dogs as a protection or warning against burglars (*attention: chien méchant*) and have triple-locked and steel-reinforced doors. However, crime in rural areas remains relatively low and it's still common for people in villages and small towns not to lock their cars.

Car theft and theft from cars is rife in Paris and other cities, where thieves on motorcycles reach through open car windows to snatch bags and mobile phones. Car burning has also become a popular 'sport' among urban youth gangs. Foreign-registered cars are a popular target, especially expensive models, which are often stolen to order and spirited abroad.

The worst area for crime is the Mediterranean coast (one of the most corrupt and crime-ridden regions in Europe), particularly around Marseille and Nice, where most crime is attributable to the vicious underworld (*Milieu*) of the Côte d'Azur racketeers and drug dealers.

Although the increase in crime isn't encouraging, the crime rate – especially in rural areas – is relatively low, particularly violent crime. This means that you can usually safely walk almost anywhere at any time of day or night and there's no real need for anxiety or paranoia about crime.

 Note that it's a criminal offence not to attempt to help someone who has been a victim of crime, at least by summoning assistance.

See also **Home Security** on page 300, **Security** on page 292 and **Household Insurance** on page 268.

HEATING & AIR-CONDITIONING

Even in the south of France, there can be extremes of weather and winters can be cold. Unless you plan to visit a property only in the summer, you need to consider central heating, although air-conditioning is a luxury.

Heating

Central heating systems in France may be powered by electricity, gas, oil, solid fuel (usually wood) or even solar power (see below). According to the Ministry for Industry, 100KWh of heating costs around €11 for electricity, €4.20 for natural gas, €8 for bottled gas and €4.50 for oil. Whatever form of heating you use, it's essential to have good insulation, without which up to 60 per cent of heating is lost through the walls and roof. Insulation is given a high priority in France, particularly in new homes. Some 65 per cent of French homes have central heating, which is essential if you wish to let your home during winter. Many people keep their central heating on a low setting (which can be controlled via a master thermostat) during short absences in winter to prevent pipes from freezing.

If you need to install a hot water boiler and immersion heater, ensure it's large enough for the size of the property, e.g. one room studio (100 litres), two rooms (150 litres), three to four rooms (200 litres) and five to seven rooms (300 litres).

Information

Information and advice on alternative heating systems and cost-saving can be obtained from the Agence de l'Environnement et de la Maîtrise de L'Energie – look in the information pages of your telephone book or contact ADEME, 27 rue Louis Vicat, 75737 Paris 15 Cedex, ☎ 01 47 65 20 20 or 08 10 06 00 50, ⌨ www.ademe.fr for details of where to find your nearest *Point Info Energie* (*PIE*) – and from the CSTB, part of the Ministère du Logement, Direction Générale de l'Urbanisme, de l'Habitat et de la Construction (⌨ www.cstb.fr).

Electric

Electric central heating is the most common form in France, particularly in modern homes with good insulation and a permanent system of ventilation, and is inexpensive to run using off-peak storage heaters. However, electric central heating isn't recommended for old properties with poor insulation. If you install an electric central heating system, you must usually uprate your electricity supply (see **Power Supply** on page 327) to cope with the extra demand. Note that some stand-alone electric heaters are expensive to run and are best suited to holiday homes. See also **Electricity** on page 327.

Gas

Gas central heating is popular in towns with mains gas and is the cheapest to run. Gas is clean, economical and efficient, and the boiler is usually fairly small and can be wall-mounted. In rural areas where there's no mains gas, you can have a gas tank (*citerne*) installed on your property. You will need space for the tank, which must be installed at least three metres from the house. Tanks can be hired, from suppliers such as Total and Antargaz, for around €300 per year, or you can pay a deposit of around €1,500, which is refunded if you take out a contract for the supply of gas for a fixed period. Note that piping adds to the already considerable cost of a gas tank, the system needs regular maintenance, and having a gas tank on your property will increase your household insurance. See also **Gas** on page 333.

Oil

Around 27 per cent of French homes use an oil-fired heating system (*chauffage au fioul*). Heating oil costs around €0.35 per litre and is usually available from a number of local suppliers. As with gas, you need space to install the storage tank. A tank with a capacity of up to 2,000 litres can be located in the basement; a larger tank must be buried in your garden or stored in a separate location sheltered from frost and away from the house. Oil costs around €0.35 per litre and you should expect to use around 2,000 to 3,000 litres per year to heat a three-bedroom house (including hot water). As oil causes a rapid build-up of deposits, it's essential to have your system cleaned and checked annually (costing around €120) and to replace the jet regularly. Note also that you should wait at least four hours after an oil delivery before restarting your boiler, in order to allow any foreign bodies in the tank to settle to the bottom.

For information about the use of fuel for heating, contact Chauffage Fioul, an association of petroleum manufacturers, distributors and retailers (☎ 08 10 34 34 34, 🖥 www.chaleurfioul.com).

Solar Power

A solar power system can be used to supply all your energy needs, although in France it's usually combined with an electric or gas heating system, as solar power cannot usually be relied upon year-round for heating and hot water. The main drawback is the high cost of installation, which varies considerably with the region and how much energy you require. The cost is between €2,000 and €5,000 for an installation sufficient to operate around eight lights and a small refrigerator (a solar power system must be installed by an expert), although a 30 per cent government grant is available under the *Plan Soleil* scheme (the percentage will be progressively reduced between now and 2006). For details contact ADEME (see page 298).

The advantages are no maintenance or running costs and silent operation. A system should last 30 years (it's usually guaranteed for ten years) and can be uprated to provide more power in the future. A solar power system can be used to provide electricity in a remote rural home, where the cost of extending electricity is prohibitive. Continuous advances in solar cell and battery technology are expected to dramatically increase the efficiency and reduce the cost of solar power.

Wood

Almost a quarter of France is covered by forest, and some 7 million homes rely solely on wood-burning stoves (*chauffage au bois*) for their heating and hot water, particularly in rural areas, and millions more have wood fires for effect. Stoves come in a huge variety of sizes and styles and can be purchased secondhand from *brocantes* (see **Shopping** on page 308). Wood for fuel (which should have been seasoned for at least two years) is measured in cubic metres (*stères*) and one cubic metre is roughly equivalent to 150 litres of oil. Check whether your commune supplies wood from local forests (*affouage*); otherwise you will need to find a commercial supplier (often a local farmer), who will charge around €35 per cubic metre.

The main disadvantages are the chores of collecting and chopping wood, cleaning the grate and lighting fires. Smoke can also be a problem. Note that an open fireplace (*cheminée*) can be wasteful of heat and fuel. An enclosed hearth with a glass door (*insert*) is more effective and often has the advantage of a hot-air chamber that warms other parts of a home, plus less heat wastage, a reduced fire hazard, and less ash and dust. Chimney sweeping (*ramonage*) costs around €35 to €50 and should be done at least once a year; although you can no longer be fined for failing to have your chimney swept regularly, your house insurance may be invalidated in the event of a fire if you haven't done so.

Air-Conditioning

In some regions of France, summer temperatures are often above 30°C (86°F) and, although properties are usually built to withstand the heat, you may wish to install air-conditioning (*climatisation*). Note, however, that there can be negative effects if you suffer from asthma or respiratory problems. You can choose between a huge variety of air-conditioners, fixed or moveable, indoor or outdoor installation, and high or low power. An air-conditioning system with a heat pump provides cooling in summer and economical heating in winter. Some air-conditioners are noisy, so check the noise level before buying one. Many people fit inexpensive ceiling fans for extra cooling in the summer.

Humidifiers & De-Humidifiers

Note that central heating dries the air and may cause your family to develop coughs. Those who find the dry air unpleasant can purchase a humidifier to add moisture to the air. Humidifiers that don't generate steam should be disinfected occasionally with a special liquid available from pharmacies (to prevent nasty diseases). The French commonly use humidifiers, ranging from simple water containers hanging from radiators to expensive electric or battery-operated devices.

On the other hand, if you're going to be using a holiday home only occasionally, it's worthwhile installing de-humidifiers, especially in the bedrooms, to prevent clothes and linen going mouldy.

HOME SECURITY

Security is obviously an important consideration for anyone buying a home in France (or anywhere else), particularly if it's a holiday home that will be unoccupied for long periods. While it's important not to underestimate security risks, even in rural areas of France, where crime rates are generally low (see **Crime** on page 296), you should avoid turning your home into a fortress, which will deter visitors as well as would-be thieves! Bear in mind that your home is generally more at risk from fire and storm damage than from burglary.

Generally, the minimum level of security required by French insurance companies is fairly basic, e.g. security locks on external doors and shutters on windows (small windows generally have bars rather than shutters). If the contents of your home are worth less than around €60,000, this will normally be all that's required unless the property is in Alpes-Maritimes or the Paris area, where burglary rates are the highest in France and many insurers insist on extra security measures, such as two locks on external doors, internal locking shutters, and security bars or metal grilles on windows and patio doors.

In remote areas, it's common for owners to fit two or three locks on external doors, alarm systems (see below), grilles on doors and windows, window locks, security shutters and a safe for valuables, although such systems are rarely required by insurance companies. The advantage of grilles is that they allow you to leave windows open without inviting criminals in (unless they're *very* slim). You can fit UPVC (toughened clear plastic) security windows and doors, which can survive an attack with a sledge-hammer without damage, and external steel security blinds (that can be electrically operated), although these are expensive.

A policy may specify that all forms of protection on doors must be employed when a property is unoccupied, and that all other protection (e.g. shutters) must also be used after 22.00 and when a property is left empty for two or more days.

When moving into a new home, it's often wise to replace the locks (or lock barrels) as soon as possible, as you have no idea how many keys are in circulation for the existing locks. This is true even for new homes, as builders often give keys to sub-contractors. In any case, it's wise to change the external locks or lock barrels periodically if you let a home. If they aren't already fitted, it's best to fit high security (double cylinder or dead bolt) locks. Modern properties are usually fitted with special high security locks that are individually numbered. Extra keys for these locks cannot be cut at a local hardware store and you need to obtain details from the previous owner or your landlord. Many modern developments and communities have security gates and caretakers.

You may wish to have a security alarm fitted, which is usually the best way to deter thieves and may also reduce your household insurance (see page 268). It should include external doors and windows, internal infra-red security beams, and may also include an entry keypad (whose code can be frequently changed and is useful for clients if you let) and 24-hour monitoring. With a monitored system, when a sensor (e.g.

smoke or forced entry) is activated or a panic button is pushed, a signal is sent automatically to a 24-hour monitoring station. The duty monitor will telephone to check whether it's a genuine alarm (a code must be given); if he cannot contact you, someone will be sent to investigate. Note, however, that an insurer may require you to have a particular alarm fitted; check before buying one that may not be acceptable.

More sophisticated security systems using internet technology are now available, including cameras and sound recorders linked to your computer or mobile phone. A variety of systems, costing between £70 and £330, is offered by Dabs.com (⌨ www.dabs.com).

You can deter thieves by ensuring that your house is well lit at night and not conspicuously unoccupied. External security 'motion detector' lights (that switch on automatically when someone approaches), random timed switches for internal lights, radios and televisions, dummy security cameras, and tapes that play barking dogs (etc.) triggered by a light or heat detector may all help deter burglars. A dog can be useful to deter intruders, although it should be kept inside where it cannot be given poisoned food. Irrespective of whether you actually have a dog, a warning sign with a picture of a fierce dog may act as a deterrent. If not already present, you should have the front door of an apartment fitted with a spy-hole and chain so that you can check the identity of a visitor before opening the door. **Remember, prevention is better than cure, as stolen property is rarely recovered.**

Holiday homes are particularly vulnerable to thieves and in some areas they're regularly ransacked. No matter how secure your door and window locks, a thief can usually obtain entry if he's determined enough, often by simply smashing a window or even breaking in through the roof or by knocking a hole in a wall! In isolated areas thieves can strip a house bare at their leisure and an un-monitored alarm won't be a deterrent if there's no-one around to hear it. If you have a holiday home in France, it isn't wise to leave anything of great value (monetary or sentimental) there. If you vacate your home for an extended period, it may be obligatory to notify a caretaker, landlord or insurance company, and to leave a key with someone in case of emergencies. If you have a robbery, you should report it immediately to your local *gendarmerie*, where you must make a statement (*plainte*). You will receive a copy, which is required by your insurance company if you make a claim.

When closing up a property for an extended period, e.g. over the winter, you should ensure that everything is switched off and that it's secure (see **Closing A Property For The Winter** on page 291). Another important aspect of home security is ensuring that you have early warning of a fire, which is easily accomplished by installing smoke detectors. Battery-operated smoke detectors can be purchased for around €10 and should be tested weekly to ensure that the batteries aren't exhausted. You can also fit an electric-powered gas detector that activates an alarm when a gas leak is detected.

POSTAL SERVICES

French postal services are poor by Western European standards. The French Post Office (La Poste) is a state-owned company, although privatisation of the postal service is due to begin in 2003 and La Poste's monopoly on the handling of letters between 50 and 100g will end in 2006. There are around 17,000 post offices, 60 per cent of them in communes of fewer than 2,000 inhabitants and, as in other countries, those in the least populated areas are gradually being closed. Signs for post offices in towns vary widely and include *PTT* (the old name for the post office), *PT*, *P et T*, *Bureau de Poste* or simply *Poste*. Post offices are listed in the yellow pages under *Poste: Services*.

In addition to the usual post office services, a range of other services are provided. These include telephone calls, telegram and fax transmissions, domestic and international cash transfers, payment of telephone and utility bills, and the distribution of mail-order catalogues. Recently, La Poste has also started offering e-mail services on the internet, including free and permanent email addresses as well as e-commerce services for small businesses. The post office also provides financial and banking services, including cheque and savings accounts, retirement plans, and share prices; post offices will start offering mortgages some time in 2005. Post offices usually have photocopy machines, telephone booths and Minitel terminals (see page 320).

The Post Office produces numerous leaflets and brochures, including the handy *Tarifs Courrier – Colis*, or you can obtain information via La Poste's website (🖥 www.laposte.fr), although only limited information is available in English. The site offers a search tool to help you find the address and telephone number of your nearest post office, according to the town name or postal code. Unfortunately, the listings don't include the opening hours or the times for the last collection each day. For further details of French postal services, see *Living and Working in France* (Survival Books – see page 389).

SELLING YOUR HOME

Although this book is primarily concerned with buying a home in France, you may wish to sell your French home at some time in the future. Before offering your home for sale, you should investigate the state of the property market. For example unless you're forced to sell, it definitely isn't recommended during a property slump when prices are depressed. It may be wiser to let your home long-term and wait until the market has recovered. It's also unwise to sell in the early years after purchase, when you will probably make a loss unless it was an absolute bargain (and may have to pay capital gains tax as well).

Having decided to sell, your first decision will be whether to sell it yourself or use the services of an estate agent (see below). Although the majority of properties in France are sold through estate agents, a large number of owners also sell their own homes. If you need to sell a property before buying a new one, this must be included as a conditional clause (see page 210) in the purchase contract for a new home. Note that when selling a property in France the vendor chooses the notary who performs the completion.

The legal procedure is the same as for buying a property (see **Chapter 5**), but a few points are worth noting. You may be asked by an agent to sign a conditional clause in the sales contract that the sale is dependent on the buyer selling another property; you aren't obliged to do so and should be wary of agreeing to such a clause, particularly if the buyer is selling a property in the UK, where sales can be cancelled at any stage – you won't be able to cancel your agreement even if another would-be buyer offers you cash. Secondly, if a buyer wants to have the property inspected or surveyed, it's wise to have this done before any contracts are signed.

Price

It's important to bear in mind that (like everything) property has a market price, and the best way of ensuring a quick sale (or any sale) is to ask a realistic price. If your home's fairly standard for the area, you can find out its value by comparing the prices of other homes on the market, or those that have recently been sold. Most agents will provide a free appraisal of a home's value in the hope that you will sell it through them. However, don't believe everything they tell you, as they may over-price it simply to encourage you. You can also hire a professional appraiser to determine the market value.

If you're marketing your property abroad, e.g. in the UK, take into account the prevailing exchange rate: if the euro is strong, this will deter foreign buyers; if it's weak, you may even be able to increase the price.

You should be prepared to drop the price slightly (e.g. 5 or 10 per cent) and should set it accordingly, but shouldn't grossly over-price a home, as this will deter buyers. Don't reject an offer out of hand unless it's ridiculously low, as you may be able to get the prospective buyer to raise his offer. When selling a second home in France, you may wish to include the furnishings (plus major appliances) in the sale, particularly when selling a relatively inexpensive property with modest furnishings. You should add an appropriate amount to the price to cover the value of the furnishings, or alternatively you could use them as an inducement to a prospective buyer at a later stage, although this isn't usual in France.

Presentation

The secret to selling a home quickly lies in its presentation (assuming that it's competitively priced). First impressions (both exteriors and interiors) are vital when marketing your home and it's important to make every effort to present it in its best light and make it as attractive as possible to potential buyers. It may pay to invest in new interior decoration, new carpets, exterior paint and landscaping. A few plants and flowers can do wonders. Note that when decorating a home for resale, it's important to be conservative and not to do anything radical (such as install a red or black bathroom suite); white is a good neutral colour for walls, woodwork and porcelain.

It may also pay you to do some modernisation, such as installing a new kitchen or bathroom, as these are of vital importance (particularly kitchens) when selling a home. Note, however, that although modernisation may be necessary to sell an old home you shouldn't overdo it, as it's easy to spend more than you could ever hope to recoup in the sale price. If you're using an agent, you can ask him what you should do (or need to do) to help sell your home. If your home is in poor repair, this must be reflected in the asking price and, if major work is needed that you cannot afford, you should obtain a quotation (or two) and offer to knock this off the asking price. You have a duty under French law to inform a prospective buyer of any defects which aren't readily apparent and which materially affect the value of a property. There are also special disclosure requirements for apartments and other community properties (see page 138).

Selling Your Home Yourself

While certainly not for everyone, selling your own home is a viable option for many people and is particularly recommended when you're selling an attractive home at a realistic price in a favourable market. Saving estate agent's fees may allow you to offer the property at a more appealing price, which could be an important factor if you're seeking a quick sale. Even if you aren't in a hurry, selling your own home saves you an agent's fees, which can be up to 15 per cent in France.

How you market your home will depend on the type of home, the price, and the country or area from where you expect your buyer to come. For example, if your property isn't of a type and style and in an area desirable to local inhabitants, it's usually a waste of time advertising it in the local press.

Advertising is the key to selling your home. The first step is to get a professional looking 'for sale' sign made (showing your telephone number) and to erect it somewhere visible. Do some research into the best publications for advertising your property, and place an advertisement in those that look the most promising. If you own a property in an area popular with foreign buyers, it may be worthwhile using an overseas agent (see below) or advertising in foreign newspapers and magazines, such as the English-language publications listed in **Appendix B**.

You could also have a leaflet printed (with pictures) extolling the virtues of your property, which you could drop into local letter boxes or have distributed with a local newspaper (many people buy a new home in the vicinity of their present home). You may also need a 'fact sheet' printed if your home's vital statistics aren't included in the leaflet mentioned above and could offer a finder's fee (e.g. €750) to anyone finding you a buyer. Don't omit to market your home around local companies, schools and organisations, particularly if they have many itinerant employees. Finally, it may help to provide information about local financing sources for potential buyers. With a bit of effort and practice you may even make a better job of marketing your home than an agent! Unless you're in a hurry to sell, set yourself a realistic time limit for success, after which you can try an agent. When selling a home yourself, you will need to obtain legal advice regarding contracts and to engage a *notaire* to hold the deposit and complete the sale.

Using An Agent

Most owners prefer to use the services of an agent or notary, either in France or in their home country, particularly when selling a second home. If you purchased the property through an agent, it's often wise to use the same agent when selling, as he will already be familiar with it and may still have the details on file. You should take particular care when selecting an agent, as they vary considerably in their professionalism, expertise and experience (the best way to investigate agents is by posing as a buyer). Note that many agents cover a relatively small area, so you should take care to choose one who regularly sells properties in your area and price range.

Agents' Contracts

Before offering a property for sale, a French agent must have a signed authorisation, called a 'sales mandate' (*mandat de vente*), from the owner of the property. There are generally two types of mandate, an ordinary or non-exclusive mandate (*mandat simple* or *mandat sans exclusivité*), which means that you reserve the right to deal with other agents and to negotiate directly with private individuals. An exclusive mandate (*mandat exclusif*) gives a single agent the exclusive right to sell a property, although you can reserve the right to find a private buyer. An agent's fees are usually one or two percentage points lower with an exclusive mandate than with a non-exclusive mandate.

 Note that, if you sign a contract without reserving the right to find your own buyer, you must still pay the agent's commission even if you sell your home yourself.

Make sure you don't sign two or more exclusive mandates to sell your home. Check the contract and make sure you understand exactly what you're agreeing to.

An agent with an exclusive mandate has the authority to sign a sales contract on behalf of the vendor. Therefore, before signing a contract to sell a property yourself, you must ensure that any other agents to whom you've given a mandate haven't found a buyer and signed a contract on your behalf. Notify all agents with a non-exclusive mandate by registered letter when a property has been sold. Mandates are for a limited period, usually three months, but can be extended for further three-month periods, usually up to a maximum of a year. It's usually possible to terminate the contract after three months by giving written notice by registered letter two weeks before the end of the three-month period. Note that you must still pay an agent's fee if you sell to someone introduced by him within a year of the expiry of a mandate. Contracts state the agent's commission, what it includes, and most importantly, who must pay it.

> **SURVIVAL TIP**
> Generally, you shouldn't pay any fees unless you require extra services, and you should never pay commission before a sale is completed.

Agents' Fees

When selling a property in France, the agent's commission (5 to 10 per cent of the sale price) is usually paid by the vendor and included in the purchase price (see **Estate Agents** on page 116). Foreign agents who work with French agents share the standard commission, so you pay no more by using a foreign agent. Note that when a *notaire* is the selling agent, his sales commission **isn't** included in the asking price and is paid by the buyer. French agents don't normally charge for advertising or other expenditure, but it's worth checking in advance.

Capital Gains Tax

Non-residents must pay capital gains tax (CGT) on the profit made on the sale of a home in France if it hasn't been owned for 22 years (see page 251). Where applicable, CGT is withheld by the notary handling the sale. Before a sale, the notary prepares a form (Cerfa 2090) calculating the tax due and appoints an agent (*agent fiscal accredité*) or guarantor to act on the vendor's behalf in matters concerning tax. If the transaction is straightforward and the selling price is under €100,000, the local tax office may grant a dispensation (*dispense*) of the need to appoint a guarantor, provided the notary applies before completion of the sale. If you obtain a dispensation, the proceeds of the sale can be released to you in full after CGT has been paid.

However, if you aren't granted dispensation and in any case if the selling price is over €100,000, you must pay an agent's fee of between 0.75 and 1 per cent of the selling price plus VAT (*TVA*) at 19.6 per cent in addition to any CGT, although the agent's fee is deductible from the gross capital gain. **As when buying a home in France, you must be very, very careful who you deal with when selling a home.**

Never agree to accept part of the sale price under the table; if the buyer refuses to pay the extra money, there's nothing you can do about it (at least legally – see **Avoiding Problems** on page 20). Note also that it can be some weeks before you receive the proceeds from the sale of a property in France, although a phone call to the notary or bank involved usually speeds things up.

SHOPPING

France is one of Europe's great shopping countries, and shops are designed to seduce you with their artful displays of beautiful and exotic merchandise. Paris is a shoppers' paradise, where even the shop windows are a delight, although it isn't the best place to find bargains and is isn't the place for budget shoppers. French products are distinguished by their attention to detail, elegance, flair and quality (not to mention high prices).

Most towns have a supermarket or two and, on the outskirts of large towns, there are usually huge shopping centres with hypermarkets, do-it-yourself stores and furniture warehouses. In many city centres there are pedestrian streets (*rue piétonne*), where you can walk and shop without fear of being mown down.

For further details of shopping in France, see *Living and Working in France* (Survival Books). Books of interest to shopaholics are Frommer's *Born to Shop France* by Suzy Gershman and *Paris Pas Cher* (Flammarion). For those who aren't used to buying articles with metric measures and continental sizes, a list of comparative weights and measures is included in **Appendix D**.

Opening Hours

Shopping hours in France vary considerably according to the city or town and the type of shop. Food shops cannot legally open for more than 13 hours per day, and other shops are limited to 11 hours per day. (There are also restrictions on the number of hours employees can work each week, and French law now limits many employees' normal working week to 35 hours.) Food shops in the provinces (such as bakers) open from as early as 06.30 or 07.00 until 12.00 or 12.30, and again from between 15.00 and 16.00 until 19.00 or 20.00. Non-food shops usually open from 09.00 or 10.00 to 12.00, and from 14.00 until 18.30 or 19.30. Small shops tend to tailor their opening hours to suit their customers rather than their staff.

Large stores and hypermarkets remain open at lunchtime, although smaller stores usually close, except perhaps on Fridays and Saturdays. Most hypermarkets are open from 09.00 until between 20.00 and 22.00 Mondays to Saturdays.

France is generally closed on Sunday, although some village shops, particularly *boulangeries*, *charcuteries* and *pâtisseries*, open on Sunday mornings. There's widespread opposition to Sunday trading from the unions and small shopkeepers, although French stores **are** permitted to open on five Sundays a year and those in designated 'tourist' areas (e.g. coastal and ski resorts) can open on any Sunday.

Many shops are closed on Monday mornings or all day Mondays, particularly shops that open on Sundays. In many cities and towns, stores have a late-opening day (*nocturne*) once a week, e.g. Wednesdays in Paris, until between 20.00 and 22.00. It's generally best to avoid shopping on Wednesdays if possible, as many children are off school and either go or are taken shopping on that day.

Most shops close on public holidays and virtually all (except some newsagents) shut on 1st January, 1st May, 14th July and 25th December.

Furniture & Furnishings

Furniture (*meubles*) is generally quite expensive in France compared with many other European countries and the choice is usually between basic functional furniture and high quality designer furniture, with little in between. Exclusive (i.e. expensive) modern and traditional furniture is available everywhere, including bizarre pieces from designers such as Gaultier for those with money to burn. Many regions of France have a reputation for quality hand-made furniture.

If you're looking for antique furniture at affordable prices, the best bargains are to be found at flea markets (*foire à tout*) in rural areas. However, you must drive a hard bargain as the asking prices are often a joke. You can often buy good second-hand and antique furniture at bargain prices from a *dépôt-vente*, where people sell their old furniture and courts sell repossessed household goods. Look under *Dépôts-vente Ameublement et Divers* in your local yellow pages. There are also companies selling furniture repossessed from bankrupt businesses at bargain prices.

Modern furniture is popular in France and is often sold in huge stores in commercial centres (inexpensive chain stores include But, Conforama and Fly) and hypermarkets, some of which provide the free loan of a van. Pine furniture is inexpensive. Beware of buying complicated home-assembled furniture with indecipherable French instructions (translated from Korean) and too few screws. If you want reasonably priced, good quality, modern furniture, you need look no further than Ikea, a Swedish company manufacturing furniture for home assembly with a 14-day money-back guarantee (note that the price of Ikea furniture varies with the country and most items are much cheaper in France than, for example, in the UK). If you're buying a large quantity of furniture, don't be reluctant to ask for a reduction, as many stores will give you one.

When buying furniture for a home in France, don't forget to take the climate into consideration. The kind of furniture you buy may also depend on whether it's a permanent or holiday home. Note also that, if you intend to furnish a holiday home with antiques or expensive furniture, you will need adequate security and insurance.

Household Goods

Household goods in France are generally of good quality and, although the choice is not as wide as in some other European countries, it has improved considerably in the last decade. Not surprisingly for a nation that spends much of its time in the kitchen (the rest is spent in the dining room!), French kitchenware in particular is among the best in the world. Prices are also more competitive than previously, with bargains to be found at supermarkets and hypermarkets such as Auchan and Carrefour. Apart from hypermarkets, one of the best stores for household appliances is Darty, which has outlets in most towns.

Interest-free credit or deferred payment is common and goods can usually be paid for in ten monthly instalments. (Note that, if you choose to buy outright a product advertised with an interest-free credit period, you're entitled to a discount in proportion to the length of the credit period, e.g. 2.31 per cent for a six-month period, 4.23 per cent for 12 months and 7.92 per cent for two years.) You can also obtain an extended guarantee (for an extra charge), which enables you effectively to 'trade in' nearly new articles for the 'state-of-the-art' model.

Bear in mind when importing household appliances that aren't sold in France that it may be difficult or impossible to get them repaired or serviced locally. If you bring appliances with you, don't forget to bring a supply of spares and refills, such as bulbs for a refrigerator or sewing machine, and spare bags for a vacuum cleaner.

Note also that the standard size of kitchen appliances and cupboard units in France isn't the same as in other countries, and it may be difficult to fit an imported dishwasher or washing machine into a French kitchen.

SURVIVAL TIP

Check the size and the latest French safety regulations before shipping these items to France or buying them abroad, as they may need expensive modifications.

If you already own small household appliances, it's worthwhile bringing them to France, as all that's usually required is a change of plug. However, if you're coming from a country with a 110/115V electricity supply, such as the US, you'll need a lot of expensive converters or transformers (see **Power Supply** on page 327) and it's better to buy new appliances in France. Small appliances such as vacuum cleaners, grills, toasters and electric irons aren't expensive and are of good quality (the label 'NF' indicates compatibility with appropriate safety standards). Don't bring your TV without checking its compatibility first, as TVs from many countries won't work in France (see page 322)

Subject to electricity supply compatibility, foreign computers will work in France. Those who don't know the difference between a *fiche* and a *fichier* may be interested in an English-language computer service called Computers4brits (☎ 01273-602623 in the UK or ☎ 02 33 90 42 64 in France, 🖥 www.4brits.net), which will (hopefully) solve your computer problems for £35 per hour and even supply you with British plugs! If you need to buy a computer while in France but don't want it to have French software or an AZERTY keyboard, you can order one from an international supplier such as Apple (🖥 www.apple.fr) or Dell (🖥 www1.euro.dell.com) or buy one in the UK or Ireland. (You may be able to avoid paying VAT if you provide a French address.)

If you need kitchen measuring equipment and cannot cope with decimal measures, you will need to bring your own measuring scales, jugs, cups and thermometers. (See also **Appendix D**.) Foreign pillow sizes (e.g. American and British) aren't the same as in France, and the French use duvets and not blankets to keep warm in winter (besides more 'natural' methods!).

Shopping Abroad

The information in this section applies both to French residents shopping outside France and to foreign residents shopping in France. Shopping abroad can save you money and, if you live in France, make a nice day out for the family. Many families, especially those living in border areas, take advantage of lower prices outside France, particularly when it comes to buying alcohol (e.g. in Andorra, Belgium and Italy). Whatever you're looking for, compare prices and quality before buying. Note that if you buy goods that are faulty or need repair, you may need to return them to the place of purchase. When you buy expensive goods abroad, have them insured for their full value.

Don't forget your passports or identity cards, car papers, dog's vaccination papers and foreign currency, if applicable (e.g. if shopping in the UK or Switzerland) – Schengen agreements notwithstanding!

Since 1993, there have been no cross-border shopping restrictions within the EU for goods purchased duty and tax paid, provided goods are for personal consumption or use and not for resale. Although there are no restrictions, there are 'indicative levels' for certain items, above which goods may be classified as commercial quantities and therefore subject to scrutiny, although the onus is on customs to prove this. For example, people aged 17 or over may import the following amounts of alcohol and tobacco into France (or the UK) without question:

- 10 litres of spirits (over 22° proof);
- 20 litres of sherry or fortified wine (under 22° proof);
- 90 litres of wine (or 120 x 0.75 litre bottles) of which a maximum of 60 litres may be sparkling wine;
- 110 litres of beer;
- 3,200 cigarettes and 400 cigarillos and 200 cigars and 3kg of tobacco.

There's no limit on perfume or toilet water.

Never attempt to import illegal goods into France and don't agree to bring a parcel into France or deliver a parcel in another country without knowing exactly what it contains. A popular confidence trick is to ask someone to post a parcel in France (usually to a *poste restante* address) or to leave a parcel at a railway station or restaurant. **THE PARCEL USUALLY CONTAINS DRUGS!**

Duty-Free Allowances

Duty-free (*hors-taxe*) shopping within the EU ended on the 30th June 1999, although it's still available when travelling further afield. According to new guidelines introduced in 2003, travellers aged 17 or over (unless otherwise stated) are entitled to import into an EU country the following goods purchased duty-free:

● One litre of spirits (over 22° proof) or two litres of fortified wine (under 22° proof) or two litres of sparkling wine;

● Two litres of still table wine;

● 200 cigarettes or 100 cigarillos or 50 cigars or 250g of tobacco;

● 50g of perfume;

● 250ml of toilet water;

● 500g of coffee (or 200g coffee extract) and 100g tea (or 40g tea extract) for people aged 15 or over;

● Other goods, including gifts and souvenirs, to the value of €182.94 (€91.47 for those aged under 15).

Duty-free allowances apply to both outward and return journeys, even if both are made on the same day, and the combined total (i.e. double the above limits) can be imported into your 'home' country.

Since 1993, duty-free sales have been 'vendor-controlled', meaning that vendors are responsible for ensuring that the amount of duty-free goods sold to individuals doesn't exceed their entitlement. Residents in towns bordering non-EU countries (e.g. Switzerland) and international lorry drivers are subject to reduced allowances.

If you live outside the EU, you can obtain a VAT refund on purchases made in France if the total value (excluding books, food, services and some other items) is above a certain amount (around €300; check the exact figure at the time of purchase).

TELEPHONE SERVICES

France enjoys a high standard of telephone services, (including fax, Minitel, internet and mobile phones). The telephone service is operated by France Télécom, which is 55 per cent state-owned (and one of the world's most indebted companies!). France Télécom maintained a monopoly on 'local' calls until 1st January 2002, but several companies now offer services for local as well as inter-departmental and international calls. For general information in English about France Télécom services contact ☎ 08 00 36 47 75. For further details of French telephone services, see *Living and Working in France* (Survival Books – see page 389).

Installation & Registration

If you're planning to move into a property without an existing telephone line, you will need to have one installed. In this case, you must visit your local France Télécom agent, which you will find in the yellow pages under *Télécommunications: service*. You will need to prove that you're the owner or tenant of the property in question, e.g. with an electricity bill, confirmation of purchase (*attestation d'acquisition*) or a lease. You will also require your passport or residence permit (*carte de séjour*). France Télécom publishes a *Set Up Guide* in English.

 If you buy a property in a remote area without a telephone line, it may be expensive to have a telephone installed, as you must pay for the line to your property. Contact France Télécom for an estimate.

If you're restoring a derelict building or building a new home, you should have trenches dug for the telephone cable if you want a below ground connection (you may be able to have an above ground connection via a wire from the nearest pylon). This work can be carried out by France Télécom, but their charges are high and it's possible to do it yourself, although you must observe certain standards. Details of the required depth of trenches and the type of conduit (*gaine*) to use, etc., can be obtained from France Télécom.

When you go to the France Télécom agency, you will need to know what kind of telephone sockets are already installed in the property, how many telephones you want, where you want them installed and what kind of telephone you want (if you're buying from France Télécom). If you want a number of telephone points installed, you should arrange this in advance. You may also want to upgrade a line (e.g. to ADSL – see **Broadband** below).

You may be given a telephone number on the spot, although you should wait until you receive written confirmation before giving it to anyone. Note that it isn't possible simply to take over the telephone number of the previous occupants. If you own a property and are letting it for holidays, you can arrange to have outgoing calls limited to the local area, or to regional or national calls only, but you cannot limit the service just to incoming calls.

To have a line installed takes from a few days in a city to weeks or possibly over a month in remote rural areas, although 90 per cent of new customers have a line installed within two weeks. Business lines may be installed quicker than domestic lines.

When moving into a new home in France with a telephone line, you must have the account transferred to your name and a telephone number issued to you. Note that France Télécom always changes the telephone number when the ownership or tenancy of a property changes. To do this, you can simply dial 1014 or go to the France Télécom website (🖥 www.francetelecom.com and follow the links to *l'agence sur le net*). Some information is available on the English-language section of the website, but it's limited to business services and investment details. France Télécom publishes two English-language telephone information service numbers (☎ 08 00 36 47 75 from within France only or 01 55 78 60 34), open Mondays to Fridays from 9am to 5pm, but neither can be relied upon to provide you with an English-speaker – or indeed anyone to talk to in any language! English-language assistance can also be obtained via email (✉ engft.paris@francetelecom.fr).

SURVIVAL TIP

Always check that the previous occupant has closed his account before you take over the line.

If you move into a property where the telephone hasn't been disconnected or transferred to your name, you should ask France Télécom for a special reading (*relevé spécial*). If you're taking over an existing line, you can usually have it connected within 48 hours. The cost of installing a new line (known elaborately as *frais forfaitaire d'accès au réseau*) is normally €104.

Broadband

There are two types of 'broadband' connection: Asymmetric Digital Subscriber Lines (ADSL) and Integrated Services Digital Network (ISDN). France Télécom is committed to extending the availability of ADSLs, but it isn't available in all areas and may even be available in one part of a village but not another! To find out if ADSL is available in your area, go to 🖥 www.agence.francetelecom.com/eliadsl_ftbynet/html/popup_eli.html and enter your current telephone number (or a neighbour's) or the number of the department in which you live or intend to live. If available, it's possible to upgrade an existing line to an ADSL (known as *le haut-débit* or *l'ADSL*) at no extra charge, although you must pay higher line rental charges (see page 315); if it isn't available and you aren't in a 'cabled' area, ISDN (*RNIS* but referred to by France Télécom as *Numéris*) is the only option. Note that an ISDN 'line' actually provides you with three telephone numbers but only two lines (at least, you can use only two at once!). France Télécom also offers various combined phone and internet access packages for compulsive internet surfers (see **Internet** on page 321). Installation of an ADSL costs the same as a standard line (normally €104), but an ISDN line costs an additional €90 (for private use) or €123 (for business use).

Alternative Providers

There are currently around 20 alternative telephone service providers in France, some of which advertise in the English-language press (see **Appendix B**). If you wish to use another provider (or several different providers, for different types of call), you will need to open a separate account with each one. Note, however, that you must still have an account with France Télécom for line rental.

Telephones

You can buy a telephone (*téléphone*) from France Télécom or any retailer (e.g. a telephone shop). Cordless (*sans fil*) telephones are widely available. The standard French telephone connector is a large block with a single blade-like plug. Adapter plugs allowing you to connect a standard RJ11 phone plug to a French phone point aren't easy to find in France, although they're available in some airport shops and larger computer shops, and it's preferable to buy them before you move to France (e.g. from Maplin, ⌨ www.maplin.co.uk, Radio Shack/Tandy or RSComponents, ⌨ www.rs-components.com, or TeleAdapt, ⌨ www. teleadapt.com). Note, however, that they cost around €40, so it may be cheaper to buy a new telephone! See also **Modems** on page 322.

Using The Telephone

Using the telephone in France is simplicity itself. All French telephone numbers have ten digits, beginning with a two-digit regional code (01 for the Ile-de-France, 02 for the north-west, 03 north-east, 04 south-east and 05 south-west), and followed by another two-digit area code. Note that, if you're calling within France, you must **always** dial all ten digits, even if you're phoning your next-door neighbour.

Numbers beginning 06 are mobile (*portable*) numbers (see **Mobile Phones** on page 320), and those beginning 08 are special rate numbers see *Living and Working in France* (Survival Books) for details.

International Calls

It's possible to make direct IDD (International Direct Dialling) calls to most countries from both private and public telephones. A full list of country codes, plus area codes for main cities and time differences, is shown in the information pages (*les info téléphoniques*) of your local yellow pages. To make an international call you must first dial 00, then the country code, the area code (*without* the first zero) and the subscriber's number. For international dialling information and directory enquiries call 3212, but note that this service costs €3 per call and you may obtain only two numbers. If you have internet access, it's cheaper to find an online telephone directory for the country you need.

France subscribes to a Home Direct service (called *France direct*) that allows you to call a number giving you direct and free access to an operator in the country that you're calling, e.g. for British Telecom in the UK dial ☎ 08 00 99 00 44. The operator will connect you to the number required. Note, however, that this service can be used only for reverse charge (collect) calls. To obtain an operator from one of the major US telephone companies dial ☎ 08 00 99 00 11 (AT&T), ☎ 08 00 99 00 87 (Sprint) or ☎ 08 00 99 00 19 (Worldphone).

These companies also offer long-distance calling cards that provide access to English-speaking operators, and AT&T offers a 'USA Direct' service, whereby you can call an operator in any state (except Alaska). To reach an operator in any other country from France, you must dial ☎ 12 and ask for the relevant *France Direct* number; there's no longer a list of Home Direct codes in French telephone directories. You can also use the *France Direct* service from some 50 countries to make calls to France via a France Télécom operator.

France Télécom publishes a useful free booklet, *Guide du Téléphone International*, containing information in both French and English.

An increasing number of expatriates (and French people) make use of what used to be called 'callback' services, such as those provided by Eurotelsat (🖳 www.eurotelsat.com) and Kallback (🖳 www.kallback. com). In fact, it's no longer necessary to wait to be called back and, as with an alternative provider, you simply dial a local freephone number or a code before numbers. Calls are routed via the cheapest provider, and companies claim that you can save up to 70 per cent on international calls.

Charges

Deregulation of the telecommunications market has resulted in an intense price war, and considerable savings can be made on national as well as international calls by shopping around for the lowest rates.

However, as there are around 20 alternative providers in France, it's impossible to list all their tariffs here; in any case, each company offers different packages, which disguise the charge per call in different ways. Comparisons between the rates offered by a number of service providers can be found via the internet (e.g. 🖥 www.comparatel.fr and www. budgetelecom.com) or you can contact the Association Française des Utilisateurs de Télécommunications (AFUTT, BP1, 92340 Marne-la-Coquette, ☎ 01 47 41 18 56, 🖥 www.afutt.org – in English) on Mondays to Thursdays between 10.30 and 12.30. Line rental and call charges are explained below; for information about installation and registration charges, see page 314.

Line Rental

The monthly line rental or service charge (*abonnement*) payable to France Télécom varies according to the type of line and the length of the contract, as follows:

- **Standard Line** – €13;
- **ADSL** – €26 for a 512k line or €30 for a 1,024k line unless you commit to a 12-month contract, in which case you benefit from a reduction of €18 on the former (strangely, there's no reduction on a 1,024k line!); a 2,048k line is available only on an annual contract and costs €30 per month for the first year and thereafter €35 per month;
- **ISDN Line** – €25.50 (private); €41.50 business.

If you use an alternative telephone provider (see page 316), there may be a separate monthly fee in addition to your call charges, although most providers have dropped these.

International Calls

France Télécom has eight tariff levels for international calls, listed in telephone directories and on their website. All international calls are subject to an initial charge (*mise en relation*) of €0.11 or 0.12 for a period varying from 5 to 27 seconds, depending on the tariff. Calls to adjoining EU countries, Liechtenstein, the Netherlands and Switzerland come under tariff 1 (the cheapest) and cost €0.22 per minute during peak periods (see above) and €0.12 per minute off-peak. Calls to North America come under tariff 3 and cost €0.48 per minute at peak times and €0.33 per minute off-peak. There's a reduction of up to 30 per cent on international call charges if you opt for a call package called *Les Heures*, which costs from €6 per month. Other packages allow 'unlimited' phone use for a fixed monthly charge (e.g. €35).

Other telephone providers have different tariff structures for international calls. Most alternative providers also offer a variety of discount plans, such as half price on all calls to a designated 'favourite country' or to specific overseas phone numbers frequently called.

Emergency & Service Numbers

The national emergency numbers (*services d'urgence et d'assistance*) in France are:

Number	Service
15	Ambulance (*Service d'Aide Médicale d'Urgence/SAMU*)
17	Police (*police-secours*)
18	Fire (*sapeurs-pompiers/feu centrale d'alarme*)

Other emergency numbers are listed at the front of telephone directories. Useful telephone service numbers include the following:

☎ 1013   After-sales service and line problems;

☎ 1014   Private customer services;

☎ 12   Directory enquiries;

☎ 3000   Details of your phone bill and of call plans;

☎ 3212   International directory enquiries.

Fax

Fax machines can be purchased (but not rented) from France Télécom and purchased or rented from private companies and shops. Shop around for the best price. Before bringing a fax machine to France, check that it will work there (i.e. is compatible or *agréé*) or that it can be modified. For example, some British fax machines won't work, although it's possible to buy adapters for UK phones and fax machines (see **Telephones** on page 316). Note also that getting a foreign fax machine repaired may be impossible unless the same machine is sold in France.

Public Telephones

Despite the increasing use of mobile telephones (see page 320), public telephone boxes (*cabine téléphonique*) can be found in all towns and villages: in post offices, bus and railway stations, airports, bars, cafés, restaurants and other businesses, and of course, in the streets. Most telephone boxes are aluminium and Perspex kiosks, and most public telephones (*téléphone publique*) accept telephone cards, *Carte France Télécom* (see below) and bank (i.e. debit) cards, although many won't accept credit cards, particularly those without a microchip.

Mobile Phones

Lower prices due to increased market competition have ensured rapid growth in the use of mobile phones, and there are currently three mobile phone service providers: Bouygues – pronounced 'bweeg' – (☎ 08 10 63 01 00, 🖳 www.bouyguestelecom.fr), Orange – actually France Télécom in disguise – (☎ 08 00 83 08 00, 🖳 www.orange.fr), and SFR (☎ 08 00 10 60 00, 🖳 www.sfr.fr).

As in most countries, buying a mobile phone is an absolute minefield as, not only are there different networks to choose from and the option of a contract or 'pay-as-you-talk', but there's also a wide range of tariffs covering connection fees, monthly subscriptions, insurance and call charges. To further complicate matters, all four providers have business ties to one or more of the fixed telephone services (SFR, for example, is part of Vivendi, which owns and operates Cégétel) and offer various deals for those who combine mobile and fixed phone services.

If you want to use a foreign mobile in France, it's usually possible to buy a SIM card which will give you a French mobile number and allow you to make and receive calls. You pay around €20 or €30 for connection to one of the French networks and can choose between a monthly contract and a 'pay-as-you-talk' card, which can be topped up (in values of €10, €20 and €35) as required. (Note that you **must** top it up at least twice a year, or you will lose your number and have to be reconnected.)

Minitel

Minitel (launched by La Poste in 1985) is a computer-based videotext/teletext information system that can be linked to any telephone. Minitel, which is unique to France and has no international ramifications, is slowly but surely on its way out, gradually succumbing to the relentless march of the internet, to which it may soon be linked. It is, however, still in widespread use (there are an estimated 6.5 million Minitel terminals) and references to Minitel numbers are commonplace (even in this book).

In order to access Minitel you must rent a terminal from France Télécom, which normally costs between €1.50 and €2 per month, although basic terminals are free. The latest versions include a slot for you to insert a credit card to pay for goods and services you order. It's also possible to access Minitel services from your home or office computer, using 'emulation' software that allows your computer to function as a Minitel terminal. The software is often included free with new modems purchased in France; it can be downloaded from 🖥 www. minitel.fr. You can even set up your own e-mail address via Minitel and access your messages via 🖥 http://mail.minitel.net.

Further information about Minitel is available from the Association pour le Commerce et les Service en Ligne (ACSEL, ☎ 01 49 26 03 04) and from France Télécom, which publishes an English booklet, *A Selection of Minitel Services*.

Internet

The internet in France got off to rather a slow start due to Minitel competition (see above) but use is now widespread and the availability of broadband connection is among the highest in the EU (see below). There has recently been a proliferation of internet service providers (*fournisseur d'accès/FAI* or *serveur* or, sadly, *provider*), over 200 currently offering a variety of products and prices. Contact details of some of the major French ISPs are given below. Wanadoo is the package offered by France Télécom, which includes email (see below), Minitel (of course) and on-line shopping. AOL Compuserve France is the other major internet contender (between them, Wanadoo and AOL have some two-thirds of the market).

- AOL (☎ 08 92 02 03 04, 🖥 www.aol.fr);
- Club Internet (☎ 3204, 🖥 www.club-internet.fr);
- Free (☎ 3244, 🖥 www.free.fr);
- FreeSurf (☎ 08 26 00 76 50, 🖥 www.freesurf.fr);
- Tiscali (☎ 08 25 95 95 95, 🖥 www.tiscali.fr);
- Wanadoo (☎ 08 10 22 25 55, 🖥 www.wanadoo.fr).

For details of all the French ISPs, go to 🖥 www.lesproviders.com; for a comparison of ISP services and charges, consult one of the dedicated internet magazines, such as *Internet Pratique* and *Net@scope*, or visit the Budgetelecom website (🖥 www.budgetelecom.com), which carries a list of internet access providers in France, with information on current offers, customer evaluations and direct links to provider websites.

One advantage of French internet services is that junk mail is strictly controlled and therefore less of a nuisance than in many other countries.

Charges

France has a number of 'free' internet access services, where you pay only for your telephone connection time, not for access to the internet provider. Alternatively, most service providers (including the free ones) offer various monthly plans which include all telephone charges for your online connections, usually at a rate that's lower than the telephone charges alone. For as little as €6 to €10 per month, you can usually have five or ten hours online. Note that, if you already have an AOL account with a fixed monthly fee for unlimited access, you may (or may not!) have to pay for connection time in France but, if you're registered in another country, you won't be able to change your registration but must cancel your email address(es) and re-register new ones (or the same ones if you're lucky!).

Broadband

For faster internet connections, you can have an ADSL or ISDN line installed (see **Installation & Registration** on page 314). Most providers, including France Télécom, offer combined telephone and internet access packages (*forfaits*). In Paris, and other urban centres with cable television, it's often possible to have cable internet access, which offers speeds comparable to a broadband telephone line.

Modems

Foreign modems will usually work in France, although they may not receive faxes (Big Dish Satellite, ⊠ www.bigdishsat.com, sells converters for this purpose); French modems (e.g. Elsa Mircolink and Olitec) generally work better. Note also that, if you have an ISDN line and want your computer to connect to the internet at maximum speed, you will need an ISDN terminal adapter.

TELEVISION & RADIO

Before taking TV sets, VCRs, DVD players and radios to France, you should consider both costs and compatibility. Further details of television and radio services in France are contained in *Living and Working in France* (Survival Books – see page 389).

TV Standards

The standards for TV reception in France aren't the same as in some other countries, and TV sets and video recorders (see below) operating on the PAL system or the North American NTSC system won't function properly (or at all) in France.

Most European countries use the PAL B/G standard, except for the UK, which uses a modified PAL-I system that's incompatible with other European countries. France has its own standard, called SECAM-L, which is different from the SECAM standard used elsewhere in the world, e.g. SECAM B/G in the Middle East and North African countries, and SECAM D/K in eastern European and many African countries.

If you want a TV set that will work in France (and other European countries), you must buy a multi-standard TV. Most new television sets available in France contain automatic circuitry that can switch between PAL-I (the UK), SECAM-L (France) and PAL-B/G (rest of Europe). If you have a PAL TV, it's also possible to buy a SECAM to PAL transcoder that converts SECAM signals to PAL. If you decide to buy a TV in France, you will also find it advantageous to buy one with teletext, which apart from allowing you to display programme schedules, also provides a wealth of useful and interesting information. Note, that a SECAM standard TV isn't required to receive most satellite broadcasts, which are different from terrestrial broadcasts.

A portable colour TV can be purchased from around €150 for a 36cm (14in) with remote control. A 55cm (21in) TV costs between €200 and €1,500 depending on the make and features, and a 82cm (32in) model from €750. Special offers can be up to 50 per cent cheaper than the prices quoted, particularly at hypermarkets such as But, Cora and Auchan or at appliance discount chains such as Darty and Boulanger.

VCRs

A British or US video cassette recorder (VCR) won't work properly with a French TV unless it's dual-standard (with SECAM). Although you can play back a SECAM video on a PAL VCR, the picture will be in black and white. Most video machines (*magnétoscope*) sold in France are multi-standard PAL and SECAM and many contain an NTSC playback feature, allowing Americans to play video tapes via a PAL or SECAM television.

Some multi-standard TVs also have an 'NTSC-in' jack plug connection allowing you to play American videos. If you have a PAL TV, it's also possible to buy a SECAM to PAL transcoder that converts SECAM signals to PAL. Video recordings can be converted from PAL or SECAM to NTSC or vice versa, although the cost is prohibitive. Some people opt for two TVs, one to receive French TV programmes and another (i.e. PAL or NTSC) to play their favourite videos.

TV Licence

A TV licence (*redevance sur les postes de télévision*) is required by most TV owners in France, costing €116.50 a year for a colour TV and €74.31 for a black and white set. The licence fee covers any number of TVs (owned or rented), irrespective of where they're located, e.g. holiday homes, motor vehicles or boats (although the government is considering levying the licence on each set). Note also that, even if you have a foreign TV which you can use only for watching videos, you must have a valid licence!

Cable TV

Cable TV is available only in and around 100 or so cities and large towns, although, since connection to the internet was combined with a numeric cable television service, interest in cable TV has significantly increased. Over 1,600 communes now have cable service (which sounds impressive until you realise that there are over 36,500 communes in France!). To check whether your town or commune is currently wired for cable television, internet or telephone services, check the website of AFORM, a French cable industry association (💻 www.aform.org and follow the link for '*Les villes câblées*').

Satellite TV

France is well served by satellite TV (*télévision par satellite*); there are a number of satellites positioned over Europe carrying over 200 stations broadcasting in a variety of languages. BBC channels can now be received unencrypted (as can CNN, Euro News, Sky News and a few other channels); information is available on the BBC's main website (💻 www.bbc.co.uk). The BBC's commercial subsidiary, BBC World Television (formerly BBC Worldwide Television), broadcasts two 24-hour channels: BBC World (24-hour news and information) and BBC Prime (general entertainment). BBC World is free-to-air, while BBC Prime is encrypted.

For more information and a programme guide contact BBC World Television, PO Box 5054, London W12 0ZY, UK (☎ 020-8433 2221). The BBC publishes a monthly magazine, *BBC On Air*, giving comprehensive information about BBC World Television programmes; contact BBC On Air, Room 310NW, Bush House, Strand, London WC2B 4PH, UK (☎ 020-7557 4899) or, for subscriptions, BBC On Air, PO Box 326, Sittingbourne ME9 8FA (☎ 01795-414787). A programme guide is also listed on the internet (💻 www.bbc.co.uk/worldservice/programmes)

and both BBC World and BBC Prime have their own websites (🖥 www. bbcworld.com and 🖥 www.bbcprime.com). When accessing them, you need to enter the name of the country (e.g. France) so that schedules appear in local time.

Note that, if you live in the Nord-Pas-de-Calais region and have the appropriate aerial, you may also be able to receive British stations without a satellite system.

Satellite Dishes

To receive programmes from any satellite, there must be no obstacles (e.g. trees, buildings or mountains) between the satellite and your dish, so **check before renting or buying if being able to receive satellite broadcasts is important to you.** You should also check whether you need permission from your landlord or the local authorities. There are strict laws regarding the positioning of antennas in urban areas, although in rural areas they're more relaxed. Dishes can be mounted in a variety of unobtrusive positions and can be painted or patterned to blend with the background. It may be possible to bring a dish from another country and install it in your French home; for more information, visit 🖥 www.wotsat.com.

Video & DVD

Video films are expensive in France and there aren't many available in English. French video rental shops may have only a few English-language titles. However, there are specialist English-language rental shops in the main cities, and mobile and mail-order services in rural areas. Films can be rented for around €5.50 for three days from video shops and postal video clubs such as Prime Time Paris (🖥 www.prime-time.org). Rental costs can often be reduced by paying a monthly membership fee or a lump sum in advance.

Most shops that rent or sell video tapes also offer DVDs, which are gradually superseding videos and have the advantage of providing soundtracks and subtitles in several languages. Films can be rented for around €3.50 per day. A new facility is the automated 'kiosk', from which DVDs can be rented at the touch of a few buttons for as little as €1.70 (for six hours).

Most hypermarkets carry a large selection of French-language videos and DVDs, costing around €20 and €25 respectively. English-language titles can be purchased by mail-order or via the internet (e.g. 🖥 www.amazon.co.uk).

Radio

Around 60 per cent of popular music broadcast on French radio is in English. On the other hand, there's little English-language radio although in a few areas there are English stations run by expatriates (e.g. Riviera Radio on 106.5FM in the south of France, Sud Radio on 96.1FM in the south-west and Lot radio on 88–89FM). Radio France Internationale (RFI) broadcasts in English for three-and-a-half hours every day in the Paris region on 738MW.

BBC

The BBC World Service is broadcast on short wave on several frequencies (e.g. 12095, 9410, 7325, 6195, 3955, 648 and 198kHz) simultaneously and you can usually receive a good signal on one of them. The signal strength varies according to where you live in France, the time of day and year, the power and positioning of your receiver, and atmospheric conditions. The World Service is also available on medium wave (648MW) in the northern 'half' of France. You can also receive BBC national radio stations (on long wave) in some northern and western areas of France, and all BBC radio stations, including the World Service, are available on the Astra satellite (see below). BBC radio stations can also be heard via your PC using a Radio Player (which can be downloaded free from 🖥 www.bbc. co.uk/radio). If you're desperate, you can also hear recordings of BBC radio programmes on your computer via 🖥 www.bbc.co.uk/ worldservice/schedules/frequencies/eurwfreq.shtml. The BBC publishes a monthly magazine, *BBC On Air*, containing comprehensive information about BBC World Service radio and TV programmes. For a free copy and frequency information write to BBC On Air, Bush House, Strand, London WC2B 4PH, UK (☎ 020-7240 3456) or refer to the main BBC website (🖥 www.bbc.co.uk).

Satellite Radio

If you have satellite TV, you can also receive many radio stations via satellite. For example, BBC Radio 1, 2, 3, 4 and 5, BBC World Service, Sky Radio, Virgin 1215 and many foreign-language stations are broadcast via the Astra satellites (see page 324). Digital satellite TV subscribers also have a choice of many French and international radio stations. Details are usually available in the monthly satellite subscriber newsletter. Satellite radio stations are listed in British satellite TV magazines such as the *Satellite Times*.

UTILITIES

As well as electricity and gas, French homes use oil (*fioul* or *fuel*) and wood (*bois*) for heating and hot water (see **Heating & Air-Conditioning** on page 297), and the government offers tax credits for the installation of energy systems running on renewable fuel (e.g. wood and solar energy). Electricity and gas are supplied by the state-owned Electricité de France/Gaz de France (EDF/GDF), although there are local electricity companies in some areas, and by 2004 commercial gas and electricity users will have a choice of private suppliers (the domestic market will have to wait a little longer!). The price of gas and electricity is reasonable and has lessened in real terms over the last decade. EDF's electricity charges were increased (by around 1 per cent) for the first time in eight years in November 2001, and there are no plans to increase the price of gas.

For information about making the most efficient use of electricity and gas, contact the Agence de l'Environnement et de la Maitrise de l'Energie (ADEME), 27 rue Louis-Vicat, 75015 Paris Cedex 15 (☎ 01 47 65 20 00 or ☎ 08 10 06 00 50 or ☎ 08 00 31 03 11, 💻 www.ademe.fr), who will advise you where to find your nearest *Point Info Energie* (*PIE*).

Electricity

Unlike other western countries, France generates some 75 per cent of its electricity from nuclear power, the balance coming mostly from various hydro-electric power stations. This means that France's electricity is among the cheapest in Europe (it supplies electricity to its neighbours for less than they can produce it themselves and owns nine other European electricity companies, including Seeboard in the UK). Due to the moderate cost of electricity and the high degree of insulation in new homes, electric heating is more common in France than in other European countries.

Power Supply

The electricity supply in France is delivered to homes at 380/440 volts through three separate phases (not one as in some countries) and is then shared across the three phases at 220/240 volts with a frequency of 50 Hertz (cycles). Some appliances, such as large immersion heaters and cookers, draw power from all three phases. Older buildings may still have 110/120 volt supplies, although these have been converted to 220/240 in most areas.

If you're moving from a country with a 110V supply (e.g. the US), your electrical equipment will require a converter or a transformer (*transformateur*) to convert it to 240V, although some electrical appliances (e.g. electric razors and hair dryers) are fitted with a 110/240 volt switch. Check for the switch, which may be inside the casing, and make sure that it's switched to 240V **before** connecting it to the power supply. Converters are suitable only for appliances without circuit boards or microchips that don't need to be plugged in for long periods (e.g. heaters, hair driers, vacuum cleaners and coffee machines). Electronic appliances such as computers, fax machines, TVs and video players must be connected to the supply via a step-down transformer. Add the wattage of the devices you intend to connect to a transformer and make sure that its power rating exceeds this sum. Converters and transformers can be bought in most DIY shops, although in most cases it's simpler to buy new appliances in France (see **Household Goods** on page 310).

An additional problem with some electrical equipment is the frequency rating, which in some countries, e.g. the US, is designed to run at 60 Hertz (Hz) and not France's 50Hz. Electrical equipment without a motor is generally unaffected by the drop in frequency to 50Hz (except TVs, see page 322). Equipment with a motor may run with a 20 per cent drop in speed; however, automatic washing machines, cookers, electric clocks, record players and tape recorders are unusable in France if not designed for 50Hz operation. To find out, look at the label on the back of the equipment. If it says 50/60Hz, it should work. If it says 60Hz, you might try it anyway, but first ensure that the voltage is correct as outlined above. Bear in mind that the transformers and motors of electrical devices designed to run at 60Hz will run hotter at 50Hz, so you should ensure that equipment has sufficient space around it for cooling.

In many rural areas the lights often flicker and occasionally go off and come back on almost immediately (just long enough to crash your computer!). Power cuts of several minutes or hours are fairly frequent in some areas, particularly during thunderstorms, and in some departments (e.g. Gers) there's a high risk of lightning strikes. If you live in an area with an unstable electricity supply, it's prudent to obtain a power stabiliser for a computer or other vital equipment to prevent it being switched off when the power drops. If you use a computer, it's also wise to fit an uninterruptable power supply (UPS) with a battery back-up, which allows you time (around five minutes) to save your work and shut down your computer after a power failure. If you're worried about lightning strikes, you can install an 'anti-lighting' device (*parafoudre*) in your fuse box. (You should also keep torches, candles and preferably a gas lamp handy!)

If the power keeps tripping off when you attempt to use a number of high-powered appliances simultaneously, it probably means that the rating (*puissance*) of your power supply is too low. This is a common problem in France. If this is the case, you must ask EDF to uprate the power supply to your property, although this can increase your standing charge (see below) by up to 40 per cent. The power setting is usually shown on your meter (*compteur*). The possible ratings are 3, 6, 9, 12, 15, 18, 24, 30 and 36 kilowatts (KW or Kva).

To calculate the power supply required, you need to list all the electrical appliances you have (plus any you intend installing, such as an electric shower or dishwasher) and the power consumption of each. Add the power consumption of the appliances you're likely to operate simultaneously to obtain the total number of kilowatts required. The three lower rates (3, 6 and 9KW) don't cater for electric heating, which needs a power supply of 12KW to 18KW. If you have an integrated electrical heating system, however, you can have a gadget called a *délesteur* installed, which momentarily cuts off convectors, under-floor heating and water-heater (etc.) when other high-consumption appliances are in use but without noticeable temperature fluctuations; it may therefore be possible to avoid a higher supply rating.

If you have appliances such as a washing machine, dishwasher, water heater and electric heating in an average-size house (e.g. two to three bedrooms), you will probably need an 18KW supply. If you have numerous high-wattage electrical appliances and electric heating, you may need the maximum 36KW supply.

Wiring Standards

The electrical system in older properties is often eccentric and may even be dangerous, with exposed sockets and bare wires evident. One of the most important tasks after buying a property is to check that the electrical system is in good condition and adequate to meet your needs (see **Power Supply** above). You can get an EDF representative to check the wiring in a property.

Homes in France are wired differently from those in many other countries (for example, they don't use a ring main system, which is prohibited). French regulations regarding the fittings and appliances in bathrooms are specific: although electric switches and sockets are permitted (unlike in the UK), they mustn't be placed within 2.25m (7ft 6in) of a bath or shower. Note also that all metalwork (e.g. pipes) in bathrooms must be earthed; this often isn't the case in older buildings.

Make sure also that you have enough power points fitted; even in new properties it's common for developers not to install enough points (although it's possible to run up to around five separate, low-wattage appliances from one socket via a multi-plug connector).

It's essential to use a qualified French electrician for electrical work (look under *Électricité générale* in the yellow pages). The electricity supply to a new property or a property that has been rewired will be connected by EDF only on receipt of a certificate (*certificat/attestation de conformité*) approved by the Comité National pour la Sécurité des Usagers de l'Électricité (CONSUEL). This can be arranged by a French builder or a registered electrician.

Plugs, Fuses & Bulbs

The first thing to check before moving into a home in France is whether there are any light fittings. When moving house, some people don't just remove the bulb, but bulb-holders, flex and even the ceiling rose! Depending on where you've come from, you may need new plugs (*fiche*) or a lot of adapters. Plug adapters for imported lamps and other electrical apparatus may be difficult to obtain in France, so it's wise to bring some with you, plus extension cords and multi-plug extensions that can be fitted with French plugs.

Most French plugs have two round pins, some with a female socket (*prise*) in the plug forming a 'third' earth connection. Small, low-wattage electrical appliances up to six amps, such as table lamps, small TVs and computers, don't require an earth. Plugs with an earth must be used for high-wattage appliances up to 16 amps, such as fires, kettles, washing machines, refrigerators and cookers. These plugs must be used with corresponding three-point sockets and will also fit two-point sockets.

Electrical appliances that are earthed have a three-core wire and must never be used with a two-pin plug without an earth socket. Note that many French sockets aren't earthed and many electrical appliances are operated without an earth, with the exception of washing machines, dishwashers and dryers. French plugs aren't fitted with fuses.

 Always make sure that a plug is correctly and securely wired, as bad wiring can cause fatal injuries (and is also a fire hazard).

In modern installations, fuses (*fusibles*) are of the resetting pop-out type or earth trip system. When there's a short circuit (*court-circuit*) or the system has been overloaded, a circuit breaker (*disjoncteur/coupe circuit*) is tripped and the power supply is cut. Before reconnecting the power, switch off any high-power appliances such as a washing machine or dishwasher. Make sure you know where the trip switch is located and keep a torch handy so that you can find it in the dark (see **Power Supply** on page 327).

Electric light bulbs in France are either of the Edison type with a bayonet or a screw fitting and both are readily available in shops. You can also buy adapters to convert from one to the other. Bulbs for non-standard electrical appliances, i.e. appliances that weren't made for the

French market, such as refrigerators and sewing machines, may not be available in France, so bring some spares with you.

Converters & Transformers

Electrical equipment rated at 110 volts AC (for example, from the USA) requires a converter or a step-down transformer (*transformateur*) to convert it to 240 volts AC, although some electrical appliances (electric razors, hair dryers) are fitted with a 110/240 volt switch. Check for the switch, which may be inside the casing, and make sure that it's switched to 240 volts **before** connecting it to the power supply. Converters can be used for heating appliances, but transformers are required for motorised appliances. Add the wattage of the devices you intend to connect to a transformer and make sure that its power rating **exceeds** this sum.

Generally, small, high-wattage electrical appliances, such as kettles, toasters, heaters and irons, need large transformers. Motors in large appliances, such as cookers, refrigerators, washing machines, dryers and dishwashers, need replacing or fitting with a large transformer. In most cases it's simpler to buy new appliances in France, which are of good quality and reasonably priced. Note also that the dimensions of imported cookers, microwave ovens, refrigerators, washing machines, dryers and dishwashers, may differ from those in France, so they may not fit into a French kitchen.

An additional problem with some electrical equipment is the frequency rating, which in some countries, e.g. the US, is designed to run at 60 Hertz (Hz) and not France's 50Hz. Electrical equipment without a motor is generally unaffected by the drop in frequency to 50Hz (except TVs, see page 322). Equipment with a motor may run with a 20 per cent drop in speed; however, automatic washing machines, cookers, electric clocks, record players and tape recorders are unusable in France if not designed for 50Hz operation. To find out, look at the label on the back of the equipment. If it says 50/60Hz, it should work. If it says 60Hz, you might try it anyway, **but first ensure that the voltage is correct as outlined above.** Bear in mind that the motors of electrical devices designed to run at 60Hz will run hotter at 50Hz, so you should ensure that equipment has sufficient space around it for cooling.

Connection & Registration

You must usually apply to your local EDF office to have your electricity connected and to sign a contract specifying the power supply (see below) installed and the tariff (see page 332) required. To have your electricity connected, you must prove that you're the owner by producing an *attestation* or a lease if you're renting. You must also show your passport or residence permit (*carte de séjour*). If you wish to pay your bill by direct debit from a bank or post office account, don't forget to take along your account details (*relevé d'identité bancaire*).

When moving house, most people tell the EDF a few days before they leave (EDF requests at least two days' notice) and EDF assumes that someone else is taking over the property. To ensure that your electricity supply is connected and that you don't pay for someone else's electricity, you should contact your local EDF office and ask them to read the meter (*relevé spécial*) before taking over a property. If the property has an existing supply, you must pay an 'access' fee (*frais d'accès*) of €13.55. Residents don't usually pay a deposit, although non-residents may be required to pay one. When payable, the deposit is refundable against future bills.

When buying electrical appliances, the label PROMETELEC (Association pour le développement et l'amélioration des installations intérieures) indicates that they're safe. The safety of electrical materials is usually indicated by the French safety standards association's initials 'NF' (*normes françaises*). EDF/GDF publish a number of leaflets detailing their services and tariffs, including one in French and English, *Le Service du Gaz et de l'Électricité*. EDF publishes a useful free booklet (in French), *EDF répond à vos questions*, available from any EDF office. Your local electricity board may also have a booklet (*livret de l'usager de l'électricité*) explaining the electricity supply and apparatus. If you have any questions regarding the electricity supply, contact your local Électricité de France office (listed in yellow pages and searchable on 🖳 http://particuliers.edf.fr – enter the name of your commune in the box top right). Information can also be obtained via a local rate telephone line (☎ 08 10 12 61 26).

Tariffs

Your standing charge (*abonnement*) depends on the rating of your supply and the tariff you choose, which also affects the amount you pay for electricity consumed (calculated in kilowatt-hours or KWh). EDF offers three domestic tariff options: basic (suitable only for those who use little electricity), off-peak (with different rates for day and night-time use), and *Tempo* (most suitable for those with second homes that are unoccupied for long periods). Details of tariffs are given in *Living and Working in France* (Survival Books – see page 389).

Note that, since January 2003, a tax called the *contribution au service public* has been applied to all electricity bills at the rate of €0.33 per KWh.

Meters

Meters are usually installed in a box on an outside wall of a property. However, if your meter isn't accessible or a house isn't permanently occupied, make sure you leave the keys with a neighbour or make special arrangements to have your meter read. (You can have your meter connected to an exterior box for around €75). If your meter cannot be read, you will receive an estimate based on your previous bills, although it **must** be read at least once a year.

Bills

You're normally billed for your electricity every three months but may receive bi-monthly or monthly bills if your consumption is above a certain level. A number of bills (*facture*) received throughout the year, e.g. alternate bills, are estimated. Bills include a standing charge (*abonnement*), VAT and local taxes (*taxes locales*). VAT is levied at 5.5 per cent on the standing charge and 19.6 per cent on the total power consumption. Local taxes (*taxe commune/département*) are around 12 per cent and where applicable are levied on around 80 per cent of the consumption and standing charge total before VAT is added. VAT at 19.6 per cent is also levied on the local taxes.

Bills can be paid by direct debit (*prélèvement automatique*) from a bank or post office account. It's also possible to pay a fixed amount each month by standing order based on your estimated usage; at the end of the year you receive a bill for the amount owing or a rebate of the amount overpaid. These methods of payment are preferable, particularly if you spend a lot of time away from home or you're a non-resident. If you're a non-resident, you can have your bills sent to an address outside France. If you don't pay a bill on time, interest (*majoration*) can be charged at 1.5 times the current interest rate. If your bills still aren't paid after a certain period, your electricity company can cut your service.

Gas

Mains Gas

Mains gas (*gaz de ville*) is available only in around 80 towns and cities and is supplied by the state-owned Gaz de France (GDF), part of the same company as Electricité de France (EDF). (Gas supplies to businesses were privatised in July 2004 and private supplies are due to be privatised in July 2007.) If you buy a property without a mains gas supply, you can obtain a new connection (*raccordement*), provided of course mains gas is available in the area. If the property is within 35m (115ft) of a supply, connection costs are around €840 if you're on *base* or *B0* tariff, or around €420 if you're on the *B1* tariff (see below). Contact GDF for an accurate estimate.

When moving into a property already connected to mains gas, you must contact GDF to have the gas switched on and/or have the meter read and to have the account switched to your name. This can usually be done at the same time as you arrange for your electricity supply (see page 327). There's a connection charge (*mise en service*) of around €14 (or €28 if you have gas and electricity connected at the same time).

As with electricity, you must decide on the type of supply you require, e.g. *base* for cooking only, *B0* for cooking and hot water, *B1* for heating (in a small house) and *B2I* for heating (in a larger house). The annual service charge (*abonnement*) is lower for a limited supply (e.g. €23.64 for *base* compared with €182.81 for *B2I*) but you're charged more per kWH (€5.85 for *base* and between €3.27 and €2.91 for *B2I* depending on the town you live in).

Details of charges in each town where mains gas is available can be found on the GDF website (🖥 www.monagence.gazdefrance.fr). Further information about gas supplies is provided in *Living and Working in France* (Survival Books – see page 389).

Bottled Gas

Most rural homes have cookers and some also water heaters that use bottled gas. Cookers often have a combination of electric and (bottled) gas rings (you can choose the mix). Check when moving into a property that the gas bottle isn't empty. Keep a spare bottle or two handy and make sure you ask how to change bottles, as this can be quite a complicated procedure, involving safety switches, etc.. Bottled gas is more expensive than mains gas. Bottles come in 35kg, 13kg and 5/6kg sizes. A small one used just for cooking will last an average family around six weeks.

Bottles can be bought at most petrol stations and super/ hypermarkets, but you should trade in an empty bottle for a new one; otherwise it's much more expensive. An exchange bottle costs around €19. If you need to buy new gas bottles, you will be asked to register and pay a deposit (e.g. €40 per bottle). Some village shops also sell bottled gas. Note, however, that there are several different types of bottle (e.g. Antargaz, Butagaz, Primagaz and Totalgaz, each a different colour) the supplier of one type won't accept an empty bottle of another type. (Check **before** you unload your 35kg bottles!) Note also that the connectors usually turn in the opposite direction to most threaded devices.

Some houses keep their gas bottles outside, often under a lean-to. If you do this you must buy propane gas rather than butane, as it can withstand a greater range of temperatures than butane, which is for internal use only (in fact, propane gas bottles **must** be kept outside a house). Note also that butane requires a different demand valve (*détendeur*) from propane, i.e. 28M.bar 1300g/h instead of 37M/bar 1500g/h.

If you're planning to buy or rent an apartment, check whether gas bottles are permitted, as they're prohibited in many new apartments.

Gas Tanks

Gas central heating is common in France, although in rural areas the gas supply comes from a gas tank (*citerne*) installed on the property, rather than a mains supply or bottles. Tanks can be hired, from suppliers such as Total and Antargaz, for around €300 per year, or you can pay a deposit of around €1,500, which is refunded if you take out a contract for the supply of gas for a fixed period.

 If you take over a property with a gas tank, you must not only pay the deposit but also have it filled and pay for a full tank of gas, irrespective of how much was left in it!

Note also that having a gas tank on your property will increase your insurance premiums.

Water

Mains water in France is supplied by a number of private companies, the largest of which are the Saur group (part of Bouygues, which also supplies mobile phone services, 🖥 www.saur.com), Suez Environment (formerly Lyonnaise-des-Eaux, 🖥 www.lyonnaise-des-eaux.fr) and Veolia Environment (part of Vivendi, 🖥 www.generale-des-eaux.fr), who between them supply some three-quarters of the water in France. Suez and Veolia being global suppliers with some 235 million customers. The water supply infrastructure, however, is owned and managed by local communes, so rates vary across the country. Most properties in France are metered, so that you pay only for the water you use and are charged per cubic metre (1,000 litres). If you need to have a water meter installed, there's a small non-refundable charge. When moving into a new house, ask the local water company to read your meter. Note that owners of a *copropriété* can have individual meters installed.

Supply & Connection

If you own a property in or near a village, you can usually be connected to a mains water system. Note, however, that connection can be expensive, as you must pay for digging the channels required for pipes. Obtain a quotation (*devis*) from the local water company for the connection of the supply and the installation of a water meter. Expect the connection to cost at least €800, depending on the type of terrain and soil (or rock!) which must be dug to lay pipes. If you're thinking of buying a property and installing a mains water supply, obtain an estimate **before** signing the purchase contract.

Water shortages are rare in towns (although they do occur occasionally) but are fairly common in some rural areas during long hot summers, when the water may periodically be switched off. It's possible to have a storage tank installed for emergencies and you should also keep an emergency supply for watering the garden or recycle your house water.

If you rely on a well (*puits*) or spring (*source*) for your water, bear in mind that these can dry up, particularly in parts of central and southern France, which continue to experience droughts.

 Always confirm that a rural property has a reliable water source and check it or have it checked by an expert (see Inspections & Surveys on page 154).

If the source is on a neighbour's land, make sure that there's no dispute about the ownership of the water and your rights to use it, e.g. that it cannot be stopped or drained away by your neighbours. You don't pay water charges for well water or water from a stream or river running through your property. If a supply is marked *eau non potable*, the water should not be drunk.

Cost

It's usual to have a contract for a certain amount of water; if you exceed this amount, you incur a higher charge. There's no flat fee (*forfait*), which has been abolished, although 'special charges' may be levied. French water varies by up to 100 per cent in price from region to region, depending on its availability or scarcity, and is among the most expensive in the world, although rates include sewerage charges. If your property is on mains drainage (*tout à l'égout*), your water can cost as much as €3.60 per cubic metre or as little as €1.75; the national average is around €2.75. If it has a septic tank (*fosse septique*), on the other hand, your water bill will be much lower, e.g. €0.75 per cubic metre.

Bills

You're billed by your local water company annually or every six months and can pay by direct debit. If an apartment block is owned *en copropriété*, the water bill for the whole block is usually divided among the apartments according to their size. Hot water may be charged by adding an amount per cubic metre consumed by each apartment, to cover the cost of heating the water, or may be shared among apartments in proportion to their size.

Sewerage

Properties in urban areas are normally connected to mains drainage (*tout à l'égout*), whereas those in rural parts usually have individual sewage systems: either cesspits (*puisard*) or septic tanks (*fosse septique*, also known as a *puits perdu* – a 'lost well'!). Note, however, that according to a law passed in January 1992, which comes into force in December 2005, mains drainage must be installed wherever it's considered cost-effective, which generally means in the centre of all French villages.

Where mains drainage is installed, there will be a one-off charge for connection made to all properties within the area of the system, which must be connected within two years of the installation, plus an annual service charge. Charges for mains drainage are normally included in property taxes (see page 247).

If you have a septic tank, you should use enzyme bio-digesters and employ bleach and drain unblockers sparingly, as they kill the friendly bacteria that prevent nasty smells.

A *fosse toutes eaux* must be emptied at least once a year, depending on whether a property is permanently inhabited or not, a *fosse septique* every three to five years; the cost of emptying is around €200. Note that you mustn't use certain cleaning agents, such as ammonia, in a septic tank, as they will destroy it, and you may need to put specially formulated products into the tank to keep it working properly.

SURVIVAL TIP

Before buying a property with its own sewage system, you should have it checked by an expert. Before buying a property or plot without a system, you should obtain expert advice as to whether such a system can be installed and what the cost will be (see Septic Tanks on page 164).

APPENDICES

APPENDIX A: USEFUL ADDRESSES

Embassies & Consulates

Foreign embassies are located in the capital Paris (those of selected English-speaking countries are listed below), and many countries also have consulates in other cities (British provincial consulates are listed on page 340). Embassies and consulates are listed in the yellow pages under *Ambassades, Consulats et Autres Représentations Diplomatiques*.

Australia: 4 rue Jean Rey, 15e (☎ 01 40 59 33 00).
Canada: 35 avenue Montaigne, 8e (☎ 01 44 43 29 00).
Ireland: 41 rue Rude, 16e (☎ 01 44 17 67 00).
Jamaica: 60 avenue Foch, 16e (☎ 01 45 00 62 25).
Malta: 92 avenue Champs Elysées, 8e (☎ 01 56 59 75 00).
New Zealand: 7ter rue Léonard de Vinci, 16e (☎ 01 45 01 43 43).
South Africa: 59 quai Orsay, 7e (☎ 01 53 59 23 23).
United Kingdom: 35 rue Faubourg St Honoré, 8e (see below) & 18bis rue Anjou, 8e (☎ 01 44 51 31 02).
United States of America: 2 rue St Florentin, 1e (☎ 01 43 12 22 22) and 2, avenue Gabriel, 1e (☎ 08 10 26 46 26).

British Consulates-General

Consulates-General are permanently staffed during normal office hours.

Bordeaux: 353 boulevard du Président Wilson, BP 91, 33073 Bordeaux (☎ 05 57 22 21 10). Covers the departments of Ariège, Aveyron, Charente, Charente-Maritime, Corrèze, Creuse, Dordogne, Haute-Garonne, Gers, Gironde, Landes, Lot, Lot-et-Garonne, Pyrénées-Atlantiques, Hautes-Pyrénées, Deux-Sèvres, Tarn, Tarn-et-Garonne, Vienne and Haute-Vienne.

Lille: 11 square Dutilleul, 59800 Lille (☎ 03 20 12 82 72). Covers the departments of Aisne, Ardennes, Nord, Pas-de-Calais and Somme.

Lyon: 24 rue Childebert, 69288 Lyon Cedex 1 (☎ 04 72 77 81 70). Covers the departments of Ain, Allier, Ardèche, Cantal, Côte d'Or, Doubs, Drôme, Isère, Jura, Loire, Haute-Loire, Puy-de-Dôme, Rhône, Haute-Saône, Saône-et-Loire, Savoie, Haute-Savoie and the Territoire de Belfort.

Marseille: 24 avenue du Prado, 13006 Marseille (☎ 04 91 15 72 10). Covers the departments of Alpes-de-Haute-Provence, Hautes-Alpes, Alpes-Maritimes, Aude, Bouches-du-Rhône, Gard, Hérault, Lozère, Pyrénées-Orientales, Var and Vaucluse, as well as Corsica.

Paris: 35 rue du Faubourg Saint Honoré, 75008 Paris (☎ 01 44 51 31 02). Covers the departments of Aube, Calvados, Cher, Côtes d'Armor, Eure, Eure-et-Loir, Finstère, Ille-et-Vilaine, Indre, Indre-et-Loire, Loir-et-Cher, Loire, Loire-Atlantique, Loiret, Maine-et-Loire, Manche, Marne, Haute-Marne, Mayenne, Meurthe-et-Moselle, Meuse, Morbihan, Moselle, Nièvre, Oise, Bas-Rhin, Sarthe and Vosges, as well as the whole of the Ile-de-France and the overseas departments and territories.

British Honorary Consulates

Honorary consulates aren't permanently staffed and should be contacted **in emergencies only** (e.g. for urgent passport renewals or replacements).

Biarritz: 7 boulevard Tauzin, 64200 Biarritz (☎ 05 59 24 21 40).

Boulogne-sur-Mer: c/o Cabinet Barron et Brun, 28, rue Saint Jean, 62200 Boulogne-sur-Mer (☎ 03 21 87 16 80).

Calais: c/o P&O Ferries, 20 rue du Havre, 62100 Calais (☎ 03 21 96 33 76).

Cherbourg-Octeville: c/o P&O Ferries, Gare Maritime, BP46, 50652 Cherbourg-Octeville (☎ 02 33 88 65 60).

Clermont-Ferrand: Résidence Carré de Jaude, 39 route de Bonnabaud, 63000 Clermont-Ferrand (☎ 04 73 34 24 29).

Dinard: La Hulotte, 8 boulevard des Maréchaux, 35800 Dinard (☎ 02 99 46 26 64).

Dunkerque: c/o Lemaire Frères & Fils, 30 rue de l'Hermitte, BP 2/100, 59376 Dunkerque (☎ 03 28 66 11 98).

Le Havre: c/o P&O European Ferries, 124 boulevard de Strasbourg, 76600 Le Havre (☎ 02 35 19 78 88).

Montpellier: 271 Le Capitole, Bâtiment A, 64, rue Alcyone, 34000 Montpellier (☎ 04 67 15 52 07)

Nantes: 16 boulevard Gabriel Giust'hau, BP 22026, 44020 Nantes Cedex 1 (☎ 02 51 72 72 60).

Nice: 26 avenue Notre Dame, 06000 Nice (☎ 04 93 62 13 56). Also deals with Monaco.

Toulouse: c/o English Enterprises, 8 allée du Commingues, 317700 Colomiers, 31300 Toulouse (☎ 05 61 30 37 91).

Tours: 7 rue des Rosiers, 37510 Savonnières (☎ 02 47 43 57 97).

Miscellaneous

Alliance Française, 101 boulevard Raspail, 75270 Paris Cedex 06 (☎ 01 42 84 90 00, 🖳 www.alliancefr.org).

Association Nationale pour l'Information sur le Logement, 2,boulevard St Martin, 75010 Paris (☎ 01 42 02 05 50, 🖳 www.anil.org).

Automobile Club de France, 6–8 Place de la Concorde, 75008 Paris (☎ 03 88 36 04 34, 🖳 www.automobileclub.org).

British Association of Removers (BAR) Overseas, 3 Churchill Court, 58 Station Road, North Harrow, London HA2 7SA, UK (☎ 020-8861 3331, 🖳 www.barmovers.com).

Centre des Impôts de Non-Résidents, 9 rue d'Uzès, 75094 Paris Cedex 02 (☎ 01 44 76 18 00).

Centre de Liaison et d'Echanges Internationaux, BP 0339, 80003 Amiens Cedex 1 (☎ 03 22 82 77 29, 🖳 www.clei.asso.fr).

Centre National de Documentation sur l'Enseignement Privé, 20 rue Fabert, 75007 Paris (☎ 01 47 05 32 68, 🖳 www.fabert.com).

Centre Renseignements Douaniers, 23 rue de l'Université, 75007 Paris (☎ 08 25 30 82 63, 🖳 www.finances.gouv.fr/douane).

Chambres des Experts Immobiliers, c/o FNAIM, 129 rue du Faubourg St-Honoré, 75008 Paris (🖳 www.fnaim.fr).

Chambre des Notaires, 1 boulevard de Sébastopol, 75005 Paris (☎ 01 44 82 24 00, 💻 www.paris.notaires.fr).

Commission de Contrôle des Assurances, 54, rue de Châteaudun, 75436 Paris Cedex 09 (💻 www.finances.gouv.fr/CCA).

Compagnie Nationale des Experts Immobiliers, 18 rue Volney, 75002 Paris (💻 www.expert-cnei.com).

Conseil Supérieur du Notariat, 31 rue du Général Foy, 75383 Paris Cedex 08 (☎ 01 44 90 30 00, 💻 www.notaires.fr).

Délégation à l'Aménagement du Territoire et à l'Action Régionale (DATAR), 21–24 Grosvenor Place, London SW1X 7HU, UK (☎ 020-7823 1895) and 2 avenue Velasquez, 75008 Paris (☎ 01 40 74 74 00, 💻 www. datar.gouv.fr).

Electricité de France/Gaz de France, 5 rue Mander, 75002 Paris (☎ 01 42 33 64 68, 💻 www.edf.fr).

Fédération Nationale de l'Immobilier (FNAIM), 129 rue du Faubourg St Honoré, 75008 Paris (💻 www.fnaim.fr).

Fédération Nationale des Gîtes de France, 59 rue St Lazare, Paris 75439, (☎ 01 49 70 75 75, 💻 gites-de-france.fr).

Fédération Nationale des Sociétés d'Aménagement Foncier et d'Etablissement Rural (FNSAFER), 3 rue de Turin, 75008 Paris (☎ 01 44 69 86 00, 💻 www.safer-fr.com).

Federation of Overseas Property Developers, Agents and Consultants (FOPDAC), 3rd Floor, 95 Aldwich, London WC2B 4JF, UK (☎ 020-8941 5588, 💻 www.fopdac.com).

French Chamber of Commerce, 21 Dartmouth Street, London SW1H 9BP, UK (☎ 020-7304 4040, 💻 www.ccfgb.co.uk).

Department for Environment, Food & Rural Affairs (DEFRA), 1A Page Street, London SW1P 4PQ, UK (☎ 020-7904 6000, 💻 www.defra.gov.uk).

Office du Tourisme, 127 avenue des Champs-Elysées, 75008 Paris (☎ 08 92 68 31 12, 💻 www.paris-touristoffice.com).

Ordre des Avocats à la Cour de Paris, 11 place Dauphine, 75053 Paris-Louvre SP (☎ 01 44 32 48 48, 💻 www.paris.barreau.fr).

De Particulier à Particulier, 40 rue du docteur Roux, 75724 Cedex 15 (☎ 01 40 56 33 33, 💻 www.pap.fr).

Union Nationale des AVF (Accueils des Villes Françaises), 3 rue du Paradis, 75010 Paris (☎ 01 47 70 45 85, 🖥 www.avf-accueil.com).

Major Property Exhibitions

Below is a list of the main exhibition organisers in Britain and Ireland. Note that you may be charged a small admission fee.

Homes Overseas (☎ UK 020-7939 9852, 🖥 www.blendoncommunications.co.uk). The largest organisers of international property exhibitions, who stage a number of exhibitions each year at a range of venues in Britain and Ireland.

International Property Show (☎ UK 01962-736712, 🖥 www.internationalpropertyshow.com). Takes place several times a year in London and Manchester.

World Class Homes (☎ UK 0800-731 4713, 🖥 www.worldclasshomes.co.uk). Exhibitions are held in small venues around Britain and include mainly British property developers.

World of Property (☎ UK 01323-726040, 🖥 www.outbound publishing.com). The *World of Property* magazine publishers (see **Appendix B**) organise three large property exhibitions a year, two in the south of Britain and one in the north.

APPENDIX B: FURTHER READING

English-Language Newspapers & Magazines

The publications listed below are a selection of the dozens related to France and, in particular, French property. Most of these include advertisements by estate agents and companies offering other services for house hunters and buyers as well as an ordering service for books about France and the French.

The Connexion, BP25, 06480 La-Colle-sur-Loup, France (☎ 04 93 32 16 59, 💻 www.connexionfrance.com). Monthly newspaper.

Everything France Magazine, Brooklands Magazines Ltd, Medway House, Lower Road, Forest Row, East Sussex RH18 5HE, UK (☎ 01342-828700, 💻 www.everythingfrancemag. co.uk). Bi-monthly lifestyle magazine.

Focus on France, Outbound Publishing, 1 Commercial Road, Eastbourne, East Sussex BN21 3XQ, UK (☎ 01323-726040, 💻 www.outboundpublishing.com). Quarterly property magazine.

France Magazine, Archant Life, Archant House, Oriel Road, Cheltenham, Gloucestershire GL50 1BB, UK (☎ 01242-216050, 💻 www.francemag.co.uk). Monthly lifestyle magazine.

France-USA Contacts, FUSAC, 26 rue Bénard, 75014 Paris, France (☎ 01 56 53 54 54, 💻 www.fusac.fr). Free bi-weekly magazine.

French Magazine, Merricks Media Ltd, Cambridge House South, Henry Street, Bath BA1 1JT, UK (☎ 01225-786840, 💻 www.frenchmagazine.co.uk). Monthly lifestyle and property magazine.

French News, SARL Brussac, 225 route d'Angoulême, BP4042, 24004 Périgueux Cedex, France (☎ 05 53 06 84 40, 💻 www.french-news.com). Monthly newspaper.

French Property News, Archant Life, 6 Burgess Mews, London SW19 1UF, UK (☎ 020-8543 3113, 💻 www.french-property-news.com). Monthly property magazine.

The Irish Eyes Magazine, The Eyes, 2 rue des Laitières, 94300 Vincennes, France (☎ 01 41 74 93 03, 💻 www.irisheyes.fr). Monthly Paris cultural magazine.

Living France, Archant Life, Archant House, Oriel Road, Cheltenham, Gloucestershire GL50 1BB, UK (☎ 01242-216050, 🖥 www.livingfrance.com). Monthly lifestyle/property magazine.

Normandie & South of England Magazine, 330 rue Valvire, BP414, 50004 Saint-Lô, France (☎ 02 33 77 32 70, 🖥 www. normandie-magazine.fr). News and current affairs about Normandy and parts of southern England, published eight times a year mainly in French but with some English articles and translations.

Paris Voice/Paris Free Voice, 7 rue Papillon, 75009 Paris, France (☎ 01 47 70 45 05, 🖥 www.parisvoice.com). Free weekly newspaper.

The Riviera Reporter, 56 chemin de Provence, 06250 Mougins, France (☎ 04 93 45 77 19, 🖥 www.riviera-reporter.com). Bi-monthly free magazine covering the Côte d'Azur.

The Riviera Times, 8 avenue Jean Moulin, 06340 Drap, France (☎ 04 93 27 60 00, 🖥 www.rivieratimes.com). Monthly free newspaper covering the Côte d'Azur and Italian Riviera.

Books

The following books about France and the French are published by Survival Books and can be ordered using the forms on pages 389 and 390.

The Alien's Guide To France, Jim Watson. A light-hearted look at life in France.

Brittany Lifeline, Val Gascoyne. A directory of services, amenities and facilities in Brittany for visitors and residents (published spring 2005).

Dordogne/Lot Lifeline, Val Gascoyne. A directory of services, amenities and facilities in Dordogne, Lot and Lot-et-Garonne for visitors and residents.

Earning Money from Your French Home, Joe Laredo. How to make money from home, including bed & breakfast and *gîtes* (published summer 2005).

Foreigners in France: Triumphs & Disasters, Joe & Kerry Laredo (eds). Real-life stories of people from all over the world who have moved to France.

Living & Working in France, David Hampshire. Everything you need to know about life and employment in France.

Making a Living in France, Joe Laredo. The ins and outs of self-employment and starting a business in France (published spring 2005).

Normandy Lifeline, Val Gascoyne. A directory of services, amenities and facilities in Upper and Lower Normandy for visitors and residents (published spring 2005).

Poitou-Charentes Lifeline, Val Gascoyne. A directory of services, amenities and facilities in Poitou-Charentes for visitors and residents.

Renovating & Maintaining Your French Home, Joe Laredo. How to realise the renovation dream and avoid nightmares.

Appendix C: USEFUL WEBSITES

Below is a list of general websites that might be of interest and aren't mentioned elsewhere in this book; websites relevant to specific aspects of buying a home in France are given in the appropriate section. Websites generally offer free access, although some require a subscription or payment for services. Relocation and other companies specialising in expatriate services often have websites, although these may only provide information that a company is prepared to offer free of charge, which may be rather biased. However, there are plenty of volunteer sites run by expatriates providing practical information and tips.

A particularly useful section found on most expatriate websites is the 'message board' or 'forum', where expatriates answer questions based on their experience and knowledge and offer an insight into what living and working in France is **really** like; these are also offered by some magazine websites (see **Appendix B**). Websites are listed under headings in alphabetical order and the list is by no means definitive.

French Property

1st for French Property (🖳 www.1st-for-french-property. co.uk). Property in most areas.

A Place in France (🖳 www.aplaceinfrance.co.uk). New property in all areas.

AB Real Estate (🖳 www.ab-real-estate.com). Property in Languedoc-Rouissillon.

Agence L'Union (🖳 www.agencelunion.com). Property in Aveyron, Lot and Tarn.

Dream Properties Dordogne (🖳 www.dreampropertiesdor-dogne.com). Property in Dordogne.

Francophiles (🖳 www.francophiles.co.uk). Property in most areas.

French Discoveries (🖳 www.frenchdiscoveries.net). Property in the north-west, including Brittany, Normandy, Poitou-Charentes and the Loire valley.

Hexagone France (🖥 www.hexagonefrance.com). Property in northern and north-west France.

Internet French Property Co. (🖥 www.french-property.com). Property in most areas.

JB French Houses (🖥 www.jbfrenchhouses.co.uk). Property in north-west and western France

KBM Consultancy (🖥 www.kbmconsultancy.com). Property in most areas.

L'Affaire Française (🖥 www.french-property-net.com). Property in Dordogne, Limousin and Poitou-Charentes.

Latitudes (🖥 www.latitudes.co.uk). Property in most areas.

Leggett Immobilier (🖥 www.frenchestateagents.com). Property in Poitou-Charentes, Dordogne, Gironde and Limousin.

North & West France Properties (🖥 www.all-france-properties.com). Property in northern and western France.

Sinclair Overseas Property Network (🖥 www.sinclair-frenchprops.com). Property in northern, western and south-west France.

Transaxia France (🖥 www.transaxia.fr). Property in most areas.

VEF (🖥 www.vefuk.com). Property in most areas.

Vialex International (🖥 www.vialex.com). Property in most areas.

Waterside Properties International (🖥 www.waterside properties-int.co.uk). Property in south-west France.

Zest Overseas Properties (🖥 www.zest-properties.com). Property on the Côte d'Azur.

General Information

All About France (🖥 www.all-about-france.com). General information about France.

All 4 France (🖥 www.all4france.com). Information about living, working and buying property in France.

Alliance Française (🖥 www.alliancefr.org). The famous French language school.

L'Etudiant (💻 www.letudiant.fr). Information for students.

French Embassy in the UK (💻 www.francealacarte.org.uk).

French Tourist Board (💻 www.franceguide.com).

Legifrance (💻 www.legifrance.gouv.fr). Official legal information.

Ministry of Culture & Communications (💻 www.culture.fr).

Ministry of Finance (💻 www.finances.gouv.fr). Economic and tax information.

Paris Notes (💻 www.parisnotes.com). Information about Paris (published in California!).

Paris Tourist Office (💻 www.paris-touristoffice.com).

Pratique (💻 www.pratique.fr). Practical information about life in France.

Le Progrès (💻 www.leprogres.fr). The site of a daily newspaper covering central France, which provides general information.

Senior Planète (💻 www.seniorplanete.com). Information for older people

Service Public (💻 www.service-public.fr). Official French government portal, with links to all ministry and other sites.

Expatriates

ExpatBoards (💻 www.expatboards.com). The mega site for expatriates, with popular discussion boards and special areas for Britons, Americans, expatriate taxes, and other important issues.

Escape Artist (💻 www.escapeartist.com). An excellent website and probably the most comprehensive, packed with resources, links and directories covering most expatriate destinations. You can also subscribe to the free monthly online expatriate magazine, *Escape from America*.

Expat Exchange (💻 www.expatexchange.com). Reportedly the largest online community for English-speaking expatriates, provides a series of articles on relocation and also a question and answer facility through its expatriate network.

Expat Forum (⌨ www.expatforum.com). Provides interesting cost of living comparisons as well as 7 EU country-specific forums and chats (Belgium, the Czech Republic, France, Germany, the Netherlands, Spain and the UK).

Expat World (⌨ www.expatworld.net). 'The newsletter of international living.' Contains a wealth of information for American and British expatriates, including a subscription newsletter.

Expatriate Experts (⌨ www.expatexpert.com). A website run by expatriate expert Robin Pascoe, providing invaluable advice and support.

Expats International (⌨ www.expats2000.com). The international job centre for expats and their recruiters.

Real Post Reports (⌨ www.realpostreports.com). Provides relocation services, recommended reading lists and plenty of interesting 'real-life' stories containing anecdotes and impressions written by expatriates in just about every city in the world.

Travel Documents (⌨ www.traveldocs.com). Useful information about travel, specific countries and documents needed to travel.

World Travel Guide (⌨ www.wtgonline.com). A general website for world travellers and expatriates.

British Expatriates

British Expatriates (⌨ www.britishexpat.com). This website keep British expatriates in touch with events and information about the UK.

Trade Partners (⌨ www.tradepartners.gov.uk). A government sponsored website whose main aim is to provide trade and investment information on just about every country in the world. Even if you aren't planning to do business abroad, the information is comprehensive and up to date.

Worldwise Directory (⌨ www.suzylamplugh.org/worldwise). This website run by the Suzy Lamplugh charity for personal safety, providing a useful directory of countries with practical information and special emphasis on safety, particularly for women.

American Expatriates

Americans Abroad (⌨ www.aca.ch). This website offers advice, information and services to Americans abroad.

US Government Trade (⌨ www.usatrade.gov). A huge website providing a wealth of information principally for Americans planning to trade and invest abroad, but useful for anyone planning a move abroad.

Australian & New Zealand Expatriates

Australians Abroad (⌨ www.australiansabroad.com). Information for Australians concerning relocating plus a forum to exchange information and advice.

Southern Cross Group (⌨ www.southern-cross-group.org). A website for Australians and New Zealanders providing information and the exchange of tips.

Women

Family Life Abroad (⌨ www.familylifeabroad.com). A wealth of information and articles on coping with family life abroad.

Foreign Wives Club (⌨ www.foreignwivesclub.com). An online community for women in bicultural marriages.

Third Culture Kids (⌨ www.tckworld.com). A website designed for expatriate children living abroad.

Travel For Kids (⌨ www.travelforkids.com). Advice on travelling with children around the world.

Women Of The World (⌨ www.wow-net.org). A website designed for female expats anywhere in the world.

Travel Information & Warnings

The websites listed below provide daily updated information about the political situation and natural disasters around the world, plus general travel and health advice and embassy addresses.

Australian Department of Foreign Affairs and Trade (📟 www. dfat.gov.au/travel).

British Foreign and Commonwealth Office (📟 www.fco.gov.uk).

Canadian Department of Foreign Affairs (📟 www.dfait-maeci.gc.ca). They also publish a useful series of free booklets for Canadians moving abroad.

New Zealand Ministry of Foreign Affairs and Trade (📟 www. mft.govt.nz).

SaveWealth Travel (📟 www.savewealth.com/travel/warnings).

The Travel Doctor (📟 www.tmvc.com.au). Contains a country by country vaccination guide.

US State Government (📟 www.state.gov/travel). US government website.

World Health Organization (📟 www.who.int).

APPENDIX D: WEIGHTS & MEASURES

France uses the metric system of measurement. Those who are more familiar with the imperial system will find the tables on the following pages useful. Some comparisons are approximate, but are close enough for most everyday uses. In addition to the variety of measurement systems used, clothes sizes often vary considerably with the manufacturer (as we all know only too well). Try all clothes on before buying and don't be afraid to return something if, when you try it on at home, you decide it doesn't fit (most shops will exchange goods or give a refund).

Women's Clothes

Continental	34	36	38	40	42	44	46	48	50	52
UK	8	10	12	14	16	18	20	22	24	26
US	6	8	10	12	14	16	18	20	22	24

Pullovers

	Women's	Men's
Continental	40 42 44 46 48 50	44 46 48 50 52 54
UK	34 36 38 40 42 44	34 36 38 40 42 44
US	34 36 38 40 42 44	sm med lar xl

Men's Shirts

Continental	36	37	38	39	40	41	42	43	44	46
UK/US	14	14	15	15	16	16	17	17	18	-

Men's Underwear

Continental	5	6	7	8	9	10
UK	34	36	38	40	42	44
US	sm	med		lar		xl

Note: sm = small, med = medium, lar = large, xl = extra large

Children's Clothes

Continental	92	104	116	128	140	152
UK	16/18	20/22	24/26	28/30	32/34	36/38
US	2	4	6	8	10	12

Children's Shoes

Continental	18 19 20 21 22 23 24 25 26 27 28 29 30 31 32
UK/US	2 3 4 4 5 6 7 7 8 9 10 11 11 12 13
Continental	33 34 35 36 37 38
UK/US	1 2 2 3 4 5

Shoes (Women's and Men's)

Continental	35	36	37	37	38	39	40	41	42	42	43	44
UK	2	3	3	4	4	5	6	7	7	8	9	9
US	4	5	5	6	6	7	8	9	9	10	10	11

Weight

Imperial	Metric	Metric	Imperial
1oz	28.35g	1g	0.035oz
1lb*	454g	100g	3.5oz
1cwt	50.8kg	250g	9oz
1 ton	1,016kg	500g	18oz
2,205lb	1 tonne	1kg	2.2lb

Length

Imperial	Metric	Metric	Imperial
1in	2.54cm	1cm	0.39in
1ft	30.48cm	1m	3ft 3.25in
1yd	91.44cm	1km	0.62mi
1mi	1.6km	8km	5mi

Capacity

Imperial	Metric	Metric	Imperial
1 UK pint	0.57 litre	1 litre	1.75 UK pints
1 US pint	0.47 litre	1 litre	2.13 US pints
1 UK gallon	4.54 litres	1 litre	0.22 UK gallon
1 US gallon	3.78 litres	1 litre	0.26 US gallon

Note: An American 'cup' = around 250ml or 0.25 litre.

Area

Imperial	Metric	Metric	Imperial
1 sq. in	0.45 sq. cm	1 sq. cm	0.15 sq. in
1 sq. ft	0.09 sq. m	1 sq. m	10.76 sq. ft
1 sq. yd	0.84 sq. m	1 sq. m	1.2 sq. yds
1 acre	0.4 hectares	1 hectare	2.47 acres
1 sq. mile	2.56 sq. km	1 sq. km	0.39 sq. mile

Note: An *are* is one-hundredth of a hectare or 100m^2.

Temperature

°Celsius	°Fahrenheit	
0	32	(freezing point of water)
5	41	
10	50	
15	59	
20	68	
25	77	
30	86	
35	95	
40	104	
50	122	

Notes: The boiling point of water is 100°C / 212°F.
Normal body temperature (if you're alive and well) is 37°C / 98.4°F.

Temperature Conversion

Celsius to Fahrenheit: multiply by 9, divide by 5 and add 32. (For a quick and approximate conversion, double the Celsius temperature and add 30.)

Fahrenheit to Celsius: subtract 32, multiply by 5 and divide by 9. (For a quick and approximate conversion, subtract 30 from the Fahrenheit temperature and divide by 2.)

Oven Temperatures

Gas	Electric	
	°F	°C
-	225–250	110–120
1	275	140
2	300	150
3	325	160
4	350	180
5	375	190
6	400	200
7	425	220
8	450	230
9	475	240

Air Pressure

PSI	Bar
10	0.5
20	1.4
30	2
40	2.8

APPENDIX E: MAPS

The map opposite shows the 22 regions and 96 departments of France (excluding overseas territories), which are listed below. Departments 91 to 95 come under the Ile-de-France region, which also includes Ville de Paris (75), Seine-et-Marne (77) and Yvelines (78), shown in detail opposite. The island of Corsica consists of two departments, 2A and 2B. The maps on the following pages show major airports and ports with cross-Channel ferry services, high-speed train (*TGV*) routes, and motorways and other major roads.

01 Ain	32 Gers	64 Pyrénées-Atlantiques
02 Aisne	33 Gironde	65 Hautes-Pyrénées
2A Corse-du-Sud	34 Hérault	66 Pyrénées-Orientales
2B Haute Corse	35 Ille-et-Vilaine	67 Bas-Rhin
03 Allier	36 Indre	68 Haut-Rhin
04 Alpes-de-Hte-Provence	37 Indre-et-Loire	69 Rhône
05 Hautes-Alpes	38 Isère	70 Haute-Saône
06 Alpes-Maritimes	39 Jura	71 Saône-et-Loire
07 Ardèche	40 Landes	72 Sarthe
08 Ardennes	41 Loir-et-Cher	73 Savoie
09 Ariège	42 Loire	74 Haute-Savoie
10 Aube	43 Haute-Loire	75 Paris
11 Aude	44 Loire-Atlantique	76 Seine
12 Aveyron	45 Loiret	77 Seine-Maritime
13 Bouches-du-Rhône	46 Lot	78 Yvelines
14 Calvados	47 Lot-et-Garonne	79 Deux-Sèvres
15 Cantal	48 Lozère	80 Somme
16 Charente	49 Maine-et-Loire	81 Tarn
17 Charente-Maritime	50 Manche	82 Tarn-et-Garonne
18 Cher	51 Marne	83 Var
19 Corrèze	52 Haute-Marne	84 Vaucluse
21 Côte-d'Or	53 Mayenne	85 Vendée
22 Côte-d'Armor	54 Meurthe-et-Moselle	86 Vienne
23 Creuse	55 Meuse	87 Haute-Vienne
24 Dordogne	56 Morbihan	88 Vosges
25 Doubs	57 Moselle	89 Yonne
26 Drôme	58 Nièvre	90 Territoire de Belfort
27 Eure	59 Nord	91 Essonne
28 Eure-et-Loir	60 Oise	92 Hauts-de-Seine
29 Finistère	61 Orne	93 Seine-Saint-Denis
30 Gard	62 Pas-de-Calais	94 Val-de-Marne
31 Haute-Garonne	63 Puy-de-Dôme	95 Val-d'Oise

REGIONS & DEPARTMENTS

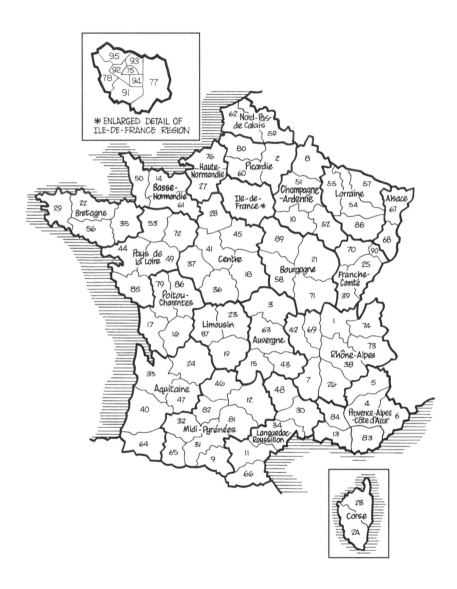

* ENLARGED DETAIL OF
ILE-DE-FRANCE REGION

AIRPORTS & PORTS

 Airports

 Ferry ports

TGV NETWORK

▬▬▬▬ Special track, on which trains can run at up to 300kph (187mph).

▬▬▬▬ Ordinary track, on which trains are restricted to around 200kph (122mph).

MOTORWAYS & MAJOR ROADS

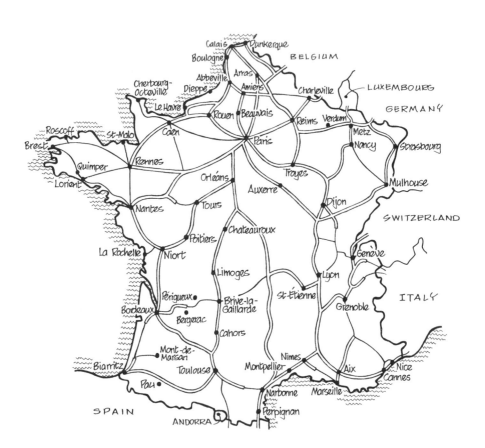

═══════ Motorways

━━━━━ Other main roads

APPENDIX F: AIRLINE SERVICES

The tables on the following pages indicate scheduled flights operating from UK and Irish airports to France. Details were current in April 2003. Airlines are coded as shown below (note that these aren't all official airline codes). Telephone numbers in italics are Irish numbers; all other numbers are UK numbers.

Code	Airline	Telephone	Website
AF	Air France	0845-084 5111	www.airfrance.com
AL	Aer Lingus	*0813-365 000*	www.aerlingus.com
BA	British Airways	0845-773 3377	www.britishairways.com
BI	BMIbaby (British Midland)	0870-264 2229	www.bmibaby.com
BM	British Midland	0870-607 0555	www.flybmi.com
EJ	EasyJet	0871-750 0100	www.easyjet.com
FB	Flybe (British European)	0871-700 0535	www.flybe.com
FG	Flyglobespan	0870-556 1522	www.flyglobespan.com
J2	Jet 2	0870-737 8282	www.jet2.com
RA	Ryanair	0871-246 0000	www.ryanair.com

	Aberdeen (0870-040 0006)	Belfast Int. (028-9448 4848)	Birmingham (0870-733 5511)	Bristol (0870-121 2747)	Cardiff (01446-711111)	Cork (021-431 3131)	Dublin (01-814 1111)	East Midlands (0871-919 9000)	Edinburgh (0870-040 0007)	Glasgow Prestwick (0870-040 0008)	Leeds/Bradford (0113-250 9696)
Beauvais						RA					
Bergerac			FB¹								
Bordeaux				FB			AF	BI			
Lyon			BA								
Nice		EJ	BA	EJ			AL	BI	FG		J2
Paris CDG	AF	EJ	AF BA	BA	BI	AL	AF AL	BI	AF BA	BA FB RA	BM J2
Perpignan			FB								
Toulouse			FB	FB				BI			

NOTES:

1. Summer only.
2. Flights diverted to Rochefort until 17th April 2005.

Thomson Fly may operate a summer service between Coventry and Nice; to check UK ☎ 0870-190 0737, 🖥 www.thomsonfly.com.

Flights between Bournemouth and St-Brieuc in Brittany via the Channel Islands are offered by Rockhopper (UK ☎ 01481-824567, 🖥 www.rockhopper.aero).

	Liverpool (0870-750 8484)	London City (020-7646 0088)	London Gatwick (0870-0002 468)	London Heathrow (0870-000 0123)	London Luton (01582-405100)	London Stansted (0870-000 0303)	Manchester (0161-489 3000)	Newcastle (0870-122 1488)	Shannon (061-712000)	Southampton (0870-040 0009)
Beauvais									RA	
Bergerac						RA				FB
Biarritz						RA				
Bordeaux			AF BA							
Brest										FB[1]
Carcassonne						RA				
Cherbourg										FB[1]
Dinard					RA	RA				
La Rochelle[2]						RA				FB[1]
Limoges						RA				
Lyon			AF BM		EJ					
Marseille			BA EJ							
Montpellier			BA			RA				
Nantes			AF							
Nice	EJ		BA EJ	AF BM	EJ		BA J2			
Nîmes					RA	RA				
Paris CDG	EJ	AF	BA	AF BA BM	EJ		AF BA	AF EJ		AF
Paris Orly		AF								
Pau						RA				
Perpignan						RA				FB[1]
Poitiers						RA				
Rodez						RA				
St Etienne						RA				
Strasbourg			AF							
Toulouse			BA EJ				BM			FB
Tours						RA				

APPENDIX G: GLOSSARY

Abonnement: Standing charge, e.g. for electricity, gas, telephone or water services.

Achat en Viager: Buying a property by paying a life annuity with the vendor as named beneficiary.

Acompte: Deposit (non-refundable). If a deposit is described as *acompte* neither party can withdraw and the sale can be legally enforced.

Acquéreur: The buyer.

Acte: Legal document or deed.

Acte authentique: The final contract (authentic deed or document) for the purchase of a property drawn up, verified and stamped by a notary.

Acte de vente: Deed of sale or conveyance document.

Acte en main: The total cost of a property including agent's and notary's fees.

Administration fiscale: Tax authorities.

Agence immobilière: (Real) estate agency.

Agent immobilier: (Real) estate agent.

Aggrandissement: Extension or enlargement.

Aménagé/aménageable: Converted/convertible.

Amortissement: Amortisation. The gradual process of systematically reducing debt in equal payments (as in a mortgage) comprising both principal and interest, until the debt is paid in full.

Appartement: Apartment or flat.

Appartement bourgeois: Spacious (usually 19th century) apartment with separate servant's quarters (*chambre de bonne*).

Appartement de standing: A luxury (usually modern) apartment. Also called a *grand standing*.

Appentis: Lean-to.

Are: 100 square metres.

Arrhes: Deposit (refundable).

Arrière-pays: Hinterland, inland.

Arrondissement: Administrative districts in Lyon and Paris.

Ascenseur: Lift or elevator.

Assurance multirisques habitation: Fully comprehensive (all-risk) household insurance .

Atelier: Workshop.

Attenant: Attached; adjoining.

Attestation d'acquisition: Proof of purchase.

Attestation de conformité aux règles de sécurité: Certificate of conformity to safety standards.

Attestation de propriété: Proof of ownership of a property.

Attribution de juridiction: The formal signing of a purchase contract.

Authentique: Authentic, i.e. a document signed in the presence of a notary and authenticated by him.

Avec tout le confort: With all mod. cons.

Avec travaux: For renovation.

Avocat: Lawyer or solicitor.

Bail: Lease.

Bailleur: Lessor, e.g. owner or landlord of a property.

Balcon: Balcony.

Ballon (à eau chaude): Hot water tank or immersion heater.

Banlieue: Suburb.

Bastide: Square or fortified stone house.

Bâtiment: Building.

Bergerie: Sheepfold or sheep pen.

Biens mobiliers: Movable property.

Bilan (de santé immobilier): (House) survey.

Bi-propriété: Shared ownership.

Bois/Boiserie: Wood/woodwork.

Bon de visite: Viewing confirmation.

Bon état: Good condition.

(au) Bord de la Mer: By the sea.

Bourg: Small town or large village.

Bricolage: Building, repairs and do-it-yourself (DIY) supplies.

Brique: Brick.

Buanderie: Wash house, laundry or utility room.

Bûcher: Woodshed.

Bureau: Study.

Bureau de vente: Sales office.

Cabinet: A small room.

Cabinet WC: Toilet.

Cadastre: Land registry/land registration.

(à la) Campagne: In the country.

Carré: Square (measurement); a *mètre carré* is a square metre.

Caution: Guarantee or security deposit.

Cave: Cellar.

Cave voûtée: Vaulted cellar.

Cellier: Storeroom or cellar.

Centre foncier: Land office.

Centre des impôts: Tax office. Also called a *bureau des impôts* or *hôtel des impôts*.

Certificat d'urbanisme: Town planning permit.

Cession: Transfer of ownership or rights, including property.

Chai: Wine cellar or vat room.

Chambre (à coucher): Bedroom.

Chambres d'hôtes: Bed and breakfast establishment.

Chantier: Builder's yard.

Charges: Utilities such as electricity, gas, water, insurance, maintenance and other services.

Chartreuse: Monastery or large manor house.

Château: Large country mansion, manor house, fort or castle.

Chaudière: Boiler (water heater).

Chauffage (central): Heating (central).

Chauffage collectif: Communal or shared heating, e.g. in an apartment block.

Chauffe-eau: A gas water heater or hot water tank.

Chaume: Thatch.

Chaumière: Thatched cottage.

Cheminée: Fireplace or chimney.

Citerne à eau: Water tank.

Citerne à gaz: Gas tank, e.g. for central heating.

Clause particulière: Special condition.

Clause pénale: Penalty clause in a sales contract.

Clause suspensive: Conditional clause in a contract which must be met to ensure its validity.

Climatisation: Air-conditioning.

Colombage: A half-timbered house common in Normandy.

Colombier: Pigeon house or dovecote.

Combles: Loft; roof space.

Commission compris (C/C): Commission included, e.g. the sale price of a property including the agent's commission.

Commission non compris: Commission not included.

Communauté: Joint estate of a husband and wife.

Communauté universelle: A marriage *régime* where all assets are owned jointly.

Commune: Town, village, district or parish.

Compromis de vente: Preliminary contract of sale for a property.

Comptable: Accountant.

Comptant: Payable in cash without a loan.

Compte séquestre: A deposit held in a special escrow account pending fulfilment of certain conditions.

Compteur: Meter (electricity/gas/water).

Concierge: Caretaker/porter of an apartment block.

Concurrence: A *concurrence* (competition) sale is where two notaries are involved, although only one can execute the deed. The notary who doesn't execute the deed (*reçoit l'acte*) is said to be in *concurrence*.

Conditions particulières: Special conditions, e.g. in an insurance policy.

Conditions suspensives: Special conditions in a contract which allow one or both parties to declare the contract null and void if they aren't met.

Congélateur: Freezer.

Conseil juridique: Professional legal adviser.

Conseiller fiscal: Financial or tax adviser.

Conservateur des hypothèques: District land register.

Constat d'huissier: A statement of fact prepared by a *huissier* (bailiff) which is irrefutable in a court of law.

Constructible: Land available for building purposes.

Contrat: Contract.

Contrat préliminaire: Preliminary contract. Same as a *contrat de réservation*.

Contrat de réservation: Promissory contract to buy a property off-plan before it's built.

Convention: Agreement.

Copropriété: Co-ownership of communal property, equivalent to a US condominium.

Copropriété financière: Co-owner finance.

Corps de bâtiments: Group of buildings.

Cour: Yard or courtyard.

Cour de ferme: Farmyard.

Cuisine: Kitchen.

Cuisine américaine: Modern fitted kitchen possibly with a dining area.

Cuisine meublée: Kitchen with fixed cooker, refrigerator, etc.

Cuisinière: Cooker/stove.

Cuve: Tank, e.g. for gas or oil.

Date de livraison prévue: Estimated date of completion.

Débarras: Box room or small store room.

Décennale: Ten-year warranty provided by a registered builder.

Déclaration de sincérité: Formal acceptance of purchase price.

Décorée: Decorated and fitted out ready for occupation.

Dédit: Penalty provided for in a contract should either party default. If a deposit is described as a *dédit* the buyer will lose his deposit if he withdraws. If the seller withdraws he must repay the deposit and a penalty equal to the same sum.

Délabré: Dilapidated or tumbledown.

Déménagement: Moving house.

Demeure: Any dwelling, but it normally refers to a grand country house with extensive grounds.

Dépannage: Emergency repair service.

Département: Administrative area roughly equivalent to a British county or an American state.

Dépendance: Outbuilding.

Dépôt de garantie: The deposit paid when buying or renting a property.

Dernière étage: Top floor.

(à) Deux étages: Two storey.

Devis: A written quotation, e.g. for work to be done on a house.

Direction Départementale de l'Equipement (DDE): Departmental surveyors, land planning and public works department.

(à) Discuter: To be discussed or negotiated.

Disjoncteur: Electricity overload trip switch or circuit breaker.

Domaine: A country estate with a stately home.

Domicile fiscal: Main residence for tax purposes.

Donation de jouissance: Legal document to safeguard the rights of the surviving joint owner of a property.

Donation entre époux: Gift between spouses, whereby a surviving spouse is given a life interest in a property in priority to children or parents.

Douche: Shower.

Droit de passage: Right of way.

Droit de préemption: Mandate to make enquiries for buyer.

Droits de donation: Gift tax.

Droits d'enregistrement: Stamp duty on a property purchase which is paid by the buyer.

Droits de passage: Right of way.

Droit de succession: Inheritance tax.

Duplex: An apartment or maisonette on two floors.

Durée: Duration or period of a mortgage.

Durée initiale: The initial duration of a lease for rented property.

Eau chaude collective: Shared hot water supply, e.g. in an apartment block.

Eaux usées: Drain or waste water.

Echange de lettres: Exchange of letters (type of property purchase contract).

Ecurie: Stable.

Emoluments d'actes: Fixed scale of fees for a notary's standard services.

Emoluments de négociation: Fees for introducing the buyer.

Emprunt: Loan.

Engagement: Commitment, usually of vendor.

Enregistrement: Stamp duty.

Entrée: Hallway.

Entreprenuer: Building consortium or contractor.

Entretien: Maintenance.

Escalier: Stairway.

Etable: Stable or cowshed.

Etage: Floor or storey.

Etang: Lake or pond.

Etat hypothécaire: Land registry search.

Etats des lieux: Inventory.

Etude: A notary's office or practise.

Expédition: A certified copy of the title deed of a property.

Expert de bâtiment: Surveyor.

Expert foncier: Valuer.

Expert géomètre: Land surveyor.

Expertise: Survey or valuation.

Expertiser: To value (a property).

Facture: Bill.

Fenêtre: Window.

Fenêtre en baie: Bay window.

Ferme: Farm.

Fermette: Small farm or smallholding.

FNAIM: The initials of the *Fédération Nationale des Agents Immobiliers et Mandataires*, the main French national association of real estate agents.

FNSAFER: See SAFER.

Forfait: Fixed price or contract with an all-in price.

Fosse septique: Septic tank.

Fosse à toutes eaux: A septic tank which filters all household waste water and discharges it underground.

Fosse traditionelle: See Fosse septique.

Four: Oven.

Four à pain: Bread oven or bakehouse.

Foyer principal: Main or principal home.

Frais: Fees.

Frais d'acte: The notary's fees for producing a deed plus stamp duty, land registry fees and other relevant disbursements.

Frais compris: Fees included.

Frais de dossier: The arrangement fee charged by a bank for establishing a mortgage.

Frais de notaire: Same as *frais d'acte*.

Garantie d'achèvement: Guarantee of completion of a property purchased off plan.

Gardien/gardienne: Guardian (male/female) or caretaker.

Gaz en boutelle: Bottled gas.

Gaz de ville: Mains gas.

Gentilhommière: Small manor house, originally a gentleman's country seat.

Gîte: Self-catering accommodation.

Grange: Barn.

Grenier: Attic or loft.

Gros oeuvre: Shell or basic structure of a house.

Habitation: Dwelling.

Hameau: Hamlet.

Hectare: 10,000 square metres or 2.471 acres.

Honoraires: A notary's fee which isn't fixed by an official scale.

Hors frais/taxes: Fees (*frais*) or taxes not included.

Hôtel de ville: Town hall in cities and large towns. See also *Mairie*.

Hôtel particulier: Elegant townhouse or mansion, sometimes better described as a palace.

HT: Abbreviation of *hors taxe*, meaning excluding tax (usually VAT).

Huissier: An officer of the court who's roughly equivalent to a bailiff and serves writs and court orders and prepares statements of fact (*constat d'huissier*) which are irrefutable in a court of law.

Hypothèque: A mortgage or loan on a property.

Immeuble: Apartment block or a legal term for immovable property.

Immobilier: Real estate; property.

Impôt: Tax.

Impôts locaux: Local property taxes.

Impôt sur la fortune: Wealth tax.

Impôt sur les plus-values: Capital gains tax.

Impôt sur le revenu: Income tax.

Indemnité de l'immobilisation: Down payment on a preliminary contract of sale, usually 10 per cent of the price.

Indivision: Joint ownership of a property or tenancy in common.

Inscription: Registered charge.

Installation: Fixture or fitting.

Installation électrique: Wiring.

Interdiction: A restriction on a vendor assigning rights to a third party.

Inventaire détaillé/état des lieux: An inventory of the contents and condition of a rented property.

Jardin/Jardinier: Garden/gardener.

Jouissance: Possession (or taking possession) or tenure.

Jouissance libre: Vacant possession.

Jumelle: Semi-detached house.

Laverie: Laundry room.

Living: Living room.

Location: Tenancy.

Location vente: Renting a property while buying some of the equity value.

Locataire: Tenant.

Logement: Lodging, accommodation.

Logis: Manor house.

Lotissement: Housing estate.

(à) Louer: To rent, hire or let.

Loyer: Rent/rental.

Lucarne: Dormer window or skylight.

Maçon: Builder such as a bricklayer or stone mason.

Maçonnerie: Brick or Stone work.

Mainlevée: Release or withdrawal of mortgage or charge.

Mairie: Town hall (or equivalent in village).

Maison: House.

Maison à étage: A two-storey house.

Maison d'amis: Second or holiday home.

Maison bourgeoise: Large period house designed for the professional classes during the 19th century.

Maison de campagne: House in the country.

Maison de caractère: House of character, often with a dovecote or pigeon tower.

Maison en carré: House built around a courtyard.

Maison de chasse: Hunting lodge, usually located on the edge of a forest.

Maison de maître: Gentleman's mansion or imposing house, usually a few centuries old.

Maison mitoyenne: Semi-detached house.

Maison neuve: New house.

Maison paysanne: Farmhouse.

Maison secondaire: Second or holiday home.

Maison de viticulteur: Winegrower's house.

Maisonette: Cottage.

Maire: Mayor.

Mairie: Town hall or office of the mayor in small towns and villages. See also *Hôtel de ville*.

Maître: Title used when addressing a *notaire*.

Maître d'oeuvres: Master builder, clerk of works or project manager.

Mandat/Mandataire: Mandate or power of attorney document. The representative or proxy who's given a power of attorney.

Mandat exclusif: An exclusive mandate, e.g. for a real estate agent to sell a property.

Mandat de recherche: An agreement with an agent to find a property.

Mandat simple: A non-exclusive mandate, e.g. for an estate agent to sell a property, meaning that the vendor reserves the right to deal with other agents and to negotiate directly with private individuals.

Mandat de vente: Sales mandate.

Manoir: Manor house.

Marchand de biens: Property developer or speculator (no longer a recognised profession).

Marquise: Porch.

Mas: A Provençal style farmhouse, usually L-shaped, often used to refer to any house built in the Mediterranean style.

Mazet: Small stone hut.

Menuisier: Carpenter or joiner.

Mètre carré: A square metre.

Meublé: Furnished. Unfurnished is *non-meublé.*

Meubles: Furniture.

Mode de paiement: Method of payment.

(à la) Montagne: In the mountains.

Montant: Amount (of money) to be paid.

Monument historique: Listed building.

Moquette: Fitted carpet.

Moulin: Mill/Watermill.

Moulin à vent: Windmill.

Multipropriété: The most common term for timesharing.

Multirisques d'habitation: Fully comprehensive (all-risk) household insurance.

Mur: Wall.

Mur mitoyen: A party wall shared with another property.

Nantissement: Collateral or security for a loan.

Net vendeur: The amount the vendor receives, excluding any agent's fees.

Non-meublé: Unfurnished.

Notaire: Notary. The legal professional who handles the conveyancing for all property sales in France (similar to a British solicitor or an American property lawyer).

Nouvelle propriété: Property under five years old..

Nu-propriétaire: Rights of owner set aside during a tenant's lifetime.

Nue-propriétée: Reversionary interest in a property.

Offre d'achat: Offer to buy.

Offre de vente: Offer of sale.

Parties communes: Communal areas (e.g. in block of flats).

Parties privatives: Private areas of a shared building or development, e.g. an apartment.

Pavillon: Small detached cottage or house, usually located on the outskirts of a town or village.

Pays: A country or the countryside.

Pelouse: Lawn.

Pépinière: Garden centre.

Période d'anticipation: The period before completion of a property purchased off-plan, during which interest is paid on a monthly basis on the amount advanced by the bank (plus insurance).

Permis de construire: Building permit.

Perron: Flight of steps in front of a mansion.

Pièce: A room.

Pièce de garantie: The amount of the financial guarantee of a bonded real estate agent, which must be displayed in his office.

Pierre (du pays): Stone (local).

Pierre apparentes: Exposed stonework, e.g. the outer surface of a wall.

Pigeonnier: Pigeon tower.

Pignon: Gable.

Piscine: Swimming pool.

Plage: Beach.

Plain-pied: Single storey.

Plan d'amortissement: Schedule for paying off a mortgage.

Plan cadastral: Cadastral plan showing the dimensions of a property's land area.

Plan de financement: Plan or schedule of purchase payments, e.g. in stages when buying a new property.

Plancher: Wooden floor.

Pleine propriété: Freehold.

Plomberie: Plumbing.

Plombier: Plumber.

Plus-values: Capital gains.

Portes-fenêtres à la française: French windows.

Potager: Kitchen garden.

Poubelle(s): Dustbin or garbage can.

Poutre: Beam (wooden).

Pouvoir: Given power to act, e.g. power of attorney.

Prélèvement automatique: Direct debit.

Presbytère: Presbytery or vicarage.

Prêt: Loan.

Prêt immobilier: Mortgage.

Prêt relais: Bridging loan.

Prix déclaré: The price of a property declared to the authorities.

Prix demandé: The asking price.

Prix fermé: Fixed price (non-negotiable).

Procuration: Power of attorney. Also known as a *mandat* or *pouvoir*.

Projet d'acte: A draft conveyance deed.

Promesse d'achat: Preliminary or promissory contract to buy a property.

Promesse de vente: Preliminary or promissory contract to sell a property.

Promesse unilatérale de vente: A property that is rented with a promise to sell at an agreed price in the future with part of the rent going towards the purchase price.

Promoteur: Property developer.

Propriétaire: Owner.

Propriété: Property.

Propriété à restaurer: Property for restoration.

Propriété en ruines: Property in ruins.

Propriétés baties: Developed or built property.

Publicité foncière: Obligatory registration of a property at the land registry.

Puisard: Cesspool or sump.

Puissance: Electricity power rating (in kilowatts).

Puits: Well.

Quartier: Neighbourhood.

Quincaillerie: Hardware store or ironmonger's.

Quittance: Receipt.

Ramoneur: Chimneysweep.

Rangement: Storage area.

Ravalement: Restoration.

Réalisation: To carry out or fulfil an agreement.

Réduit: Box room.

Réfection: Reconstruction.

Réfrigérateur: Refrigerator (often shortened to *frigo*).

Règlement de copropriété: The document containing the rules and regulations of a *copropriété* building.

Remis: Storeroom.

Remise des clefs: Handing over keys to a new owner.

Rénovation: Renovation.

Rente viagère: Life annuity.

Représentative accrédité: A guarantor for capital gains tax purposes.

Réservation: Deposit (in a *contrat de réservation*).

Réservoir: Water tank.

Résidence principale: Main or principal home.

Résidence secondaire: Second or holiday home.

Résiliation: Cancellation (of contract).

Responsabilité civile propriétaire: Third party liability of homeowners for which insurance is mandatory.

Restaurer: To restore (a building).

Révision de loyer: A revision or review of the rent payable on a property.

Renouvellement: The renewal of a rental contract (lease).

Rez-de-chaussée: Ground floor.

Ruine: Ruin or run-down property. A property in need of restoration, renovation and modernisation is referred to as a *propriété en ruines* or a *propriété à restaurer*.

SAFER: Société d'Aménagement Foncier et d'Établissement Rural; regional member of the Fédération Nationale des Société d'Aménagement Foncier et d'Etablissement Rural (FNSAFER).

Saisie-arrêt: Distraint or attachment.

Saisie-exécutions: Distraint for sale by court order.

Salle: Room.

Salle à manger: Dining room.

Salle de bain: Bathroom.

Salle de douche: Shower room.

Salle d'eau: Shower room.

Salle de séjour: Living room.

Salon: Sitting room, lounge or drawing room.

Sanitaire: Bathroom or plumbing.

Sanitation: Sanitation or main drainage.

Sans travaux: Ready to occupy.

Séjour: Living room.

Séjour principal: Main or principal residence.

Séparation des biens: Separation of property. A marriage *régime* where each spouse retains legal ownership of his or her own assets.

Service du cadastre: Land registry or cadastral survey.

Servitudes: Building regulations, rights of way or easements.

SNPI: Syndicate National des Professionnels Immobiliers, a professional association of estate agents.

Société civile immobilière (SCI): A civil company that holds voting shares in a property.

Sol: Ground.

Source: Spring (a *sourcier* is a water diviner).

Sous-seing: Preliminary contract.

Sous-sol: Basement often used as a garage or cellar.

Studio: A one-roomed apartment or bed-sitter.

Surface habitable: Habitable area excluding terraces, balconies, cellars, store rooms, etc.

Syndicat (des copropriétaires): The committee appointed to manage a community development (*copropriété*).

Système de chauffage: Heating system.

T: Abbreviation for *type* used by estate agents and in property advertisements, followed by a figure indicating the number of main rooms (i.e. excluding kitchen, bathrooms, toilets, etc.).

Tapis: Carpet or rug. A fitted carpet is a *moquette*.

Taxe d'habitation: Dwelling or local property tax based on occupancy (not ownership) of a property.

Taxe foncière: Local property tax (rates) levied on property owners. The tax is split into two amounts: one for the building (*taxe foncière bâtie*) and a smaller one for the land (*taxe foncière non bâtie*).

Témoin: Show apartment or house (*appartement/maison témoin*).

Terrain: Grounds or land.

Terrain à bâtir: Building site for sale.

Terrasse: Terrace.

Testament: Will.

Titre de propriété: Title deed.

Toilettes: Toilet or lavatory (public).

Toit/Toiture: Roof/roofing.

Toit en terrasse: Flat roof.

Toiture: Roof (structure).

Tontine: Ownership in joint tenancy under which the assets pass to the survivor. A *clause tontine* can be included in a property purchase contract (*acte de vente*).

Tout à l'égout: Mains drainage system.

Toutes taxes: Including taxes.

Travaux: Building works.

Trésor public: Public treasury or treasurer's department.

Triplex: Maisonette on three floors.

TTC: Abbreviation of *toutes taxes comprises*, meaning inclusive of tax (usually VAT).

TVA: Abbreviation of *taxe sur la valeur ajoutée*, meaning value added tax (VAT).

TVA immobilière: VAT payable on property under five years old.

Urbanisme: Town planning.

Urgence: Emergency.

Usufruct/Usufruit: Legal term for a life interest in a property.

Valeur cadastrale: Assessment of a property's value for land tax purposes.

Valeur vénale: Market value.

Vendeur: Vendor or seller.

Vente en l'état futur d'achèvement: Sale of a property off plan (on plan) before it is built.

Vente à réméré: Sale which is subject to a right of repurchase.

Vente sous conditions suspensives: Sale subject to special conditions, e.g. the sale of an existing property.

Viabilisé: (Plot) having mains water and electricity connections.

Vente à tenure: Sale of usufruct.

Véranda: Conservatory, sun-room or extension.

Verger: Orchard.

Vieille maison: An old house.

Villa: A (usually modern) detached house with garden.

Ville: Town.

Volet (roulant): Shutter (roller).

INDEX

L

P

R

LIVING AND WORKING SERIES

Living and Working books are essential reading for anyone planning to spend time abroad, including holiday-home owners, retirees, visitors, business people, migrants, students and even extra-terrestrials! They're packed with important and useful information designed to help you **avoid costly mistakes and save both time and money.** Topics covered include how to:

- Find a job with a good salary & conditions
- Obtain a residence permit
- Avoid and overcome problems
- Find your dream home
- Get the best education for your family
- Make the best use of public transport
- Endure local motoring habits
- Obtain the best health treatment
- Stretch your money further
- Make the most of your leisure time
- Enjoy the local sporting life
- Find the best shopping bargains
- Insure yourself against most eventualities
- Use post office and telephone services
- Do numerous other things not listed above

Living and Working books are the most comprehensive and up-to-date source of practical information available about everyday life abroad. They aren't, however, boring text books, but interesting and entertaining guides written in a highly readable style.

Discover what it's *really* like to live and work abroad!

Order your copies today by phone, fax, post or email from: Survival Books, PO Box 146, Wetherby, West Yorks. LS23 6XZ, United Kingdom (☎/▤ +44 (0)1937-843523, ✉ orders@ survivalbooks.net, ▤ www.survivalbooks.net).

BUYING A HOME SERIES

Buying a Home books are essential reading for anyone planning to purchase property abroad and are designed to guide you through the jungle and make it a pleasant and enjoyable experience. Most importantly, they're packed with vital information to help you **avoid the sort of disasters that can turn your dream home into a nightmare!** Topics covered include:

- Avoiding problems
- Choosing the region
- Finding the right home and location
- Estate agents
- Finance, mortgages and taxes
- Home security
- Utilities, heating and air-conditioning
- Moving house and settling in
- Renting and letting
- Permits and visas
- Travelling and communications
- Health and insurance
- Renting a car and driving
- Retirement and starting a business
- And much, much more!

Buying a Home books are the most comprehensive and up-to-date source of information available about buying property abroad. Whether you want a detached house, townhouse or apartment, a holiday or a permanent home, these books will help make your dreams come true.

Save yourself time, trouble and money!

Order your copies today by phone, fax, post or email from: Survival Books, PO Box 146, Wetherby, West Yorks. LS23 6XZ, United Kingdom (☎/🖷 +44 (0)1937-843523, ✉ orders@ survivalbooks.net, 🖳 www.survivalbooks.net).

OTHER SURVIVAL BOOKS

The Alien's Guides: *The Alien's Guides to Britain* and *France* provide an 'alternative' look at life in these popular countries and will help you to appreciate the peculiarities (in both senses) of the British and French.

The Best Places to Buy a Home in France/Spain: The most comprehensive and up-to-date homebuying guides to France or Spain.

Buying, Selling and Letting Property: The most comprehensive and up-to-date source of information available for those intending to buy, sell or let a property in the UK and the only book on the subject updated annually.

Foreigners in France/Spain: Triumphs & Disasters: Real-life experiences of people who have emigrated to France and Spain.

How to Avoid Holiday and Travel Disasters: This book will help you to make the right decisions regarding every aspect of your travel arrangements and to avoid costly mistakes and disasters that can turn a trip into a nightmare.

Lifelines: Essential guides to specific regions of France and Spain, containing everything you need to know about local life. Titles in the series currently include the Costa del Sol, Dordogne/Lot, and Poitou-Charentes.

Renovating & Maintaining Your French Home: The ultimate guide to renovating and maintaining your dream home in France.

Retiring Abroad: The most comprehensive and up-to-date source of practical information available about retiring to a foreign country – contains profiles of the 20 most popular retirement destinations.

Wine Guides: *Rioja and its Wines* and *The Wines of Spain* are the most comprehensive and up-to-date sources of information available on the wines of Spain and of its most famous wine-producing region.

Broaden your horizons with Survival Books!

Order your copies today by phone, fax, post or email from: Survival Books, PO Box 146, Wetherby, West Yorks. LS23 6XZ, United Kingdom (☎/▤ +44 (0)1937-843523, ✉ orders@ survivalbooks.net, ▣ www.survivalbooks.net).

ORDER FORM

Qty.	Title	Price (incl. p&p)			Total
		UK	Europe	World	
	The Alien's Guide to Britain	£6.95	£8.95	£12.45	
	The Alien's Guide to France	£6.95	£8.95	£12.45	
	The Best Places to Buy a Home in France	£13.95	£15.95	£19.45	
	The Best Places to Buy a Home in Spain	£13.95	£15.95	£19.45	
	Buying a Home Abroad	£13.95	£15.95	£19.45	
	Buying a Home in Florida	£13.95	£15.95	£19.45	
	Buying a Home in France	£13.95	£15.95	£19.45	
	Buying a Home in Greece & Cyprus	£13.95	£15.95	£19.45	
	Buying a Home in Ireland	£11.95	£13.95	£17.45	
	Buying a Home in Italy	£13.95	£15.95	£19.45	
	Buying a Home in Portugal	£13.95	£15.95	£19.45	
	Buying a Home in South Africa	£13.95	£15.95	£19.45	
	Buying a Home in Spain	£13.95	£15.95	£19.45	
	Buying, Letting & Selling Property	£11.95	£13.95	£17.45	
	Foreigners in France: Triumphs & Disasters	£11.95	£13.95	£17.45	
	Foreigners in Spain: Triumphs & Disasters	£11.95	£13.95	£17.45	
	How to Avoid Holiday & Travel Disasters	£13.95	£15.95	£19.45	
	Costa del Sol Lifeline	£11.95	£13.95	£17.45	
	Dordogne/Lot Lifeline	£11.95	£13.95	£17.45	
	Poitou-Charentes Lifeline	£11.95	£13.95	£17.45	
	Living & Working Abroad	£14.95	£16.95	£20.45	
	Living & Working in America	£14.95	£16.95	£20.45	
	Living & Working in Australia	£14.95	£16.95	£20.45	
	Living & Working in Britain	£14.95	£16.95	£20.45	
	Living & Working in Canada	£16.95	£18.95	£22.45	
	Living & Working in the European Union	£16.95	£18.95	£22.45	
	Living & Working in the Far East	£16.95	£18.95	£22.45	
	Living & Working in France	£14.95	£16.95	£20.45	
	Living & Working in Germany	£16.95	£18.95	£22.45	
	Total carried forward (see over)				

ORDER FORM

Qty.	Title	UK	Europe	World	Total
			Total brought forward		
		Price (incl. p&p)			
		UK	Europe	World	
	L&W in the Gulf States & Saudi Arabia	£16.95	£18.95	£22.45	
	L&W in Holland, Belgium & Luxembourg	£14.95	£16.95	£20.45	
	Living & Working in Ireland	£14.95	£16.95	£20.45	
	Living & Working in Italy	£16.95	£18.95	£22.45	
	Living & Working in London	£13.95	£15.95	£19.45	
	Living & Working in New Zealand	£14.95	£16.95	£20.45	
	Living & Working in Spain	£14.95	£16.95	£20.45	
	Living & Working in Switzerland	£16.95	£18.95	£22.45	
	Renovating & Maintaining Your French Home	£16.95	£18.95	£22.45	
	Retiring Abroad	£14.95	£16.95	£20.45	
	Rioja and its Wines	£11.95	£13.95	£17.45	
	The Wines of Spain	£13.95	£15.95	£19.45	
	Grand Total				

Order your copies today by phone, fax, post or email from: Survival Books, PO Box 146, Wetherby, West Yorks. LS23 6XZ, UK (☎/▤ +44 (0)1937-843523, ✉ orders@survivalbooks.net, 🖥 www.survivalbooks.net). If you aren't entirely satisfied, simply return them to us within 14 days for a full and unconditional refund.

I enclose a cheque for the grand total/Please charge my Amex/Delta/Maestro (Switch)/MasterCard/Visa card as follows. (delete as applicable)

Card No. _ _ _ _   _ _ _ _   _ _ _ _   _ _ _ _   Security Code* _ _ _

Expiry date _____   Issue number (Maestro/Switch only) _____

Signature _____   Tel. No. _____

NAME _____

ADDRESS _____

_____

_____

* The security code is the last three digits on the signature strip.

NOTES

NOTES

We offer a specialist search and legal assistance service, to enable you to buy your dream 'Home in France'

Our service is individually tailored to your needs and our offices in the UK and in France are available to assist you with every aspect of your purchase.

UK Office: The Old Granary, Low Lane, Cuddington, Bucks HP18 0AA
Telephone: 0870 7486161   Fax: 0870 7486162
info@ahomeinfrance.com
French Office: 34 Place de la Fontaine, 37500 Chinon
Tel: 00 33 2 47 93 12 21
ahomeinfrance@wanadoo.fr

Web Site: www.ahomeinfrance.com